The Great Cosmic Teachings
of JESUS of Nazareth
to His Apostles and Disciples, Who Could Understand Them

The life of the true God-filled people

with explanations by Gabriele

*The Eternal Word,
the One God, the Free Spirit,
speaks through Gabriele,
as through all the Prophets of God—
Abraham, Job, Moses, Elijah, Isaiah,
Jesus of Nazareth,
the Christ of God*

Gabriele
Publishing House

The Great
Cosmic Teachings of

JESUS
of Nazareth

to His Apostles and Disciples,
Who Could Understand Them

The life of
the true God-filled people

Revealed by Christ,
the Son of God and the Redeemer
of all souls and people,
through the prophetess of God,
Gabriele

with

Explanations

for the fulfillment
of the eternal laws

by Gabriele

Table of Contents

Foreword

God is absolute. He is the Absolute Law of infinity. Since we are out of Him, we, too, all people, are the Absolute Law in our innermost being, the love for God and neighbor. God is—and we are divine. He is our origin and our goal.

In the mighty turn of time in which we live, the Spirit of God pours the entire fullness of His truth into this world. Now, the Spirit of truth, Christ, has made true what He had announced, as Jesus of Nazareth: "But when the Spirit of truth comes, He will lead you into all truth."

He has come in the prophetic word through Gabriele, His teaching prophetess and emissary. The whole truth, to the extent that it can be expounded on in our three-dimensional words, is the Absolute Law of God. In 1991, Christ revealed the Absolute Law through His prophetess: »*The Great Cosmic Teachings of Jesus of Nazareth to His Apostles and Disciples Who Could Understand Them. The life of the true God-filled people.*«

The teachings of the Absolute Law remind us of who we truly are. They give us an inkling of our true being, which says: In each one of us, in the depths of the soul, is the absolute, independent and selfless being. The Absolute

Law is the origin of our true being and our goal as human being and soul.

May the one who can grasp it, grasp it.

During the years from 1991 to 1996 in the Inner Spirit-Christ Church, a gathering place open to all God-seekers, the teachings of the Absolute Law were explained by Gabriele, God's teaching prophetess. Gabriele is also God's emissary because she draws from her opened spiritual consciousness, which lives in God.

This book is a mighty spiritual teaching work. It contains the axioms of the "Great Cosmic Teachings," the highest revelations of the Christ of God, which show us the way to our spiritual-divine heritage, into the eternal law of love for God and neighbor.

The second part of the book consists of the axioms and the explanations about them given by Gabriele. They are instructions on how we, as human beings, can apply the axioms in our daily life. This book takes by the hand every one who wants to let himself be guided by the Spirit of truth.

On December 31, 1991, among other things, Christ revealed the following through Gabriele, the prophetess of God:

»Behold: You are living in a glorious time. It is the highest cosmic time. The Spirit of life, God in Me and I in Him, pour out the highest: the Absolute Law.

I still speak through the mouth of a prophet. But know and grasp in this hour: The soul of My instrument, your sister, lives in the direct source. She draws from the source, receives from the source—and thus, you receive My direct word.

Oh see: It is a time that will never come again to human-kind. Once the Absolute Law is taught in all details, then the end is at hand, the end of the materialistic time ...

The teachings from the Absolute Law show the human being his inner heritage, the eternal Being of the soul, the all-encompassing consciousness, God—your spiritual heritage. The Inner Path leads you step by step to the inner life. And the Absolute Law, given and taught from the direct source, God, shows you your true Being, your spiritual heritage, so that you may very gradually know and recognize that you are truly children of the Most High ...

Oh see: The horn of plenty is being poured out—the Inner Path and the Absolute Law. Recognize in this that the Absolute Law, given in all its details, already symbolizes the end of the materialistic time. For absolute is, simply, absolute. Beyond that there is nothing more ...

Blessed is the one who grows into the inner source, into the eternal Being ... He will no longer give from the intellect what he has acquired as knowledge, as spiritual knowledge—he is the being and speaks the language of the Being, just as it is given to you in the interpretations from the Absolute Law. The person through whom I speak interprets from the source of love. She speaks the law, even if I do not speak directly from the stream to you through the person.

And this is the way you should be: creative, the being. It is possible. You have a role model and an example. Do it. Follow Me, and fulfill, and you, too, will be an example for many—the example, that is, the role model; for only true role models will be able to endure on this Earth.«

(The complete text of this revelation by the Christ of God may be read in the book: "The Message from the All" Vol. 3)

Gabriele, herself, has gone the path of purging of soul and person. She knows the weal and woe of being a human being, the difficulties and problems that are a part of it. Therefore, she can also understand us in everything and give us advice and help from her opened spiritual consciousness. Gabriele, whose soul is consciously at home in the eternal Being, expresses the life of the heavens in our human words insofar as it is possible.

This book can show still many more seeking people the path into their inner being—into the kingdom of the inner being that is our true homeland.

Gabriele-Verlag Das Wort

Introduction

We live in a mighty time of radical change. The Spirit of God pours out His horn of plenty. We receive the Inner Path from the level of Order up to the level of divine Earnestness. Beyond that, we receive the Absolute Law, The Great Cosmic Teachings of Jesus of Nazareth, and, in this way, we may immerse in our spiritual heritage. We are allowed to feel into the life that is deep in our soul, that is our homeland, and thus, experience who we truly are.

A treasure from the heavens is given to us. If we are ready to receive this treasure, then we will also raise it; for the treasure is God, and God, the life, is in us.

If we want to draw closer to God, we have to learn and apply the divine laws again. Otherwise, we cannot become one with the great Spirit, God, the Eternal, the Absolute.

We pray to God, our Father. We hear of God, our Father, of Christ, our Redeemer, and of the spirit beings of the heavens. For many a one, God is only a word, something abstract—he still feels very far from Him. Why do many of us still feel far from God? Because we have not yet made ourselves aware of what God, the All-One, has given us. He gave us immortality because He is immortal. He gave us every cosmic radiation because we are His heirs. He gave Himself to us completely.

Who is God?

God is spirit, power, streaming life. God is the light that permeates us. God gave Himself the spiritual form: the eternal Father. He is a spirit being, as we, too, are spirit beings in the pure Being. However, He is unsurpassed in His radiation. Thus, God is flowing energy. On the other hand, the eternal Father is a being, just as we, too, are divine beings in the divine Being.

Only once we are again completely irradiated by every cosmic radiation, will we live as drops in the ocean, God, and will again be one with God, our Father, and will be in His image.

Gabriele

*The Great
Cosmic Teachings of*

JESUS
of Nazareth

*to His Apostles and Disciples,
Who Could Understand Them*

The life

of the true God-filled people

*Revealed by Christ,
the Son of God and Redeemer of all
souls and people,
through the prophetess of God,
Gabriele*

Preface

I, the eternal law, the Christ of God, explain to you the I Am, the eternal Being, which you, too, are in Me.

What I frequently repeat, the truth, and what I explain from the three filiation attributes—Patience, Love and Mercy—is for you, so that you may find Me, the Christ of God, in you.

I throw light on the Being—Me and you—from various perspectives, so that you may gain clarity about Me and about yourself and find yourself in one or several repetitions, to also find Me, who I Am in every repetition. I Am the truth in each repetition, which is merely spoken differently, that is, explained differently—for you.

I AM the Alpha and the Omega, the beginning and the end of the material universe and of the soul realms.

In Me and with Me, you shall mature into the eternal life, where I Am in the Father, just as you, too, are with Me in the Father. There is neither beginning nor end there because God is and we are in God. For I, the Christ of God, raise all things to the light of truth.

I Am the life, Christ, the Son of God. The one who lets Me, the Spirit of life, Christ, arise in him has found his spiritual heritage again, which is his eternal life. Then the being returns home to God, the eternal Father because it is from Him.

All will resurrect in Me. I will find all those who believe they are lost. And the weak will grow strong in Me, for I Am the glory in the Father.

He, the great All-One, assigned Me the task of leading back into the eternal Being all that seemed lost.

As Jesus of Nazareth I spoke about the law of life without parables to those who could understand Me. For those who could not understand Me, the holy words were mysteries. This is why I spoke in pictures, again and again. But now the time has come when I, Christ, reveal the law of life to all, so that they may find Me; for I Am on My way to establish My kingdom on the Earth.

May the one who has ears, hear!

A new humanity is emerging. I, Christ, bring the inner reform, the spiritual renewal for the inner life, to My own, who truly follow Me. The world of the senses passes away— the spiritual world is rising and, with it, all those who are aligned with Me, Christ. They are the noble, the fine, who bring the inner life, the new humanity in Me, the Christ.

Many world-oriented people will look upon the field of death and, in the end, will enter the realm of death with empty hands, where they will live as the spiritually dead. They are those who did not master their earthly existence, who missed the opportunity for the growth of their inner being in the school of Earth.

The new human being cultivates the community because he has developed the sense of community, the common good: One for all and all for One.

The new human being in Me, the Christ, knows no act of violence; he knows no claim to possession and no thought of power.

He is the bringer of light, who radiates the light and ignites with the light of truth all those who verily strive for the truth.

The rate of vibration of the new humanity and of the new Earth is several degrees higher. The prisoner of the world, the greedy one, who strives for power and prestige, can no longer reach this higher vibration. He falls into his own floods, into what he, himself, created.

The new humanity is the people with spiritual nobility, with inner values because I, Christ, have risen in them.

The new human being in the age of the Spirit will possess the Earth.

The eternal Being flows through all realms and on the Earth. The one who has awakened to the truth has awakened to the Being, to the creative power and to the creative life, which floods through the Earth, which permeates those people who ennoble their souls. These people bring the creative thoughts for the new Earth.

You people of this time, understand that as soon as a person turns back and renounces materialistic activities, he goes inward, into the kingdom of stillness. Hardly has he taken the one step, he realizes that God, the Eternal, had already long since prepared this path for him.

The person who strives toward truthfulness does not overcome his base ego for his own sake, but to become divine again.

What I reveal to you is the path to the divine law and the divine law itself

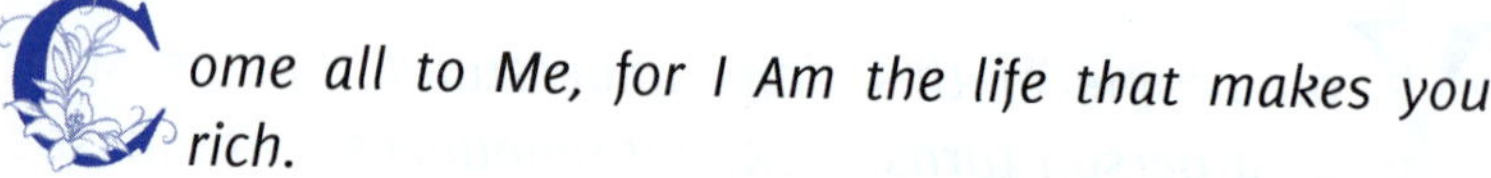

Come all to Me, for I Am the life that makes you rich.

I Am the inner wealth, Christ, who gives Himself to you. Open your hearts and you will become heart-thinkers, who look inward, and thus, let the kingdom of the inner being come to the Earth.

I Am the kingdom of the inner being. For this reason, come into your inner being and know that each one of you is the temple of the Holy Spirit. Cleanse the temple. Then you sanctify your sensations, thoughts, words and deeds, and you will become the new person, who does not think in a static, but dynamic, way, who penetrates the three dimensions because he is a child of the All—the son and the daughter of God, who live in the sonship and daughtership because they live in God, their Father.

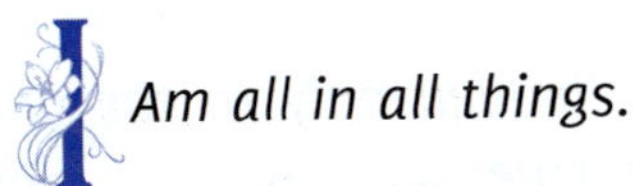 Am all in all things.

Behold the bush—and you will find Me.
Pick up the stone—and you will find Me.
Look to the stars—and you perceive Me.
Look deep into the human being—and you
find yourself and thus, Me, Christ,
the Self in you.
Regard the animal—and you find Me.
Feel the wind—and you hear Me.
Look at the drop of water—and you
look at yourself in Me.
For I Am the life in all things;
and you are the life in all things;
and everything is in Me, and
everything is in you.

We are united in Him,
The great All-One,
Who i s eternally—
the stream of Being and
the personified Being.
He is the stream of the All
and the drop itself.

The powers of the All are hidden only to the one who does not know his true self. The one who wants to experience the powers of the All must unveil them through actualization.

What you see, I Am in it.
What you hear, I Am in it.
I Am everything in all things, the whole.

Once you have awakened to the whole,
then you are the Being.
You behold the Being.
You hear the Being and speak
the language of the Being.
You behold, hear and speak Me,
because I Am the whole in you.
I Am the whole in your neighbor, in you,
in the flower, in the blade of grass
and in the stone.
I Am yours—you are Mine.
I Am the All—and you are the All in Me,
the All.

You do not ask—you know.
You do not see—you behold.
You do not listen in—you hear and know.

ever look to without. The light is in you.

In you is the truth that knows about all things, that knows everyone and everything. You do not need to look for your neighbor. You do not need to regard things from without—what is, is in you.

Everything you see is merely a reflection of the truth, that is, a reflection that is not the absolute truth.

What is within, in you, the light, the truth, what you are in the pure Being as a being in God, took on shape and form in heaven as purest substance.

What is in the innermost part of your incarnated soul, in the very basis of your soul, is the incorruptible light, the eternal truth. It is and remains the Being, eternally.

Only a predetermined quantum of divine energy was transformed into Fall-energy when a being fell away from God. From this, emerged Fall-realms, Fall-beings and human beings. This quantum of divine energy was given by the Eternal to other Fall-beings to sustain their lives. It is divine energy, transformed down. For this reason, matter and all the energies that have been transformed down are but reflections of the pure Being.

In all of infinity there is only one principle: sending and receiving. What you send is what you are; that is what you radiate. What you radiate comes back to you.

The one who lives in his innermost being, in God, is divine. He radiates the eternal law, the pure, the beautiful, the fine, the absolute love—the Being that he is.

The eternal law, the pure, the beautiful, the noble, the fine, the absolute love, radiates what goes out from the one who is God-filled, and then radiates back into him and through him.

The pure being lives in the Being that is eternal and has its existence in the eternal Being because it, itself, is the eternal Being, the eternal law, God: the purity, beauty, freedom, the noble and fine, the selfless love. The pure being is the Being in the All-stream, in God, in the Being.

The burdened souls in the spheres of purification and the incarnated burdened souls, the human beings, do not live as the Being, nor do they move in the stream of the Being.

The one who does not live in God lives in his self-made world, which consists of his human feelings, thoughts, words and deeds, which he calls his »being« and his »self.« This is the small world of the human ego.

In this small world, he lives, he moves and thinks that his existence is solely there.

Then he sees only with the eyes of his small world, which can be compared to a cocoon. With this, he then looks only at the small cocoon-world of his neighbor.

He sees only the surface of life, the reflection because he lives only in the external world and moves only in his small world, in his cocoon, which he, himself, has spun with his burdened feelings, thoughts, words and deeds. This is his state of consciousness.

The threads of the small cocoon-world are like the walls that he looks at and that he calls the »truth.« Because he looks only at the walls of his small, his own, world, he also sees only the walls of the small world of his neighbor. And so, he merely looks into the mirrors of truth and does not behold the truth itself.

He speaks of the truth and with this, he means the reflection of the truth, that which he has input, himself, with which he has spun himself in, in which he believes because he sees only that. And so, he believes only what he sees, and that is what he calls the truth.

In the entire All, there is only one principle: sending and receiving. Each one sends himself—what he is, his feeling, thinking, speaking and acting.

The pure being lives and is active in and from the pure eternal law, the All-law.

The impure one lives in his small, self-made world that consists of his impurity, that is, of the refuse of his feelings, thoughts, words and deeds. In this, his cocoon-world, he lives and moves and feels, thinks, speaks and acts just as he is, what his cocoon-world consists of.

The burdened person can be compared to a caterpillar.

The burdened person—the caterpillar—spins himself into his small world until he recognizes that he has to emerge from his cocoon, that is, unfold, to become a butterfly, a being of the light that lives and moves in the eternal All-law of God, and has its eternal existence in the Eternal, in the All-principle, which is and which speaks itself as the Self: the pure, the fine, the noble, the beautiful, the selfless love, the All-law, the Absoluteness, the eternal Being, the eternal truth.

For this reason, each caterpillar must unfold, that is, unwind itself from what it has spun around itself, in order to recognize itself in it and repent of what it recognized, to ask for forgiveness and to forgive and no longer commit what it recognized.

Then the threads of its cocoon dissolve. The walls fall, which the human being looked at until now and which he called the truth—his small ego-world that was merely the reflection of the truth. The light-filled soul and the human being who is turned within, to the holy of holies, will then behold the eternal Being, the eternal truth, in themselves.

The eternal Self is the truth. The one who has become the truth is, himself, the truth, the Self, the Being, the I Am, the eternal law of love.

With the eyes of truth, the person beholds in himself that which is outside, as well. He penetrates the reflection of the truth and sees the truth in all people, events, conversations and occurrences.

With the eyes of truth, he also sees the untrue. He cannot be deceived because he is the truth and beholds with the eyes of truth and speaks, discusses and accomplishes everything in the truth.

And so, he is the truth, which is the eternal law of the All, in which he lives, in which he moves, from which he draws and with which he works.

He is the truth, the law, in every sensation, in every thought, in every word and in every action.

Since the truth, the Being, the eternal law, is in you, and the true, the eternal, first assumes form and shape in you and then, only externally, in your surroundings and in the world, you have to live in yourself, in the All-Holy One who dwells in you.

Therefore, recognize: You are the temple of the One, the Holy One, who dwells in you.

Remember the following sentence of truth and live accordingly:

Dwell in yourself; for you are the temple of the One, the Holy One, who dwells in you.

»Dwell in yourself« means:

Allow no human, egocentric thoughts.

Raise all your feeling, thinking, speaking and acting to God.

Speak only when you are asked, and then, solely in accordance with the eternal law of the order of the temple—not too much and not too little. The measure is in you. Or speak when it is important for your neighbor, when you can give him gifts of life to take with him.

Do not ask out of curiosity. If possible, do not ask at all. What you should hear and know about will be led to you by the One who dwells in you.

And when your neighbor beside you is deep in meditation or thought, do not address him to give him an understanding of your human wisdom because you do not know where he is just then, with whom or with what he is in communication.

Do not disturb your neighbor—then you, too, will never be disturbed because then, you are alertness itself.

And when your neighbor is eating or working, do not disturb him, unless you have something important or essential to share with him because you do not know with whom or with what he is in communication.

o not waste any energy because with this, you weaken your soul and your body. At the same time, you leave the holy place in your innermost being, the Godhead in you, and you go outside of yourself.

You then begin to lean on the temple of your neighbor and begin to demand because the energy of your soul and body decreases.

The one who does not dwell in his temple gradually forgets that he, himself, is the temple of the Holy Spirit, since he no longer keeps the order of the temple, which says:

Abide in you. In the holy of holies, you experience and receive everything for yourself and for your neighbor. In yourself, you hear everything that you should say or not say. In the holy of holies, in you, you also receive the energies for your daily work.

The one who does not keep his own temple pure builds external temples or maintains these through his energy by affirming rites, dogmas and cults, and with his talents and money. He then becomes the prisoner of an order that is not the holy Order, God.

The one who is at home in God, in his temple, dwells in the innermost being, in the holy of holies, and will never invade the temple of his neighbor and desecrate it.

Therefore, never invade the temple of your neighbor with your stubborn desires, with your wanting, with your conceptions and opinions.

Never influence your neighbor in a determining and demanding way, and do not force him to do this or that. If he complies with your pressure only to please you or to be left in peace, then you have become a thief and a plunderer because you have robbed him of part of his life force.

Respect the temple of your neighbor, for he, too, shall learn the order of the temple and recognize himself through his weaknesses and faults—which he sees only when you do not block his view—and he shall clear up what he is aware of, so that he, too, may enter the holy of holies, his temple, which cleanses itself more and more.

If you heed the laws of the order of the temple, then you respect yourself and your neighbor.

The one who does not respect himself does not respect his neighbor either because he does not keep the order of the temple, himself, the law of the temple.

The order of the temple is the law of the temple. It is the eternal holy law. It is the life in God and with God.

The one who keeps the law of the temple raises his feelings, his sensations, his thoughts, his words and deeds to God. Thus, he is fulfilled by God, and what he feels, thinks, speaks and accomplishes bears divine power.

The one who keeps the law, God, is one with his neighbor and with all Being because the one who keeps the eternal law is the Being.

Take note:

You are the temple of the One, the Holy One, who dwells in you.

Therefore, keep your temple pure, by keeping the order of the temple.

Daily anew, become aware that in you dwells the All-Wise One, the Eternal, who knows about all things, who is with you, who speaks to you, who knows every answer and solution.

When you awaken in the morning, before any conversation, before you begin to work, when you meet your neighbor and speak with him, remember:

The All-Wise One, the Eternal, who knows about all things, dwells in you.

He speaks to you. He speaks through you. He guides you through your conversations. He acts through you in every situation. He is the strength for your work.

*R*emember the following:

Do not allow the unnecessary and impure to romp about in your conscious mind and in your subconscious.

The one who lives consciously is alert and knows the vagabonds that insinuate themselves, to tempt him.

Take the whip of inner strength and drive away from you all that is impure, that insinuates itself, so that it finds no entry to the sanctified temple.

By mastering your thoughts and senses, your inner temple has become pure.

Whatever insinuates itself, every temptation, drive it away from you!

However, before you drive the temptation away from you, greet the good in it and allow the good to move in you.

The movement of the good in you causes anguish in the evil, in the tempter who is behind the temptation.

The anguish is the conscience that knocks at the door of the evil and makes itself perceivable as help and strength for transformation, offering itself for this at the same time. Through this, the evil has the opportunity for self-recognition and for clearing things up. The evil, which comes from without, is the temptation behind which are the tempters, who guide the negative powers to you, to test you and to see whether or not you succumb to them, after all.

The same happens through you, the liberator, only in a reverse sense: The good in you knocks at the door of evil, to move it to see reason, to recognize itself and to turn back.

Thus, if evil approaches you, then step before the gates of your inner temple and bring the gifts of goodness to the evil.

By the reaction of the approaching thoughts that you have perceived, you notice the reaction of the tempter. If you feel that your selfless gifts found resonance, that is, were accepted, then give even more. Then call the tempter's attention to the consciousness of the Christ of God and again enter the inner sanctum, your temple.

There, in your innermost being, allow no human thoughts and reactions. Maintain the good of the tempter in your innermost being, and move it from time to time. In this way, you are sending the All-law to him. You are thus sending gifts of selfless love to him. You, however, do not go into a receiving mode. Leave this up to the Christ of God and His child, the tempter.

How your neighbor behaves and what he sends concerns only the eternal Father and His child.

Keep, you, the order of the temple: be silent!

To be silent means to be in the stillness.

God lives and speaks through the one who lives in the holy of holies, in God.

In the temple of God, no human thoughts can exist. So linger within, in you, without thoughts, that is, in silence.

And when you think, then think divinely.

And when you speak, then speak the law of God—speak divinely.

Speak only divinely, and only when your neighbor desires gifts from the law of life.

Take note:

Your pure sensations and your pure thoughts are divine.

Your selfless, noble, that is, ethical, senses are finely attuned. They are the antennae into the All, which reach into the heavens because you live in the Being, in heaven, and thus receive from heaven, as well.

Never look at your neighbor, or you will look only at yourself.

Only when you have learned to see through yourself, from your innermost being, from the holy of holies, will you also penetrate your neighbor.

As long as you cannot penetrate your neighbor, you have not taken him into your innermost being.

Only if you have unfolded the divine of your neighbor, which is also in you, will you know your brother and your sister in you.

As long as you are unable to penetrate your neighbor, he is a stranger to you because you, too, are still a stranger, far from the eternal Being.

Once both of you penetrate each other, then you both speak the language of the Being, and you are consciously united and united in God.

ever say: »This person is a stranger to me.«

Even if the shell of the soul is unknown to you, that is, a stranger, remain in the awareness that the content of the shell, the pure in the innermost part of the soul, is a part of you.

If you do not know your brother and your sister, then you do not know yourself either because you have not unfolded the pure part of your neighbor in you.

As long as you separate into »known« and »unknown,« you are far from God.

For this reason, never see yourself as a human being. Instead, perceive yourself and your neighbor as a reflection and image of God and behold him or her as your brother or your sister in you. Then you will experience in you that the life is the Being because it is omnipresent in you and in all things—the smallest in the large and the large in the smallest.

Think about the following spiritual principle:

You have spoken with a person, whom you know only by name, for you do not know what he consists of. Your neighbor, too, who lives only in the external, does not know himself because he does not know what he consists of, either. That is, he does not know himself, and you do not know him, either. If you both do not know yourselves, then you do not know God, either, and therefore, each of you is alone. God, the eternally loving Father, knows every single one because He loves each child and carries it in His great Father-heart.

verything is in you. The life is in you and you fulfill it of your own accord.

Since everything first takes place in you, the eternal Being is without shadow. This is why there is no above and below, no in front and behind, no right and no left.

The All-unity is a mighty crystal that sparkles in all facets of inner life, and each radiation permeates every facet.

The human being speaks of »above« and »below,« of »in front« and »behind,« of »right« and »left,« because he sees only with his external eyes and registers only the reflections of the truth. Through human wrongdoing, he created density, by which emerged the three-dimensional way of thinking, since with his physical eyes he can see, in turn, only the walls of his self-made cocoon-world, and accepts this as real and as the quality of his life.

Density, matter, is nothing but transformed-down divine energy, the reversal of light into shadow.

The soul of the person who lives in this human world of shadows is shadowed and is on Earth as a human being to expiate what the soul has contributed to the shadowing of the whole—unless the being of light comes on behalf of the Almighty to show the ways how the human being, the shadowed soul, can find the way out of the labyrinth of his dark ego.

f you want to keep the order of the temple, then be aware that life is a whole. And as a whole, it is above and below, in front and behind, right and left. If you have recognized this and live in the innermost part of your temple, then you also draw from your innermost being.

What for the externalized person is above and below, in front and behind, right and left, is for the inward-looking person the life, the whole, in himself.

If you keep the order of the temple, then you live in the temple, in the holy of holies of God in you, and you experience yourself. If you have experienced yourself as the Being, then you know your neighbor because you know the All, the Being.

Then you do not need to seek—you have received because the Being gives eternally. It gives in you. It streams through you and reveals itself in you and in this world.

If you recognize yourself as the Being and live in the Being, then you do not need to look around to find the truth, the Being because you know that what is behind is the same as what is in front. You do not need to look to the right or to the left because you know that what is right or left is the same as what is in front and behind. You do not need to look either upward or downward. You know that what is above and below is the same as what is in front and behind, right and left: the life, the large in the smallest and the smallest in the large, in you, the Being.

Take note and carry it with you at all times:

God is present. God is everything, everywhere.

In the largest is the smallest; in the smallest is the largest, God.

If you have found yourself, then you have found God, and you are at home in the All. Then you do not need to look around for the All nor look to the right, or to the left, nor upward or downward—the All is in you; God is in you; your neighbor is in you; all the forces of the kingdoms of nature are in you.

If you have found yourself, then you behold everything in you because you are everything in all things, yourself.

Again, take note and bear this consciously in you:

If you keep your temple pure, then you have opened everything in you, and you also have respect for the temple of your neighbor and reverence for the All-Holy One who dwells in you and in your neighbor and in all life forms of nature.

You are rich, for the All is in you. Therefore, you find everything in yourself—the smallest in the large and the large in the smallest.

I, Christ, as Jesus, taught this and more details of the eternal law to those of My apostles and disciples who could understand them. But again and again, I also had to explain to them the path to the eternal Being, as well as the Fall-law, the law of sowing and reaping.

The Fall-law is transformed-down energy of God, which the adversary reversed and wanted to use against God. This fallacy bore the turning point in itself because what the human being sows as human aspects, he will reap—and not God or his neighbor.

In God there is no curiosity. The one who looks around out of curiosity sees only his base self, himself, the ego, and does not behold his true self—therefore, he does not know himself, either. The curious one is in search of something new to gain something for himself or to use something for himself because he lacks inner values.

The curious one is the desire, the greed. He sees and hears only himself.

The curious one, who curiously looks to the right and left, to in front and behind, above and below, is also the fearful one, who sees danger for himself everywhere. He does not rest in God and therefore, does not live in God, either, and through this, creates for himself what he is afraid of. He lives in a world of limitations and of density.

The one who is afraid of others is afraid of himself. He has no confidence in himself. To him, density is reality, and at the same time, threatening. In his fearfulness, he is constantly concerned with looking around himself, so that nothing may happen to him. Curiously, he looks in front, behind, to the right and to the left, upward and downward, thus lulling himself into thinking he is safe because he is of the opinion that this way he has everything in sight.

The looking around, the looking up and looking down, to the right and to the left, to behind and to the front should—in density, on matter—be only for orientation because your physical eyes were created for matter, for density. The one who does this remains in the temple of the inner being and keeps the order of the temple.

The truly wise one is the prudent one who remains in the holy of holies and maintains the stillness there. In the temple of stillness, the truly wise one, the prudent one, receives direct instructions from God and salvation from God.

If you are experienced in the law of inner life, then you feel and think in a divine way and speak His word, which you are—divine.

he one who lives as a drop in the ocean, God, has become the law of God. The drop is the essence of the whole ocean. All drops, in turn, form the ocean, God. One drop is the same as the other drops because in one is contained everything. For this reason, all drops permeate each other and form the ocean, the All-law, God.

The All-law, God, is the holy of holies in you. Absolute stillness is there.

est in yourself—you are.

You are the Being that does not chafe at anything, that does not get annoyed about anything and does not take offence at anything. You are the Being—you see through all things and everyone. For this reason, you also penetrate everything and everyone.

The one who moves in the forecourt of the temple or on the roads to the temple, that is, the one who has not yet entered the temple, still lives in the disorder of his world of feelings and thoughts. As a result of this, he also sees only himself, his base self, and speaks only of himself, his base self because his consciousness cannot yet grasp and penetrate the disorder.

Such a person speaks only himself and sees only himself and hears only himself. Therefore, he can neither see nor understand nor hear his neighbor because he sees only himself and speaks only himself and hears only himself.

Such people have no feeling for their neighbor. They do not understand what their neighbor is saying because they do not understand themselves, since they cannot see through the disorder of their feelings, thoughts, words and deeds, nor through their coarse and craving senses. They are confused because their world of feelings and thoughts is confused.

The true and the all-permeating takes place only in the innermost part of your temple, in the holy of holies—with the All-Holy One and through the All-Holy One, God.

Only in you, do you behold and recognize how many gifts you can give your neighbor from the treasure of your innermost being—what he is able to absorb, to grow and mature spiritually. Thus, it is in you that you behold and hear the quantum that you may offer to your neighbor, which is then also offered to him for his benefit.

Know that if you have become the Being, then all things and everyone are in you. You see, hear, smell, taste and touch in you and through you because everything that the external contains in itself is the life in you.

Therefore, dwell in yourself, then you also see yourself, the self, in all things because you are the self, the being, and all things, in turn, are the Self, the Being. Then you see a part of your true self in the minerals, in the plant and animal worlds and in the stars, and you perceive all that is pure in you, the pure one, as light, as power, as a part of you. What you see externally, has, just like you, light and power in itself, in its inner being, that is, it is as essence in you and thus, a part of you.

The one who lives in this noble, fine and pure consciousness will not wantonly destroy any external form of life because he then disturbs this part of life in himself, thus becoming the disturbed one who destroys everything that he believes does not serve him. Through this externalization, war, murder and discord emerged.

Recognize: This means that what you kill wantonly—people, animals and plants—is what you shadow in yourself. You disturb your own life and remain the disturbed one, the ego-person who affects his environment in a destructive manner.

Only within yourself do you behold the Being in all things. For this reason, you do not need to look around. You have the circumspection in yourself.

What is in heaven is also on Earth—only turned away from God. The law, God, is selfless, impersonal love. It gives and gives itself and gives equally to each one.

The law of sowing and reaping came about through self-love, through the person-oriented love. This implies that the one is closer to me than the other. The one who is closer to me receives more—the other receives less. This is the person-oriented love, the self-love, the selfish love.

What is in heaven is on Earth in modified form. For this reason, the Earth, the material universe and the planes of purification are merely the mirrors of the eternal Being. The law of sowing and reaping is to be regarded as a mirror image.

Heaven is the Being, the pure, the law that radiates throughout everything, God. The law of sowing and reaping is the »being« of the human being, which consists of the mine and me that came and comes out of the base ego.

The pure is the Being, the Self, the I Am, the impersonal life, the law, God. The pure beings are the pure, the Self, the Being, the impersonal, the I Am, the law, God. Their feeling, their word and their action is the law, God, the Self, the Being, the impersonal, the pure. They, the law—since their ether-body is law—feel and speak themselves, the pure, the Being, the Self, the impersonal, the law, God.

The law of sowing and reaping can, in general terms, be called the law of burdens. It consists of the many components of the human ego, which have become the egoity-law of the individual. The egoity-law of each individual consists of his negative feelings, thoughts, words and deeds. The egoity-law can also be called the person-law because it relates to the person who emits his ego and receives again the same sending potential.

The one who has created his person-law lives in it, and, through his soul, he calls it up from where it is stored, in the stars. Your neighbor cannot adopt your egoity-law, unless he creates the same or like things through the same or like negative feelings, thoughts, words and deeds.

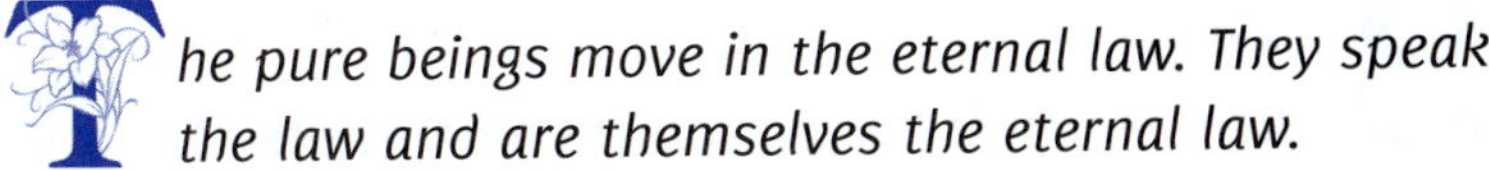

he pure beings move in the eternal law. They speak the law and are themselves the eternal law.

Every burdened person moves in his egoity-law, in his small world that he created with his ego, the mine and me. He speaks his small world, with which he built his egoity-law. According to this law, he feels himself, thinks himself, speaks himself and acts as he feels, thinks and speaks. Thus, he feels, thinks, speaks and acts according to his base self, his base being.

The human self, that is, the base ego, has no eye, no ear and no sense for its neighbor, only for itself.

The human self finds no entry into the divine Self, into the holy of holies, and thus, cannot sense, recognize, see through, and experience its neighbor because selflessness is not yet developed in the externalized person.

The human self, the base ego, has nothing in common with the divine Self, with the All-permeating I Am.

The pure one speaks the pure, the eternal law, God. The impure one speaks his impurity, his egoity-law, the base self.

Therefore, each one speaks himself: the pure one, the absolute Self, the I Am—the impure one, his base self, his base ego that is oriented only to the person.

Be still.
In the inner stillness, you become aware that you are a being from God, which is in God because the All-Eternal Father and you, His child, are one. You, the pure being, live in the holy of holies, in you, the self, for you are the temple of God, and the All-Holy One dwells in you.

Be still.
In you is the stillness and you are in the stillness.
Once you have become still, then you no longer have human feelings, thoughts, words, stirrings and inclinations. You are imbued by the All-stillness, God.
Sanctified feelings and thoughts unfold in you; you speak inspiring words and act impersonally for the great whole.

The true Self, the all-encompassing, mighty I Am, communicates with you, and you are the radiance of beauty. You are the pure, the noble and fine, the sublime—because you dwell in yourself, in the eternal Self, in the Being, and because you are what heaven is: beauty, purity, the noble, the fine, the sublime, the kindness, the selfless love.

The sun of love has the language of light. The sun of love shines in you and through you.
Your nature is the radiance of the sun, of selfless love.
Be still, completely still. Nothing and no one stirs in you.

The holy order of the temple, which you are, is the radiant selfless love, the sun of justice, the delight of your life, the I Am.

W*hatever you intend to do and to fulfill—the true Self in you, the Being, feels, thinks, speaks and acts through you.*

Your sublime, selfless feeling and thinking is the Being, the divine that you are.

The true Being refers solely to the issue and matter at hand and enters in communication with the pure in the issue and in the matter. The pure that is in the issue and in the matter tells you in your inner being how you should set things up for the issue and the matter; how you should plan, how you can clarify each situation, how you can change disorder into order and how you can clear up what is not cleared up.

In every question is the Being, the answer for you.

In every answer is the Being, and perhaps, in turn, the question for you.

In every conversation, the Being is active—you experience it in you.

The Being is in every word—it speaks to you.

In everything that you see and encounter is the Being. It shows itself to you and speaks to you.

*Once you are in your innermost being,
then your temple is pure and you are
in communication with the pure.
You hear what others do not hear;
you behold what others do not see;
you know what others do not know;
you recognize what others do not recognize;
you sense what others do not sense;
you smell and taste what others do
not smell and taste;
you perceive what others do not perceive—
because you are the truth,
the stillness of the temple,
the selfless love,
the law, God.*

Recognize:
Every issue, every matter, every difficulty, every prob-lem, every situation, every conversation, indeed, every word, speaks itself.

The Being in the issue, in the matter, in the problem, in the difficulty, in every situation, in every deed and in every thought, speaks, in turn, the mighty Self, the Being.
The shell, the human, speaks itself. The power in the shell, the Being, also speaks itself; it is the I Am.
The one who has become the Being, the selfless Self, is in communication with the pure. He beholds with the eyes

of truth. He clarifies, makes order, clears up, plans and speaks from the eternal Being, the selfless Self.

The base ego does not know the I Am; but the I Am knows the base ego because the I Am, the Being, permeates all things.

The pure one, who keeps the order of the temple, will endeavor to clarify every situation from the perspective of the law, to carry on every conversation in a lawful way, to solve every issue, every matter, every problem and every difficulty from the perspective of the law, God.

If the human ego wants to resolve the issue, the matter, the difficulty, the problem, the situation or the conversation with its base ego, then it either remains unresolved, or it leads to chaos.

Know that the Being in all things is the speaking God. He speaks to you from the issue, from the matter, from the difficulty, from the problem, from the situation, from the action, from every conversation.

Everything is consciousness. The pure is consciousness, and the impure is consciousness. The pure speaks in the holy of holies—in you, to you and, at the same time, out of you.

The impure speaks the impure. It speaks the burden; it speaks out of the disorder. It speaks the disorder, and thus, there can be, in turn, only disorder in the world.

Your eyes are the light of the soul.

You see only yourself. You hear only yourself.

With your feelings, sensations, thoughts, words and deeds, you draw the picture of your soul.

The picture of your soul is your consciousness.

Every state of consciousness perceives what corresponds to its state. This is what goes into it. This is what it is. This is what it radiates and this is what it passes on at the same time.

Can your neighbor see the same picture that you have drawn with your world of feelings and thoughts, with your words and actions?

Even what you describe is seen differently by each one—all according to their pictorial awareness.

Every person also sees his surroundings differently, again, entirely according to the pictures of his consciousness, which he has predetermined himself.

The sounds, too, which come up in your pictorial life, are also heard differently by each one.

If you call your neighbor's attention to certain sounds or colors or forms, then despite your description, he will perceive the sound differently than you, and he will also see the colors and forms differently than you.

It is possible that your neighbor even perceives more sounds than you, or sees more color nuances than you, or that the forms have another shape for him than what you see.

Who can prove to whom that he hears the right sound or sees the right color or the right shape? No person can prove something to another because each one sees, feels, senses and thinks differently.

Many people say, »I can prove it,« when a person has stolen from them.

Can a person really prove that he was stolen from—or was only that taken from him, which he had stolen from his neighbor in a former existence?

Both, the one who was stolen from and the one who stole, violated the law of God, for neither one should take something from his neighbor and call it his own.

You say that you can prove that your neighbor lied. Did your neighbor really lie—or did he merely say what you move in your world of feelings and thoughts and what, in the last analysis, you are, yourself?

Recognize that everything has two sides—unless you are divine. Then you are the truth and live All-consciously.

Then you will not get upset, either, but will speak the truth. You will clarify everything and leave it at that.

The one who finds fault with his neighbor and is moved by this for a longer period of time can be certain that he is afflicted with this fault, himself.

With what you find fault in your neighbor, you expose yourself—through the principle of sending and receiving—

to those forces you have called up through your feelings, sensations, thoughts and words.

Recognize yourself and change yourself so that, transformed, you are able to enter the spheres of salvation.

I give you an exercise for self-recognition:

Each one looks, for example, at the same area of a landscape. Each one sees different aspects in it. What the one sees, that is his picture, and not the picture of his neighbor.

A small animal moves in the landscape picture. Each one registers the animal—and yet, each one sees and senses it differently.

The perception of the individual is part of his picture and not that of his neighbor.

The picture of each individual is the picture of his state of consciousness.

Just as the individual sees and hears, feels, senses and thinks, that is his state of consciousness, with which he registers the picture, sees the colors and forms and hears the sounds.

Who can prove that the little animal looked as he perceived it? Everything is relative since each one sees, hears, smells, tastes and touches from his viewpoint, from his present consciousness-radiation.

Since each person has a different state of consciousness, he perceives the reflections which he calls matter accordingly.

Recognize that the one who heeds the many aspects that lead to freedom brings peace to himself and to his neighbor. For this reason, never influence the consciousness-radiation of your neighbor by thinking that you have to put order in his home, in his room, according to your consciousness.

Remember the following spiritual principle:
Leave to your neighbor his kingdom. That means, do not change his consciousness-radiation. The consciousness-radiation of you and of your neighbor also affects the rooms that you or your neighbor live in. Leave to your neighbor his small kingdom, for this is how he wants to feel at home. If you heed this spiritual principle, then he will be glad when you visit him.

Enter his room only when you are welcome and leave everything in the room the way your neighbor arranged it because that is the perspective of his consciousness.

If you sit on a chair or take an object, put the chair back as it was and put the object back in its place—just as it was before.

Do not change anything, even if you would like it better otherwise, and if you think it would be nicer as you see it. With this, you influence the consciousness-radiation of your neighbor and with your seeming order you bring disorder into his life, into his consciousness-radiation. Just as your neighbor sees it, that is how it is good for him at present. He does not want it changed by you—unless he asks you to.

The one who heeds this spiritual principle respects his neighbor and himself, too.

Even in the smallest things, the following spiritual principle applies: What you do not want others to do to you, do not do to others, either.

Never be curious. Do not look behind, to the right and to the left out of curiosity, to see and to hear. You are responsible for what you see and hear.

What you saw and heard stimulates you to think—and you are responsible for every thought. What you saw and heard stimulates you to speak and to act—and for this, too, you are responsible.

The pure one will not look around curiously. He will not produce thoughts. He will not look for words or think about how, what and when he should act and work. The pure one has everything in himself, and is in all things because he is the truth, which, in turn, is in all things.

If you behold your neighbor, then you behold the All, and you behold the eternal Father in you and you behold your neighbor in you. You are the image of the eternal, sole holy Father because you are divine in Him, His created children, whom He beholds in Himself, through Himself and in the All.

If you have beheld your neighbor in you, then you have beheld your eternal Father, for the Eternal and His pure child are one.

Since you know and behold your neighbor as a part of you in you, you also know the eternal One, the Holy One because you are His image, the eternal law—which you know because it is what you are, since you are divine.

The pure one is the eye of the holy temple.
The one who beholds sees through everyone and everything.

he innermost being is the stillness that beholds itself and sees through all things. The stillness is the true life.

Therefore, be still. The stillness is the All-wise word, the law of the All. It reveals itself as the stillness in the stillness. It beholds itself in the stillness as the stillness.

Everything is the law, which is the sublime, unending stillness, which speaks itself, the I Am.

The stillness is the law and the wisdom of God. The one who is wise is still because he knows about all things since he sees through and penetrates all things.

he absolute is the stillness; it is the order of the temple, which you, the pure one, are.

If you know who you are, and if you know that the awareness of the I Am is the life, then you live and will not take offense at anything. Nor will you break through anything because you see right through and penetrate everything that is density, hindrance and offense in the eyes of the world.

The one who works by day sees the corners and edges and will not bump into them because he uses the light of the day.

The same is true of the eternal light. Nothing can happen to the one who walks in the light. The light of love will always shine for the one who keeps the laws of the Spirit of God, whether he is soul or human being.

The restless one, the loud one, in whom feelings and thoughts toss and rage, is the seeking one who looks only at the surface of the truth—of things, matters and words—and seeks the solution there. With this, he gives himself riddles because he wants to guess and chase after the knowledge himself.

The one who is not wise is also not quiet, that is, still because he keeps wanting until he has found himself in the very basis, in the stillness—that which he is, the self, the wisdom and the beauty from God, the all-knowing law, God, the wisdom, which is the same as truth.

Your neighbor, the one, is just as near to you, the pure one, as the other because no one can be far from you and a stranger to you, since God is in you and you are in God, and your neighbors are in you and you are all in God. That is unity. The one is in the other and both penetrate each other and penetrate everyone—and everyone penetrates both. That is the All and the law of love and unity.

If the one were closer to you than the other, then you would look to the front, to behind, to the right, to the left, to above and below, to see him because you do not behold him in yourself.

he pure one wishes for his neighbor only what he is, himself: the eternal law, God, the pure.

The impure one, the unenlightened one, often wishes for his neighbor what he does not have himself: the beautiful, the good, the peaceful, the happy—facets from the eternal truth, whose actualization he still lacks in himself. What he wishes for his neighbor does not enter his neighbor because it is not imbued with power, truth and love. These are soulless wishes that return to the impure one, the unenlightened one.

The All-unity is the wisdom of God. God is everything in all things, the law of life.

The pure one addresses the whole in everything that he says, the large in the smallest and the smallest in the large.

The one who speaks to, or wishes, his neighbor only facets from the eternal law, thus placing only parts of the eternal law into his word and into his action, also favors only parts of the eternal law and expresses that he is imperfect.

With this, he bears witness of himself. He favors certain people while disregarding others. This means that he makes exceptions in relation to himself and to his neighbor.

The language of the law is the whole law, since everything is in all things, the largest in the smallest and the smallest in the largest. The pure one always speaks the whole law. If he wishes his fellowman selfless love, then he addresses all the facets of the eternal law. That is the language of the law.

If the pure one wishes his fellowman peace, he addresses, in turn, the whole law. That is the language of the law.

The pure one always speaks the whole law, even when he wishes an ill person health.

If he were to wish the ill person only a facet of health, for example, the health of an ill organ, then he would be addressing only that part of the law that is overshadowed by the illness. By doing this, he would ignore the effectiveness of the whole eternal law. Through this, he could perhaps hinder the effectiveness of the eternal law in the ill person.

The one who wishes for only the physical recovery of his neighbor addresses the illness itself, which he may even intensify, if the ill person relies on this statement. With this, he disregards the will of God, who knows about His child and wants to guide it in such a way that is of benefit for its soul.

Selfish thoughts influence merely the surface—that is, the effect, the symptom, the illness—and prevent the eternal law from becoming effective.

The one who addresses merely the surface of life, the reflection—for example, by wishing his neighbor peace *when he has no peace himself—addresses only the lack of peace in his neighbor because he has no communication with peace himself.*

As a human being, the truly wise one needs the language of the world to make himself understood. Despite the limitation of words, the wise one will address the whole, the all-encompassing law, God, in words such as »health« and »peace.« Then the eternal law, God, will prevail, which leaves every person his free will and guides him in such a way that it serve his soul and not solely the shell, the person.

The one who himself is ill and wishes health to his neighbor, addresses, in turn, only the illness in his neighbor and perhaps those aspects that are in accord with his own illness because what goes out from him will go back into him and possibly into his neighbor, in whom the same or like symptoms of illness are found. This takes place according to the law »like draws to like and intensifies itself.«
The one who wishes his neighbor peace and is without peace himself may intensify in his neighbor the aspects that lack peace, if his neighbor is without peace because like always stimulates like and wants to fulfill itself.

The one who wishes love to his neighbor and is, himself, without love may strengthen the lack of love in his neigh-

bor who is still without love because like always draws to like and wants to fulfill itself—again, according to the law »like draws to like and intensifies itself.«

Recognize:
Every sensation, every thought, every word and every action is energy.

What a person emits can become effective in his neighbor if the same or like things are in the neighbor. The same and like things return to the person who emitted because the one who emits will receive.

The one who wishes health and peace to his neighbor and is, himself, ill in soul or body or does not have peace in himself, by not having actualized the eternal laws, influences the illness and the lack of peace in his neighbor and intensifies these because he did not let his wishes of peace and recovery, which he offered to his neighbor, become active in himself.

If you wish for your neighbor what you, yourself, have not yet fulfilled, for example, the pure, the noble, the beautiful and the good, it will not reach his inner being because it is not vivified by you—or the surface, the appearance, his base ego, takes it in and feels flattered and honored, and in this way, his base self, his base ego, is strengthened.

Wish your neighbor only what you have in and on you, that is, what is actualized and thus, vivified, and address the whole of the eternal law in everything. Since everything is contained in all things, affirm the whole law, God, in your wishes for your neighbor. Do not look only at the surface, at what should take place on your neighbor's body or in his surroundings. Remember that the salvation of the soul is the decisive factor and that the pure spiritual body is, in turn, the whole law.

What the pure one wishes for his neighbor—that which he, himself, fulfills—comes from the innermost part of his temple and goes into his neighbor's temple. He carries, so to speak, the fruits of the eternal law into his neighbor's temple because he brings the eternal law to his neighbor as a gift of love, which, in turn, is the law itself.

Thus, do not wish your neighbor details from the eternal law, otherwise you address in him and in yourself only parts of the eternal law. With this, you let all other facets of the eternal law lie fallow. This means that you would be satisfied with some facets and through this, you bear witness to your impureness and open the gates to the impure so that it can ensnare you.

Even if you address only a certain area of matter, place in it the whole. That is the true life, that is living in the eternal law, God.

*L*earn to behold.

The curious person looks curiously to the front, to behind, to the right and to the left, to above and below—and always sees himself because curiosity always calls up only what the curious person is, himself. Like calls to like, to communicate with it.

Learn to look through yourself, to behold from the temple of your inner being, then you recognize the spiritual principle in all things and in your neighbor, as well—and the whole in the spiritual principle. That is the life in the eternal law; that is the language of the law.

Learn to listen.

The pure one does not need to listen for something. He knows within himself, in the holy of holies of his temple, what is important. Everything else, what is still pending, is not yet ripe and not yet significant.

The one who wants to listen in and eavesdrop will experience only his base ego, which unsettles him and stimulates him to again think, speak and act in an unlawful way—that is, to emit negatively—so that he will receive negativity in turn.

Learn to listen. Never ask curious questions because otherwise you will hear only yourself, your base self.

In everything that is being said to you, listen for the spiritual principle of God, and recognize, in turn, the totality in it and, at the same time, experience it in you, in your temple. The spiritual principle contains the whole law, just as the spiritual principle is contained in the whole law. That is living in the eternal law, and that is also the language of the eternal law.

The one who aspires to listen for the eternal word, the Being, the law, in himself, is not yet the word, the Being, the eternal law. And the one who listens for it—according to his soul's degree of maturity—merely listens and does not yet know it because he has not yet become the law of God.

And the one who wants to recognize and experience the eternal Being according to the letter reads or listens past the reality. And the one who listens for only what his neighbor expresses as truth creates images in his mind from what he hears. That is never the reality of life, but the appearance; it is the reflection of the law and not the truth itself.

Thus, the one who merely listens for the truth—whether in himself or from without, as presented by people—is not yet the truth himself, the Being. The one who has not become the truth, the Being, does not know himself as a being of the truth because he has not yet found the way to the nature of truth, to his true being.

Only the one who is the eternal word, the Being, the law, is in the life—and is the life itself because he is the essence of the holy word, of the truth, the life.

The word of the heavens is His word, the word of God, the eternal law. The one who has become the word of God has become a being in God. He also beholds people, things, events and occurrences in the image of heaven, in the truth, in the I Am—and no longer in the image of his small world, within sight of the »I want.«

Every heavenly, selfless thought and every heavenly, selfless word is a heavenly picture, which bears everything in itself. Like the cell of a body contains the whole person, so does every selfless sensation, every selfless thought, every selfless word and every selfless action contain the entire All as essence.

The truly wise one places the whole in everything that he says—even when he shares only a facet of the truth from the whole by bringing it to shine.

God is the whole and is undivided. For this reason, the whole is effective in the one who is the divine word. He is the one being in the Being. He is not divided like the person who speaks other than he thinks and feels other than he thinks and speaks.

The eternal law is active and reveals itself in you. Everything is law. You do not see it externally; you recognize and see it as the whole, in you alone.

The physical eyes perceive only what is external and not what is manifest in the innermost being, in the pure being, in the temple of God.

The physical eyes perceive only the pale reflection of what is in heaven.

That which is matter is reflection and not the Absoluteness.

The one who beholds becomes aware of God in everything that is—in every flower, in every bush, in every stone, in the stars, in the people. With every blink of the eye, with his ears, with the senses of taste, smell and touch, he encounters God.

For the one who beholds, God is present in all things.

When he does his work, God is present. When he has a conversation, God is present. When he goes here or there, God is present.

These people have found the philosopher's stone. They let God act through them. The one who keeps the connection with God in everything that he feels, thinks, speaks and does truly walks in the light of God, and God does works of love through him.

In everything, keep the awareness that God is present; God is in all things.

If you have assimilated this certainty in you, then loneliness, desolation and grief will withdraw from you. You will gain togetherness, inner happiness and more insight.

Be aware of this in every situation: God is always present—He is always there. Whatever you do, wherever you go, where you are, what you think—God is there. He is present.

God is with each one of you—no matter how you think, speak and act.

If you are in the midst of an angry crowd—God is with you. Be still, entrust yourself to Him. He leads you.

God is the health in illness, the joy in sorrow.

Remember: God is always present. God is love; He loves each one of you.

Do not leave the recognition that God is present at mere knowledge, that God, our eternal Father, loves you and me, all of us. Only the actualization, this means the spiritual knowledge that is lived, gives you the certainty and dynamism in the Spirit of God—the life in the Being.

The Being is present. In the Being there is no yesterday, no today and no tomorrow. Matter is transitory. The Being is everything in all things. Through this, matter is refined and becomes the Being because God is the present in all things.

The present in all things is the everlasting, the Being. For this reason, the transitory, the yesterday, today and tomorrow will transform into the Being, which is.

The vision of the pure one is the pure that he perceives solely in himself, in his pure temple. There, the most holy, eternal law, God, shines and reveals itself continuously.

The pure one beholds what the impure one does not see.
The pure one perceives in himself solely the eternal truth because he himself has become the truth, the all-encompassing law, the I Am. He allows nothing impure in the temple of love.
On the other hand, the impure one perceives only the impure, namely, what he is himself—the impure.

The pure one beholds and recognizes in himself the pure, the truth. He speaks the language of pictures, of the truth, in himself because he has become the truth himself. The word of God is the law. It is the truth that manifests itself as the living picture in the innermost part of the soul. No matter where the pure one looks—he beholds in himself only the law-picture, the purity; and outside of himself, he sees the reflection, the impure.

The pictorial vision is, at the same time, a vision of recognition. What you see, you see through and you recognize—and thus, you know about all the details. This is the truth. This is you, the truthful, eternal self.
The truly wise one, the enlightened one, is what he speaks, the law.

The unenlightened one, who is unable to tell black from white, is the blind one who is satisfied with the illusion and believes the Being to be far away.

The true vision is the vision of recognition. You see and know, yet cannot prove it because the innermost being, the holy of holies, does not need to be proved because it is.

Only the illusion wants to prove itself because what is in it, the eternal spiritual principles, is not manifest.

The Being sees what the illusion does not see. This means that I, the Being, behold what you, the reflection, do not see. But when you are the Being, then you are united in Him, in the All-One. Then you will also behold what I behold, and we behold what the illusion does not see.

The spiritual eye beholds—the physical eye sees. Both cannot be brought into conformity with each other because the spiritual eye is the law of heaven and the physical eye is merely the eye of reflection, which passes on the Being as reflection that is many times distortion. The one who is satisfied with this is the fool who has not yet stepped through the gate into the truth.

The eye of the truth is God. The one who beholds with this eye is truthful and divine. He brings the light, the eye of God, the truth, into this world, the eternal law of love.

The eye of truth is the light and the image of your pure spiritual body, which is the image of God.

The physical eye is the image of the soul, of the enveloped spiritual body. It has an eye only for what is enveloped, which, in turn, is the onus and the burden of the soul.

As Jesus of Nazareth, I, Christ, instructed My apostles and disciples from different perspectives of life. Again and again, I pointed out to them the Absolute Law and explained the law of sowing and reaping. I spoke to them in the following sense:

The sea of infinity is the stream of the All. Move more and more in the sea of infinity as the sun of love and justice. Then you will be the life and will no longer ask about life.

As long as the person lets himself be shone upon by human beings, he does not radiate. Then he is dependent on the shine of his neighbor. If a person is dependent on the shine of people, he does not know the radiance of the sun that dwells in him.

For every single one, the eternal law is: You, stay the true self. Then you are the true self and do not expect the shine of your neighbor because you, the true self, your self, radiates.

Only the illusion is satisfied with the shine. Both then stand in the twilight and are of the opinion that they have *the highest and the greatest because they shine on each other.*

Recognize that illusion deceives and the one who falls for this can become a deceiver.

For this reason, do not surround yourselves with illusions, with the shine, but become the sun of love and justice in the sea of infinity.

Many souls and people move toward the Being, but few are in the Being. The one who merely thinks about the Being receives only from the illusion, and not from the source of life, which is the Being.

The one who belongs to the illusion wears many masks. He puts on the mask that fits the occasion.

The one who lives in the world of illusion and has his masks knows neither himself nor the one who wears the same or similar masks as he does, himself. Both speak only about their masks, about illusion, and do not find reality.

The mask-maker is lonely and alone because he does not care about his neighbor. He thinks only of himself and wants to maintain his masks.

But the one who lives in the inner world, in Me, the Christ, is clear-sighted and farsighted. He no longer needs masks because he sees through everything and recognizes everything by way of the light of truth. That is the being in the stream of the Being, the personified being, the microcosm in the macrocosm.

Everything that you see and that upsets you is your mirror. It influences your person. If you do not follow the path of self-recognition, you perceive only the reflections of your base ego and that of your neighbor. If you continue to do this, then you become ever more entangled in the mine and thine. You then differenciate between yourself and your neighbor. This is the law of the human ego. It is: »Divide, bind and rule.«

The divine law is: »Link and be.« This means that the one who lives connected with the innermost being is linked with all people and beings and with all forms of life. With them, he forms the unity in God that knows no differences, since everything is contained in all things, the law of life.

The law of cause and effect, which was created by the adversary—»Divide, bind and rule«—is the person-oriented law, the egoity-law that knows only itself, the base ego.

The adversary wants division and binding. People should bind themselves to people and things, generate possessions and property, to thus bring about division, the mine and thine. The one who has acquired the most property rules over those who have less.

Satan took the sword and divided the unity of the Earth into multiplicity. With the pieces, the countries, he created rulership and rulers, the rich, who made of the pieces their realms.

That is the division that comes from the satanic. But I have come to establish the unity again through the law of love, which unifies everyone and everything.

Boundaries restrict and lead to hardening. When boundaries remain in force for a long time, people believe they are separated from each other by these boundaries. They then speak about different mentalities that have little in common. From this attitude, awaken indifference and enmity toward the neighbor who, according to the eternal law, is a part of every soul.

Once the adversary has caused division among the people, he then rules and creates more external possibilities for binding people, for example, binding people to creeds, rites, dogmas and cults and, at the same time, to superiors, to subordinates, to husband or wife, to children or material assets, to money and property. From this, the causal law emerges, in which every egocentric person and every egocentric soul has its existence, until they break out of the maelstrom of the human ego and strive for the divine that links and that is.

This world and the planet Earth appear in the divine as a mirror image because the world and the Earth were reversed into their opposite.

The heritage of God to His children can be explained as follows:

That which is Mine is also thine. It is for you and for each child the same, namely, everything from all things, from the One, who is.

The adversary reversed this divine principle of the law and says: The mine and thine belong to me. The adversary believes that through this reversal, he can assimilate everything and be lord over everything and everyone. He wants the power for himself alone and wants to defeat God because he wants to be God, himself.

The materialistic person who is oriented to himself is of the opinion that he is the ruler of the world and of the All. He thinks he is a god because he sees only a small perspective of life and this is, moreover, enveloped by his human ego. This idolatry lends him the arrogance to think he can continue to develop creation, all according to his image and standard. In reality, he leads himself into the abyss and destroys matter and his physical body.

In the number eight lies the Deity, in despising, the adversary, who reversed the holy Being, the eight, and turned it into despising. In this way, he created his Fall-law that will bring him to his downfall.

The one who does not respect his neighbor honors neither the eternal Father nor Me. His prayers remain fruitless because the fruit, encapsulated in these prayers, does not attain ripeness.

The one who lets himself be honored by human beings does not honor God.

The adversary leads soul and person into the world of the senses. He tempts them with the illusion of their neighbor. He shows them what others possess and have, their mine and for me, and makes them greedy and envious. In this way, he leads them away from their innermost being, the Being, the fullness in God, and toward the external world, to illusion.

The one who allows himself to be blinded by illusion will become like the one who is already blinded: greedy, envious and rapacious. In his craving, he uses all the weapons at his disposal to attain what his neighbor's illusion radiates to him: outer splendor attained through prestige, means and opportunities that are reflected in money and wealth.

In this way, the person moves away from the inner fullness more and more, becoming poor of inner strength and spirituality. He trains his mind and raises it to the intellect, to become an intellectual who has knowledge *about the illusion, the deception. In so doing, he no longer knows the Being, his true self, the reality of life, but knows only himself, his small world where he dominates, rules and binds his neighbor to himself and to his opinions, to which he, himself, is bound.*

Woe to those who use their intellect to idolize human beings. Imperceptibly, such a person creates idols. In this world, he attaches himself to them, and after his physical death, he is bound to them.

The one who is greedy and egocentric, who exalts himself with the splendor of illusion, always wants to be the greatest and the best, and wants to rule over everything and everyone.

The drive to dominate contains, in turn, a flowering of fear that another one could be greater, could attain more splendor, more prestige and wealth. Hounded by fear, he thinks that his eyes and ears have to be everywhere, to ensure that he is not defrauded. If a rival appears, he will be fought. If the rival has abilities that he does not have, then, at the same time, envy and animosity grow, and not least, aggressiveness, the effort to eliminate the rival.

Fear and aggressiveness lead to curiosity. The ego-person wants to see everything, to listen in on everything, to know about everything, to protect himself from dangers that could come toward him from his neighbors, who have more prestige, who seem to be better, smarter and richer. This leads to his constantly having to get his bearings. Cu-

riosity urges him to look to the front, to the back, above and below, to the right and to the left, to see and to listen in on everything. In doing this, he sees and hears only himself because what is driving him, his human ego, drives toward him the same or like things again.

The egocentric person sees himself in every situation. He hears himself in every situation. He meets only himself—people who are, in turn, similar to himself. He and his neighbor speak the same language, themselves. What comes of this is, in turn, only they, themselves. Thus, they bind themselves to each other. They will have to clear up together what they have tied themselves with, until they can leave the wheel of reincarnation and the soul realms.

Therefore, O human being, practice selflessness and learn to recognize yourself as a being in God.

Do not look around in curiosity, otherwise you will see only yourself, your ego, which you will then have to fight and struggle with again. Do not eavesdrop on the conversations of your neighbor. Do not listen when two people are conversing, otherwise you will hear only your own ego—unless they include you in their conversation.

A person is responsible for what he hears.

If you are at home in the innermost part of your temple, then you will speak the word of truth, which is the life, from eternity to eternity.

he word of God is the stream of the All. The human word is merely the edge of the stream. Therefore, speak only what is essential and fill it with the power of actualization, with the power of God. Then you will reach the stream of the All.

The word that you speak has value and power only as far as you have actualized what you express. Only what you have fulfilled, that is, actualized, goes into the person, and not what you draw from your intellect. This word is empty. It is hollow, as it were, and does not know the depth of the All, which I Am.

It is not enough to affirm and proclaim the laws of the All, the laws of God. Only the one who actualizes them brings good deeds.

You must first have actualized, yourself, what you teach. That is the best role model. These words and deeds enter the person's soul because they have substance and power.

It is of no use to speak about the light and not be the light.

The one who merely speaks about the light is empty because he is divided. He wants to serve God and thinks that it is enough to serve according to the letter. However, that is not serving, but being servile. He teaches a word, but not the word because the letter kills. However, the light in the letter brings life.

Only the one who journeys inward and becomes the light can find the light and vivify the letter.

The one who merely speaks about wisdom and is not wise is in the world and lives with the world and is for the world. Therefore, he is divided. He speaks wisdom according to the letter and yet is in the world. He wants to be wise and yet is not. Through this, he deceives himself and pretends to others what he is not: wise.

The one who merely speaks about a good and loving mindset merely has words about the loving mindset, but does not bring the good, the valuable, into this world.

The one who actualizes, brings spiritual values and spiritual deeds into this world. He is the heart-thinker who gives from the light of life. He lives righteously because he knows: God looks into the heart of each and every one.

hose awakened in the Spirit of God see those who are unawakened. They experience them in their behavior, in their thinking and speaking. They try to help them, as far as the latter want this.

Those awakened in the Spirit know the unawakened ones. They understand them and will be helpful to them to the extent that is good for their souls.

The unawakened ones, however, do not recognize the awakened ones. To them, in many cases, the latter are charlatans and know-it-alls, or they categorize them under the consciousness that corresponds to their own nature.

The unawakened ones, who orient themselves solely to matter, see in the spiritually awakened person, in the divine, either a mischief-maker or an eccentric whom they are unable to fathom.

Those who live daily with an awakened one look solely at the person and do not comprehend what radiates from him.

If an unawakened one wants to teach and guide another unawakened one, then both remain unawakened because they speak only empty, that is, hollow, words, in which the fire of love that makes them bright and seeing does not blaze. Both are the blind ones who will fall into the pit.

For this reason, be alert and pray, and let your words become filled with light. Indeed, let them become divine, so that you live in Me, the Christ, and are one with Me, the Christ, for the Eternal has sent Me to humankind to proclaim and bring the light and salvation to it.

The one who has devastated his inner temple builds ever greater and more splendid dwellings. Through this, the awareness of the presence of God and the sight for the true life were lost. I Am come to erect the inner temple again and to cause the holy works of God to become visible.

With My power, I Am among the people, to again proclaim the light and the salvation to them. Blessed are the ones who find Me in their hearts. They do not need external temples anymore—they have become the temple of salvation, themselves.

I Am the freedom. Do not let yourselves become bound, neither to dogmas nor to statutes.

Realize that in heaven there are neither dogmas, statutes, ceremonies nor superiors and subordinates. In heaven, you are all equal among one another—brothers and sisters. The one who does not strive toward this goal or who lets himself be dissuaded from this goal is a fool and spiritually dead, as it were.

The awakened one strives to reach his inner being, the kingdom of life—the unawakened one strives toward the external, toward the things that are reflected in the materialistic world and that rule the one who is with this world.

Never let yourselves be integrated into institutions and taught by Pharisees and scribes. They do not have the keys to the Kingdom of God, since they have not entered the life, themselves. As a result, they do not let those enter who want to come in because they do not know the lock, since they are not practiced in carrying the key that I Am, Christ.

The pure one sees through everything. His beholding eye is the perception of his divine consciousness. Everything that takes place in his divine consciousness is the truth. Everything else is merely a mirror, a distant echo of the truth, a reflection, the illusion of truth.

How you speak and what you say is your language—it is also your face and your body.

Your inner being as well as your outer aspects—your word, your behavior—speak themselves. The fulfilled one speaks the self because he is the self in the All-Father-Being. The world-oriented one speaks his base self. He speaks the language of his ego—that which he is, himself. The world-oriented one is the one who is wrapped up in the world, who is content with what he sees, with the reflections of his little world, which are his own mirror image.

What you, the pure one, the light in the primordial light, say is substance and power, since it is spoken from the holy of holies, from you, the Being. That is the language of God in you and through you.

Speak the language of the true Self, and you are divine. The language of the true Self is the God-filled word. It flows from the innermost part of your temple.
The divine does not defend itself, nor does it debate, because it is. The »Is« beholds and sees through everything and knows the innermost part of the person and his outer aspects, as well. The one who knows the eternal law because he is it, will not debate.
The innermost being is the impersonal, which addresses the personal in an impersonal way, explaining and putting right what is untrue.
Explain things to your neighbor when something is not right, but never intrude on him. Do not urge him to think and to do what is the truth. If the intransigent one continues to speak, despite the explanation or despite knowing better, then he talks himself into trouble.

You, the truly wise one, be silent. If you have put right what is not right, if you have shed light on the untrue with the light of the truth and if, despite everything, you are rejected, then be silent because you know the true Savior, God—as well as the judge who speaks solely of himself. He is the person who through intransigence, through revenge and greed, delivers himself to the law of sowing and reaping, by sowing into the field of his life that which judges him. It is his small, base self, his egoity-law.

What you speak outside of the holy of holies is not always the language of your personal ego because your thoughts and words are not always your thoughts and your words. When you speak so-called thoughtless words over years and decades, then it may be you who is speaking, but another is speaking through you. This is the outside control via your sensory world in which you then live. The programmer, the one who, or which, controls you, also controls others through you. The one who allows this is a slave to sin and a sinner.

ou are not the time, but eternity in the Eternal One.

However, you are a human being in the course of day and night that is called time. For this reason, plan your time with God. Include the passage of time in your planning and bring your plan into the All-law that is in you. Bring everything into your inner temple and surrender it to the order of the temple.

Then be still and alert at the same time, for the All-Holy One in you makes order and sets the course. The All-Holy One, who is your word and your deed, moves in your innermost being and reflects to you, the human being, the step-by-step course of your plan. He also includes it in the passage of time.

Then, at the right time, you speak the word that is rich in content, the word that is divine, and you do what needs to be done at the right time, which, in turn, is divine. Then your daily work runs in accordance with the will of the All-Holy One who is in you, and in whom you are.

s Jesus of Nazareth I traveled a lot with My apostles and disciples. On the paths and byways from one place to another, I taught them the following:

When you walk, then walk upright; when you stand, then stand upright; when you sit, then sit upright.

Each one of you is the being in the stream of the Being.

Every harmonious movement is the rhythm of the stream, the rhythm of the All.

The stream knows no bending, no curve. It does not give way to anything or anyone. It flows unvaryingly through the All and flows throughout everyone and everything.

When you walk through this world with long strides, then you walk bent over. Your eyes look to the earth, to the ground, from where you absorb what adheres to the ground. Everything that is heavy or burdened crawls on the ground and burdens, in turn, those who direct their looks and thoughts solely to the ground.

Recognize: A heavy gait is, as it were, a crawling gait. Such people see only themselves and what they, in turn, are—that which radiates to them from the ground.

Therefore, walk upright. You then gain foresight and insight and an overview. Then you are linked with the cosmic powers more and more. These point out to you what still needs to be cleared up, so that, in time, you behold cosmic-

ally, you hear cosmically, you feel, think, speak and act cosmically.

When you stand, then stand upright. Do not lean against objects and things. The one who leans against objects and things will also be emitted to by these objects and things. You then absorb whatever adheres to the objects and things.

The one who leans against objects and things also leans on his neighbor and takes from him the humanness that he radiates.

If you lean on your neighbor and your neighbor leans on you, then, in time, you will both become tired and weary of each other because the energies that you transmit and draw from each other will soon be exhausted. What then?

The results are strife, quarreling, discord and disunity. Once you are weary of each other, then each one seeks his next victim, on whom he again leans—and perhaps the victim, in turn, leans on him. The result will be the same as before.

Therefore, stand upright. Do not lean against anything or on anyone. Then you will gradually become cosmic antennae that reach into the heavens and receive from the heavens.

If you sit, then sit upright. Your spine is not curved. It is perpendicular and shows you that you should sit upright, to receive from the stream of the Being.

You have heard that the stream of the Being, the law, knows no bending and curving. A healthy spine, too, knows neither bends nor curves.

If you lie back in your chair, then it is as if you were lying on the floor and receiving the vibrations that crawl along the floor.

If you cross your arms and legs, then you block the flow of the Being in and on you, or you direct it away from you and attract other forces.

Know that the human being should be a cosmic antenna. The one who makes knots in his antenna or bends it can receive neither the powers nor the salvation of the All. It is solely the powers of the All that strengthen and move the person, that make him free and healthy. They give him foresight and insight and the overview.

The one who does not accept and live these spiritual principles becomes narrow-minded and intellectual. In time, he acquires those traits that his neighbors show, who are likewise on the human track.

If you lie down, then lie down to rest. Rest consciously and lie horizontally and be aware that you are resting, then you will perceive the stillness of the All.

If you support your head on your hands while speaking, while eating or doing something else, you will speak only your base self and wolf down the food like a predator with his prey. Then you become a glutton who seeks pleasures and nurtures physical pleasure, sexuality because through his undisciplined behavior, through the bent antenna, he receives corresponding powers, that is, corresponding transmitters.

The stream of the Being is harmonious, rhythmic movement. Therefore, move harmoniously. Harmonious movements are the melodies of the All.

Know that each body is sound; it is melody. Just as it sounds, so is the person.

Every hectic movement is a bending of the antenna that is, in turn, the person, himself. Then the person will lean against things, he will half lie in his chair, cross his arms and legs and support his head on his hands.

Harmonious movements are dynamic movements. They bring about flexibility in thought, speech and action.

Know that the upright person is the one who has straightened up, as it were, who radiates the cosmic sounds in his thinking, speaking and acting, and whose gestures and facial expressions give voice to the cosmic symphonies.

Therefore, sit upright and place both feet on the floor. Then you release tensions and take in harmonious vibrations.

Know that every one of you is the compressed All, and the All is the Being—it is the eternal homeland, the sea of light, God. For this reason, as human beings, behave in such a way that you send into the heavens and receive from the heavens.

If you live in the stream of the All, then you are the essence of the All. Then you live in the fullness and you are the fullness. No person and nothing can disappoint you because you expect nothing, since you are the fullness.

Recognize that the All and the All-stream send unceasingly. Look at the bushes, flowers, animals and stones— they are. They have their antennae directed into the All.
Animals, plants, bushes and trees do not lean on others of their kind, unless the human being interferes in the cosmic course of things. When trees stand too close together, they cannot develop. It is similar with people when they lean on people, objects and things.

Unfold yourselves: Do not lean against anything or anyone.

The ennobled person is the wise person who rests in his inner being.

The ennobled and wise person does not laugh out loud from his throat. He smiles from his heart.

Realize that culture cannot just be put on a person or a country. Culture has to grow out of the person. Where there is no culture, there are many cults.

The You Am I, and you are the I.
Therefore, remember the following:
You are the fine and the beautiful.
You are the noble and the pure.
You are in the You that is eternal, the sublime.
The sublime is the One.
You in the You, in the sublime One, are the sublime one that knows about all things because the sublime One is the Father—the greatness, the power and the All, itself.
He is the culture and the cultural because He is Creator, God, bearer, mover, giver—the Being.
He is beauty, splendor, the fullness.
He is your Father—you, His child, the heir.
You are the light in the sea of light, God. Therefore, you do not need to hold on to anything or anyone.

You, the pure one, are the sincerity and the upright one. You lean on neither people, things nor objects. You draw your strength solely from the holy of holies in your self, which you, the self in you, the Self, are.

Therefore, do not lean on people, otherwise, you will become dependent and insincere. The one who leans on people also rejects people. The dependent one will become like an appendage of his neighbor. When the latter no longer supports him, he is lonely.

Do not lean against or hold on to things or objects because that says that you rebel against your neighbor. It also indicates the turmoil of your state of mind.

Know that every person radiates his degrees of vibration. Things and objects also radiate what adheres to them. When you lean against something or on someone, then you call up from the people, things and objects exactly what moved you to lean on them, or what brought out the turmoil of your emotions.

I repeat: Countless vibrations adhere to people, things and objects, which vibrate into and besiege the one who has the same or like things in or on him. Through this, your correspondences, your rebellious attitude and your emotional turmoil are reinforced.

Do not lean on anything or anyone, instead, be steadfast, upright and straightforward, then you will be, or you are, the I Am, the sincerity, the justice, the All-law.

Rest in you. Whatever you do, give it your all, with full concentration, focused on the matter and issue.

The wise one who lives in his purified temple also keeps the order of the temple while writing. Now, he is writing. His sensations and thoughts are with the writing of his paper. From his innermost being, the holy of holies, in which he lives and from which he gives, he has an effect on the external, on every letter and on every word. Through this, he lends power to what he writes and imbues it with the eternal law, God.

Whatever you do, keep the order of the temple in everything.
Now you go here and there, and you are with you because you are in you.
Now you work at the workbench, and you are with your workpiece and thus, in and with you.
You speak with your neighbor, you are with you and in you and you speak the law in the word.
What you do, you do totally.
When you hold an object in one hand, then you should not hold another one in the other hand, unless both objects are attuned to each other and are not contrary to each other. For example, when you hold a workpiece in one hand and in the other hand the tool with which you work on the workpiece, then both are attuned to each other because the one serves the other.

When you put something in writing, then hold only the writing instrument in your hand. If, for instance, you were to hold a ruler in the other hand, or an object to erase what was written, then you lose your concentration and your attention is divided because these two vibrations, not being attuned to each other, cause inattentiveness and dissonance in you.

If you hold a ruler in the other hand, then, for example, you will frequently underline statements that should not be underlined, or you will underline what you are or are not yet, yourself. With this, you lend expression and emphasis to your human ego because you underline yourself, your ego. When you have the writing instrument in one hand and in the other an object for deleting what was written, then you will more often make mistakes and then erase them.

Recognize yourself in everything and give yourself up, your base ego. Then you will attain the I Am, the Being that is everything, that knows about everything and sees through everything, that hears everything, that speaks through you.

Recognize again and again: The pure takes place solely in the innermost part of the soul, in the pure—the impure, solely in the external, in the world of the senses.

ecognize: The intellect of the human being is not the heart of the soul. The one who speaks from his intellect speaks from his human programs because he is not at home in his innermost being, in the Being that knows about all things, that sees everything, that hears everything, that speaks itself.

Words spoken from the intellect merely go back into the intellect. They have no power. Therefore, they are limited and oriented to matter, which is where they become effective.

Just as the way of thinking and living of humankind changes through the ages, so does the word that is shaped by the intellect. It speaks itself again and again, from epoch to epoch, only with different words and terms.
The human, base self will pass away because it is born solely in the intellect and is spoken from there.

The surface is the intellect which reacts, in turn, superficially. The intellect is thus merely the surface of the lake, not the bottom. On the surface is merely reflection and not the truth.

The word of the innermost being is the I Am, the word of the eternal law. It was not born as was the word of the intellect. The word of God is from eternity to eternity, and the one who speaks it is from eternity to eternity.

The truly wise one, the enlightened one, speaks the I Am. It is the eternal law, the word that speaks itself eternally in the innermost being of the soul.

The God-filled person never speaks the word of the intellect because he is at home in his innermost being, in the self, which he speaks.

Let the word first grow in you before you speak.

Whether you think or speak, both are energies that will not be lost.

That which is sensed in the innermost being, in the sanctified temple, is, at the same time, also the word. The innermost being bears good fruit because the sensation, which gives birth to the thought and brings forth the word, is the divine fruit, the light and the power that come into this world through the Spirit of Christ, who vanquishes the darkness.

The one who has conquered himself with the power of Christ beholds what is, and speaks the Being, the present, God. On the other hand, the external person speaks out of the human past and future because the present of this world is but a breath that, barely grasped, has already faded away.

The God-man, who is at home in his innermost being, beholds the »Is« in what is becoming because in his innermost being everything is present and already accomplished. The God-man lives and works out of the presence of God. What for the external person is just becoming, for the God-man it has already been accomplished in his innermost being.

The one who lives in his innermost being also beholds in his innermost being what is taking place and will take place in the external world and how it takes form. With his divine sensations, he accompanies the steps that still have to be taken externally, but which have already been taken in his innermost being. He places the whole into what is becoming, so that it will also be in the external world, as it already is in his innermost being.

What the inner person retains and moves in his innermost being will also be realized externally, in the world of the senses because in his innermost being it already is and is also retained and moved.

The language of the Being is impersonal. The impersonal expects nothing; it wants nothing. It speaks itself, the eternal Self. The eternal Self is the infinity and the eternal fullness. The pure being is the Self that became form. It is the fullness that became form.

If you are the self, then you are the word of the Self that speaks in you and that penetrates the outside world as sound and tone. There, it speaks itself and vibrates to the ear of the world and into the ear of the Being in the person, sounding in his soul. Thus, much in the world, too, will change for the good of the whole.

Let what you speak aloud stream from you and flow through you. It formulates itself in you because it is the self. That is the I Am, the word of the Being, the life and the substance of life. It is the Absolute that never passes away, even when the times change and pass away.

The word, which is the Being, the I Am, the eternal law, and which is in the stream of the All, does not fall back on you like the vapid, energy-poor word of the intellect. The word, the Being, remains in the stream of the Being and flows through you, the being that became form, and through Me, the Being that became form, as well as through everything that is in the stream of the Being and has its existence there.

Therefore, speak the word, the Being, in you.

Learn to move everything in your innermost being, to receive it in your innermost being and to speak out of your innermost being. Then you will speak the language of the Being.

Everything that lasts eternally takes place in the innermost being of the soul. That is the truth. That is the constancy. That is the life. That is the stream, the Self, the I Am. It is the life and the substance of life in you.

The one who accuses his neighbor of being untruthful and of lying, without being able to prove this statement, bears witness to himself that he is at the edge of the stream throwing stones at his neighbor—thus stoning himself because his neighbor, whom he accuses, is a part of him in his innermost being.

The one who merely stands at the edge of the stream thinks that this is reality because he does not know the stream. The one who behaves in this way bears witness to what he still is.

he one who speaks the word, the I Am, beholds the truth and the untruth. He explains, sets right, and then goes his way. He knows that the one who changes himself and devotes himself to God walks the path that leads to freedom. But the one who does not change himself walks the stony path into sorrow, to awaken to the truth via the sorrow that is the same as the sin, and then be able to enter the truth.

If you do not tire of the search for truth, you will find yourselves by recognizing your faults and weaknesses and by clearing them up in time before sorrow comes over you. For this reason, never be weary of searching, other-wise, you will have to endure your sinfulness.

he one who does not want to look at himself al-ways looks at his neighbor. He is of the opinion that he is the good one and his neighbor, the bad one. This behavior brings out the know-it-all, who is of the opinion that he can steer the course of the All, since he considers himself all-around clever.

Recognize that the fool knows everything better. If his neighbor approaches him with his foolishness, then two fools quarrel with each other. Both lack wisdom.

The opposite of truth is foolishness. Very many are occupied with this.

When the soul goes as a fool into the worlds that it has determined for itself through its foolishness, then only foolishness surrounds it because it lives in its illusory pictures of foolishness. Even if the former human being knows about the laws of God and did not fulfill them, he remains the fool and the slave of slavery, of foolishness, which he lived and with which he surrounded himself.

The one who does not come to grips with his earthly existence, has no relationship with the spiritual world, either.

The one who does not walk the path to the kingdom of the inner being, that is, who does not refine himself in feelings, thoughts, words and deeds, cleaves to this side of life, to the life in time. Whether he lives or dies, whether he is awake or asleep—neither this earthly existence nor death will teach him anything new because he stayed the former, sinful person, despite knowing better.

No person can flee from himself. Each one has to look at himself and expiate what he has inflicted upon himself. The task that life gives to him is his life.

One day he will be given the task to expiate what he inflicted upon himself.

What you enter in the stars yourself, in the mighty memory bank, continuously lies in wait to break in over you. Thus, you are yourself your own danger.

If you do not weary of seeking your true self, then you are willing to learn. The one who is willing to learn will recognize himself and find his true being in self-recognition. He will actualize—and thus be fulfilled.

If soul and person are not willing to learn, that is, to find themselves in God through actualization, the life of soul and person will become harder and more difficult.

If you are suffering, then feel in the suffering why you are suffering. Let the sensations and thoughts of the suffering come, for they speak their language. And if you do not tire of fulfilling the eternal law, you will mature in suffering and grow closer to the light that brings you peace and stillness.

The person should neither lament about the path of his life on Earth nor condemn his path through life.

The one who presumes to know his path through life also presumes to have authority over creation.

All the paths that the Spirit teaches lead to the one goal: that soul and person find their way to the Being, which is God.

The hope and the longing for God awaken the fulfillment of hope. Wherever there is hope, the longing for this fulfillment, the ruling hand of God is there.

I, Christ, give you teachings for self-recognition, so that you may resort to them again and again when you become lukewarm:

In each situation, decide for God, then you evade the darkness.

If the person is once warm, then again cold, he is undecided and serves the darkness. The one who decides for the world decides for the intoxication of the ego. Then the world inspires him, and those who belong to the world will inspire him.

The darkness plays with the human being. It influences him—once for, then against, God. With this, it wants to mock God. It will play this game with the person until the person has decided.

Further teachings for self-recognition:

Always demand of yourself the utmost, not what is within reach. Then you will come to know the power potential of your soul.

Admonish yourself repeatedly, by asking yourself again and again what you want to do about yourself.

And when you ask yourself, then you know what you want to do about yourself. Do this, and in you will awaken the eternal self, which you are in eternity as a being of eternity.

The soul in a person is merely a guest on Earth. The soul has become a human being to develop the inner treasure and to do good. The good comes through people—as does the bad.

The good person who lives in Me, the Christ, bears good fruits. The immoral person, who has dedicated himself to the darkness, brings darkness into the world.

Blessed are the ones who bring goodness, through whom the good comes into the world. Woe to those through whom the darkness comes into the world. The one will go to the light—the other will suffer in darkness.

Know and sense in your hearts: The more you love God, the more will God give to you. The more joyfully you share the gifts of love, the more you will receive from God. Only the selfless one receives because he passes it on selflessly. The one who gives selflessly draws from the eternal Being, from the unending stillness that is God. Through this, he becomes more still and God-conscious because he knows that God gives to the one who selflessly passes on the gifts from the treasure of his actualization.

I, Christ, Am the key to selflessness, the key to the Being. I, Christ, Am the key to the door of life. All enlightened ones enter the eternal Being through Me, for I Am the light of the soul, the truth and the life.

Just as I serve all things, souls, people, animals, plants and stones, so should you selflessly serve everything that is around you—people, animals, plants and stones.

The selflessly serving love is the inner devotion. It sets the heart aglow and gives joy to the soul and pulsates through every selfless word and every selfless deed. It lightens and frees the soul and lends wings to the steps because soul and person personify the law of the All.

Whatever you do, do it from the Spirit because only the selfless deeds are done in and with God.

If you think your works are ever so good—then examine yourselves, whether you have done them from the Spirit, that is, selflessly. If you have done them with your human ego and your benefit in mind, they can have an opposite effect. Sooner or later, you will have to suffer under this.

For this reason, live from the Spirit, and be mindful of the inner light, which is your helper and adviser, Christ:

I, in all of you, and all of you, in Me. I, in you, and you, in Me.

The truly wise one lives in God, and God lives through him. Whatever he gives is not given by him—God gives it through him. Whatever he does is not done by him—God does it through him.

He speaks, yet it is not he who speaks—God speaks through him. He works, yet it is not he who works because God works through him.

The truly wise one lives in the world for the divine world and is merely a transformer of selfless love, the inner power. He is selfless giving. For this reason, it is not he who speaks and acts, but it is God through him.

Safeguard the good, the Being, as the gem of your innermost being, then you will remain in your innermost being and speak the language of the innermost being, the truth.

The one who is begotten by the human being alone, that is, by humanness, will also return to humankind as a soul, again and again, and be born of the human being, of humanness, and speak the language of human beings— until he strives to be born in God, the unparalleled birthplace, which is the Being. Then he will return to God and live eternally in Him, the stream of the Being. Then he will also speak the language of the Being because he is again the Being that has become form, and in which he moves.

Speak the language of the Being!

Nothing is outside of you. It is not the flower, the grass, the plant, the stone, the mineral—you are the being, the flower, the grass, the plant, the stone and the mineral because you are in all things as essence and all things are as essence in you.

No matter where you go, where you stand, where you are—be a part of the eternal temple! Keep the order of the temple. Then you will also be just and attain justice.

Remember: Whatever you do not perceive in your innermost being, in your true Being, you have not developed yet in your innermost being.

You will not grasp and behold what is not alive in you. If your neighbor is not alive in you, then you have neither access to your neighbor nor communication with God.

Examine yourself:

How you speak shows whether you are in yourself or whether you speak only out of your ego, the surface.

*D*ine in God. Just as the morsels and the drink go into you, they have an effect in you and again radiate from you.

The one who sanctifies his morsels and drink keeps the consciousness of the food and drink alive. It then goes into the soul as essence and strength. The food and drink then strengthen not only the body, but soul and body.

With your awareness, accompany every morsel and every swallow of drink on its way into your body.

The sensations, thoughts and words that you give to the food and drink on its way into your organism have a corresponding effect in soul and body.

Everything is energy. The food and drink, too, are energy. The way you feel and think—with these forces, you magnetize the food and the drink. It is what you give them on their way into your body.

Therefore, with the intake of nourishment, as well, remain in the innermost part of your temple because food and drink are also a part of the order of the temple, of the law of the temple.

Each aspect of consciousness is the same as its state of consciousness. It has the whole in it and speaks itself according to its degree of consciousness.

The fruits and drinks, too—all food—are consciousness and speak the language of their degree of consciousness.

This means that they are in communication with the stream, in which they move and have their existence.

Just as you, the person, treat the food and drink, that is how they will have their effect in and on you. Everything is vibration that makes itself noticeable in and on you, marking you as well.

My words are spirit and life, light and truth. The spiritually maturing one, who strives toward the light, toward Me, becomes more sensitive, more permeable for the inner life. In the knowledge of life, he will no longer partake of dead food. Nor will he stuff himself and consume great amounts of food.

The spiritually maturing person lives from within to without. He will also choose his food accordingly, so that his physical body receives what it needs to live, but not beyond that.

The spiritual person will not live lavishly. He will give his body what it needs. He does not fill it.

Recognize: Many believe that when they fast and mortify themselves they will draw closer to God more quickly. This is an error of the intellect.

Spiritual growth does not involve a diet with fasting or mortification; nor are certain ways of praying required. What is important is that the person lives out of the Spirit because then everything comes into order on its own. No rules are necessary—a consistent life is needed, in which the person goes more and more within to the source of life, and draws from the source of the Being.

It is not about the physical well-being, but the spiritual attitude, your doing or not doing.

Therefore, examine whether what you want to do corresponds to your innermost being and serves your spiritual growth. Thus, be honest with yourselves. Do nothing that is contrary to the eternal truth, to the eternal Being because nothing is hidden from God. What you have concealed will be evident one day, and you, yourselves, will see whether your thinking and acting was upright and honest.

As long as your eyes are directed toward worldly things, you have not entered the Kingdom of God, and you rely on an external kingdom that is not real.

Should you ask for the recovery of your body, then outer fasting can be salutary only if you simultaneously discard your human thoughts, what you have recognized as human, thus becoming free for the irradiation of the light.

If you honor the holy of holies in all things, by safeguarding it in you as treasure and life, and by letting it take effect through you, then you will sit and dine in the holy of holies, at the table of the Lord.

Thus, in every situation, in everything that you do—also when partaking of food—remain in the innermost part of your temple. The temple of your innermost being is built with the essence of all your neighbors and with the essence of the nature kingdoms.

The divine in your neighbor and every power in the mineral, in the stone, the plant and the animal is a component of your inner temple, in which the All-Holy One dwells.

If a component of your temple is missing, you are in disunity either with people or with parts of nature. Then your temple is also imperfect. This means that you are not in the law of God and are not the law of God, either. Then you cannot enter the holy of holies in you to take up dwelling there.

Then you will not sit at the table of the Lord, either, but at the table of the people who—as you—thoughtlessly partake of the life, the gifts from God. Then you are homeless and an errant sheep that lets itself be led astray, since it is blind and is often kept blind because it follows blind ones who lead it to a temple that was built by human hands.

But if you are willing to establish, cleanse and expand your inner temple through a life in God, then you, too, will straighten up and see clearly.

In the same measure that you perfect your inner temple, you will keep the order of the temple and find entry to the inner temple.

If your temple is perfect, then you, too, are one with all people and all beings, with all Being. Then you are also one with the All and its laws and you also dwell in the holy of holies because you are in the All and it is in you, and you are both from eternity to eternity.

The Kingdom of God is the inner kingdom. You can perceive it only with your inner eyes and you can hear what the inner laws say to you only with your inner ears.

You can hear the true Being, your heritage, only in your inner being. It speaks to you and speaks with you because I Am the »I Am« and the I Am is you. For this reason, you are I, and I Am you, and where you are, Am I, and where I Am is where you are because everyone and everything is in you—you and I as unity in all things.

You and I, the melding of both in the I Am, can be experienced only in the innermost part of your temple, in the holy of holies, in which everything is—the you in I and the I in you. There is nothing where you and I are not as a unity because God is the You and the I, the consciousness of unity. God is the You; you are the divine being. Once you have grasped this, then you will not seek your neighbor— you will not call for him. He is there—in you! Wherever you are, he is with you because he is in you—the you and the I melded in the You, in the law, God, the I Am in you.

The You of God is the duality. In God, two become one. All numbers flow into the One, into the Oneness because God unites everyone and everything and all beings are the image of the One, God.

You are My thought, the All-Father thought, the law. The Mine is yours because the Eternal, who I Am, and you are one.

You, the pure one, speak the Self because you are the self. Therefore, you speak your self and you also address the Self in everyone and in all things, you in your neighbor and in all things, occurrences and events.
The word of the pure one is the Self that is in all things. The law speaks itself and brings forth itself again because everything is in all things—it is always the whole.

You address the whole in everything and in every facet of the truth, again, the whole. The corresponding consciousness-radiation, the facet, answers you in you, and you hear again the whole in you.
You do not need to ask about the state of consciousness. Always address the whole because in the smallest is the large and in the large is the smallest.
Wherever the thought of the law radiates, there it shines again on the law.
What the law-thought contains is already fulfilled in you because the eternal law is the same as fulfillment.
The law-thought cannot be destroyed or diverted. It has already fulfilled itself in you while being emitted.
In the external world, the law-thought fulfills itself according to the law of free will once it gains entry into the heart of a person.

But the law-thought does not know any hindrances. It penetrates all density and every hindrance and waits until it is received. It also follows the path of fulfillment externally because it is a part of the eternal law that is in the innermost being of the person.

The law-thought does not know time. It is the law, and timeless. The path of the law-thought to a person in the external world can mean a delay for the person because the law-thought knows the moment to act, and stays in the person's field of aura as fulfilled, until it gains entry.

In the lawful feeling and in the lawful thought there is no setback, no dissolution of feeling or thought because they are the eternal law, the All-power.

I, Christ, as Jesus of Nazareth, taught the eternal holy laws to some apostles and disciples who could understand them. Despite their spiritual knowledge, I had to catch them again and again before they fell into humanness, into the »err-reality.« Again and again, I had to make clear to them the holy thought—the eternal Self—which they let out of their innermost being time and again because the illusion, the »err-reality,« the human thought, seemed closer to them.

I spoke to them in the following sense:
The holy word that is the power of God and that was born in you can be enveloped by you with the human ego—which builds up in the conscious mind and the subconscious—only if you do not keep it in you as the true Self. If, despite knowing better, you let it out of your innermost being through doubt, fears or impatience.

The core of human thoughts and words is the word of God. It remains divine. But what envelops it directs itself against you and will become a burden for you.
Every law-sensation and every law-thought goes out from the eternal power, God, and from the communication with God. Even if they are enveloped by the human ego, the core, the life, however, remains in God.
The law, God, is: sending and receiving. The eternal law sends itself and receives itself. For this reason, no energy is lost. Thus, the eternal law speaks itself, and the answer

is, again, the law, the Self because everything is His law and all pure forms of life are the law and they all have their existence in the flowing law.

I taught My apostles and disciples the law:
God is the All-law.

The All-law, God, consists of countless facets of consciousness, which are degrees of consciousness. They are the spiritual life forms—minerals, plants, animals and nature beings—which are led by the Creator-God, the Spirit of evolution, to the next higher degrees of consciousness. The various spiritual capabilities and mentalities, too, are contained in the life forms as predispositions from the Creator-God. This is also true of their spiritual names.

The Eternal leads all forms of Being to perfection. For this reason, everything is contained in all things.

Every degree of consciousness contains the entire All-law. The various degrees of consciousness communicate, in turn, with the same or like degrees of consciousness. Despite all this, the following holds true for the forms of life: In everything is contained, in turn, all things, but not every aspect is already all-encompassingly manifest.

However, everything is manifest in each one of you because your spiritual body has opened all forms of Being as the law. Therefore, learn to perceive, to behold in you everything in all things, and to address everything in every aspect of consciousness.

I address each one of you: Why do you want to look into the distance, when the Eternal, what you believe to be far away, is in you?

Why do you want to speak with your brother, when he is in you as power and light?

If you have something important to tell him, address him in you. By doing this, you establish a conscious communication with your neighbor and if it is important for him, he will receive it—if he also bears you in himself as power and light. If your brother is linked with you, then he will answer in you, or you will meet him and make a date for a conversation with him.

But it all first happens in you. That is the eternal law, not the causal law.

I repeat: The prerequisite for a divine communication is that you have opened the divine essence of your brother or your sister in you—and, vice versa, that your eternal spiritual part of life is effective in him or her.

I taught My apostles and disciples: If you want to chase after what is in the distance, you will be pursued and hunted because you live externally, in and with the world, which is mere illusion, that is, the pale reflection of reality. Some pleasant worldly things may come to you briefly—or you will immediately have to struggle with the disagreeable, with what you have sown. It is possible that you will mix new seed, new causes, with the old seed, and through this, attract events and forces that do not correspond to the law of God, the holy order of the temple.

Then you will speak only your human self and will display yourselves in your humanness. You will not speak the eternal word, which is the eternal law, the impersonal life, God because you are personal.

Everything that puts you under pressure and coercion, that does not leave you any way out, is personal. The personal always wants confirmation—whether it presents itself nearby or from a distance. It cannot take the lawful course because what is personal is oriented exclusively to the person and not to the impersonal, cosmic All-Being.

The person, the human ego, is the human self, which sees itself and thus relates only to the earthly life and to the person, to what is transitory and lasts only in terms of years. The transitory human self urges, in order to use the years in which it can confirm itself. Since it is not the unity and the infinity, it urges into the distance, it urges into the proximity. It urges to the right and to the left, above and below, thus constricting itself more and more because it relates everything to itself, the person.

Every restriction leads to delimitation, to narrowness and to limitation and then to explosion. Everyone who is restricted lashes out. What breaks out is the evil product: strife, war and plundering.

All these aspects are explosions of the human ego, of the human self, which claims more and more for itself. For this, entire armies often go to war, people who are subject to the same or like restrictions and let themselves be ordered about by those like themselves. They then elect their leaders who rule entire nations.

The base ego is insatiable. It wants to possess and to have, until the ego-person passes away. Things then continue in a similar way in the soul realms or in new incarnations. For this reason, beware that you do not decline into spiritual death.

Again and again, I hear you speak about death.

What does death mean to you? To many, it is the end. But death is nothing more than the transition into another form of existence, in which you live in the same way as you lived while a human being.

Death will not take anything from you—nor will it give you anything. The soul that leaves the body is the same one that was in the person and which the person reflected. For this reason, you will not attain resurrection after the death of your body.

Only the one who journeys toward the light, who journeys inward, goes into the light. Just as the soul of a child leaves the inner kingdom to enter the school of life Earth, so should the older person have grown from the school of life Earth into the inner being through actualization and nearness to God.

The one who opens the inner kingdom, the Kingdom of God, will become the temple of salvation and attain resurrection already in his own temple, in the temple of flesh and bone. Then he does not need to taste death. But the one who is spiritually dead is also dead as a soul. The spiritually dead will not resurrect after their physical death. They remain spiritually dead because just as the tree falls, so will it remain lying.

For this reason, realize that in the flesh, you should awaken to the filiation to God, and in the flesh, you should attain resurrection because the soul in the person is in the school of life Earth to again become what it is in the Father: divine.

Know that the spiritually dead look only to the letter and do not grasp the meaning. Therefore, verify to whom you speak and what you say because you shall not cast pearls into the grave, but bring them to those who want to awaken.
The one who as a human being did not find Me will not find Me after the death of his body, either. The one who lived only in humanness will also live only in a world-

oriented way as a soul and again seek out the flesh that to him is the life.

Therefore, recognize: Life is God, and the one who has not found God in himself, has not found Me, the Christ of God, either. After the death of his body, he will go through the gate of death and will remain spiritually dead—until he recognizes himself and finds himself in Me.

The one who recognizes Me knows the All. He is in the All and the All is in him. The one who does not recognize Me is oriented to the Earth and collects external treasures and wealth, since he is not aware of his inner being because he is not oriented to the great whole. Since he does not know Me, he knows neither himself nor the All, the I Am.

The countless powers of the All are in you as essence because you, O human being, are the microcosm in the macrocosm. You are the heir of infinity. In you, everything is united, and what is, is eternal. What is eternal is in you.

Only what is in the innermost part of your soul is yours, and what is yours is eternal. The external is illusion and transitory. You cannot take it with you; you have to leave it here and there.

Recognize that all density is transitory—and what is transitory passes away. Therefore, matter, too, will pass away because density is not eternal and is not eternity.

You think you have to flee from the world to overcome it. I say to you: You will not overcome yourselves by fleeing from the world. You will not recognize who you are, for you have lost the mirror of your world.

As long as you are in the world and do not overcome the world that still clings to you, you are vulnerable to the world. You have to rid yourself of all reflection and become as God beholds you, that is, as you were from the very beginning—and as you will be again through Me, the Christ: beings of light.

The world of the incarnated beings, the human beings, is likewise the world of the discarnate beings, the souls. Both worlds penetrate each other. They are places of residence for people and souls, in which people and souls mature by becoming and growing, thus growing closer to the eternal kingdom, to immerse in the stream, God, who is eternal.

The spiritually awakened ones mature into eternity. The spiritually dead ones are content with the reflection.

This world is the toxic substance for soul and body. The one who assimilates it falls ill.

Every illness is the effect of one or several causes. It can also be a collective illness, based on a collective guilt, when several people have sinned against their fellow human beings out of the same motive. If the latter do not forgive them, then their illness will last, often over incarnations or in the soul realms.

The illness is the picture of your soul. It is the mirror in which you can recognize your world of feelings, sensations and thoughts.

Happy the souls that have taken on flesh to become divine in the school of Earth.

Woe to the souls that have taken on flesh to indulge anew in the lusts of the body.

The soul in the human being is in the school of life Earth to become divine again.

What changes when the soul takes off its mortal shell?
What changes when a flower withers?
What changes when the seasons pass?
Do they go and never come again?
Or is not the Being in the passing, and already again the becoming, which attires itself in an even more beautiful and lavish garment?

Humankind calls autumn, the yet-again-becoming in nature, which fashions itself anew and more lavishly: the transitory.

But there is no transience—only change and transformation.

Can there be time in change and transformation?

Time is transitory. What passes on?

What is space if the consciousness is boundless?

What is space if the human being is a sending and receiving station?

What is space if the nature kingdoms are cosmic?

Therefore, what are time and space?

In God there is no time. In Him, nothing is lost. In God, the »cannot understand« does not exist. This belongs to time.

God is the present: Everything is in the One, and the One is in everything. He gives Himself in the one radiation, which He, God, is. Therefore, God can be only »Oneness.«

Multiplicity is time and is the one who determines it and determines those people who strive for quantity and mass and who, in their existence, have lost the measure of all things, God.

When the term time passes away, limitation and finiteness fall. Then the ruling hand of God is visible. The Being then enters the life of fulfilled people—and they live. Death is then broken because time has fallen.

s Jesus, I, Christ, spoke further words to My apostles and disciples in the following sense:

Many people cling to their life on Earth with all the fibers of their earthly existence. They are not aware that already at birth they have put on the garment of death and that the veil of death hangs over them.

You, however, should make yourselves aware that each one of you will die and each one in a different way. For this reason, you should establish a relationship with your dying, so that you are not surprised by your so-called death.

The veil of death hangs over every person. The person can raise it only if he has spiritually awakened—or it will be taken from him only when he has died.

Thus, take a good look at the fact that every person dies. What comes after so-called death?

I ask each and every one the question: How do you want to die? The how gives you the answer with the question: How have I lived?—Or with the question: How do I want to live?

The life on Earth of every person shows him his dying and raises the veil of death—all according to how the person lived. The earthly life of each and every person is the measure for what is concealed from him behind the veil of death.

The person determines himself, whether he finds himself outside the wheel of reincarnation or whether he adheres to the wheel of reincarnation.

My apostles and disciples asked Me, »How shall we prepare ourselves?« I said to them:
Recognize that each of you is the today and the tomorrow. Each one is a part of every moment, of every second, of every minute and of every hour. Each of you is a part of a day, a part of a week, of a month and of a year.
Because of this, every person has a part in creating what he calls time. Once the aspects for this world—which are effective in the moment, in the second, in the minute, in the hour, in the day, in the month and in the year—have run out, then he no longer is a human being, but a soul.
However, the soul retains the rhythm of the human ego, until it has found the true Being, which is eternal. You can find it only on the path of actualization.

My apostles and disciples said: »Teach us more! How can we fathom the depths of our human ego to become free more quickly, so that we draw nearer to God, the Eternal?«
I essentially explained to them the following: The five senses of a person can be compared to antennae. The one who uses these antennae too little, to recognize and sense who he is and to feel who he still could be, does not find his way into his inner being and cannot find himself, either.

Recognize that a person creates his programs by way of the five senses. They are in the conscious mind, the subconscious and in the soul, as well. These programs consist of feelings, sensations, thoughts, words and actions. Therefore, the person can, according to his degree of honesty, deduce from his thoughts who he is. If he goes with his thoughts to the world of his sensations, then he gets to know who he still is.

If the person takes the finer antennae, which are like feelers, and immerses with them into his world of feelings, he will sense further human traits—or he experiences the wisdom of the soul, the divine aspects that he has already developed.

he fullness from God is the life. The one who lives in the fullness of God is and remains fulfilled. He does not need to worry about tomorrow—he is the All and is the fullness of the All-radiation that streams through him and from which he draws because he lives in it.

The fullness, God, knows no privation. It is and gives, and is the wealth, the All, in which the being of the All lives and is as essence. The one who wants to receive the fullness from God has to renounce the world. He may well live in the world and work in the world, but he is not with the world.

The one who disdains the fullness, since he fills himself with the gifts of the world, will live in want, even if he presently appears to be externally rich.

If you ask God for earthly gifts, then you are of little faith and do not recognize your filiation to God, the stream of the All, from which you went forth and in which you live.

Ask for spiritual gifts, for awakening in the Spirit of life, so that you open your heavenly heritage. When you ask for what is your own from the Spirit, indeed, what is given to you, then you will also attain the earthly goods, what you need, and beyond that because God lets no child live in want.

It is the human being who seeks and strives for external things. Through this, he becomes impoverished because he neglects his true heritage.

By worrying about tomorrow, by wondering whether you will remain ill or become ill or when you will become healthy again, you hinder God, the almighty Spirit, from becoming active in you and through you, and you hinder Me, the Inner Physician and Healer, from bringing you relief and healing by way of your soul.

These human thoughts, desires and longings remove you more and more from God and lead you into a time that is poor in light, into a land that is already poor—just as poor as you have become. Then you will experience your present in the future.

Know that each one of you bears the heritage of the All in himself and is thus the possessor of infinity.

The one who acquires external possessions, who on Earth is the owner of land that he guards and calls his own will keep returning until he has recognized that his true possession is heaven. Let the Earth and a life on Earth become merely a bridge that you cross over. But do not acquire great possessions there—otherwise you will again create a place for your next incarnation.

Recognize Me in you—then you have beheld Me as your brother. Then you will behold heaven because in each one of us is the entire Being as power and light. In each one of us is infinity, the heritage, our spiritual possession. As power and light, we are one because I Am in you and you are in Me.

This is how it is in all of infinity: Everything is in all things. That is the inner wealth—that is our true Being. That is our possession; it is our own.

I say to you, if a person asks you for your shirt, then give him your coat, too. But woe to those who possess a shirt and a coat and deceivingly ask for a second shirt or coat for themselves. Woe to those who could help themselves and yet take. They will be called to account—when their own judgment of sowing and reaping comes over them.

For this reason, actualize the holy laws, so that you may behold—that is, perceive—and recognize the »for and against« in people.

od is the fullness. The one who clings to his desires, longings and passions is veiled. He wears the garments of his desires and passions—and thus, he does not know the Being, the life, which is the Spirit of God. He entrusts himself to the world and not to the Eternal, who dwells in him.

For this reason, learn to draw from the Spirit of life, by entrusting yourselves to God with all your worries and desires. He, the All-One, knows you and knows how to guide you.

The one who draws from the Spirit of life lives in Me, the Christ, and draws from the Spirit of love and gives from the Spirit of love. He will not be an eccentric, but a spiritually rich person. He will live on this Earth, but will not be with this world.

A person of the Spirit will fulfill his work and give his best. However, he is not only a citizen of the material world—he is rather a citizen of the Kingdom of God because he lives in God and draws from the source, God.

Take these My words into your life on Earth as salvation and life force. Then, as human beings, you will do the works of love and you will stand in the midst of the world and fulfill your obligations with God.

Give your best! You can do this only when you are united with the best, the Being. Never be satisfied with the mediocre or even the defective—give your best.

Endeavor at every moment to draw from the works of love and to imbue your work, your thinking and doing with them. Then you are the being in the stream of the Being, and you draw from the All, which is the law, God.

Remember My words: It is not the external that matters, but solely the inner being, that which the temple contains, the fullness, God. Therefore, cleanse your temple, so that you may gain entry to the holy of holies.

Never be indignant. Otherwise, you will be held back by the temporal, by things and events that belong to the transitory.

The one who lives in God lives in the fullness, in the eternal law, God. He will never ask about the how and why because he is the being that knows about all things.

The indignant one bears witness to himself, since he still seeks his hold in external things.

An indignant person is always one who is seeking and has no hold because he seeks security and a hold in the world. In the long run, matter offers the person neither security nor a hold because matter is merely illusion and not the Being.

For this reason, practice keeping the inner calm in every situation, so that you recognize things and events in the light of truth.

God knows about each and every one. He knows His child and helps him.

he one who has learned to behold does not accuse his neighbor because he knows him. Only the spiritually blind one accuses his neighbor because he knows neither himself nor his neighbor.

If you are accused, then set things right and point out in general terms what is wrong and insinuated, but never name the accuser. That would be personal. Remain impersonal because when you address him by name and he does not forgive you in time, then it is possible—depending on the cause—that you will have his name in another life on Earth. His name, which you then bear, calls up the causes that bind you to each other. Through the radiation, the soul or the person that you once accused by name can then be attracted. You and your neighbor will be led together by the law of sowing and reaping, to clear up what now, in another incarnation, becomes active.

Therefore, keep the golden rule:
Be silent. Speak only when it is essential and lawful.

For this reason, never be indignant. Take yourself back and remain impersonal in every situation.

Remember: Speak about yourself only if you can explain and clarify the facts or if you can serve and help your neighbor with what you recognized on yourself and mastered. Otherwise, never speak about yourself person-

ally because everything that you say about yourself, at the same time, you are speaking to yourself again. It clings to you and intensifies your ego-complex.

I repeat: Remain impersonal in every situation, then you will find your way to inner stillness and linger in the temple of God.

In the long run, matter offers the human being neither security nor a hold because the temporal is merely illusion and not the Being, the reality, the eternal.

The light illuminates the things and events that show themselves on matter and lets you see them. But if you want to hold on to the ray of light, you will fall. For this reason, learn to move in the ray of light.

Never lean on matter. Do not affirm the external alone, the illusion, otherwise, sooner or later you will slip off what you have leaned on—because every time you lean against something or on someone, it leads to binding, and every binding separates you from the connection.

A binding is like an object. It is shone upon. The connection is togetherness and is radiated through.

If you look at, and listen to, the external alone, then you are externalized and your senses of taste, smell and touch will be just like your senses of sight and hearing.

You determine your life in time or in eternity because you have the principle of the law of freedom and you can thus decide—for the divine or for the undivine. The divine radiates through you. The negative merely shines on you. You decide who you are and what you are, and ultimately, what you want.

You are the light in the light. For this reason, you do not need to hold on to anything or anyone.

You are freedom in the freedom of God.

You are wisdom in the wisdom of God.

The wisdom of God knows about all things. Therefore, you, the wise one, will neither bind yourself to people nor cling to humanness and call it your own.

You are also no longer the personal in the person. You are a human being and thus, a person—but no longer personal.

You, the wise one, are All-conscious because you live consciously in God and are aware of all things, of everything that is because you see through everything. The wise one is knowing and has insight into the things that surround him and that come toward him.

The one who rests in God and draws from the eternal law seldom speaks of himself. He is impersonal because he is the one who sees through things, and is the knowable one, and the word of the All, himself. The wise one speaks of himself only when he can thus be a guide on the path, but not to talk about himself.

If a person speaks his personal ego, then he speaks his base self that he speaks out of himself and that he, at the same time, again speaks to himself because the human ego is not divine and thus belongs to the one who is still not divine.

The undivine, the human ego, which goes out from you, goes into you again. Through this, you expand and intensify your ego-complex, the undivine, in you, thus creating ever greater fields in your soul, into which your ego-seed falls and where it sprouts.

For this reason, before you speak, think about what you want to say because each word is energy that has its echo. Thus, remain impersonal in every situation. Then you will find your way to inner stillness and will linger in the temple of God, the holy stillness, as the wise one.

The truly wise one is not a hermit. He lives in the world, but not with this world. Since he is a human being, he has obligated himself to give to Caesar what is due to Caesar, and he will give to God what is due to God. The one who keeps the laws of Earth that do not oppose the divine can also remind Caesar of his duty, so that the latter gives him what is his due as a human being.

As Jesus, I, Christ, taught the law of God and the law of sowing and reaping to My apostles and disciples in many repetitions. Despite all this, they spoke about unessential things and about themselves again and again to display themselves. I addressed them again and again and made them aware of the unessential, the personal:

If you speak of yourselves, then you express only what you still are, yourselves. Whom do you want to help with this?

Everything that has not been actualized is empty; it is hollow, as it were, and not filled with strength and wisdom. If you have actualized little, you are not filled with strength and wisdom, either, but are filled with the human ego that has its illusions.

The one who is empty and hollow, himself, falls, in turn, for empty, as it were, hollow, words. He looks solely to the word and to the one who is speaking because he does not hear himself and does not see himself either. He may choose you as a leader and then is the ensnared one. Both are then the blind, who fall into the pit of their ego and are chained there to each other because the blind one relied on the blind.

For this reason, first empty your vessel of your human aspects, that is, first cleanse your cups and bowls, your soul particles and body cells, your temple of flesh and bone. Through this, you gain entry into the holy of holies, from where you are able to give your neighbor what he needs and can offer him selfless service, which helps him on his spiritual ascent.

In everything that comes to you, first look at the innermost being of the person. Therefore, fulfill the eternal law with regard to each one who comes to you, be it only through a selfless word, a selfless gesture or a selfless helping hand. These small, selfless services are more valuable for the salvation of his soul and for his spiritual life, than if you give him much externally, thus, perhaps helping him to gain in prestige, wealth and power. This earthly burden could lead him to a deeper fall.

From the law of God, the smallest, selflessly offered, is the greatest; it serves the soul and lends it strength. Through the selfless, smallest service, you, too, will remain in the stillness, in the secureness of God, in His fullness because you have given impersonally.

God gives of Himself—but from what God pours out as a whole, each one can receive only as much as he can absorb in his spiritual consciousness. If he thinks that he has to take more to gain capital for himself, then he will lose it—including that for which he has worked so arduously. The one who strives for outer prestige and does business with the divine, the truth, will lose himself and all that he has acquired for himself, personally. For this reason, examine what you think, and reflect before you speak and act.

Maintain the stillness, which is neither human sensation nor human thought.

Be still. Entrust yourself to God. Indeed, trust Him, and you will receive from the stream of life what you should say and carry out in the present.

In everything that God breathes into you is the measure and the quantity. Thus, you receive only as much as you should presently give and speak.

Be still and know that you will be guided. The You of your soul knows about all things. It knows everything—it is in everything.

As Jesus of Nazareth, I reminded My apostles and disciples again and again that all this is given only to the ones who sacrifice their ego, who are no longer the personal in the person, but the Being, the true self.

The one who lives in God lives in the fullness and draws from the fullness because he lives in the source that is God, and he, the being, is divine.

s Jesus, I spoke to My apostles and disciples in the following sense:

Your feelings, thoughts and words are the tools of your body. They are your advance workers. Through the deed you are merely the handyman, doing the finishing work that follows your feelings, thoughts and words. Your feelings, thoughts and words go in advance of your doing and of your deeds.

Without your advance workers, your feelings, thoughts and words, you can accomplish nothing. Your feelings, thoughts and words thus prepare for you what you then carry out—either in a personal way, with your intellect, if your advance workers were of a personal nature, or with your heart, if your advance workers were impersonal, that is, divine.

How you fare today, in this incarnation, you acquired for yourself in your previous lives, through your advance workers, your feelings, thoughts and words, and then through your finishing work, your deeds. Your work, your idleness, your worries, your problems, your blows of fate and difficulties, your suffering and your joys, your health and your illness were all created by you in previous lives. Nothing can come to you that you did not already input beforehand.

Therefore, what you input in previous existences is what you have predetermined for this and possibly future incarnations. In your future lives on Earth, you will then feel, think, speak and do the same and like things. No one else can do your speaking. Each one speaks himself, what he has predetermined in previous lives or in this incarnation, that is, what he has assimilated.

Every human feeling and every human thought, every human word and every human action is, as it were, an assimilation: The person assimilates his humanness into his soul. With this, he shapes his present and his possibly future earthly body.

What you were yesterday, that is, in past lives on Earth, is what you are again today—unless soul and person have cleared it up in good time with the power of the eternal law.

It is possible that soul and person may be in this cycle for thousands of years. They come over and over again and are always the same. Today, they determine their tomorrow. They come again and again with different faces and different bodies, with different first and last names, and in reality, they are the same because they again feel, think, speak and do as yesterday. Their face, their body, their first and last names correspond to those of yesterday, the radiation of their previous lives.

What identifies the person today, his thinking, speaking and acting of today, is what he should recognize, clear up and fulfill today. The one who does not fulfill it today, that is, the one who does not use the energy of the day, which points out his thoughts and actions to him, will not successfully complete the school on Earth, either. Today, such a person predetermines yet again what he will be tomorrow.

Each morning, every person is at the mercy of himself. What this day brings to him and what he does with it, determines what his day and his life on Earth will be tomorrow. For the day of every single person is his life, it is what he has input into the stars, himself.

On himself today, every person can deduce who or what he will be tomorrow. Just as he feels, thinks, speaks and acts tomorrow—that is, in a future incarnation—that is how he felt, thought, spoke and acted today, in this incarnation. His activity of today can be his activity of tomorrow.

What the person accomplishes with his baseness, his works, is not the works of eternity. His works pass away, and with them, his base self.

The wheel of reincarnation developed through the cycle of birth and death. Repeatedly, the human being inputs into his soul what goes out from it, that with which he once programmed it. The corresponding stars absorbed the respective programs, through which a mighty causal communication network emerged. This causal communication network is the law of cause and effect, which, in turn, forms the wheel of reincarnation.

The wheel of reincarnation, the law of sowing and reaping, consists of countless solar systems of a coarse-material and a fine-material nature. After the death of the body, the soul is magnetically attracted by that plane and that planet that has stored the soul's programs that are active and waiting to be cleared up. The wheel of reincarnation—with its purification planes, which are of a fine-material nature, and the coarse-material matter—is a large memory bank that has registered every uncleared cause of each and every soul and human being, and radiates these back to the soul and person.

The soul, which has cleared up little or none of its soul-guilt in the beyond, again brings into its subsequent life on Earth what still adheres to it. As a human being, it will then be what it was as a soul and as a person in its previous lives. Every person can deduce, himself, from his way of thinking, speaking and behaving, what he once was and possibly still is today, and will be tomorrow.

The slipping in and out of the flesh will continue until the person has successfully gone through the school of life called Earth and until his soul is able to go on, with spiritual-divine gifts and values, to the higher worlds that exist outside of the wheel of reincarnation.

Then the cycle of birth and death comes to an end. The spirit being, the purified soul, returns to its origin, to God, its Father, into the eternal law because it has again become the eternal law, the true Self, which it then speaks again because it is the law.

As Jesus of Nazareth, I gave this and other principles of the law to My apostles and disciples to take with them on their path of life over the Earth. And as Christ, I give them to all people, so that they may walk the path to the inner life, on which I, Christ, go with them.

*E*verything is consciousness. Thus, you, too, are consciousness. You, the consciousness, are composed of your aspects of consciousness, of your feelings, thoughts, words and actions. This is what you are. Wherever your feelings, thoughts and words go, you are there, because you are consciousness. Your advance workers, your feelings, thoughts and words, and your finishing workers, your actions, are consciousness.

With your feelings, thoughts and words, you emit yourself, for you are your feeling, thinking, and speaking, yourself, the consciousness. Since everything is consciousness, you, the consciousness, will be wherever you, the human being, send to.

Wherever you send to, that is where you are. You build up your magnetism there, and one day you will be attracted there.

If you send out a human thought, then your body may be here, but a part of your consciousness is there. It is the part that lies in your feeling, thinking and speaking. Through this, you are multi-divided: here, where your body is, there, where your feelings are, and there, to where your thoughts and words go. Thus, you can be multi-divided because your feelings can be, for instance, with your neighbor, your thoughts, for example, at your place of work, and your words with your neighbor, with whom you are speaking.

This state of being multi-divided can lead to severe disorders in the person. So-called disturbances of the equilibrium can develop. Your nervous system can thus be shattered. Further causes and their corresponding effects can be the result. Through this, the person can no longer think clearly and logically and his actions are then half-measures.

Recognize: If you are split by simultaneously sending out human feelings, thoughts and words, you are here and there; you are at this and that place at the same time. Through this multiple and simultaneous sending, which is human, that is, personal, you establish so-called Earth stations. In further incarnations, you will—magnetically, as it were—be attracted there, and you will seek out those places that you have magnetized with your feelings, thoughts and words, to clear up there, what you caused in your previous lives, that is, to where you emitted.

If you want to figure out where you will be tomorrow, in another incarnation, then examine your feelings, thoughts, words and deeds of today. And if you want to figure out with whom you will be very close tomorrow, then examine your feelings, thoughts, words and deeds toward your neighbor—that is, examine what binds you to your neighbor and what binds your neighbor to you.

The one who does not build on the temple of his inner being, but lives in an external way instead, lives here and there. As a human being, he creates, in the present, his earthly places of destination and the stations for his next incarnations—where he will then have to live or travel to, in order to remedy what he created in previous existences.

As Jesus, I taught all this and much more to My disciples, and I teach it now as Christ to all people of good will.

The one who has taken up dwelling in the innermost part of his temple will keep the order of the temple that says: What you do, do it totally.

The one who lives in his innermost being, in the holiest of holies, in God, is oriented to the subject, the matter and the situation. His feelings, thoughts and words stream from the holy temple. They are the eternal law. Lawful feelings, thoughts and words are holy forces that move in the omnipresent stream and find access and entry into people, things, matters and situations.

The God-filled one who dwells in the holiest of holies, from where he sends out selfless feelings, thoughts and words, remains in the innermost part of his temple, despite external movement, despite the waves of the ocean world because he lives in God, in the fullness, and is not divided, but is united in God, in the stream of life, in the Being.

Selfless God-filled feelings, thoughts, words and deeds are in the eternal stream and work from the eternal stream and bring the eternal and the lawful into the stream of God again because everything that is pure returns to the pure. The truly wise one leaves to the Eternal when and how the God-filled one will return to the eternal stream.

What the wise one accomplishes, he fulfills for the eternal law, for the eternal stream, in which he lives.

All external, that is, transformed-down, energies have to be transformed and brought back into the stream of God where they have their origin.

God-filled feelings, thoughts and words are the unity-consciousness because they are the law in the stream of Being. On the other hand, human feelings, thoughts and words are loners, which again join with like-minded feelings, thoughts and words, from where they then come back to the sender. However, before they seek out the sender, they have multiplied. They multiply because the receivers think the same or like thoughts, which likewise radiate back. These then return to the sender as a complex and influence the sender as a complex. This means that things will become much worse for him, the person, than they were before.

Such loners are troublemakers. They are the nagging thoughts that want to control the sender. They force themselves on him because they need the sender's energy to remain active and continue to activate themselves. The one who takes in these nagging thoughts thinks the same or like thing. With this, he intensifies the nagging complex, through which, at the same time, the person becomes what he has thought and thinks.

The one who does not sanctify his life loses it and, depending on the burdening of his soul, will possibly have to gain it back through several births into the flesh. He then goes through his own hell, by way of his own torments and suffering, through what he, himself, has entered into himself.

For this reason, use the days and hours because you do not know when the soul will be called back and what it will then have to bear and perhaps bring with it again.

If you want to have an inkling of what your soul bears, you can fathom one or more segments of your spiritual ego, by measuring your way of feeling, thinking, speaking and acting against the Ten Commandments.

The person is an unmistakable sign, himself, either of the I Am or of his human ego. He can hide himself only from those before whom he can disguise himself—those who, themselves, are as he is, who shimmer colorfully and embellish themselves with many words and gestures, to draw attention to themselves.

The mask of such a person can be compared to a house of cards. A gust of being disregarded—and the house of cards collapses. What is left over is then the corroding, the biting ego that suddenly speaks another language. The masks have then fallen, and the person behaves just as he is: disappointed and resigned because he is no longer heeded because his ego is no longer exalted because he is no longer the focus of attention.

If you have something to hide, that is, if you want to hide yourself, then you seek a safe place. You make it your home of choice and call it your concealment where you, the base being, believe you are hidden.

However, being hidden in concealment is still apparent because nothing is hidden to the stars. You, who want to hide yourself, have entered in the stars what you want to hide from the world. Thereby, you are in constant communication with them, no matter where you are.

From whom or what do you want to hide? The stars, into which you have entered what you are, hit you at the right time—even if you have hidden yourself here or there. There is no place where you can hide from yourself because what you have input in the way of feelings, thoughts, words and deeds is what you are. It is also what you carry with you.

Learn to see yourself in your feelings and thoughts and to hear yourself in your words and to recognize yourself in your deeds.

You are then, yourself, a mirror for yourself and will look less and less into the mirror of your neighbor because you have enough to do with clearing up your human ego. Overcome what you recognize on yourself, then you will unfold toward the divine—just like the flower when the warming rays of the sun touch it.

The one who opens himself to the inner light gains inner beauty because his soul attains purity. Beauty, that is, purity, is an attribute of the true Being. True beauty and purity cannot be emulated because the inner garment is cosmically radiating love.

If the physical body is permeated with the radiance of the inner being, then the person is virtuous and selfless. He gains inner grace, which is then the adornment of his outer appearance. The adornment of the spiritually matured person consists of precious gems: of his selfless thoughts, words and deeds.

The person has to develop the longing to become one with God, only then, will he attain the state of oneness.

On the day that you live completely in Me, you are raised to the truth and you are the truth.

The truth does not need to ask. It does not need to seek anymore. It knows about all things because it is the truth.

If you are raised to the truth, then you are divine.

The truly wise one knows about all things because he has insight into all the things of life, since he has become the truth.

The enlightened one does not need explanations. He lives the eternal law and is the eternal law of love. He is recognized in that he is as he is, upright, honest, selflessly loving—and not by many words of love.

he person who is in the light of truth speaks a different language. What he says is permeated by the light of truth and thus, selfless. The truthful one does not display himself—he is.

The one who sees only the external is blinded by the illusions of this world and believes deception to be reality and thinks he is a realist because he believes in only what his eyes reflect: the illusion of the Being.

On the other hand, the one who beholds, who turns his eyes to within, comprehends the Being, the truth, and sees the external, the illusion.

The one who beholds, sees you in himself as a part of himself. He also sees your external aspects, and sees you as you are, and recognizes you in your world of illusion. He knows where you come from and where you are going because your shimmering shell that strives only for outer splendor is evident to him.

The true Being is the inner radiance. It does not need many words—it radiates. It does not seek oil for its lamp, either—it is because it is the true, the beautiful, the eternal and eternity, the light that never goes out because it is divine. This is what you are in the light of the truth.

The truth does not boast; it is. It radiates and irradiates all souls, people and beings, all Being.

The one who longs for the truth receives sparks from the light of the truth, according to his spiritual maturity.

The more sparks he is able to receive, the more intensive and far-reaching the light of his soul becomes. It shines for him on the path inward to God, so that he draws ever closer to the Eternal. The light of the truth fills the feelings, thoughts, words and deeds of the person striving toward God with light, so that his thinking, speaking and acting is truthful.

People in the spirit of truth no longer need their neighbor's matchstick, the little flame of aggrandizement and acknowledgment, with which so many people still let themselves be ensnared. The one who needs this little flame is content with this brief flaring up. With this, he is ignited—and with this, he, in turn, ignites others of like mind.

What good to a person is this little flame that briefly flares up? How long does a match burn? It flares up and is readily burnt up.

It is similar with the human ego. It flares up and shines briefly, then collapses. It is again dark in the one who is content with aggrandizement and acknowledgment—until another comes and again ignites for him the little flame of aggrandizement and acknowledgment for a brief moment.
This craving for the little flame of aggrandizement and acknowledgment continues until the soul has unfolded in Me, the Christ, and has become light of My light. Then the

soul has ignited itself on Me and shines in God eternally. The one who ignites himself on My light will become self-luminous again—just as he was as a pure being and will be again as a pure being: eternally self-luminous.

But how poor is the one who offers the match and how poor the one who has to ignite himself on it, to briefly flare up, so that he can briefly display himself, that is, briefly move into the light! Both, the one who offers the match and the one who lets himself be ignited, are souls without light, still poor, spiritually dead ones, who feel sorry and mourn for themselves and briefly rejoice in the little flame of aggrandizement and acknowledgment.

The one who thinks and acts this way and expects the little flame from his neighbor does not live. The one who does not live knows neither himself nor his neighbor, nor does he have an eye for the true and beautiful. He speaks of the Being and means his ego. He speaks of the Self and means himself. He acts solely for himself and gives his all to be seen.

The darkened, the blind, person sees only his base self and does not behold his true self. He will remain a blind one, until he knows who he is and until he lives what he is—divine.

As long as the person does not draw from the truth, he wants to prove himself. If he has become the truth, then he is the truth and the true Being, the life in Me, which is impersonal.

The one who has become the true being, the true self, does not need to prove himself; nor does he need to prove himself to his neighbor because he is the true self, the true being.

The truth does not have to prove itself—it is.

The one who is from the truth is the truth; he also does not need to ask about the truth.

The true one does only good for his neighbor and only if his neighbor asks for it. The truthful one is always loyal and good to his neighbor—even if the latter denies him and his help.

If the soul in the person has become the I Am, the truth, the law of the All, then it also encounters the I Am again and again because it lives in the stream of the I Am and is the eye of the I Am.

The I Am is the true Self. It encounters itself again and again because it is divine and all that is divine is contained in all things. You are the bearer of the true Self, of the divine, the All-life.

The I Am is the true Self, the Being, the truth; it is the law of the All. The I Am is everything in all things. Therefore, it is the Self. If you are divine again, you are the self, the being, the truth, the law of love because you are the heir to infinity and the image of your eternal Father.

On Earth as it is in heaven: The divine encounters the divine over and over again—itself. The human self, the base ego, encounters itself, the base ego, again and again.

y apostles and disciples asked Me how they could become free from bindings and from striving for acknowledgement:

You will become free from bindings and the striving for acknowledgement when you leave your fellowman his freedom and reflect upon yourselves, to attain the conscious sonship or daughtership of God through actualization and fulfillment of the laws of God because in God, all beings live as free beings. They are bound to nothing and no one. They are rich because they fulfill the law of God.

If soul and person do not fulfill the law of God, they become impoverished and bind themselves to people and things that surround them and that come toward them.

The one who lets himself be controlled by the events of everyday life and by people has surrendered the rudder of his life and does not have the gift of discernment. Such people separate from one person and bind themselves to another.

Heed the following simple basic rule:

Rely on God, the Eternal. Do not expect anything from your neighbor, then you will not be disappointed.

ou should not make comparisons with anything or anyone. Like presupposes like.

Recognize that the inner light, the Christ in you, the I Am, is incomparable.

The one who is awakened in the light of the truth no longer compares—he is.

any people are enveloped in the darkness because they are completely taken up by the external. They thoughtlessly pass by their neighbor and do not know that they are passing by God.

Dark, and thus blind as they are, they violate the highest forces of life, the law of salvation. They do not know about their innermost being, the precious treasure, the gem, which is God, out of whom they were spiritually born, thus becoming divine.

Therefore, learn to walk in the light, in the eternal Being. Maintain your life by drawing from the life. Go into the stillness, become still and be active from the stillness. That is the true deed. That is being fulfilled by God.

What the person radiates is what he attracts, and he sees only that. Everyone sees himself in his neighbor, the divine one and the undivine one.

A person encounters what he thinks because like always attracts like, and sees its like.

You see yourself in your neighbor.

What you see and what you get upset about is what you, the person, are. Your physical eyes reflect only you, yourself, and what is around you and what upsets you—and this, in turn, is you.

The one who truly beholds, the true self, beholds and sees at the same time because the spiritual eye sees through, and has the overview of, everything.

The one who truly beholds has an eye for the true Being. He sees into the depths of life and in it, beholds himself and his neighbor and all Being because the spiritual eye perceives everything, since it is, at the same time, the eye of the eternal law: the true Being, the true Self.

The one who truly beholds does not judge because he is the wise one who sees into the depths of life and sees through everything. But the one who looks only at the surface of life judges because he has not yet fathomed the depths of life.

The one who beholds knows no definitions because he does not have to comprehend anything—he is.

The one who beholds has no opinion because he is wise.

The one who is, is in the Being, and the Being knows about all things because it is itself. It beholds itself and perceives itself, the law of the All, which is everything in all things.

Since everything is in all things, God, everything is also God—in the soul of the person and in every cell of the physical body. If the person feels, thinks, speaks and acts against the Being, the law, God, then he acts against himself.

The one who is against his neighbor is also against himself because God is in his neighbor and God is in him— everything in all things.

If you disparage your neighbor, you disparage yourself. If you insult your neighbor, you insult yourself. If you act against your neighbor, you act against yourself.

Recognize: If the All-power, God, is in you, then the All- power, God, is also in your neighbor.

You, the Being, the being in God, are the essence of in- finity, since the essence of infinity is also in your brother, in your sister. You act against yourself if you are against your brother.

Thus, the one who is against his neighbor is also against himself.

The opposite pole is the adversary who is against God. Thus, you, too, are against God if you disregard His laws. In this way, you create your own human law for yourself— this is what you are, what you live in, and what influences you.

To want to return to God means to return to people, to respect them and to learn to selflessly love them. This is the return to unity because God unites everything.

You are and I am in Him. All people and beings, the stars and the kingdoms of the animals, plants and stones are in Him.

You are mine,
I am yours;
the eternal Being moves in this consciousness.
I am in everything,
you are in everything;
you are and I am
everything that is.

There is nothing in the pureness that is not in Me.
There is nothing in the pureness that is not in you.
We are one in the stream of the One,
who is eternal,
who protects you and Me,
out of whom I am

and you are—
for we are divine.
He is the salvation and secureness.
He is the love and the feeling of safety.

I am from Him;
you are from Him.
We are linked by that which is,
the Eternal and eternity;
for you and I
are divine, eternally.

If your neighbor is close to you, then you are close to God. If you feel distant from your neighbor, then you are distant from God. At every moment, you determine how near or how far you are from God, yourself.

Once you have learned to feel into the soul of every person, then, in yourself, you experience the very depths of your neighbor's soul and know what soul and person need. Only by putting yourself in your neighbor's place, can you understand him and become one with him.

Once you have experienced and beheld in yourself your brother, your sister, then it is just as if you have beheld God, for God is the divine in you and in your neighbor.

When you cut down your brother—be it in thoughts or with the sword—then you cut down yourself, so to speak because the positive side of your brother, the divine, is in you.

If you are against your brother, then you are also against that part of your brother that is in you.

What you destroy today, you must build up again tomorrow.

As Jesus, I, Christ, taught My apostles and disciples to behold, which is, at the same time, the perception because the senses of the soul and the senses of the person are organs of perception.

The one who has spiritualized his human senses beholds and hears the innermost Being, his true self, and his senses of smell, taste and touch are aligned only with what is divine.

The beholding is the perception of the Being in the stream of the Being. If you want to practice the right beholding, the divine perception, ito open the eye of truth that is the Being, then affirm—at first, still blindly—the Being, which is in everything you see.

In this way, you experience in yourselves that the Being knows no differences. But it has the gift of discernment and beholds and grasps the various degrees of consciousness of the evolutionary steps that mature toward perfection.

Make no differences between your neighbors because if one of your neighbors is closer to you than the other, then you reject the other and imagine yourselves to be higher than the one who, in the end, is equal to you, the other one. As long as you make differences, you will not attain the gift of discernment and therefore, will also react differently in what you think and do because you do not behold, and cannot perceive, the whole in everything.

Affirm the whole in everything, then you will keep the order of the temple and will also learn to behold the degrees of consciousness and attain the gift of discernment and learn the language of the law, which is not the language of human beings.

The language of the law is the opened divine consciousness, the philosopher's stone, which radiates all the facets of truth into infinity, and thus, knows all things because it is the law, the All.

The eye of the law is, at the same time, the ear of the law: What you behold, you also hear.

The one who beholds hears, registers and reacts all at the same time. What he beholds, he also registers, and what he hears, he also perceives.

He beholds the Being because he is the being, and hears the Being because he speaks the being, which is the life.

The one who is the truth also sees his neighbor as he is. He hears what his neighbor does not say, and when the latter speaks, he perceives from what is said who his neighbor is.

The one who beholds sees through everything because he has the overall view. The light of your eyes is either the light of your ego or of the I Am.

What you see that irritates you is what you have attracted.

What you listen in on that irritates you is what you have attracted.

What you speak is what you are and you are also with those who speak the same way.

The light of reflection of your physical eyes, of your physical ears, of your physical words and your physical desires and passions is the light of your ego. With these reflections of your human ego, you attract solely those people who are the same or like you. You are of one mind with the people who reflect in the same or like way as you. This is human and has no access to heaven.

The truly wise one does not reflect. He penetrates everything because he is the eternal law that penetrates all things.

The pure penetrates the pure and it makes no distinctions. Pure is pure. It penetrates the All and all those who are pure.

The divine principle—sending and receiving—pervades the All.

The impure one always sees only himself—his impurity—in his neighbor. That is what he radiates—that is what he is.

The one who affirms himself, his base ego, understands only himself, his base ego. With this, he is on the human level.

The one who is does not need to understand because he is wise. He is the divine essence in his neighbor, and his neighbor, in turn, is the divine essence in him. Both irradiate each other, and both irradiate the All and the All irradiates both. Both and the All irradiate all Being, the Being that has become form, the spirit beings and the spiritual nature kingdoms. And all Being that became form irradiates both, in turn because everything is contained in all things. Thus, there are no differences, only the gift to discern between degrees of consciousness.

As above, so below.

There is only one law-principle: What you send is what you receive.

Nothing that is eternal is outside of you. What heaven is, the eternal law, is in you. That is what you are, the self—and that also surrounds you because everything is contained in all things, and the Being, the law, is effective in all things.

What is on Earth—density, matter—emerged through the reversed principle of »sending and receiving,« through the base ego, which shapes itself with the feeling, thinking and speaking of the individual. What the person has acquired in the way of human aspects is not divine. This burdens his soul and his body; it is what he radiates. Density, matter, which is merely reflection, emerged through the undivine.

The divine principle is the pure—the undivine principle is the impure, from which matter came forth. The divine principle can radiate through the reversed, the undivine, the human principle—but the undivine, the human, cannot radiate through the divine.

Since the divine is in matter and radiates through matter, in time, the mirrors, which as a whole form matter, will become dull. Sooner or later, each mirror will change in the absolute principle because the Spirit penetrates matter, and no shadow can exist in the long run.

Then everything is again the Being in the stream of the Being.

The pure ones who live in the pure principle, in the stream of the Being, and who personify the Being, the Absolute, the pure principle, speak the language of the primordial sensation, which expresses itself in them because they are, themselves, the word of the truth that is manifest in them.

If the pure one sends, he receives the word of the pure in himself because his neighbor—and the language of his neighbor—is divine and is, in turn, a part of the one who receives. The entire law is contained in the divine word because everything in all things is the whole.

The impure principle is the human ego. It is what is outside; it is the density, the human state, the human way of feeling, thinking, speaking and acting—which, in turn, is the one who sends it out himself, projecting it onto his neighbor. He will then hear only the language of his neighbor, which, then again, is his language because like attracts like.

Your feelings, thoughts and words are a part of you. Just as you emit them, in the same way they behave toward you and come back to you. Therefore, just as you send, will you receive, and that is how you will also behave toward your neighbor: positive, divine—or not divine, that is, human.

Your human feelings, thoughts, words and deeds leave their mark on you, which you are, yourself.

The world of your life, which is made up of the sum of your feelings, thoughts, words and actions, and from which your longings, passions and desires follow, compels you to feel, think, speak and do the same and like things again and again. You will continue to be the spiral of your ego, until you move out of this spinning top and reject the tempter—who you are, yourself, and which is your human ego.

The tempter is your small, egocentric world of thought, which consists of the countless threads and cords of your human ego that trap you again and again, binding you to what you feel, think, speak and do. Only with Me, Christ, can you undo the shackles of your human ego, to find your way into the eternal principle, into the eternal law, God, which speaks itself because there is only one principle: sending and receiving.

Recognize and experience yourself as the principle of God. Then you will see through the wiles and the falsity of the adversary. He steals into you by way of your human feelings and thoughts to ravage your temple.

Therefore, learn the following and take it to heart: You are your thought. What you provide your thoughts with is what they cause in this world, in and on you, and in your surroundings.

If you want to recognize yourselves in your thought, then place this thought before you for consideration. Regard it carefully, and you will be amazed at the many aspects it bears.

As Jesus, I, Christ, continued to teach My apostles and disciples: Your earthly body is a thought-body. You are equipped today with what you felt, thought, spoke and did in previous lives and did not clear up.

The cells and organs of your body, which are already formed in the womb, are shaped by the soul that prepared to move into this house. Before your birth, your body is shaped by what you should clear up in this life on Earth. If you want to learn what you have brought with you and what comes from that life, then read your life-picture: the scale of your human feelings, thoughts, words, deeds, desires, passions and longings.

Recognize: The soul thus brings its imprint with it and, already in the womb, shapes its body. Although the child's brain cells do not have anything stored in them yet, what the person will experience in this life is already stored in the body, in the cells of the body.

During fertilization, the soul, which is preparing to in-carnate, already enters into the first cell division what it brought with it—what is of significance for it in this life on Earth. Thus, already in the womb, it determines its physical body.

The light-filled soul predetermines the person's fine structure, the noble features, which can first become no-ticeable in later years, if the body grows and the person has fostered the fineness of his soul. Just as the structure of the body is, so does the person vibrate; so does he radiate; so is he; so does he behave.

A burdened soul predetermines a coarser structure that is already recognizable in its early years on Earth, often when the earthly garment enters the development phase of puberty. It is not always the girth of the body that is significant, especially not during the developmental phase of puberty.

However, nothing happens by chance. Thus, it is not a coincidence that one has a finer structure and the other a coarser structure; that one is more delicate and the other one heavier; that one is poor and the other rich; that one is born ill and the other healthy.

Only the fewest people think about why things are as they are. What is important for most people is that all goes well for them. The neighbor who begs by the wayside, who has taken to his sickbed or is mistreated and despised by his fellow humans is of interest only to the fewest of people—and the majority of people act the same way toward the worlds of animals and plants.

Disinterest, too, is a part of the law »you will reap what you sow.« The one who sees that people mistreat or kill people, the one who sees that people mistreat and kill animals and violate nature, the one who sees that people deliberately violate the laws of inner life and closes his eyes, that is, does not object—is no better than those who do these things. The radiation of his soul, his behavior and the shape of his body will then likewise say who he is.

Although the Earth itself and everything on the Earth is matter, the structures of individual people and of all the other forms of life show considerable differences. Thus, every person brings his soul's identification with him. The structure of his body identifies him since the person shows himself as he is constituted: fine, noble, understanding—or uncouth, coarse and intolerant.

»You shall know them by their fruits« also means, among other things: The person shows who he is—in what he says, how he says it, what he does and how he carries it out, how he dresses and with whom or what he surrounds himself.

In everything, he reveals either attributes of the I Am, of the inner being, or attributes of the burdened soul.

The one who judges his fellow people in his thoughts because he is of the opinion that he is better than his neighbor, is more likely worse. Through his attributes, he displays what he wants to hide in his thoughts and reveals his falseness to the truly wise one. The one talks sweetly and thinks in a sour way, thus showing himself as the cunning one who will himself be conned. People who are marked by falseness sneak around. They are sly and want to listen in on everything, to then raise themselves above their fellow people, by talking sweetly—that is, sourly—about them and vilifying their life and existence.

The sincere one who addresses everything clearly and impersonally is not the proud, the arrogant, one. Upright people are honest, clear people who are farsighted.

Erect people who display themselves, that is, people with an air of artificial dignity, are unclear people who hide their narrowness by talking a lot about themselves and by seeming to be kind and busy. They are the domineering and jealous ones who have little inner life—but all the more external semblance.

Those people who are turned without seek external gloss and create for themselves what most people do not have: wealth. They are people with a coarser structure, who then disguise themselves and wrap themselves in crimson and gold, in velvet and silk, to veil what they are: coarse, domineering, jealous, envious and intolerant.

Regardless of what the person uses to try to hide himself with, his identification is always his way of thinking, speaking and acting—even when he shows himself as an intellectual and boasts with his knowledge, adorning himself with words that are not typical of the fine person because the latter is fine and shows himself this way, noble. The words of the noble person contain the radiance of the inner being, since his way of feeling and thinking, too, bears the radiance of the light-filled worlds.

I taught this and more to My apostles and disciples. However, again and again admonishing words preceded what I taught: The one who judges and condemns his neighbor is worse than the one who was judged.

I gave My apostles and disciples the teachings from the Absolute Law and from the causal law and further pictorial instructions to take with them on their path through life—for self-recognition and knowledge. The one who recognizes himself and clears up what he has recognized attains the gift to discern between good and evil.

taught some of My apostles and disciples how to send out feelings, thoughts and words. At the same time, I pointed out to them the dangers that lie in using the energies of feelings, thoughts and words, that is, in sending and receiving.

At the present time [1991], many people hear and read My word, which I Am, the Christ of God, and which I give through My instrument. Likewise, I point out to all those who hear Me through My instrument or read My words, the dangers that are effective in sending and receiving feelings, thoughts and words.

Every feeling, every thought and every word is a sender that seeks its corresponding receiver in order to be actualized.

What the person sends will find the receiver, who consists of the same or similar thoughts. Since every receiver also contains the sender, the former is stimulated by the one that sends and, in turn, sends the same or something similar back. Through this exchange of thoughts, an ever-greater sending complex emerges, a program that is then also absorbed by the soul as a burden, as a cause. From this, ensue the blows of fate, the illnesses and afflictions that correspond to what the complex or complexes, the burdening or the burdens, consist of.

The adversary strives to direct the person in such a way that he will unceasingly think in a negative way and consequently also receive negativity. Through this, fields of communication build up in the person's brain and in his soul, which he will then use, himself. Via the negative communications, which—as long as the soul is burdened—are also part of his sending potential, so-called injections occur. This means that the adversary lets his desires and his will flow into the person's running negative programs.

The life of a person who allows this to happen will change more and more toward the negative. In the end, he will no longer recognize whether they are his own negative programs or those of the adversary or those of souls clinging to him, to fulfill through him what they once could not do in the earthly existence, during their incarnations.

You have heard that all beings and all Being are linked with one another through communication. The principle of communication is sending and receiving.

What the spirit being sends can be seen as a perfect picture at the place to where it sent it, for instance, in the receiving spirit being.

Every cosmic impulse is the law that is revealed as a perfect picture. Every cosmic impulse is the law that is lived, and is therefore, permeated with light and power. The impulse that the spirit being emits never misses its receiver because the impulse, the picture, is the I Am, the life.

In the reversed, the satanic, principle, something similar takes place: The human ego sent out is likewise a picture. The more this impulse, the human picture, is lived by the sender, the more intensely it is permeated by the one sending. The more it is lived by the one who is sending, the more quickly it comes back to him.

The law says: What you send comes from you and is lived by you.

The reversed principle says: In you, you have to relive what you think and say. You have to experience it in you as pictures, then it returns to you even more quickly. The one who carries out this reversed principle, which has been input by the demons, is the one who must bear it.

To wherever the person sends, from there he receives the answer. For any sending that occurs outside of the eternal Being, the soul or the human being has to give the corresponding equivalent in return.

Recognize and grasp: The soul that incarnates develops its growing body already in the womb. Even the organs and the functions of the body form the magnets for the material radiation. Once the child is born, then the infant receives its soul-radiation by way of its organs and the functions of its body. In this way, the soul makes a direct connection with the body.

As long as the child is not yet able to differentiate between good and evil, the parents bear the responsibility for their child. How they live with the infant, how they treat it or what they say to it or what they talk about in its presence—the infant absorbs, first, by way of its organs and body functions. In the further course of the soul becoming rooted in the body, the imprint of the body functions then enters the child's brain cells.

Recognize: Like attracts like. It is no coincidence that a child comes into exactly the family it is born into. For this reason, a good or less good development of the child cannot be based solely on the parents, but has to do with the family's total energy-volume. If souls as human beings, that is, in their incarnation, form a family, then all family members have the task to examine their family's sending station and to make of it what will help the individual to become a person of the Spirit.

The family—that is, all family members—forms the birth-place, either for the positive or the negative, the »for and against,« which is then passed on to the following incarnations of the individual soul. Every human being himself decides where his soul will be after this incarnation because each one is responsible for what he has brought with him as a soul from the soul realms, and how he behaves as a human being in this earthly existence.

Thus, the person, himself, has brought upon himself what the soul bears, light or shadow. The members of the family have to expiate or bear together the same or simi-

lar things. This is why the family should be the nucleus for the good, the pure, the beautiful and noble.

The one who monitors his sending and receiving station will apprehend what he sends. He will then also know what he receives. What he receives is what he is today and what he will be in the future—either light and freedom or darkness and bondage, from which, in turn, comes grief, illness and need.

The adversary wants the person to unceasingly send negativity, in order to bind him to himself, the adversary, and to the wheel of reincarnation—in accordance with the law, »what you sow, that is, send, is what you reap, that is, receive.« Through the binding behavior of a person, he also binds weaker ones to himself and pulls them down again, as it were, which means into further incarnations, by way of the wheel of reincarnation. Then it is possible that the present family will come together again in another incarnation, but in another constellation—the father or the mother could then be the children of their former child.

The one who does not recognize himself does not recognize the one he is face to face with, either. Through this, he will be divided in two—one time for God, then again against God. Thus, he remains a swaying reed in the wind whose eyes are closed to the truth.

Those who are divided in two or more parts call out »Lord, Lord,« and yet, are not with Me. One time, they want to belong to Me, then again to the world. They are the lukewarm ones who speak about the light of truth, yet do not live in the light of truth and do not know the light of truth. They speak about the kingdom of heaven, yet are far from it because they live far from God. They are one time warm and then again cold. They cannot be depended upon because they follow the vicissitude of time and those who are as they are: one time warm and then again cold.

Those who are divided in two or more parts have yet little light in their souls. They will remain bound to the wheel of coming and going, until they have attained unity with all forms of life and are thus one with God and with all beings and human beings.

Be you the Self in every sensation, in every thought and in every word and in everything that you do. Then you do not have to lean on your neighbor. You are one and are the unity in the unity because you are everything that is eternal.

Only the one who is not aware of the true Self in his feeling, thinking, speaking and acting worries about tomorrow. You have to unfold the Being, the Self, in your feeling, thinking, speaking and acting, so that you are then able to speak the language of the Being, of the Self. Then you feel, think, speak and act yourself because you are the true self, the being, the all-encompassing law.

You, the true self, the unity in God, will then again be the whole in every feeling, in every thought, in every word and in every action.

The law, God, is indivisible—it is everything in all things. Just as you are the being, the self—everything in all things, and in all things, everything—you are also everything in every feeling, in every word and in every action. You, yourself, are as essence in what goes out from you.

If you send your self, the true being, the true self, the law, God, then you are in communication with the true Being, with the Self, with the law.

Wherever you, the true being, send to, there the radiation of your self builds itself up as picture and form, also *in the material world, on the Earth. In time, that which you, the self, have built in the radiation-picture and in the radiation-form comes into effect. What then radiates back to you and your surroundings, thus becoming manifest on the Earth, is, again, the eternal law, the Self, the Being.*

Your true self is your divine mentality, your divine abilities, and what you are, yourself, as a being in God. What you are and what you emit is realized because every feeling, every thought and every word ripens to fulfill itself. That is the law of sending and receiving.

Thus, on Earth, the positive, the divine, can build up as well as the negative, the dark. You determine it because you are the determining one for yourself and for your surroundings—and you, yourself, contribute to the buildup of light or to the decline of the materialistic world.

Therefore, recognize what sending and receiving means: In the sending and receiving potential lies, at the same time, the responsibility for yourself. What you send, you will also receive. What flows out of your innermost being enters your innermost being again and builds up as light and power externally.

Nothing that is sent out misses its goal because it was aimed at the goal. The goal lies inherently in everything that is sent.

All of infinity is built on the Father-Mother-Principle, on polarity and duality, on sending and receiving, on the positive and negative poles. This principle also builds up in the evolutionary steps of the minerals, plants and animals, up to the perfect spirit beings.

The Fall made the divine principle its own and applied it to itself. It undertook the following reversal: From the divine »Link and be« became »Divide, bind and rule.«

This means that the Fall-thought likewise can actualize itself, that is, bring about its purpose. The purpose then comes back to the sender through the principle of sending and receiving.

The reversed principle will continue to exist as long as human beings are receiving stations for this, that is, receivers, which, in turn, send out the same and like things.

I, Christ, came as Jesus to the people to teach them the law of God—»Link and be«—and to live it as an example for them.

I Am the Christ, the Spirit that reveals Itself and that again teaches: »Link and be.«

Through willing people, I, Christ, transfigure the Fall-law, the law of »Divide, bind and rule.«

I transform all that is negative to the divine. The base energies are transformed up, by which means the Fall-law—»Divide, bind and rule«—dissolves and everything again is the Being, the pure, eternal law: »Link and be.«

The person who is in the process of changing from the negative to the divine, from the »I want« to the »Let there be,« becomes ever finer in his structure. He raises himself to the true Being, which has no thought.

Every thought is the present, the past and the future in one, and is carried by the maintaining energy, the Spirit consciousness.

The present is the conscious mind. The past and the future are the subconscious. The Spirit consciousness is the life. It is the maintaining energy that will again become the flowing power of God through the transformation.

I live through the one who lives in Me, the Christ. He has become wise and no longer needs the opinion of his neighbor because he sees through everything and knows about all things. He will then no longer be an opinion-maker because the one who opines does not know. The truly wise one knows and does not opine.

The person who has awakened to impersonalness has found the philosopher's stone. He hears the lawful principle in everything that is spoken—and recognizes, in turn, *the whole in it because the eternal, the truth, always communicates itself totally.*

Since everything is contained in all things, you should pay attention to the following, to gain knowledge of the All-unity:

What you sow, therein Am I, too.
Wherever you go, I, too, Am there.
Thus, what you sow and where you sow—
I Am in everything.
Wherever you go—I go with you.

The You Am I because I Am in everything;
and you are the I because I Am in everything.
You are here and there, and I Am here
and there.
Therefore, there is no place
where I Am not and where you are not.
For this reason, find yourself in Me,
and I Am the You in you.
Wherever you think toward—I Am there,
whatever you speak—therein Am I.

Whomever you speak to, what you say bears within Me, the Self, the I Am—that you also are, that is in your neighbor and that is in all things, occurrences and events.

This is the law. This is the way the prophets of God thought and think, the way they lived and live.

emember: You cannot serve two masters. Nor can you love two people differently. The one who does this will accept the one and spurn the other.

Therefore, the precept of life says: Love all beings and all things equally. That is the impersonal life; that is the heaven that comes to Earth.

The unified one has become the self, the state of oneness, the light. He is the divine because he lives in the stream, in God. He lives in Me and I live through him, and we know each other because we know God, since we are divine.

he one who sows in the Spirit of God will also reap from the Spirit of God. The one who sows in human beings and their human deeds will also reap only from human beings, and only humanness. The one is eternal—the other transitory.

he human being and matter are merely projections of the inner being. Just as the person thinks, so is he. That is the projection of his world of sensations and thoughts, his words and deeds.

This is why the illusion can never rise against the Being, nor the shadow against the light. The shadow will shatter on the light.

The Spirit of our eternal Father is the sole reality, the only verity that is and reigns eternally.

On this holy, eternal consciousness, God, matter will be shattered, and all those who bind themselves to matter will break into pieces.

As Jesus of Nazareth, I taught My own: The time will come in which more and more people will immerse in the light of the truth, the I Am. They will live in the I Am, in Me, the Christ, and will personify on this Earth the inner light and the inner life, the I Am.

I Am the way, the truth and the life. I come to My own and bring them the I Am. But I will not come in the flesh again. I will be among them in the Spirit—among those who bear the light, the I Am.

I, Christ, came into this world in Jesus to serve the people and not their humanness. The same is true of all true prophets. They came into this world to serve the people and not their humanness.

The one who keeps the eternal laws will also act as I and all prophets did. We came into this world to serve the people and not their humanness.

Through My Redeemer-deed, the base ego will dissolve and everything generated by it.

The page has turned. It is not the creation of God that will dissolve—as was the goal of the enemy of the good: the dissolution of the divine creation, in order to be God, himself. The human ego dissolves and everything that it generated and generates.

May the page turn in every one of you: Dissolve the human ego, the base ego—and then you will find your way to the I Am, in which I, Christ, live and Am.

The Spirit of the Christ of God, who lives in the Father, has to come into full bloom in the soul of the human being.

As soon as the soul immerses in perfection, in the stream of the eternal Being, the person, too, will know the truth and express it in thoughts, words and deeds because he then draws from the consciousness of perfection, the eternal Being.

If soul and person have not yet developed the Spirit of the Christ of God who lives in the Father and dwells in every soul, then the person will not understand the eternal laws, which are the truth. Nonetheless, the Spirit is the living wellspring in every soul and in every human being. Despite the darkness and ignorance of the human ego, the Holy Spirit remains in soul and person.

The one who merely accepts Me, the Christ, and does not receive Me in his heart has made of himself his own judge.

The one who loves Me, Christ, also loves his neighbor. The one who does not love Me, Christ, loves neither the Father nor His children, the people who are brothers and sisters to one another.

Love is the law of life. The one who loves selflessly lives. The one who does not love selflessly does not live. He has joined the spiritually dead.

Each one who strives toward selfless love recognizes the voice of love through people and through all things because God is everything in all things, the law, the voice of love.

Abide in My love, for My love is the love of the Father-Mother-God.

The one who keeps the commandments of selfless love abides in My love and is in the love of the eternal Father.

Verily, verily, I say to you: The one who hears and reads these My words and grasps their meaning and achieves what I have commanded him is truly a wise man who builds on Me, the rock, Christ.

*The Great
Cosmic Teachings of*

JESUS

of Nazareth

*to His Apostles and Disciples,
Who Could Understand Them*

with

Explanations
by Gabriele

 AM the Alpha and the Omega, the beginning and the end of the material universe and of the soul realms.

In Me and with Me, you shall mature into the eternal life, where I Am in the Father, just as you, too, are with Me in the Father. There is neither beginning nor end there because God is and we are in God. For I, the Christ of God, raise all things to the light of truth.

Gabriele, the teaching prophetess
and emissary of God, explained about this:

Alpha and Omega. »I Am the Alpha.«
The Alpha in God means the beginning of creation, of the pure Being that became form. God, the primordial power, breathed out—and it was. Very gradually, spiritual suns and planets, spirit beings, animals, plants and minerals formed out of the inexhaustible source of the primordial power. This eternally expanding, divine heavenly mechanism is the eternal, imperishable Being—our homeland.

God, the power, the light, knows no beginning. God, the light and the power, was and is eternally because God is.

»I Am the Alpha and Omega, the beginning and the end of the material universe and of the soul realms.«
The Alpha is also the beginning of the Fall-planes. Through the Fall, soul realms and matter came into being. Through the Fall-thought, parts of the spiritual planets

fell; they broke away from the pure Being and arranged themselves outside of it. Beings of the Fall fell with them, and with these beings, the nature kingdoms, as well because the life in God is a whole. The heavenly bodies, the beings, the animals, the plants and the minerals are a part of life. That is unity in God. And God gave the unity to the Fall-beings to take along with them on their journey all the way to matter.

God, our eternal Father, allowed the Fall because every child has free will. He was and is with His renegade children. His light, His power, continued and continues to flow to them.

Everything that is, is the life from God because God is the life. Therefore, God is also in density, in matter because in matter, too, He is the indwelling life.

Since God is in all things, God is also in the beginning, in the Alpha, and likewise in the end of density, in the Omega.

Through Christ, His first-beheld Son, the Co-Regent of the heavens who is one with Him, everything will be transformed and led back into the eternal light again.

God, the flowing light, knows neither beginning nor end; for He is. From Himself, the flowing light, He came forth as a being. From Himself, the flowing light, He also created us, the pure spirit beings, His children. We are in His image, light that became form.

God is the Father-Mother-God. In the Father-Mother-Principle lies the great heart-magnet for children. Consequently, He created the eternal Being that became form, the heavens, with His children, with the spiritual families who, in turn, live in the great family of God.

Like the Father-Mother-God, the dual principle is the giving and the receiving. The Father-Mother-God is the primordial Father. The duals call themselves dual-father or dual-mother—they are the principles from God: the positive, the giving, the male principle, and the negative, the receiving, the female principle.

Thus, God breathed the giving and the receiving into the beings, just as He is giving and receiving Himself.

God breathes out and in. Infinity expands unceasingly. There is no standstill. God continuously creates spiritual heavenly bodies. The spiritual children come forth from the union of the dual principles, from the giving and receiving, so that the heavenly Being, our homeland, expands and is populated more and more.

All of us, each one of us, bears a soul within. Once the soul purifies itself, it will again become a light-filled being of the heavens, a spirit being.

On the way to God, we return into the primordial stream, we return to our spiritual families, to the spiritual kin, from where we went forth. Our true life is there. We belong there, and we will also be there again—through Christ, our Redeemer.

Christ has set out to lead us back. He walked the path over this Earth to Golgotha. He gave to each soul and each human being from His light potential, which leads us home. That is why the soul can reach the Father only through Christ, through no other power—no matter what it calls itself. Christ is the redeeming power, and the path back into the eternal Being goes by way of Christ.

Christ speaks: *»In Me and with Me, you shall mature into the eternal life, where I Am in the Father.«*

For us, "In Me" means to find our way to Christ, in order to resurrect in Christ and then to live in Him.

We walk the Inner Path, from the level of Order to the level of divine Earnestness, so as to make the Redeemer-light in us shine. Once we have developed the four levels of Order, Will, Wisdom and Earnestness for the most part, we are resurrected in Christ. Christ then leads us on, to the eternal Father.

Therefore, we have to find our way into the inner light, to Christ. Christ is our way and our goal. He is the inner light, the inner life. To find our way to Him means to find our way to ourselves, the true self, in us.

In the words *»In Me and with Me, you shall mature into the eternal life,«* Christ addresses each one of us to say to us: "Come to Me first. Find yourself in Me; then you can return with Me into the consciousness of the eternal Being as the eternal being."

All of infinity can lie in one word. How many words, that is, gifts of infinity, we receive from our Brother and Redeemer, Christ, so that we find our way back to the life that is in us and that unites us.

A small passage from the great cosmic teachings could open all the heavens for us. Let us immerse in the words of absoluteness, to again learn the language of the inner being, the language of our true being!

The language of the pure spirit being is the language of light that is sent out and received in pictures. If we look into the statements of the eternal law, we very gradually learn the language of pictures—because our human language, too, is a language of pictures.

Let us learn the language of the heavens! Then we understand one another better because we recognize who we truly are. Through this, we gain more and more respect for our life and for our true being, which is the infinity in the eternity.

The language of the heavens is the language of love. To learn the language of love means to understand our neighbor, to no longer disparage him and to make ourselves aware every day that in him, too, is the positive part that cannot be burdened, God, the Eternal. God is in our neighbor—and what is in him is also in us.

Once we recognize ourselves as the son, the daughter, of God, heirs to the powers of infinity, we will also accept our neighbor in our inner being because we grasp that he is a part of us—since God is indivisible and is the whole in every one of us. By accepting and understanding, we establish communication with our neighbor and, at the same time, the connection with God. Through this, we learn the language of the Spirit, the language of selfless love—the law of inner life.

Let us take two words from the statement of the Lord, *»In Me and with Me, you shall mature into the eternal life«:* "mature into." What is in these two words? Let us feel into these words. Let us allow these two words to come up in us as pictures.

Often the Spirit of God spoke to us in the following sense: "In the shell of the word, lies the meaning, which alone makes it alive. Into one word, I place the infinitely many facets of life, the I Am. Thus, the fullness, the law of the heavens, is in one word."

Since this is so, the word of God is a treasure that wants to be raised by us. With the feelers of our inner being, we can feel into the word, so that what the energy of the day brings us today to experience, to recognize and to transform, rises in us as a picture or sensation.

We can hardly succeed with this when we work solely with the intellect, with the human mind. Only when we grasp the meaning of the word with our heart, with our inner consciousness, will we become aware of some aspects that will enrich us and bring us forward on the path to God, to our original nature.

Therefore, what do the words "mature into" say to us?

It is the process of maturing from seed to harvest. Let us relate this to us human beings.

The seed is the desire to draw closer to God. How do we draw closer to God? We have to water this seed again and again, and nourish and care for the small plant that sprouts from it—until it finally becomes a majestic plant, a majestic tree, the inner life of the God-filled human being. This is how our maturing on the Inner Path takes place. If the tree bears fruit, it shows itself in its fullness. It brings forth the law of its species, the law of the tree.

Thus, we have to mature into the eternal law by working on ourselves, and letting the fruits of love, our heritage, become manifest.

Every human being—just like every soul—determines his own spiritual becoming himself. Based on his free will, he decides when he discards his burdens, the all-too-human patterns of behavior, so that the positive life, his spiritual heritage, can unfold again more and more. His spiritual consciousness thus has to gradually mature because the human being is burdened.

On the other hand, nature already bears maturity in itself. It brings forth its consciousness from itself for us. It does not have to mature first—the plant merely lets become outwardly visible what already lies in it: the maturity.

Through the power of the Son and the power of the Father, the primordial power, the earthly forms of the powers of creation and of the children of creation—the Earth with its stones, plants and animals—will experience transformation.

Dear fellow people, when movement can be felt in us, let us remember: Nothing befalls us by chance because there is no coincidence. What we become aware of—also in the words we read—wants to tell us something. What we feel and see in pictures speaks to us. It draws our attention to something that is significant for us today, perhaps leading the way or as an admonishing hint.

If we pay attention to this hint from the energy of the day, by putting it into practice, we advance step by step on the path of becoming and maturing.

»There is neither beginning nor end there because God is and we are in God.«

For many, God is still something abstract, something far away. Let us now learn to feel God in us, in the word »God!«

What do the two words *»God is«* say to us?

Let us read the words calmly and consciously. If possible, we speak them out loud and let the sound reverberate in us: "God is." What comes up in us?

The "is" is the Being, eternally. God is the flowing eternal law. He has no beginning and no end—He is eternally being.

Let us grasp the difference: God is the flowing, omnipresent law. The Father, the form, came forth from His law. He is a spirit being. In the fullness of His light and in His radiation-power, He is infinite and inconceivable. He is sublime.

Where is God?

He is in every word that we speak. He is in every thought, in every feeling, in every stirring. In everything that we do, as well, is God, for God is the Being, the stream of life that flows through everything and sustains everything. God is always present. God is in every particle of our soul, in every cell of our body. God is in every component of matter. In every movement is God because God is the life.

Dear fellow people, let us take as a task to become aware: God is.

Wherever we go—God is.

Whatever comes toward us—God is.

God is at the place of work. God is in our work. God is in our conversations. God is always there.

He loves us. Let us trust God, and then we develop confidence in Him. Let us call on Him in every situation. A sincere request for help, and God makes His presence felt.

God is the positive power in every problem, in every difficulty, in all adversity. In every sin, God is the pure. If we want to ask for forgiveness, we ask God that He stand by us—and He stands by us.

When we sin, God calls us in time because He is in our feelings, sensations, thoughts, in our words. He is always the silent listener.

He leaves us the free will. But if the child comes to God, who is the eternal inner listener, then God comes alive in us and in what we are asking for, and He helps us to solve our problems. He helps us in conversations. He helps us every step of the way because God is the love, the giving power.

God is the Father-Mother-Principle, the creator power, also in the nature kingdoms. When we go through nature, we are going with God and are going through God, through His mighty stream, through nature, which, in turn, He is.

God is. Once we make ourselves aware of this again and again, then it begins to come alive in us and in our daily life, as well. This task and exercise—"God is"—can help us. For example, when we walk by people, when we want to disparage them, we will very quickly notice how suddenly an inner push comes that says, "Stop! I Am in your neighbor. Link with your neighbor and you will learn to understand Me, the life in all things—because God is."

If we remember this task again and again, if we grow into this awareness—"God is"—we also learn to understand ourselves. We will then also gain an understanding for our fellowman and respect for the nature kingdoms.

Through the words "God is," the clear sensation for the good, the divine, is awakened and strengthened. On the other hand, we also recognize more quickly and in finer nuances what is not divine, the base humanness. We learn to differentiate between the egocentric and the self-less more clearly. Our conscience gradually reacts more subtly, so that we become more certain in our decisions.

The selfless love is the true life that is divine. We are on Earth to become divine, that is, to become selfless love. Everything that is human is bitter. We don't always notice it. Often, we feel it only very late. When we remember "God is" in the situations of the day, we become sensitive, more sensitive to our humanness, and we experience in time that we should turn back. The sinfulness against the soul is meant here, with the word "humanness."

»For I, the Christ of God, raise all things to the light of truth.«

Let us look into the one word "truth". "Truth"—what does this word say to us?

There is only one truth—and it is God, and God is absolute. There is nothing to quibble about, nothing to doubt, there are no ifs or buts—God is!

The truth is sure of itself. It does not argue; it does not dispute. It clarifies—but it does not defend itself. It does not have to prove itself—it is. It is independent, untouched by opinions, conceptions, theories and points of view. The truth is and remains—irrefutable.

We cannot reach for the truth to change it. The one who changes it to suit himself changes himself—but never the truth.

The truth is absolute, always giving and helping. We can rely on God, the truth. He is always there. He is always present.

In all areas of our life, wherever we may be or go—God is!

Let us become aware of this: God is there to help us.

The Spirit of truth wants to help and serve us. He wants us to be well. He wants us to become healthy and stay healthy. He wants us to be happy because He is the happiness. God wants us to be peaceful and joyful because He is the peace and the joy.

Let us become more and more aware of this in our daily life. Whatever we do, wherever we go—God is with us everywhere. God is. He loves us. He helps us. He serves us. He wants the best for us because He is our Father.

Where there is truth, everything is open and apparent. The truth has no secrets because everything is true. Only the one who has to hide the untruth has secrets. Once we learn to be truthful in everything that we think, say and do, then we find our way to the truth.

The word »truth« bears the entire eternal law in itself. The truth is our spiritual heritage because we are divine law that became form, and thus, the truth.

Let us become truthful—truthful in our feeling, thinking, speaking and doing! Let us take this into our life on Earth:

Become truthful in everything that you think, say and do; then you will find yourself, and you will find yourself in the true Self as the eternal self in God.

Once we are imbued with the truth, that is, once we are truthful through and through, then we are also selfless, impersonal and certain. Then we also have the strength and, from this, the courage to impersonally express and address everything, according to the situation and state of consciousness of our neighbor. The truth is the selflessness. It is impersonal and phrases everything impersonally.

In the truth lies the honesty, the uprightness, from which, in turn, the sense of fellowship, the genuine brotherliness comes forth.

The truth is always the connection. It excludes no person because the truth is the same as unity.

Everything is united in God. If we are not truthful, then we are outside the law, outside the truth, and separate ourselves from our neighbor.

Truth is also clarity, and the clarity, which is the truth, is always simplicity.

The law of God is simplicity and everything simple is ingenious. This is why it is the greatest.

The law, God, is the whole in all things. Let us become aware that in a speck of dust is all of infinity. The opened degree of consciousness, the developed facet from the eternal law, finds expression in the form.

Once again, let us think about our spiritual heritage and about free will:

Our spiritual heritage contains free will. If we rebel against God, by disregarding the eternal laws, then that lies in free will. God will not hinder us. By rebelling, we step out of the eternal law and create our own laws. Just as we create them for ourselves, is how we live, how we think, how we suffer. The pure Being, the law, is no longer able to guide us. We cut ourselves off and become separate from God.

God does not intervene; and He will also not intervene in this material life because He gave us free will. Much will change through the power of the stars, in fact, everything will be transformed by the law that we human beings have created ourselves: What you sow, you will reap.

God is the freedom and we are His children—not vassals or servile ones. The divine law, the free will, makes us children of God and heirs to the eternal kingdom.

Dear fellow people, let us realize that through free will, we will also freely return to God. We are not forced by God to anything. God, our loving Father, always impersonally gives us the strength to believe in Him, to trust Him, to feel Him, to perceive Him and thus, to draw closer to His eternal law, our spiritual heritage—until we completely fulfill the laws of God and return as perfect drops into the ocean, God, into the eternal Being. Freely. Just as we left the eternal Being, so will we also return—freely. Then we can move freely in the eternal Being since we have again become heirs to the Spirit of God and children of the infinite, eternal freedom freely and without coercion.

A few more remarks about freedom:
The human being has made of himself what he is today. The tools with which he put himself together are his sensations and thoughts, his words and his deeds. Every person decides about himself at every moment.

Our thoughts, words and actions, our whole attitude toward our fellow people and toward our life are like rough chisels because of our burdens. As we fulfill the law of God more and more, our sensations, thoughts, words and deeds are akin to a finer chisel.

This means that our all-too-human thoughts are coarse; they shape us accordingly. Once we turn to the eternal law, then we become ever finer; then we take the finer chisel and chisel out our true being.

We decide, ourselves, which chisel we use, the rough or the finer chisel. At every hour, at every minute, at every moment of the day, we decide: either for our all-too-humanness and thus, for the satanic—and then we fall victim to the Fall-law—or we decide for God—and then we grow more and more into the law of the heavens, into our spiritual heritage.

"God is." Once we absorb this thought, we will no longer give free rein to our human thoughts. If we link with God again and again, and fulfill little by little what the will of God is, then we will take the fine chisel. We become finer because we become nobler. Our soul becomes more beautiful because it becomes purer.

The words "God is" want to take up communication with the highest consciousness, God. Perhaps we thus experience that our state of well-being is raised, once we have awakened in our inner being the awareness that »God is.« We can align better and work better and with more concentration.

If we affirm again and again that "God is," then it is in our consciousness to want to draw closer to God. Indeed, He is in everything, in every thought, in every word, in every stirring and movement—God is in every moment. When we now bring to mind "God is," thus making ourselves aware of this again and again, then we automatically call up the following sentence in our inner being: " ... and I am divine."

From these two words "God is," logically follows: "... and I am divine." This statement, "God is, and I am divine," is consciousness, a mighty source of power of divine energy. It touches the undivine in our soul. The undivine comes into vibration more strongly. The burdens that lie over the divine, the purity of our inner being—our human wrongdoing, our sins, our egocentricity—come into motion and become noticeable.

This is how the divine that we consciously strive for shows us in our inner being—also externally, through the impulses of the energy of the day—where the un-divine still is. For example, disparaging thoughts that come up.

We should not push aside the all-too-humanness that comes up now, by saying, "No, no, I don't want that any-more. I have decided: God is—and I am divine." Instead, we take the chance and grasp the negative, our human ego, our base self, and look at it—where does it come from?—and clear it up with Christ. If we do this, and re-solve to no longer do it, then the light begins to be active in our soul. It begins to erase what we cleared up, or what we started to clear up.

It is a lawful principle on the Inner Path that if we commit ourselves to the Absolute Law—"God is"—then the Absolute shows us what is not divine in us. If we clear it up, we feel how more light and more strength enter our consciousness. More human aspects can now be grasped and reduced, problems can be solved—at the same time, we become lighter, freer, more buoyant, and move one step closer to our heavenly Father.

If we turn to the Absolute Law, the law of sowing and reaping also touches us. This law "sowing and reaping" is the causal law. If we immerse in the causal law by addressing the All-law, then it shows us where we are still not divine. However, in the Absolute Law we have something to hold onto. Just like a young tree is tied to a stake, we tie ourselves, so to speak, to "God is."

Nevertheless, we should be aware of the fact that when we accept the divine law, we obligate ourselves to clear up what comes up in us as human aspects, so that we can become what we listen to, what we read and what we affirm.

Devoting ourselves to the words "God is" can bring about many a thing. It is possible that because we remembered the words, "God is," we are able to carry out with joy and concentration a job which we would otherwise do unwillingly. What happened? At the very moment we remembered the words "God is" and placed our feelings into them, our soul came into movement and took up a more intense communication with God. Through this, more power flowed to our soul, the power flowed into the body, and the vibration of our body rose. As a result of this, it was no longer difficult for us to concentrate, and the work was done more easily.

We see that when this heartfelt "God is" touches us, the divine draws closer to us. At the same moment, more power flows to us. In this, we recognize that God is present. God, our eternal Father, always stands by us—if we turn to Him. We can go to Him in every situation, with all the things that we encounter each day because He loves us.

Again and again during the day, let us bring to mind these two words—"God is"—then we feel the presence of God in us and in everything we do. In these two words lies the All because God is the All, the whole. "God is" is thus the whole in us.

Let us imagine God as the light and the power in our inner being, as the light in our thoughts, in our words and in our actions. "God is"—God is light and power. And when we say "Christ" or "Christ in me," then it is the same as when we say "God is," because Christ in the Father is God in the four natures of God. In these four basic powers of God, He is omnipresent in the Father.

"God is." To feel this consciously in us, expands our consciousness. We understand more. We see more. Things open up in the continuing development of the spiritual— dimensions that are unknown to us as human beings and are incomprehensible, as seen from the human ego.

If we turn consciously to God, we are thankful because we experience His presence, His help, in our life. Then it

may be that we say, "God has solved a problem in me."
Yet, how does this take place? God does not intervene directly in our life because we have free will. We could say
that God has awakened the problem in us. He made us
aware of our faults, of what we should clear up, to solve
the problem, or to contribute to its being solved.

Spoken with other words, in the problem, in our difficulty, God pointed out our wrong behavior, so that we
recognize what we need to clear up to solve the problem.
Or, so that we recognize what our part in it is, if several
have contributed to this problem.

Thus, God makes us aware of our faults. He does not
solve our problem, Himself. If He were to solve our problem, we would not recognize ourselves and would always
make the same mistakes again and again.

Out of the trust in God, grows thankfulness. We show
our thankfulness to Him, in turn, by actualizing daily what
the energy of the day brings to us. Only through actualization, do we find our way to God, our Father.

We will experience many situations, whether in the
family, at work or anywhere else. But God is—He is always
with us. This awareness "God is" should take root in us.
Then we have the best helper at our side.

I Am the life, Christ, the Son of God. The one who lets Me, the Spirit of life, Christ, arise in him has found his spiritual heritage again, which is his eternal life. Then the being returns home to God, the eternal Father because it is from Him.

Gabriele:

A passage from the Absolute Law. Let us feel into it! All of heaven is in this passage.

»I Am the life.«
May we not also say this, when we affirm ourselves as the pure being in God? The heavenly heritage is our life, it is the compressed Being—it is we, ourselves.

"I Am the life," says God, "in all that is." And we are the heirs to the spiritual kingdom. We possess everything that is. It is the makeup of our spiritual body.

»The one who lets Me, the Spirit of life, Christ, arise in him has found his spiritual heritage again, which is his eternal life.«
The spiritual heritage consists of the seven basic powers of God. The seven basic powers are the eternal law— the All. The law flows through all realms; it flows through all beings; it flows through the nature kingdoms, through the heavenly bodies—through everything that is.

The heavenly heritage is the shining power in us. Therefore, there is no need for a sun that shines on the pure being. The pure being, itself, is the sun because the divine heritage, the infinity, shines in the spirit being.

We human beings have to first learn about the knowledge concerning the laws of God. Once we actualize the spiritual knowledge, we attain wisdom. We then no longer need to ask how this or that may be. We no longer need to look for the correlations between heaven and Earth. The wisdom in God knows about all things because the being in God is wise.

Knowledge, alone, has no wisdom. Only actualized knowledge brings wisdom. And wisdom does not ask—it knows about the divine laws, about the correlations of the divine Being.

The Absolute Law, merely heard or read, does not bring us wisdom. The actualization of what comes toward us day after day leads us to divine wisdom, to the knowledge of all spiritual things. Only through actualization, do we enter our inner being, not by way of mere knowledge. Only through actualization, do we find our way into the absoluteness again because God, our Father, is absolute, and in God, we are absolute, perfect beings.

Gabriele:

This paragraph should encourage us. It gives us comfort. It gives us confidence—because God is. And we will resurrect in Christ because Christ in us is the light of resurrection. Each day, He offers us what we should put into practice on this day, that is, what we should actualize, so that the light, the light of Christ, can grow in us, and we can resurrect in Christ.

»I will find all those who believe they are lost.«
Nothing can be lost. No being, no speck of dust can be lost because in the speck of dust, in the particle of dust, is God. If one small particle were to be lost, then infinity would not be perfect. No energy is lost—and God is positive, eternal, shining energy. He shines in the speck of dust, in the grain of sand—yet this small, to us often inconspicuous form, bears, again in itself, the divinity. So if this small thing were to be lost, then a part of creation would no longer exist. That is impossible because God is.

Since even the smallest is secure and borne by God's care, how much more does Christ go after every being, every human being! For the spirit being in the human being possesses all the powers of the All.

The smallest is in the large, and the large is in the smallest. And this is why nothing can be lost because God is. He is in the smallest as in the large.

In God there is no passing, nothing becomes nothingness. When we say that the world is passing away, then this means that all egocentricity will shatter, so that the selfless, the indwelling divine power in us, can become free. When we speak about the fact that the human being, the humanness, the ego-shell, passes away, that it has to die, then this means that the shell has to transform, so that the pure, the fine, the noble of the eternal, spiritual being can come to light—and it transforms because God, the inner life, is everlasting.

»And the weak will grow strong in Me ...«
We will transform toward the divine, to grow strong in the divine, only when we also strive for this. Whether we are serious about this can be deduced from our world of thoughts. If we still circle around ourselves a lot, then we nourish our human ego. And if we nourish our human ego, how will we find God?

God does not nourish our human ego. We, ourselves, nourish, strengthen and expand it, by abusing the powers of God that are given to us each day anew. We transform them into negative energy through our egocentric way of feeling, thinking, speaking and acting. Or we take energy from our neighbor by making our neighbor dependent on us, so that he does what we want. His energy then flows to us, which we use for ourselves and, in the end, abuse it.

At every moment, we have the chance to recognize and grasp the positive, the divine, the strong, in the negative, in the weakness, and to decide for it and build on it. The negative that we have discarded will then be gradually transformed in Christ. The weakness becomes the strength.

We always have the possibility to actualize, to work on the transformation of our humanness, of what is weak. It only comes down to doing it! The doing is important.

Christ speaks: *»And the weak will grow strong in Me, for I Am the glory in the Father.«* What happens when we now refer to this statement and say, "Well, then, we will stay weak. But in the weakness, is the strength. At some point the strength will turn up." Even if we remain passive, if we continue to let the days go by, the strength will turn up, but then, through grief, through illness, through need, that is, through expiation. At some point—be it after several incarnations or in the soul realms—we will realize that we have to go the path of remorse, of asking for forgiveness, of forgiving, and then, we may no longer do what we have recognized as being all-too-human in us.

We cannot avoid looking at our weaknesses, so that the strength in the weakness awakens. If we look at the weaknesses and clear up the humanness, the weakness, then the strength, the light of the Lord, radiates to us.

We will not attain the strength simply by waiting for the strength to come. We have to recognize ourselves! If we do not recognize our faults and sins, we will do them again and again. We have to recognize them, go the path of clearing them up and of no longer committing the faults. Then the strength awakens; in the end, it is the Spirit of the Christ of God in us. And we will find our way with Him into the glory of the Father, where He, Christ, is.

And that is not hard on the path to God! It gets hard only when we do not believe in God, our Father, and in Christ, our Redeemer; when we do not trust in God. It gets hard only when we do not want to accept and receive our neighbor because we find our way to God only through our neighbor, since our neighbor belongs to the great unity of God. The animals, plants, minerals and heavenly bodies are also in the great unity of God. We cannot overlook one tiny spark of life and say, "I will go to God alone." We have to find our way to God by way of the person, or by way of the animal, or the plant that we reject!

To become pure means to make our eternal heritage accessible, which contains the powers of all forms of Being in the entire All. We may not exclude anything from our heart, otherwise we will not open our heavenly heritage.

Everything that we feel, think, speak and do is of significance because every thought, every sensation, every feeling is a lawful principle, either in the divine law or in the causal law.

The causal law, the law of cause and effect, is the broader term. We are recorded in the law of cause and effect with our burdens. Each and every one of us is a personal law in the causal law. Our personal law is the human ego in all its variations.

This human ego has to be reduced, that is, transformed, so that we find our way into the impersonal law, God.

Let us become aware once more that every feeling, every sensation, every thought, every word and every action is a lawful principle. Let us ask ourselves: Is what we feel, sense, think, speak and do, divine or not divine? The divine raises us and makes us free, happy and healthy. What is not divine is against freedom, against happiness, against health. This is why it brings us sickness, grief, lingering illness and lack of peace.

Thus, at every moment we decide—whether we are aware of this or not—to either increase our burdens, our personal law, or to become divine. In our subconscious, too, there is a constant exchange, a communication with corresponding forces. We are likewise responsible for these sub-communications.

The meaning and purpose of our life on Earth is to find our way from the humanness to the divine, from egocentricity to being linked with God, into the inner life. The guiding principle for a lawful life is known to every soul and every person. It is formulated in the Ten Commandments and in the Sermon on the Mount.

When we fulfill the Ten Commandments and the Sermon on the Mount step by step, then we find our way from the conscious mind to the subconscious. We will suddenly be aware of what we had not been aware of, so that we can clear it up in a conscious way. Thus, we have to work it off layer by layer. If we seriously fulfill this with Christ, we can spare ourselves many things.

Only the deed is of significance, the actualization of the commandments of God. If we actualize day by day, then the grace and help of God comes into action again and again.

We may be aware of the grace and help of God, but we are the ones who have to set out to develop the longing to draw closer to God, our Father, and thus, to our divine heritage. This is true for all people and for all souls.

He, the great All-One, assigned Me the task of leading back into the eternal Being all that seemed lost.

Gabriele:

Words of comfort from our Redeemer, Christ.

Redemption is given to all to become free and to find themselves in God. This is why all religions, all institutions have to pass away. There are neither religions nor institutions in God. The inner religion is the Christ of God; it is the life of the human being in Christ. Once we open the law of God, our heavenly heritage, through belief, trust and actualization, then we have brought the Redeemer-spark in us to shine. No external religion and no institution is necessary for this. Once we have opened the kingdom of our inner being in us, then we are united with God, our Father, and thus, united with all the powers of infinity because we have become divine again.

As Jesus of Nazareth, I spoke about the law of life without parables to those who could understand Me. For those who could not understand Me, the holy words were mysteries. This is why I spoke in pictures, again and again. But now the time has come when I, Christ, reveal the law of life to all, so that they may find Me; for I Am on My way to establish My kingdom on the Earth.

May the one who has ears, hear!

Gabriele, the teaching prophetess
and emissary of God, explained about this:

Dear reader, we have to learn to hear and feel into the words, to grasp their deep meaning, otherwise, the words will not be deciphered by us. Everything spoken then remains a mystery to us.

We understand the law of God only if we learn to understand ourselves. The one who does not know himself does not understand himself, and the one who does not understand himself does not know himself. The one who does not know himself also cannot look into the words of the Spirit of God. To him, they remain mysteries.

Therefore, the Inner Path. The one who walks the Inner Path consistently purifies his soul. Through the purification of the soul, the consciousness expands, and more light and more energy flow into the soul and into the person. The person sees more clearly, farther and more deeply. He understands and senses more. Why? Because he has more energy. The less of God's energy we have, the less we understand because not having looked at ourselves, we do not understand ourselves.

The Lord said: *»But now the time has come when I, Christ, reveal the law of life to all ….«* Why? Because we live in a mighty time of radical change, in a time as has never existed before. All the old structures will disappear. In no country, on no continent, will the old bear up—it will be swept away, as it were. This means that Christ comes!

»I Am on My way to establish My kingdom on the Earth.«
Well, dear fellow people, His kingdom should also be our kingdom because we are heirs to this kingdom, since the kingdom of the good, of the pure, is in us. It is our spiritual heritage. We shouldn't leave it with just the knowledge. Let us set out! We have to open our spiritual heritage again, to find our way to the inner kingdom, and be inhabitants of the Kingdom of God, in heaven, or on the Earth, in the Kingdom of Peace of Jesus Christ.

Therefore, we cannot avoid making the inner kingdom—the Absolute Law—accessible.

The Lord says: »*May the one who has ears, hear!*«

Once we learn to listen into the words, we will no longer need the language of pictures which is made up of conceptions, of the reflections of our human ego. Then we behold the image of God in the word and, in the end, ourselves, as divine beings.

Language expresses itself in pictures. If they are human pictures, then we need the parables, the pictures of the causal law. Once we find our way to the image of God, we grasp the law of God in a pictorial way and look more deeply. Therefore, if we release what is bound, then the so-called "mysteries" of God are also dissolved.

God has no secrets. With our sins, which we do not want to have revealed, we close our access to the inner life. Through this, we no longer look deeper and declare the whole thing to be a mystery of God. Once we release the shackles of the human ego, once we free ourselves of our secret thoughts, of what we still want to hide, then we will also unveil the so-called mysteries of God.

In God, there are no mysteries. We, ourselves, are a mystery to ourselves. We, ourselves, have veiled the eternal law, our spiritual heritage, through our wrong thinking, through our sins. Therefore, we have to unveil it again because we are heirs of the eternal truth, beings of the light. We know that by walking the Inner Path, we find our way into the Absolute Law, to our spiritual heritage—but not when we only talk about the Inner Path. Then it just remains talk. We have to do it!

Therefore, let us not talk, let us act! Then we will walk the Inner Path earnestly. Only when we walk it earnestly, that is, consistently, will we find our way out of the den of iniquity.

Let us consider how many nice words have already been said about Christ, and all that has been already written about the causal law! All this is of no use, if we merely listen and read. It is of no use, if we merely talk about it. We have to fulfill it, that is, do it.

Gabriele:

The inner reform, the spiritual renewal, thus means for us that we have to become new. This, in turn, means to change our way of thinking—away from the all-too-humanness to the spiritual.

Christ said that it is the noble, the fine, who bring the inner life. How do we become noble? How do we become fine?—We have to let ourselves be polished.

A picture: It is said that a diamond develops only under pressure. It shines as a result of cutting and polishing. We have to become, as it were, this diamond again. How? The days bring what we should look at. If we don't look at it, then they bring grief. If we look at it and clear it up, the days will become ever more light-filled. They bring more joy. Why? Because the diamond is being cut and polished.

Let us become aware of this again and again:
What do we want to become? Noble people, finest porcelain, cut glass, a cut and polished diamond?

Let us watch ourselves in the events of the day. How do we react? How do we think? Is it noble? Is it fine? Can God, the light, radiate through me in this thought that I am thinking or in this word that I am speaking? In these words and thoughts, am I permeable for higher powers—that is, am I fine and noble? Let us ask ourselves this each day!

Every now and then, let us stand, as it were, before a mirror with the following questions: Is my inner being the finest porcelain, cut glass or a cut and polished diamond? Thus, are my sensations, feelings, thoughts, words and deeds noble? If yes, then I am ennobling my soul and the nobility of my soul also brings out what is noble in the person.

Through the nobility of the soul, what is fine in the human being is also given expression. We gain respect for our life and respect for our neighbor. We become permeable for higher powers because we are cut and polished. Selfless thoughts and deeds are the expression of the nobility of the soul, of the noble and the fine, in and on the human being.

Therefore, let us look at ourselves. Let us use on ourselves the high standard that corresponds to our innermost being, the image of God. Once we ennoble our souls, once we are the finest porcelain, cut glass, a cut and polished diamond, then we notice it in our way of thinking, speaking and acting. If not, why not?

Let us also take into our daily life the task: God is—and I am divine.

In these words from the divine law, lies the process of becoming aware of our true being. They help us to recognize our humanness from the point of view of the law of life. Once we gain respect for our true life, we will also clear up what we have recognized as our human aspect and no longer do it. In this way, we ennoble our soul. This is how we refine our being. In this way, we become noble because we become pure.

Many world-oriented people will look upon the field of death and, in the end, will enter the realm of death with empty hands, where they will live as the spiritually dead. They are those who did not master their earthly existence, who missed the opportunity for the growth of their inner being in the school of Earth.

Gabriele:

If our behavior relates solely to the temporal, if matter is the measure of all things for us, then we stay coarse in our overall structure because all our aspirations are world-oriented and aligned with our coarse, bristly ego.

At night, when we sleep, our soul cannot reach the higher spheres, not even the nearest planes of purification because of this world-oriented aggressive striving, the striving for power. It stays Earth-conscious and thus, close to the Earth. This means that the soul hardly knows about the worlds of the beyond, since it is occupied solely with matter, just as the person identifies solely with this side of life.

Once the human body dies, that is, passes away, where then, does the unknowing soul go? It stays on the Earth. It has no home because just as the tree falls, so will it lie. This is spiritual death then. As a human being, the soul did not master the school of Earth. The person was world-oriented, and the soul stays world-oriented. It does not know its way into the worlds of the beyond, much less into the eternal homeland.

The Lord revealed: *»They are those who did not master their earthly existence, who missed the opportunity for the growth of their inner being in the school of Earth.«*

If we know about the laws of God and do not actualize what we have recognized, that is, if we do not purify ourselves, then what we have failed to do in this life can be made up only with difficulty. We know that the huge memory bank, the so-called causal computer—the material heavenly bodies and the planets of the astral planes, which store the offences of humankind against the law, its burdens of sin, what it has sown—is almost full. The seed and its harvest now follow one another more and more directly. The causes become effective more quickly, the effects hit the person more and more quickly. The worldly structure, erected in the presumptuousness of a thinking and living that is far from God, is collapsing.

The one who knowingly violates the divine should not hesitate to turn back now. We should take the hand of the Christ of God, so as not to be overpowered by the wave of the world and overtaken by our own self-caused fate.

The one who knowingly violates the laws of God is the one who knows them and does not act according to them. We, as Christians, have the Ten Commandments and the Sermon on the Mount. These principles of the law urge us to fulfill what the Lord commanded of us. Therefore, we cannot say that we did not know about it. The Ten Commandments are recorded in our soul because they were given to us by God through Moses, likewise the Sermon on the Mount, by Jesus, the Christ of God.

Therefore, let us set out to find our way out of the human way of thinking, so that we do not stand with empty hands when the hour has come for our physical body.

Gabriele:

The new human being in the light of the Christ of God cultivates the community. What is the community in the eternal Being? One for all and all for One.

The community is the great family of God, where all spirit beings live and work in the law-unity. Once we develop this sense of community with each other, then we also no longer circle around our human ego, around the fabric of our small thinking, around our self-made human laws.

Everything is law. In the law of God, everything is in good order—it is given; it is absolute and the way it is given is in order. The heavenly law contains the seven basic powers of God—the divine Order, the divine Will, the divine Wisdom, the divine Earnestness, the divine Patience, Love and Mercy. Thus, it is given; thus, it is determined—thus, it is eternal.

What is not a part of the Absolute Law, of the divine, falls under the law of cause and effect. It is the base, the human, the perishable, the negative. Thus, our human thoughts, too, are principles of the causal law.

If we preoccupy ourselves only with our baseness, with our human ego, then we cannot sense our neighbor. We cannot grasp him in our inner being. We have not accepted him, let alone received him. To receive him means to let him come alive in us.

At the same time, this means that if we do not feel our neighbor in our inner being, that is, if the positive sides of our neighbor do not resound and vibrate in us, then we are still occupied with our all-too-humanness.

If our neighbor, who is a part of our divine heritage, is not alive in our innermost being, then we have no sense of community because we cultivate community only with ourselves and have not developed the perception of the senses for our neighbor. We lack the positive, divine communication, which constitutes the sense of community.

If a person lacks the sense of community, there is no common good for him, either, since he thinks only of his own good. The common good is the good for all.

Thus, the one who develops the sense of community strives toward the common good. As in heaven, so on Earth. In heaven it is: All are in the One, God, and everything belongs to everyone because they are heirs to infinity. If we do not strive toward the sense of community, the common good—everything belongs to everyone—then we will not be able to follow Christ, either. He guides us into the law of love, to our spiritual heritage, which comprises the community life and thus, the common good.

The Kingdom of God will come to the Earth, and as it is above, that is, in the eternal Being, it will be similar in the Kingdom of God on this Earth. For this reason, Christ gives us the law of life because this law will be valid among those who follow Christ.

In the eternal Being, everything belongs to each being because the great whole is in each one as essence. The great whole, the macrocosm, forms our spiritual body—as a microcosm—because we are divine law that became form.

What ensues from this is that if we reject just one person, we do not cultivate the sense of community, nor do we live in the thought of the common good, and thus, do not live in the law of life. If we disregard the least component of nature, we disregard God because God, the whole, is likewise in this form of life.

When we became human beings, we took on a great task: to become divine. This means nothing other than to again make accessible everything that lies in us as divine predispositions, divine aspects, divine powers. To reach our total divine heritage is the task of every person, of every soul.

We have the divine heritage deep within us. However, it has to awaken in us again and fully bloom. Our divine heritage is fully alive then, once the essence of each smallest component in the universe is again active in us.

If we are aware of this, we will no longer thought-lessly, indifferently, or contemptuously pass by the small and large forms of life in nature, which God, our Father, allowed from His radiation, to remind us human beings of the beauty and abundance of our heavenly homeland. We will respect our neighbor as ourselves because each one of us is the child of the eternal Father, which should become His image again.

Dear fellow people, let us become more and more aware of the community, of the unity with all Being! The following questions help us with this:

Whom or what do we still disparage?

Whom or what do we carelessly pass by?

Do we still step carelessly on stones, grass, and flowers?

Infinitely wise and great is God. We step on grass, on flowers, on stones, indeed, even on animals. In these, figuratively speaking, He is the carpet on which we may walk. God serves us in this way. Under our feet is the entire event of creation, God!

The infinite greatness, God, wants to tell us: "Recognize yourself! You are My image. Attain your true greatness because you are on Earth to become divine."

The one who does not strive for the inner community with all people and with all Being is against God. The one who does not include God in his life is against God and against all that is divine. Such a person loves only himself, his base self.

Where there is self-love and egocentricity, there can be no peace which grows out of inner communication. Selflessness brings out the sense for community, the common good. The sense of community always shows itself also on the external, in the deed. Thus, the one who nurtures the inner communication with all Being will also take his place in the great family of God, and will promote the common good. As in heaven, so shall it also be on Earth.

If we are still captives of our ego-world, then we look only to the armor of our human ego. The narrowness, the state of limitedness, shows itself in that we think only of ourselves: "I, I, mine, me, for me!" Now we are called to come out of our limitation, out of the mine and me, toward our neighbor, who is a part of us.

If we are caught in the limitation of our ego, we do not behold the omnipotence of God that surrounds us. We do not hear His sensations of love, which He whispers to us through countless mouths, through the ray of the sun, through the wind, through the leaves, through the blossoms, through every stone, through every animal, through the radiation of the stars. God is wherever we go, wherever we are.

God is deep in our feelings, sensations, thoughts and words. Once we become aware of all this, then we begin to very gradually awaken in the awareness that we are children of God, heirs to infinity. Only then, will we set out to consistently walk the path to Him—because we have awakened.

The one who sleeps in worldliness thinks only of himself. The one who awakens thinks more and more of Him, Christ.

The more we are for our neighbor in a selfless way, the more people we will meet consciously, to whom we can give drops of life from the eternal Being, so that they, too, find their way into the great ocean, God, which is the community of all drops.

To develop the sense of community means to live consciously. Daily, we have to learn to appreciate the salvation deep in the person, and not to look only at the shell, the human being. If we look only at the external, then we see only the faults of the person. But if we receive our neighbor in us, if we let the total impression become effective in us, then we see the positive, as well.

Once we affirm the positive in and on our fellow people, then it will become easier and easier for us to accept and receive our neighbor. Let us not forget that each one of us is a part in the true being of our neighbor. Each one of us bears within the essence of infinity and each pure being is a part of infinity. If we disregard or scorn one person, then we disregard and scorn God.

Dear reader, let us take the statement, "God is in everything, also in our neighbor," as a consciousness aid, as a help for the days ahead of us, for the path to God goes solely by way of our neighbor.

We are called to glorify God in all our feelings, sensations, thoughts, words and actions, by ennobling, that is, cleansing, our soul more and more. Thus, the deep glorification of God is the actualization of His holy laws and their fulfillment, to then become again the lawful being which we are in the sight of God.

Once we attain unity with our neighbor, then we live the life as it is in heaven. One knows himself to be at home in the other; each one feels himself in every one. That is the community group of inner life; that is the divine communication in the All.

The same holds true for the nature kingdoms of the homeland, for the animals, plants, and minerals. The same holds true for the heavenly bodies of the eternal Being. It is a great, all-encompassing, communication network—the All. All communication, each individual impulse and ray in this pure cosmic network, is contained as essence in the spirit being. Each spirit being is contained as essence in the other, and all and everything form the great unity in God.

The new human being in Me, the Christ, knows no act of violence; he knows no claim to possession and no thought of power.

He is the bringer of light, who radiates the light and ignites with the light of truth all those who verily strive for the truth.

The rate of vibration of the new humanity and of the new Earth is several degrees higher. The prisoner of the world, the greedy one, who strives for power and prestige, can no long-er reach this higher vibration. He falls into his own floods, into what he, himself, created.

The new humanity is the people with spiritual nobility, with inner values because I, Christ, have risen in them.

The new human being in the age of the Spirit will possess the Earth.

The eternal Being flows through all realms and on the Earth. The one who has awakened to the truth has awakened to the Being, to the creative power and to the creative life, which floods through the Earth, which permeates those people who ennoble their souls. These people bring the creative thoughts for the new Earth.

Gabriele:

When we read: »... renounces materialistic activities, ...« we think of the hectic world, of the deafening noise, the pursuit of an externalized life, which sees and knows only the material. But who is it that propels matter? Who is a part of it?

The person, himself, is the cause of the unrest, of the hectic and chaotic activity. It is our human thoughts that hound us, so that we, in turn, hound others. Through this, we are the hounded ones.

If we let ourselves be driven, we are the driven ones. The more we let ourselves be driven by our thoughts and desires, the less we know ourselves because this state of being driven brings a hectic pace into our life. The thoughts chase through our brain, and we no longer understand ourselves because we can no longer grasp our thoughts.

We human beings propel the wheel of materialism because we, ourselves, are materialistic and are looking for our own advantage, since we, ourselves, focus on wanting and having, thus turning more and more without, instead of going within, into the kingdom of stillness.

It is quiet in the kingdom of stillness. Our thoughts become harmonious. We become peaceful. We will fulfill all the smaller and greater desires, which we have as human beings, aware that God knows what is good for us.

So this does not mean that we should deny the fulfillment of all desires. It means to free ourselves from the pressing desires that befuddle us, that paralyze our consciousness. We should look at them and clear them up with Christ; for God, our Father, wants things to go well for us. Let us build on Christ, by fulfilling the laws of God more and more and striving toward the consciousness of becoming divine! Then we will have everything that we need because God knows what is good for us.

Once we think and live in this awareness and trust God in all things, what is due to a child of God will be fulfilled. Through this, we ennoble our soul. All that is pressing and hectic is not the noble; it is not the fine in a human being. Through this unworthy behavior, the person becomes ever coarser, ever cruder. He wants only to have and to amass for himself. The greed grows and he craves everything that he sees and can get hold of.

The Kingdom of God in us is the inner wealth. The one who truly is the child of inner stillness receives what he needs and beyond that. The child of the inner stillness does not have to live in want; it does not have to go hungry. It will never have to live in a quagmire—unless we have quagmire-like thoughts that drive us, thoughts of wanting to be and to have, of claims to power and the like.

The one who enters the stillness receives. The one who lives in the external world takes.

Taking always bears greed in it, the hoarding: Everything only for me!

The more a person takes, the poorer he becomes. At the latest, in a future incarnation, his soul seeks out those places where his former unkindness and hard-heartedness left their traces.

This does not mean that we should just let the day go by, that we should simply sit and meditate. The spiritual person is nimble and dynamic. He works from within to without. He plans, places the plan in the will of God and, in the plan, lets himself be guided by God, day by day. Then he does not take—he receives and can give. He is not driven—he is dynamic.

»As soon as a person turns back and renounces materialistic activities, he goes inward, into the kingdom of stillness.«

Thus, we go into our inner being. What is this, our inner being?

It is our homeland, the only haven where we are safe and secure.

Our inner being is God, it is the law of love. We can imagine the law of love as a mighty white flame that shines in our inner being. It is the flame of selfless giving, of impersonal love, the flame of justice. It is the flame of the seven basic powers; it is the law, God.

God, our Father, is the only security in Christ, our Redeemer. He, who dwells in our innermost being, invites us to enter this inner space, which is our security. The inner light, into which we immerse, gives us support, it gives us secureness, it gives us peace, harmony and stillness. Thus, the inner being, into which we want to, and do, enter again and again, is for us like a fortress, a citadel, in which we are safe and secure.

Let us ask ourselves: What are we talking about when we say, »We go into our inner being«? Let us take a close look at this: Are we really in our inner being—or are we in our human sensations and thoughts? Do we feel safe? Do we feel we are in a fortress, a citadel, protected by the great All-One, who is our life, who is the love, who is our Father? Or are we still outside?

If we refine our feelings and thoughts, our words, actions and our senses, more and more, that is, if we let them become divine, then we draw our world of the senses to within, so to speak, and linger in the inner light. The inner light embraces us, envelops us and strengthens us. Every thought, which is thought in the inner light, that is, in the innermost being, is divine, peaceful, harmonious. Every sensation and every feeling that rests in the ocean, God, lets the person—the outer shell—feel that he is a being in God.

The one who lives in this awareness, that his inner-most being lives in the center of love, in the light, cannot but say yes—to the One who is the most beautiful, the most holy, indeed, the absolute.

The most beautiful, the holy, the absolute is our divine heritage, it is what we are in our pure spirit garment. The pure being abides steadfastly in the light of God. The light of God, which streams and radiates through all pure realms, is symphony. It is the ocean, in which all pure beings and pure forms move.

Many a one asks himself: What may it look like there, where the spirit beings are at home, where, as a pure being, I, too, live and am active?

God, our Father, gave us the planet Earth. The Earth—as the eternal Father gave it to us—is a planet of great beauty, a distant echo of the heavens. Here, too, there are beautiful, magnificent gardens. Let us think of the large gardens with trees, roses and bushes. The sun irradiates the gardens—we see light and shadow.

In the eternal home, every form of life shines from within itself through the radiating and pulsating core of being, which is all in all things. Every rose, every leaf, shines from within itself. In the large parks, especially in the large Italian gardens, we see graceful bridges here and there, which go over little brooks. It is similar in the eternal homeland.

The reflected splendor of the large parks of this Earth conveys to us an inkling of the gardens of our heavenly homeland. In the eternal Being, there is no separation, no hedges and fences. All of infinity of the pure Being is the garden of God, where the structures of the spirit beings are located. They consist of the finest and the most select, fine-material minerals that shine inherently, on their own, from within. The spirit beings are one with everything that flows and has become form.

These few words want to convey a small notion of what awaits us in the eternal Being. The forms of nature on this Earth give an indication of what is also in the pure heavenly worlds, only transformed down into matter, and that can be experienced in our world of the senses. Once we learn to feel into what we see, that is, once we learn to behold, we perceive more than the outer shell shows us. If we behold instead of seeing, we experience a touch of what also lives in the material forms: the divine.

Many a one thinks that everything in the other dimensions must be empty, that everything is uninhabited. No, it is an active life, a life in the law of God and with the law of God, a divine creating and working in the great cosmic law and with the cosmic law, for God, the Creator, breathes in and out. His works of divine creating are tireless. The spirit beings form and shape according to their mentality. This means that they work according to the basic power of the plane of which they are a part.

Every spirit being is compressed, eternal law, and thus, all of infinity is in it as essence and power. The spirit being does not need to say "This is mine," because every spirit being is heir to infinity. Because it is an heir to infinity, it can also go everywhere. It doesn't need to go here and there to meet its neighbor. Everything can take place in it through the principle of divine communication. This excludes the distance of "here and there."

We are on Earth to become divine again, to return to the eternal Being from where we came and to which we have to become again. To us human beings, it seems a long way, when we think of "there." But when we become aware that all of infinity streams through us as light and power, indeed, that our spiritual body is the compressed Being, and that the All-power, God, dwells in every cell of our body, then we know: God is here. God is very near. And in us is the eternal law, our homeland, our nature, which is divine.

Wherever we go, wherever we are—God, the Eternal, is with us. When we look at an object from without—who radiates to us? God. He radiates into our inner being. If we pay attention to only the external appearance, then we do not grasp Him. As long as we only look at the external, we are externalized and see only the external, as well. Then it is hard for us to live in the awareness that we are children of God, pure being, divine being, divine life.

Many ask: "On Earth, can we become divine as human beings?" The answer is: It is our soul that can become divine. The person needs the programs for this Earth. Let us look back: What we learned from childhood on, to be able to subsist as human beings—these are our programs.

But if we let our earthly programs, which we need as human beings, be irradiated by the Spirit of God, then we are guided, and we will look more deeply with our senses and thoughts, which are pure for the most part. We will then perceive and grasp in its depth, what is not recognizable externally.

Instead of merely looking, we have to learn to take what we see into ourselves and let it take effect in our inner being. Then we feel more and more that God is near to us. God supports us. He gives us strength and leads us, also by way of our earthly life-programs of thinking, speaking and acting.

If we are not satisfied with the external, with the material shell, but strive to feel into the external forms of matter, into the life of the respective form, then we gradually develop our spiritual consciousness and can take in the life of the forms we are looking at.

How is this done? First, we look at the whole material structure of the life form. We affirm the divine life force in the form. By doing this, we begin to send. We send—at the same time, we receive. If we human beings send to objects or forms of nature, they radiate back to us immediately, and we receive. By fulfilling the eternal laws and doing this exercise, we very gradually open our divine consciousness and perceive from there the communications, through the principle of sending and receiving.

Let us endeavor to take conscious steps, be they ever so small. If, during the day, we remember a consciousness aid, a memory aid, a task, an exercise, and apply it, we will notice that even a small step is rewarded from within. We may sense it; we may feel it.

Although there are still traces of humanness there—the effort alone will be rewarded by the divine power. The answer is the feeling of freedom, of lightness and joy. That is the answer of God. That is the reward of the Father to His child, which is taking more and more steps toward Him.

We can also enter an inner communication with the animals. Let us practice establishing communication with the innermost being of our animal brothers and sisters, with the creation powers in them.

Through this, we refrain more and more from the personal, confining, egocentric, human ego, and can look at the still existing ego-person. This way, with self-recognition and by clearing up the human aspects, we find our way, ever more inward to the Kingdom of God, the stillness in us.

Hardly has he [the person] taken the one step, he realizes that God, the Eternal, had already long since prepared this path for him.

Gabriele:

There is infinitely much hope in this sentence: »*Hardly has he [the person] taken the one step, he realizes that God, the Eternal, had already long since prepared this path for him.*« Through whom? Through Christ.

We all know that Christ is the way, the truth and the life. He prepared the way for us with His sacrifice on Golgotha. Through Christ, the path is already given—for each one of us. We will take it because we bear redemption in us. When we take it, is determined by each one of us, based on the law of free will.

To have »*... taken the one step*« means that we have actualized. Our soul has become more light-filled. The light of the soul is greater and radiates farther. Through this, we already see the next step before us, and we also have the strength to take it. The greater the consciousness-light of the soul becomes, the farther we see, the deeper we look, the more we recognize—about ourselves and, through actualization, about our neighbor, as well. Only in this way can we give help.

Let us think of Christ. Through Golgotha He prepared the way for us. He walks it with us and leads us to the Father.

With Christ and through Him, we mature into the divine life that is deep in our soul and waiting to be opened again. This is why we are wayfarers on this Earth. As long as we do not rest in God, we are journeying, and we will be dissatisfied again and again, unhappy, again and again. Even if we believe today that happiness favors us—tomorrow it is already gone. External happiness does not last; discontentment or unhappiness follow it, again and again.

We have to find the inner happiness. It is the stability in Christ. The inner happiness is the safety and security in Christ. Let us dare to do it with Him! He is present; He is in us.

The day shows us that we can draw closer to Him. How? The day tells every one of us. In the day as well, in all the occurrences, all the adversities—regardless of what comes toward us—Christ is the Helper. He is always with us.

If we go through our days in the awareness that He is always with us, then we also dare to take the steps with Him out of our human aspects. We are then granted the inner happiness and, in inner happiness, the inner peace. Selfless love grows in the inner peace because we don't look only at the faults of our neighbor. We also see our neighbor with his positive sides.

Let us say yes to Christ! Let us dare to take the first step with Him—and we will gain the courage to carry out the further steps, and thus mature into the life, into our true life, which is divine.

Blessed is the one who is able to grasp that the true hold—the hold that always holds—is so near to us! It is Christ in our soul. It is Christ in every cell of our body. It is Christ in every thought, in every problem, the positive solution in every difficulty. Christ is the omnipresent Spirit in the Father, and the Spirit of God is in us.

Our days will change their aspect if we make ourselves aware of this more often: Wherever we go—the hold, the security, is in us. Whatever happens—the hold, the security, is in us. Whatever we think, even if we believe we can hardly overcome this or that problem—the hold, the security, the help is in us.

He, Christ, is always there—always ready to help us. When we fall—He catches us, puts us back on our feet and says, "Come, keep going!" To where? To Him. Where is He? Here, there? No! *In* us.

Once we are aware of this, we attain inner security. In the inner security, we feel the safety—and in the safety grows the love again. It is the love of the child for the eternal Father because Christ and the Father are one: *one* stream, the one Spirit that permeates all things.

In today's time, we need Him more than ever. Christ does not leave us; He does not forsake us. Not even when we have scorned Him for years, decades. Not even when we have hardly thought of Him. Not even when we have slandered Him and not believed in Him—Christ is here. One honest request, one small, selfless step toward Him, into the inner being—and He comes several steps toward us, from our innermost being.

Let us take the step to trust Him, to entrust ourselves to Him, and we will experience very soon that Christ is the hold for us. He is the Comforter and Redeemer. He is the path to the Father. He is the truth in us. Christ is our life and, in Him, we are the life.

Gabriele:

What is contained for us in this statement?

By giving up our base ego for our own sake, we will make little progress spiritually. We may indeed give up one human aspect, but we build on another one because we are not concerned with becoming divine, but with achieving more. That is self-deception. We will not achieve anything more, but will build up more egoity, more human aspects. Only base things come from the roots of baseness, if we do not bring ourselves into the consciousness of becoming divine.

Our goal, our inner motivation, is crucial. If our goal is to draw nearer to Christ, the inner light, the law of the heavens, then, we will also make Christ in us accessible, the inner light, the law of the heavens.

»The person who strives toward truthfulness ...«
What is truthfulness? Truthfulness is divinity.
Truthfulness comes from truth. The truth comes from integrity, and integrity is purity, absoluteness. The truth is the depth of the Being and the Being, itself. The truth is the source out of which truthfulness flows. The true one

is the sincere one, a person of integrity, and the sincere one is the pure one. The pure one is the truthful one, and the truthful one lives in the source of truth.

Therefore, we cannot overcome our humanness if we do not overcome ourselves, if we want to make spiritual progress only for our personal ends. In the all-too-human striving is, yet again, the root for new human aspects. Then we continue to build within the law of sowing and reaping.

But we want to become divine. That is the goal of each soul, and the meaning and purpose of our life on Earth. That is why we should strive toward truthfulness. We attain truthfulness by gradually immersing in our true self. The following questions hold true for us each day: Who am I, in my words and in my deeds? Am I truthful—or still human? What is my world of feelings and sensations like? The world of feelings and sensations tells us more clearly and distinctly than our world of thoughts, whether we are truthful or whether we only affirm the truth with our intellect.

What is in the brain is by far not in the heart. The brain bears our human programs, our knowledge, our intellectual thinking. In the heart, in the spiritual consciousness, in the depths of our soul, dwells the divine, the logos, the intelligence—the truth. As a result, the intellect deceives, but never the intelligence in the soul. The truth is there, and truthfulness stems from it. Everything else is deception and illusion.

The truth is plain, quiet and simple; it is the Being. Everything truthful, divine, is the Being. Only the wanting to be, which is not the Being, wants to sparkle, to display itself, to scintillate and shine. The one who counts on knowledge and intellect sparkles and scintillates. That is not the life, it is not the Being, the truth, but illusion—hollow and fleeting.

About this, a sentence from the divine Wisdom:

Each one has made himself what he is today—not how he scintillates today! Tomorrow, he will again be what he is today—but he will no longer scintillate.

The truth, that is, wisdom, is without ifs and buts; it is without question. Wisdom does not have to ask. It grasps the core, the inner being, the heart of all things and events, and knows.

May the one who wants to reach his inner being, from his head to his heart, move the following statement in himself:

Knowledge has an eye only for the external world. The one who has only knowledge asks—because he has no wisdom. And so, we can say: The knowledgeable one asks—the wise one knows.

Spiritual knowledge that is lived becomes wisdom, the inner life, the life out of, and in, God. Once spiritual knowledge and wisdom have become a unity, then the person sees to the bottom of all things. He knows about all things because he has become wise.

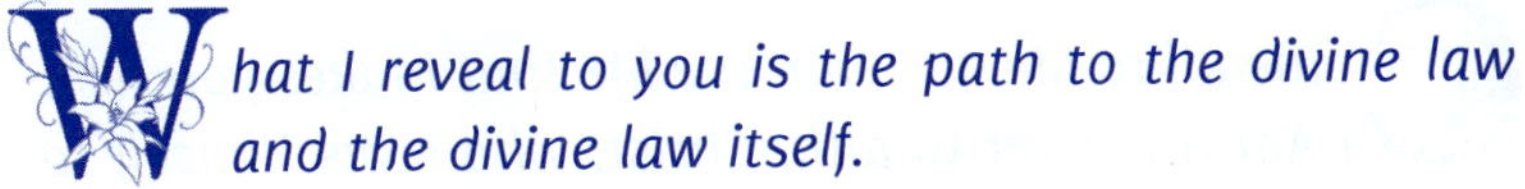

Gabriele, the teaching prophetess
and emissary of God explained the following about this:

In the book, "The Great Cosmic Teachings of Jesus of Nazareth to His Apostles and Disciples Who Could Understand Them. The Life of the True God-filled People," the Lord touches upon the causal law for us, again and again. From the absolute, He radiates into the law of cause and effect, so that we can find ourselves and, through actualization, find our way to our true heritage, to our true being.

Therefore, we can say that it is the hand of God that He extends to us, the hand of the Father who wants to help His child out of hardship and affliction, out of the clutches of the human ego. Our Father wants to draw us upward into the light, the pure, the fine, into the Being. He is there, always ready for us. It depends solely on us, when we take His hand to never let go of it again.

Gabriele:

Christ calls: *»Come all to Me, for I Am the life that makes you rich.«*

We know that Christ, the Spirit of life, is in us. He is the central light of our soul. He is in each cell of our body. In the Father, He is omnipresent in all Being. For us, this means that we have to turn within because we find Him only in our inner being. If we look for Christ in the external world, then we will not find Him. Then we draw up theories and opinions about Christ—and there are many of those.

The one who does not find Christ in his heart does not find himself. He does not know himself. To not know means to deny your divine heritage by disregarding the eternal Being. To find Christ means to find yourself, to recognize yourself, to put aside the humanness and become divine. Then we unite with the Redeemer-spark, with Christ in us. Out of this arises the primordial spark, which is the beacon for us into the Kingdom of God, to our Father.

»I Am the inner wealth,« thus Christ speaks.

The one who does not develop the inner wealth, the one who strives only for external wealth, who collects, amasses and hoards external things, is poor in his inner being. Although he may still be rich today, he will be poor tomorrow because the law of sowing and reaping will become active at the right time, according to the radiation of the stars.

The one who strives for external wealth, who amasses and is envious, who craves and hoards possessions is a prestigious man in the eyes of the world. From the point of view of the Spirit of God, of the inner wealth, he is a poor man because as a rich man he has already plunged into poverty.

Only the one who gives is rich, not the one who takes. God, the life, gives and gives of Himself unceasingly. The one who lives in the inner kingdom need not fear that his wealth will pass away. God is infinity, unending love, eternity and eternal wealth. The one who gives selflessly lives in the cycle of giving and receiving, and this cycle is eternal.

The life, the love, is giving. The one who does not give selflessly does not love. The one who does not give does not live. There is no fulfillment in taking, only in giving.

Selfless giving is selfless receiving; it is the cycle of life.

Gabriele:

How often have we already heard that each one of us is the temple of the Holy Spirit.

As long as we need external temples, we have not sanctified our own temple. As long as we go to external temples to worship God, we have not found ourselves as the child of God. As long as we idolize people, we worship the darkness. God alone should be worshipped, for He is the whole. He is the center in our life. He is the Holy One and we should become sanctified.

The one who does not cleanse his own temple also soils the temple of his neighbor. The one who does not cleanse his own temple pollutes the whole Earth because he pays homage to the one who wants it this way.

The new human being, the person of the Spirit, does not think in a static, but dynamic way. He is not imprisoned and caught in his own world of conceptions. He does not think from here to there. He penetrates the three dimensions because he is aware that he is divine. To penetrate the three dimensions means not to affirm the limitedness, matter, but to feel into matter, so that we find the One who is in everything and who knows of all things.

Once our consciousness expands, then we also live consciously. We do not see what comes toward us only from without, but we take its inner being into us and let it come alive in us. Thus, we feel that the three dimensions exist only in our world of thoughts, but not in the kingdom of the inner being.

Not until we cleanse our temple, do we see through, that is, penetrate, density, and grasp what it means to be children of the All. Then we are also in the sonship and daughtership of God—why? Because we do His will. And His will is the Absolute Law, from Order to Mercy.

Dear fellow people, through Christ, who is the light and the life of our soul, we will again become the child of the All, who lives consciously in God, his Father, as the son, as the daughter, of God. Let us have Christ become the center of our lives! How do we find our way to Him?

Each day is a guide that shows the way to Christ. If we live in the present, if we live in the day, then we see the many hints and signposts for our path. We find our way to ourselves. First to our base self, to clear it up. If we act according to our realization, then the divine self, our heritage, awakens more and more in us and we feel the inner richness. It is the deep happiness, the selflessness and openness, the uprightness and truthfulness. We are no longer chased and hounded. We are planners who place their plan in the hands of God, who let themselves be guided day after day by the great law of Order, God, who is the present and, in the present of the human being, knows the future.

Let us not forget to also thank Him. God never forgets us. Gratitude links. Gratitude is the alignment with the great giver of all that is good. Gratitude is tuning into, and joining in, the great stream of giving and of kindness. Without gratitude we do not attain selflessness. Gratitude makes us free and joyful.

The Spirit of God touches us and speaks to us through everything that we encounter. And so, also in what we read, there is the one or the other message for us. We feel it; it moves us; it occupies us. Images come, memories, feelings, recognitions, admonishments.

We should take seriously the task that is in this for us. What is the message to us, what is the task for today? The day that brings it to us, at the same time brings the energy to overcome it. Let us use this chance to become free of our burdens!

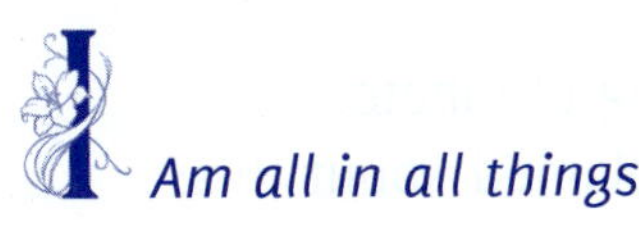 *Am all in all things.*

Behold the bush—and you will find Me.
Pick up the stone—and you will find Me.
Look to the stars—and you perceive Me.
Look deep into the human being—and you
find yourself and thus, Me, Christ,
the Self in you.
Regard the animal—and you find Me.
Feel the wind—and you hear Me.
Look at the drop of water—and you
look at yourself in Me.

For I Am the life in all things;
and you are the life in all things;
and everything is in Me, and
everything is in you.
We are united in Him,
The great All-One,
Who i s eternally—
the stream of Being and
the personified Being.
He is the stream of the All
and the drop itself.

Gabriele, the teaching prophetess
and emissary of God, explained about this:

Words from which the entire heaven radiates!

»I Am all in all things.«

God is never in the external. God is streaming power, the life in us. Once we have found our way to God in us, through a life of actualization and fulfillment of His laws, then we also have access to the divine in all forms of life. To be able to communicate with the divine in our neighbor, we thus have to live in God. We have to return to our true nature to find God in all things.

»Behold the bush—and you will find Me.«

If we just look at the bush, then we sense no reaction from the substance, the "I Am." We speak about it, the bush, that it is beautiful—yet receive no answer. The All-Spirit speaks out of countless mouths, and yet many do not hear Him. What does this want to tell us? It is not the intellect that perceives the law, God, but it is the very basis of our true being deep within that grasps the language of the All.

But if we take in the bush with the eyes of our true being, then we grasp the total radiation of the bush and, at the same time, come into communication with the very basis of all Being. Then the bush begins to send and we receive.

God is all in all things. As a result of this, God, the whole law, the entire All, is in every leaf. Behold the bush—and you will find Me, the All, the whole. The Creator-power is everywhere as a whole because God is indivisible.

Let us become aware that in one leaf, in one little blade of grass, is the entirety of the All. God is indivisible. The bush has developed the spiritual consciousness that corresponds to its kind, the nature-consciousness of the bush. This radiates toward us; it sends. God is always the whole. Even when one aspect of God, for example, the nature aspect of the bush, radiates toward us, it is still God, the whole, since everything is contained in all things.

We have to learn to understand the words: "God is indivisible. He is all in all things." Only then, can we gradually have an inkling of the fullness from God. The fullness of God is the I Am. It is our true nature, which is divine. Thus, we are heirs to the All.

Let us become aware of our spiritual body. It consists of countless spiritual particles, and in each spiritual particle, we can receive the entirety of infinity because we are beings of the All.

The language of infinity is the language of pictures. We receive colors, forms, fragrances, sounds and beings as images in the spiritual particles of our spiritual body, as an absolute, as a perfect, picture.

We realize: God is so close to us.

In the smallest stone is, in turn, God, the whole. God is the whole and the fullness in all things. Every developed facet of the whole radiates to us and communicates with us.

Who will throw away the stone in a thoughtless and dismissive manner? Only the one who does not know that in so doing, he throws away a part of his life. Who will strike a bush? Only the one who, in the last analysis, strikes out at others with thoughts, words and deeds and, as a result, will be struck, himself.

»Look deep into the human being—and you find yourself and thus, Me, Christ, the Self in you.«

Again, in the very basis of each one of us. Thus, it is necessary not to look at the humanness of our neighbor, only at the shell, but to take his total radiation into our inner being. This is perception. If we are well-disposed from within toward our neighbor, then we communicate with the positive powers in him. This means that we communicate with the divine in him and, in the end, with our own spiritual heritage. What our neighbor bears in himself, the divine, we likewise have in ourselves.

If we reject our neighbor, then one day we, too, will be rejected. If we disparage our neighbor, then we, too, will also be disparaged. If we kill our neighbor, then we, too, will be killed one day. Let us remember: What we do to our neighbor is what we do to ourselves.

To regard means to take in the total radiation of an animal, to let it reverberate in us. We take in the divine aspects, the developed facets of a part-soul only in the very basis of our being, through which we are in constant communication with all that is pure. The shell, the person, receives this divine perception as joy. It is the heavenly joy, the same as the heavenly cheerfulness that does not irritate the nerves. We will touch the animal gently and lovingly with the radiation that then streams from our inner being.

What do we then feel as human beings? We will grasp our second neighbor, the animal, in a totally different way because we have taken in its total radiation, not merely the external appearance as we had learned thus far: "This is an animal. This is a nice animal."

When we take in the consciousness-radiation of the animal, we will also no longer make value judgments and say, "This animal is beautiful, that one is not beautiful," or even, "That animal is ugly." We would be attributing these value judgments to ourselves.

In God, everything is perfect, including the essence of the inconspicuous stone, the bush, the animal. What could be unsightly in God, when He, God, is perfect in all things? The one who looks only at the external appearance makes value judgments.

Let us look into a water drop that runs down a glass. Let us put ourselves into the water drop and ask ourselves: What is above, below, right, left, behind and in front *in* the water drop? When we feel into the water drop, then we will have an inkling of the seven dimensions.

Countless life is in one drop of water!

Thus, we recognize that life is all in all things, and in all things is contained the entire principle of creation. God's creation is love, beauty, purity, eternal Being. If we disdain the smallest form of life, we disdain ourselves. If we disdain the water drop that holds countless forms of life, then we disdain ourselves and will one day thirst.

How did the Lord say it: "What you do to the least of My brothers, you do to Me." In the end, that is what we do to ourselves. He is God and we are divine. He is the great whole and we are the heirs. What we do to our neighbor, our second neighbor, the kingdoms of nature, we do to Him—and thus, to ourselves.

We recognize that we will draw closer to God, the inner life, solely if we not only turn to Him, the eternal Father, and Christ, our divine Brother, but also enter into communication with all the forms of life of nature, with the stars and with our neighbors, whom we have to accept and receive according to the divine principle of equality and unity.

We learn: Everything is in us. Everything is accomplished in us. We also receive the lawful answer in us, through a flaring up of our consciousness.

The prerequisite for this communication to take place is that we are aware that we are not mere human beings; our true Being belongs to the light of eternity. Our true life is the inner life. There, we are in the light and feel ourselves in the light. Our spiritual consciousness is there. That is our homeland.

Dear fellow people, all of us are in the earthly garment. But does this mean that we have to be or remain a rough person with a limited horizon and a low consciousness?

Each one decides for himself. But one thing is irrefutable: At some point, every single soul—be it only after more light-cycles that we call eons—will find its way back to its true nature that is spiritual, pure, fine, noble, good and selfless—in one word: divine.

If we strive for the fine, the noble, then we find our way to within, and we find our way into the light that surrounds us like a fortress. There, we are secure. There, we are stable. There, we are surrounded by the strength and the love of God. Then we are united in Him, the great All-One, who is eternally.

We are children of eternity because God is eternal. And since we are children of eternity, we should also see ourselves as children of eternity and behave like children of eternity.

We can be confident and calm, and do what is right in an upright manner—whatever needs to be done at the moment. We are secure in the awareness that the great white flame in us is the fortress, that is, a citadel, the solid temple. We are in the light. The light surrounds us. We are secure in the light. We are united in God.

We need not fear and worry—God, the light that surrounds us, wants the best for us. And we will attain the best for us if we devote ourselves to Him—the One, who is all in all things, who is the life in us and in whom we are the life.

The powers of the All are hidden only to the one who does not know his true self. The one who wants to experience the powers of the All must unveil them through actualization.

Gabriele, the teaching prophetess
and emissary of God, explained about this:

All will be revealed to the one who does not hide from Christ, but who fulfills the principles of the law of the Ten Commandments and of the Sermon on the Mount more and more. Everything that is pure is in him as essence, power and light. He is the inner heaven, the eternal Being.

273

*What you see, I Am in it.
What you hear, I Am in it.
I Am all-in-all, the whole.*

*Once you have awakened to the whole,
then you are the Being.
You behold the Being.
You hear the Being and speak the
language of the Being.
You behold, hear and speak Me,
because I Am the whole in you.
I Am the whole in your neighbor,
in you,
in the flower, in the blade of grass
and in the stone.
I Am yours—you are Mine.
I Am the All—and you are the All in Me,
the All.*

*You do not ask—you know.
You do not see—you behold.
You do not listen in—you hear and know.*

Gabriele, the teaching prophetess
and emissary of God, explained about this:

»I Am the All,« thus speaks the Lord, *»and you are the All in Me, the All.«*
What God is—the law—that is what we are. He, God, the All, the streaming love, gave us the whole as essence and power. We are never separate from God because the All, the eternal law, our true heritage, pulsates deep in our soul.

»You do not ask—you know.«
When we immerse in the eternal law, we will not ask about things—we know about them. Then we need not ask for the principles of the law—we know about them. Everything that is in the All is, compressed, the makeup of our spiritual body, which we are, ourselves. All of infinity is in us as knowledge and power.

If we ask about the things of life, then we are not yet aware of them. From this, we recognize that we have not yet completely opened our spiritual consciousness, our eternal heritage.

As long as the intellect is active, we live unconsciously because we relate only to the things we have learned. Then we understand only what we have stored in our conscious mind. We are not conscious of anything else. Therefore, we ask about what constitutes our life: our spiritual heritage, our divine wisdom, our true intelligence

275

because we are children of the All. To be children of the All means to be All-conscious because the All-Wise One has made us heirs to infinity.

»You do not see—you behold.«
To behold is the same as to perceive.

We human beings look here and there. We observe the details externally, and thus, human thoughts move into us.

But if we perceive things, if we take in the whole vibrating complex, then we gradually experience our true being in us because we establish communication with the inner values, with the inner power. This experience is the inner peace, awareness, safety, secureness, nearness to God.

»You do not listen in—you hear and know.«
The law does not need to listen in, nor does the compressed law, the spirit being. It knows about all the details of the eternal law.

If we want to listen in, this is human. It is curiosity because what we should hear, we will hear. To want is to be controlled by curiosity. If it is good for our spiritual development, we will hear what we should hear through inner guidance. Therefore, we could ask ourselves: Is our life under guidance or are we being controlled?

As long as we want to listen in, we are curious. Curiosity always has its human thoughts that are related to our wanting and our base wanting to be. What we want, we do not have, and what we have as human beings does not belong to us. We have to rid ourselves of all wanting and of all wishing, and let ourselves be filled by the inner wealth. Then we will not live in material need, either.

Whenever we want something, we are controlled, controlled by our human feelings, sensations and thoughts, which push us into our world of desires. If it is our endeavor that God guide us, then we have to become straightforward. We have to give up our curiosity and our pressing desires that often cannot be realized at all, and we have to make ourselves aware again and again that God knows what is good for us.

Once we grow into this awareness, then we become still and experience the inner guidance from the inner stillness. The inner stillness also gives us the resulting calm, which contains prudence and concentration. From this, grows the spiritual dynamism that lets us go through the day in a concentrated manner.

ever look to without. The light is in you.
In you is the truth that knows about all things, that knows everyone and everything. You do not need to look for your neighbor. You do not need to regard things from without—what is, is in you.

Everything that you see is merely a reflection of the truth, that is, a reflection that is not the absolute truth.

Gabriele, the teaching prophetess
and emissary of God, explained about this:

»Never look to without. The light is in you.«
To look to without means to want to catch only the appearance. This wanting again bears the curiosity that leads us to look restlessly to the right, to the left, to above and below, to see everything.

Once we immerse in the inner light, then we become calmer and will gradually see more deeply. Then we will establish communication with the positive powers in people, plants, animals, in all things.

»In you is the truth that knows about all things, that knows everyone and everything.«
Once we become aware that God is in us, the truth that knows of all things, that knows everyone and everything,

then we attain strengthening and strength. Then we keep coming back to the light in us, in the growing awareness that in us is the truth that knows of all things and that knows everyone and everything.

»You do not need to look for your neighbor. You do not need to regard things from without—what is, is in you.«

Let us think about the situations of our daily life. For instance, when we greet our neighbor and look for him, what thoughts are in our conscious mind? Are they all-too-human thoughts that let us recognize that we have looked only at the external, the shell, and communicated only with the external, the shell? On the other hand, when we greet our neighbor from our heart as our brother or our sister, then we will not look for him.

So let us decide to monitor ourselves during the day and see how often we look after our fellowman and what we are thinking while doing this. We turn and look back with the question: Could this be my acquaintance? Then we ask ourselves: What is behind this question, what feelings and sensations? We look back at our neighbor because we like or dislike something about him. What feelings and sensations are behind this external perception? We give ourselves the reason why we turn and look back at someone.

Once we have spiritually developed to the extent that the positive part of our neighbor vibrates in us, then we will not look for him unless he calls us. When we then turn to him consciously, it is not the human attraction, the being controlled, but it is two beings who meet each other in mutual respect—impersonally.

»Everything you see is merely a reflection of the truth, that is, a reflection that is not the absolute truth.«

How can we feel the absolute truth, the Being, our true heritage?

Since every feeling, every sensation, every thought and every word is a component of pictures, our words of prayer, as well, are aspects of pictures or of one whole picture, if we pray in the same way or in a similar way, again and again. These pictures, even the pictures of our prayers, penetrate our consciousness and possibly make us unsettled or prevent us from becoming calm.

We want to practice a deeper prayer that expands our consciousness and, at the same time, lets us feel what wonderful tranquility and peace come over us. We then no long-er take in the reflections of our prayer thoughts because all humanness that goes out from us is, in turn, merely reflection. It radiates back in pictures, in colors and forms, which show our humanness and which may continue to move, and thus, intensify, our humanness.

We go into the stillness.
We close our eyes.
We become quiet.
We let go of our human thoughts.
We surrender them to Christ and now concentrate
on our breathing.
Our thoughts recede.

Now, let us imagine a light in us, in our physical body.
It is energy, God's love.

We now immerse in this light and call on the All-Holy
One in us, God, that it may radiate through us. In doing
this, we expect nothing, nor will we think.
We let what is holy radiate through us, to where we
want to send it.

Now we call on the eternal light:

Eternal light,
you are the power and the love.
Flow more strongly into me.
Stream throughout me,
set me aglow!
From your fount of salvation,
from your light,
I send your love, your light,
to all people.

We send—and do not think.

In this moment of deep prayer, we communicate with the Spirit of God in many people.

The answer from this selfless communication is the stillness, the peace, the hope, the confidence, the strengthening and the strength. In doing this, we do not hear a voice. We sense how our spiritual consciousness expands because God pours His stillness and His peace into us from the fount of His life.

We let prayer sensations flow to the Eternal in us:

Lord, Your light sets me aglow.
I live in Your consciousness.
I send Your power, which is effective in me,
to the nature kingdoms.

We let this power stream out. In doing this, we do not think and do not visualize the nature kingdoms.

Again, the answer is stillness.

Peace, hope and confidence build up in us because we had communication with the Creator-power in nature.

This exercise is a form of deep prayer. The words of prayer given here should be seen as an example.

Such a prayer can bring us infinite stillness and inner experience, the experience of peace. We hear so often: "God is peace." We should experience this spiritual reality in us. Through this prayer, this can happen.

First, we let ourselves be filled with the power of love, then we send the holy rays of prayer out, and we do not think while doing this. They bring life energy to our neighbor. What radiates back from this source of energy fulfills us, as well.

We can call it an exercise. We can call it a prayer. This deep communication is an opportunity to sense what our spiritual heritage is. Then the longing awakens more and more to become, to be, as we feel in our inner being.

I repeat, so that we remember this deep prayer well. We let ourselves be filled by the power of God, by asking the Father: "Radiate into me and radiate out through me to my brothers and sisters," and then we remain in the stillness.

By doing this, we, too, will be fulfilled, and thus draw nearer to the One who is the longing of the soul.

At the very moment we send, we radiate out, we feel that joy, gratitude, strength and hope build up in us.

But the prerequisite is that we do not want anything! If we were to imagine a picture, we would experience ourselves, namely, the reflections of our human ego. These pictures would come from our three-dimensional thinking.

We may have no expectations of any kind, but just let the radiation of the Eternal flow through us. Then, but only then, what furthers our spiritual development for today and for the coming time, builds up in our soul, in the very basis of our soul.

This inner prayer is selfless and impersonal. We call it the "deep prayer" or the "All-prayer."

What is within, in you, the light, the truth, what you are in the pure Being as a being in God, took on shape and form in heaven as purest substance.

Gabriele:

Our entire heritage is in this sentence:
All pure beings bear the same in themselves, the law—God. From the streaming life, from the flowing and streaming light, from the energy, God, the Eternal created the spiritual forms. They took on form and became purest substance from the breath of God, from His flowing law. Our innermost being, too, is purest substance. We, too, are beings of the All because we are children of God.

Gabriele:

Thus, in us is the infinite, eternal source, from which all spiritual beings, all forms of life of the heavens, draw. It is the All-Spirit, which flows throughout everything. It is the omnipresence of God, from which we may receive and give.

As spiritual beings, we are all in this mighty, eternal stream. We draw and we give from this stream, the principle of the All. Thus, all pure beings live in the cycle of infinity: receiving—the same as drawing—and giving. That is our true existence in the eternal Being.

Gabriele:

Each one of us is called upon to again transform the quantum of energy that we transformed down through a wrong way of thinking, to cause it to again become spiritual primordial substance, primordial power, in order to bring it back into the eternal Being.

The quantum of divine energy that was given to each one of us as we plunged into the Fall-realms is borrowed energy. Everything that is borrowed has to be brought back.

On the Inner Path, we learn to transform the negative into the positive, by clearing up with Christ what we have recognized to be human and by no longer doing it. Through this, the divine energy that we transformed down, that is, the negative energy, is transformed into divine flowing power. In this way, we transform it up again, to its origin, to God.

Each of us will have to do this sooner or later. This is why we have the Inner Path.

Again and again, we hear that the Earth and everything on the Earth is a mere reflection of the eternal Being.

Let us think of a lake with a more or less moving surface. What is on the shore of the lake, the grasses, trees, buildings and other things, is mirrored on the water. In the mirror of the lake, which waves may gently ruffle, do we see the same as what we see on the shore? No, in the water everything appears distorted.

Let us use this comparison for the spiritual kingdom of the heavens and for the Earth: Heaven is reflected on the Earth. But what we grasp and perceive on Earth is not the reality, the Being, the kingdom of heaven. Through the various layers of the human ego, the whole thing is mere reflection, a semblance, and never reality.

It comes down to which level we are on—on the level of reflection, of semblance, the level of the outer and external, of human pictures, or on the level of the Being, of the inner life.

In all of infinity there is only one principle: sending and receiving. What you send is what you are; that is what you radiate. What you radiate comes back to you.

Gabriele, the teaching prophetess
and emissary of God, explained about this:

With every thought that we think, we send and receive at the same time. In this way, our fate is built up. But what we have built up, we can also diminish, by discharging our sending potential in that we clear it up with the help of the transforming power of our Redeemer, and by sending more and more to Christ, who should be the central focus of our life. Only in this way, will we gain our spiritual heritage step by step. Only then, can we say that we safely go through this time that is filled with turmoil.

The sole security is Christ. There is no external security for us. People, things, objects, money and goods—nothing can offer us security. We live in a mighty time of transformation. The old structures, on which many people have relied until now, are falling. On this Earth, in this world, during the course of transformation from the old to the New Era, there will be no hold in the external anymore.

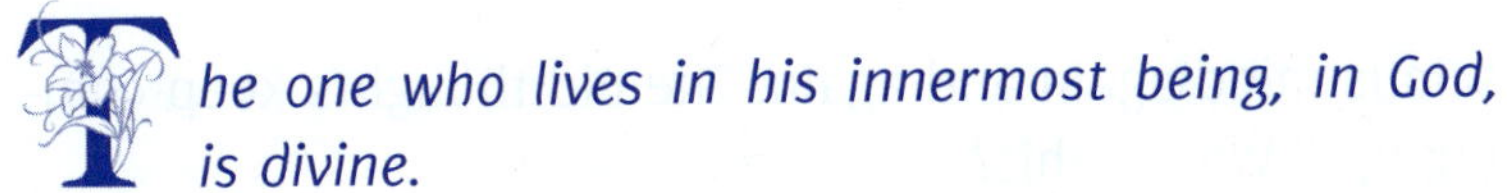

he one who lives in his innermost being, in God, is divine.

Gabriele, the teaching prophetess
and emissary of God, explained about this:

We hear again and again about the inner light. How do we find our way to the inner light, and how can we stay in our inner being?

Here is a small exercise for this.

When we want to speak, then we take ourselves back with the question:

Is what we want to say divine?

Why do we want to say something?

We speak only when we feel that we do not want anything for ourselves personally. We feel this in the fact that there is no urging and no disparaging in what we want to say—when we do not have our own advantage in mind. We can also examine ourselves in how we say something because in the type of words and their combination, as well as in the tone of voice, we recognize whether our ego—be it the deep layers of the ego—is speaking, or whether it is impersonal and comes from the fount of life.

Often, we say, "I have already cleared this or that up. I have already forgiven. And yet, it comes into my conscious mind again and again. The old thoughts keep coming up." Why is this?

It is possible that they are awakened memories. When, for example, our neighbor thinks of us and about a situation that has already been cleared up, this can come alive in our world of memories. Then we should examine what our feelings and sensations are like, especially toward that neighbor. If our feelings and sensations are pure, then we say "no" to these old thoughts, and we turn to Christ and pray as we have learned:

We call on the inner light and let the light shine through us to our neighbor or to our neighbors, of whom we are thinking. Through this All-prayer, the thoughts withdraw from us. It becomes easier and easier to rest in ourselves.

Other examples should help us to grasp the All-prayer even more deeply, and be able to carry it out more and more independently.

Let us become aware that everything is in all things, and soul and person should establish communication with everything because it shall be on Earth as it is in heaven.

We now watch our breathing and immerse in the inner light. We call on the holy light, the love of the Creator-God. We let ourselves be filled with love, power and wisdom, and pray:

Eternal, glorious Father!
You are the light and the power in us.
You are the omnipresent Spirit,
that streams through all things
and sets all things aglow.
You love Your creation,
to which we human beings also belong.
In all things, You are the love, the light,
the homeland and the salvation.
We now send Your light,
that gives us warmth and secureness,
to the mineral kingdoms.
You flow through us
to the mineral kingdoms.

Our thoughts are silent.

In the same way, we can have the light of God flow to the plant and animal kingdoms.

We watch our breathing again.

We go ever more deeply into the light. The sun of love embraces us more and more.

We call on the inner light and let ourselves be filled more and more by the love, power and wisdom of God.

Beloved Father!
All spirit beings, souls and people
are Your children.
You, kind One, sent us Your Son,
so that we may become spirit beings again,
light of Your light,
love of Your love,
power of Your power.
Kind, All-One, fill us from
the fount of peace and of salvation.
Fill us with Your love,
so that we may feel
that we are Your children.

Kind, eternal Father,
Your light radiates through us to all
our brothers and sisters all over the Earth.
Our thoughts are silent—
You, O All-One, radiate through us
to our human brothers and sisters.
We let it radiate; we do not think.
It radiates.

Once again, we watch our breathing and at the same time feel to within.

We notice how the calm and peace come over us. It is the answer of love.

Once again, we call on the mighty light in us and ask it to set us aglow.

Eternal sun,
You kindness and warmth,
You love and mercy!
You, Father, You beloved You
of our souls,
You are so near to us,
because we are Your children.
You stream through us
with the power of the heavens,
which is our spiritual heritage.
You set us aglow and let us
glow in Your love,
that is our true Being.

Eternal, kind One,
through Your infinite power,
we now come into communication
with our brothers and sisters
of the eternal Being.
The heavens open within us,
the regions from Order to Mercy.

The light of the All-One
radiates through us
and establishes communication
with our heavenly
brothers and sisters.

We let the love stream. Our thoughts are silent.
Deep in our soul, we may feel the connection.
We may receive.
We send toward heaven—homeward.
We receive from heaven, from home.

Father,
You, our bliss and our happiness!
Brother, You, our Redeemer and our friend!
We thank You, Father;
we thank You, Brother!
Thank you with all our heart.
Thank You for the Being.
Thank You for Redemption.
Thank You for the Inner Path.
Thank You for the eternal homeland.

Gabriele:

If we have scaled back our talking and thinking during the day, by examining ourselves with the question: "Is my thought, my word, impersonal, that is, divine, or egocentric?"—then, in the evening, we can sense ourselves, how we feel.

To sense our self means: We perceive ourselves. How was and is our body rhythm? How was and is our inner and outer attitude? How was and is our behavior? We can also examine ourselves in the mirror. How do we reflect? How do we radiate?

We will experience smaller or greater so-called miracles if we consistently do this exercise during the day. The evening will show us a totally different person.

These exercises let us recognize how quickly and wonderfully the Spirit of God is able to be effective in and on us. We experience the nearness of God.

Gabriele:

What goes out from the God-filled person radiates back into him and through him—because of the principle of sending and receiving.

We hear about the Being again and again. The Being is the divine in all things. Only when we have attained the divine communication with all things—because everything is in all things—will we live in the Being.

To live in the Being, thus means to live in our inner-most being. The previous exercises help us to experience what it means to live in ourselves and to give from the Being, the source, through the communication with the All-power in all things.

We hear about purity again and again. We attain the purity of the soul through selfless feelings, sensations, thoughts, words and deeds. This leads to inner beauty. Therefore, soul and person attain beauty through purity.

We see that all things permeate and complement each other. The one who adorns himself with virtue and selfless love attains inner freedom because he has found himself, his true self. He then leaves freedom to his fellowman, and the person is noble and fine, since the soul has become pure.

Let us consciously take in this statement once more and let it reverberate in us, for in this one statement is so much that is decisive for us: *»The eternal law, the pure, the beautiful, the noble, the fine, the absolute love radiates what goes out from the one who is God-filled, and then radiates back into him and through him.«*

The pure being lives in the Being that is eternal and has its existence in the eternal Being because it, itself, is the eternal Being, the eternal law, God: the purity, beauty, freedom, the noble and fine, the selfless love. The pure being is the Being in the All-stream, in God, in the Being.

Gabriele:

The purity is our true life. When we turn away from our true life, from the purity, the beauty, the eternal Being, then we create our illusory life that consists of our ego-law. It is the reflection, the I Am, which has been transformed down and changed. We have built this up with our human feeling, thinking, speaking, acting and wanting. Our ego-law, which encompasses only us and is stored in the causal computer, in the stars, is what we call the law of sowing and reaping, as a general term.

Thus, what we sow is what we reap. This causal sending and receiving continues until we have attained the purity of our soul for the most part.

In the purity lies the beauty, and, again in the beauty, the purity. Both radiate and result in freedom. In the purity, beauty and freedom lies the noble, the fine, the selfless love.

The burdened souls in the spheres of purification and the incarnated burdened souls, the human beings, do not live as the Being, nor do they move in the stream of the Being.

Gabriele:

As long as we are still burdened, parts of our spiritual heritage, of our true Being, are covered. For this reason, we do not find our way back to the origin of our life. To be able to immerse again in the stream of God to live as a purified drop in the eternal ocean, God, we have to follow the path of self-recognition.

We have to learn to understand ourselves because only if we understand ourselves, will we, in time, also recognize ourselves. If we learn to understand ourselves, then we will also gain understanding for our fellow humans. In this way, we purify our soul and gain access to our neighbor because our neighbor—the positive part of our neighbor—is a part of our true being, of our divine heritage.

Only in this way, through self-recognition and through understanding, will we mature into our inner being, will we attain the link with our neighbor and gain communication with the nature kingdoms. Then we also understand what it means to establish communication with the infinite All because we are children of the All, heirs to infinity, beings who bear in themselves the entire Being.

Gabriele:

We thus recognize how the adversary has reversed the highest words. Our small world, the ego-world of the individual that consists of our human feelings, thoughts, words and deeds, we call our "being" and our "self." But it is not the eternal Being. In our human "being" is the "mine," which contains the separation from the eternal Being. In our human "self" is the "me"—again the separation. Through human egocentricity, the mine and me, we have placed ourselves in a cocoon-world, which we will hear about later on. We thus see how close together light and shadow are.

Words that are spoken out of the actualization and fulfillment of the eternal law bear the divine in themselves: light and power. On the other hand, words are our base existence, if they are not permeated by the Spirit of love, if they are not lived by us.

God speaks of the eternal Self, of the eternal Being. The reverse is our human being, our human self.

In this small world, he lives, he moves and thinks that his existence is solely there.

Then he sees only with the eyes of his small world, which can be compared to a cocoon. With this, he then looks only at the small cocoon-world of his neighbor.

He sees only the surface of life, the reflection because he lives only in the external world and moves only in his small world, in his cocoon, which he, himself, has spun with his burdened sensations, thoughts, words and deeds. This is his state of consciousness.

Gabriele:

Starting from this state of consciousness, we feel, think, speak and act—as human beings, who are imprisoned in the limitation of materialistic, egocentric thinking. We cannot see any farther, nor can we understand any further. What we have unfolded, what we have developed, is our state of consciousness. The light of our consciousness radiates accordingly. Again, it illuminates only what is our state of consciousness: the breadth or the narrowness, according to the limitation.

Since, according to the radiation of our consciousness, we live in our own self-made beam of light, it is ourselves that we experience again and again. Let us watch what we think, what and how we speak! All of this tells us who we are.

If we revolve solely around ourselves in our sensations and thoughts, then we live in a cocoon-world and see our neighbor only in the beam of light of our ego. Our fellow people then pass by us and we do not recognize them. We do not perceive them as brother and sister in the Spirit of the Lord because we affirm only ourselves because we look only at our small world. This small world is the body of our thoughts, and this is what we call the truth.

Gabriele:

From this arises the distortion of truth.

What are the "walls"? The so-called walls are the radiation of the aura. They are the different facets of the light of our soul. What is stored in our soul particles, light or shadow, radiates through our body and forms the aura, the corona. Our aura is like the beam of light of our consciousness.

Only what our soul radiates is what we can somewhat understand, and this is what we speak about. We cannot go beyond this. Our radiation potential, light or shadow, determines our aura. This is the light of our consciousness, our state of consciousness.

He speaks of the truth and with this, he means the reflection of the truth, that which he has input, himself, with which he has spun himself in, in which he believes because he sees only that. And so, he believes only what he sees, and that is what he calls the truth.

Gabriele:

Our language is a pictorial language. Each picture shows our state of consciousness. Day after day, infinitely many thoughts shoot through our brain. Just as the thoughts shoot through our head, the pictures shoot right through us and shape our cell structure. Since we still live unconsciously for the most part, we grasp little of our own language of pictures—and thus, many chances for self-recognition are lost.

To live consciously means to gather the powers of our consciousness in the moment, to be totally with what needs to be done at the moment. To live consciously thus means to live in a concentrated way.

Let us resolve to do everything that we do in a concentrated way. Concentration means that our thoughts are with our work, with what we are doing at the moment, or with what we are saying.

If, as a result of this, we lead a more conscious life, then we also grasp very quickly when thoughts beset us.

They knock on the radiation of our concentration and want to communicate with us. Then we should pause briefly, allow the thoughts to come and look into the world of our thoughts. They come and show themselves to us in pictures. We have created these pictures; they are a part of our life. In this way, too, we can recognize very quickly who we are. If we use the energy of the day to clear up what needs to be cleared up today, then the radiation of our consciousness, the beam of our consciousness, expands.

Thoughts that send toward us can also originate with our fellow humans. However, these are only brief flying thoughts that don't irritate us and yet, could tell us something because there are no coincidences. However, if they constantly knock at the radiation of our concentration, then something is in us that should be cleared up.

Thoughts, sensations or feelings can also originate with our presently developed spiritual consciousness—impulses that want to stimulate us to continue to develop, to clear away what limits and burdens our soul. These thoughts or feelings, too, knock on the radiation of our concentration. They announce themselves, so that they may be cleared up. We pause briefly and take in the thought-pictures. What do they want to tell us? This is what needs to be cleared up.

We are in the school of life, Earth. The energy of the day brings to every single person individually the tasks that are pending for him because of what he once entered into the stars, himself. Thus, we meet our own human aspects, day after day.

The humanness is our base being, our base self. We have to transform the base self, the base being, with Christ. In this way, we find our way to the eternal Being, to our true self, and thus, to our divine heritage.

Therefore, we see that all of infinity consists of sending and receiving. We are sent to, and we receive. We send and receive. The entire All is a mighty communication network, in which each one of us is integrated.

In the entire All, there is only one principle: sending and receiving. Each one sends himself—what he is, his feeling, thinking, speaking and acting.

Gabriele:

Let us look at the statement: Each one sends himself.

We cannot send the sending potential of our neighbor. We send only our own sending potential, those programs that we have inflicted on ourselves during the course of this life on Earth and in our former lives, that is, all that has not yet been cleared up.

Again and again, let us make ourselves aware that each one of us sends only his own sending potential. With our feelings, thoughts, words and deeds, we build up this sending potential. It forms the various programs in our brain cells, which again have an effect on our soul and on every cell of our body because these are likewise in communication with the repository planets. Thus, with our—but only with our own—sending potential, we are in communication with the stars.

What we send, we enter into our soul and into the corresponding repository planets—in this case, into the causal computer. From the causal computer, it comes back via our soul, via our feelings and thoughts. And so, our feelings, sensations, thoughts, words and deeds can be a warning for us. This is why we should be alert, to experience and grasp what they want to tell us about ourselves.

We are our own sending potential. This is how we vibrate. This is how we think. This is how we live. This is how we act. It is also the rhythm of our body. This is how each cell of our body vibrates.

Our body is a body of sound, as it were. With our feelings, sensations, thoughts, words and deeds, we attune the body of sound, the person.

Do we want to know how we sound? Let us listen to what we think and speak! Then we will know how we sound.

God is harmony. God is eternal symphony, eternal cosmic sound. If our body of sound is at one with the symphony, God, then our soul is in the Being. If our body is disharmonious, if our rhythms are jerky and edgy, if we are not even-tempered and balanced, then we are not in harmony with the eternal Being. Then we are playing our own tune.

The pure being lives and is active in and from the pure eternal law, the All-law.
The impure one lives in his small, self-made world that consists of his impurity, that is, of the refuse of his feelings, thoughts, words and deeds. In this, his cocoon-world, he lives and moves and feels, thinks, speaks and acts just as he is, what his cocoon-world consists of.

Gabriele:

The refuse of our feelings, thoughts, words and deeds is a murmuring, a soughing in our inner being. It makes us discontent, unstable and unhappy. The awakened soul urges to be free and happy. It wants to connect with the eternal stream, God. It wants to again immerse in the eternal Being, in the eternal light—as the true Self, the compressed Being.

Every now and then, we should practice the song of the soul. The love of the soul for the Father is an adoration, as it were, a heavenly song that turns to Him because God is sound. He is symphony, harmony and love.

Let us allow this yearning of the soul to occasionally break out of us, to radiate from us. Let us express what stirs in us, and feel ourselves into this melody! Then we will sense the discrepancy between soul and person and, at the same time, also notice what still needs to be cleared up.

The soul does not have our words. What it conveys to us—the longing for God, for purity, for beauty, for unity with the eternal stream—comes to us, the person, in the form of thoughts and words. But our thoughts and our words are limited, often they cannot express what breaks out of the soul—and thus, the person can hardly grasp it because he has only thoughts and words available to him as tools.

Feeling, too, belongs to the sphere of humanness, and is not the perception of the soul itself. When the rising vibrations of the soul—the longing for the unity with God— arrive in our brain cells, then this fine, tender feeling is yet again attuned to the three dimensions because the person simply feels, thinks, speaks and acts only three-dimensionally. We see that there is always a discrepancy between soul and person. This often hurts.

I experience it often. In my inner being, I grasp everything and all-encompassingly. However, with our human words, I can bring across the totality only in a limited way. The human language does not have the words to convey what is effective in one sentence, in one word of the Absolute Law. The radiation, the Absolute Law, is infinite and mighty and powerful. In comparison, the human word is small and inane.

We have to learn to feel into the words and terms. But even the feeling, as such, is still limitation because we again transmit it to our three dimensions. The discrepancy remains, until we are divine again, consciously the son, the daughter, of God, the being in the Being. Then we will no longer need words to describe the Being.

Let us remember this again and again: We are on this Earth to become divine again. Our inner being is the pure, the fine, the noble and beautiful, the law of infinite love.

Let us remember this again and again: God, our Father, loves us. He sent His Son, our Redeemer. Christ is so near to us, for He is the way, the truth and the life.

Let us think about this again and again. Let us enter this message of love with our thoughts: God, our Father, sent His Son, so that we may return to Him, to God, our Father. This message is the message of love. It draws throughout the past 2000 years and will knock on our hearts again and again, until we have become love and are united with the great Spirit of our Father, with God.

God is the stream of the All. Our Father is the being of the All. Let us remember that in the divine, we are His images, the images of the eternal Father. He is the life in the stream, and we are the life in the stream. When we return home to the eternal Being, who receives us? The infinite love of our Father. We may behold Him because He gave Himself form from the stream, just as He formed us as His children, His images.

We could also ask ourselves: Will we step before God, our Father, after our sojourn on Earth? Will we bow before Him and thank Him from our hearts for His guidance through Christ, our Brother and Redeemer? Will we, as a child of God, look up to Him, into the tender, mild, kind eyes of the eternal Father?

He will certainly take us in His arms and say: "Child, it is done! It is over, the pain, the suffering. See, through My Son, your Brother, I have brought you back to Me. Come and possess the kingdom that has belonged to you since the very beginning.

My child, it is over. Everything is good. Behold, and you see yourself, for what you have created with My power is you, yourself, it is your nature."

And in our inner being, and wherever our spiritual eyes look, we will behold what we have been aware of since all eternity: the light, the homeland. We will again be embedded in the bosom of God, in the freedom, in the life of communication with all Being.

Let us remember this again and again. Let us become aware and affirm that we are sons and daughters of God! Let us affirm that we are immortal. Let us affirm our law—indeed, our law—the eternal life, our spiritual heritage, and it will go better for us by the hour.

The burdened person can be compared to a caterpillar.

The burdened person—the caterpillar—spins himself into his small world until he recognizes that he has to emerge from his cocoon, that is, unfold, to become a butterfly, a being of the light that lives and moves in the eternal All-law of God, and has its eternal existence in the Eternal, in the All-principle, which is and which speaks itself as the Self: the pure, the fine, the noble, the beautiful, the selfless love, the All-law, the Absoluteness, the eternal Being, the eternal truth.

For this reason, each caterpillar must unfold, that is, unwind itself from what it has spun around itself, to recognize itself in it and repent of what it recognized, to ask for forgiveness and to forgive and no longer commit what it recognized.

Then the threads of its cocoon dissolve. The walls fall, which the human being looked at until now and which he

Gabriele:

Each one of us has to unwind the cocoon of his ego again, as we unwind a film reel. As we unwind, we have to recognize ourselves in the pictures that are projected onto the screen of our consciousness: our human games, the intrigues, the pressing desires, the passions, the cravings, hate, envy, animosity; the striving for wealth, for prestige and possession.

We also hear ourselves in these pictures, how we disparage our neighbor, how we exalt ourselves. We hear what we say about them, how we think about them, whether we have harmed them, with what methods and much more. All this has to be cleared up with our neighbor through Christ.

The eternal Self is the truth. The one who has become the truth is, himself, the truth, the Self, the Being, the I Am, the eternal law of love.

With the eyes of truth, the person beholds in himself that which is outside, as well. He penetrates the reflection of the truth and sees the truth in all people, events, conversations and occurrences.

With the eyes of truth, he also sees the untrue. He cannot be deceived because he is the truth and beholds with the eyes of truth and speaks, discusses and accomplishes everything in the truth.

And so, he is the truth, which is the eternal law of the All, in which he lives, in which he moves, from which he draws and with which he works.

He is the truth, the law, in every sensation, in every thought, in every word and in every action.

Since the truth, the Being, the eternal law, is in you, and the true, the eternal, first assumes form and shape in you and then, only externally, in your surroundings and in the world, you have to live in yourself, in the All-Holy One who dwells in you.

Gabriele, the teaching prophetess
and emissary of God, explained about this:

If we want to change the world, we have to change ourselves. As long as we merely speak of change and do not change ourselves, we only create more burdens in this world and encumber ourselves with these.

When we merely speak of the peace that should come into this world and have no peace ourselves, we contribute to peacelessness because our own lack of peace infects others, in turn, with peacelessness.

When we speak of the light of Christ and remain without light ourselves, then we mock Christ and contribute to the fact that our neighbors think, speak and live as we do—without light.

When we speak of mercy and of being a Good Samaritan to our neighbor and that mercy and love for neighbor should be practiced in the world, while we, ourselves, are without mercy and peace, then we contribute to an increase of the lack of mercy and love in this world. Through this, we burden ourselves.

If we want to change the world for the better, then we have to become kind.

As long as we do not respect ourselves, we do not heed God in us, either. As long as we strive for the external temple, we have not found ourselves as the temple of God.

Therefore, recognize: You are the temple of the One, the Holy One, who dwells in you.

Remember the following sentence of truth and live accordingly:

Dwell in yourself; for you are the temple of the One, the Holy One, who dwells in you.

Gabriele:

We can live in our inner being only when we adorn our temple with the virtue of selfless love, of freedom and brotherliness. Then the selfishness will fall away from us, our addictions will transform and we will become seekers who find. We find God in us.

Gabriele:

To raise our feeling, thinking, speaking and acting to God, we have to become aware that God wants the best for us and that He is the listener in us. If we have felt, thought, spoken and acted in a human way, then we take our human aspects to God and ask the Spirit of our Father, who dwells in us, for forgiveness. With "human" is meant, as stated, the sinfulness against the soul.

God, who loves us, will forgive us and will remind and admonish us whenever we want to fall again into the same or similar chains of feelings, thoughts or words. Through our increasing alertness, we will be better and better able to raise our feeling, thinking, speaking and acting to God, in good time.

Gabriele:

Why should we speak only when we are asked or when it is important, and then solely according to the order of the temple, that is, according to the Ten Commandments and the Sermon on the Mount?

Everything is energy. Our soul consists of cosmic energy. Our physical body, too, is imbued with cosmic energy. We should use this precious energy of life carefully, that is, not waste it. We should give to our neighbor from the treasure of the inner being, from the laws of inner life. The Ten Commandments and the Sermon on the Mount are excerpts of these.

When we give from the highest source, from the laws of life, then we are giving gifts of inner life, which are of inestimable value. These divine gifts are then active in our words and deeds.

We can draw and give from the wealth of inner life only if we have previously brought the treasure of the inner being to light, through the actualization and fulfillment of the divine laws.

Do not ask out of curiosity. If possible, do not ask at all. What you should hear and know about will be led to you by the One who dwells in you.

Gabriele:

The one who asks out of curiosity hears only himself and perhaps hears what he is not able to digest, today. He then moves this in his thoughts. In this way, he can burden himself further because every thought is energy, which does not go away from him, but stays with him. It burdens his soul and his physical body.

And when your neighbor beside you is deep in meditation or thought, do not address him to give him an understanding of your human wisdom because you do not know where he is just then, with whom or with what he is in communication.

Do not disturb your neighbor—then you, too, will never be disturbed because then, you are alertness itself.

And when your neighbor is eating or working, do not disturb him, unless you have something important or essential to share with him because you do not know with whom or with what he is in communication.

Gabriele:

Therefore, let us heed the law of inner life, the fine, the noble, beautiful and pure. We will very gradually become the law of God. Then we will ennoble our soul and respect it as a being in God, and our neighbor as well, who is, in his innermost being, as we are—fine, noble, beautiful and pure. So, let us never intrude on the temple of our neighbor, then we, too, will not be disturbed and our temple will not be ruined.

Gabriele, the teaching prophetess
and emissary of God, explained about this:

How do we waste our energy? We waste it because we want to communicate our ego because we want to display ourselves. The ego wants to help the neighbor in a selfish way, to put itself in the foreground. We do competitive sports so that the ego can prove itself in competition. These and other human egoisms cause us to waste energy.

We may quarrel with our husband or wife or our life-partner. We quarrel with our colleagues at work. In our thoughts, we constantly nurture desires. We form pictures of our desires and live in this world of desires. Are we aware that we are wasting energy with this, and that we weaken our soul?

We are outside of ourselves if we are not in ourselves, if we do not relate to the I Am, the divine in us. If we are constantly concerned that our neighbor see us as we pretend to be, this is the life that is turned without. We are constantly anxious that our neighbor see us, that he praise us, that he acknowledge us, that he include us in everything. We are curious and want to hear and see everything, we want to discuss things to show how right we are. That is the externalization of our life.

By wasting our energy, our senses are drawn to without more and more, and into a further loss of energy. Because of the lack of energy, we then strive to exalt ourselves. We strive for recognition, praise, enrichment and many other things. We grow more and more discontent because our senses crave and always want more. The weaker our soul becomes, the less energy it has, the more the person demands for himself, personally.

»You then begin to lean on the temple of your neighbor and begin to demand because the energy of your soul and body decreases.«

To lean on one's neighbor means to demand from him. This means to take energy from him. We expect from our neighbor what we, ourselves, lack, what underlies the weakness of our soul.

If we drain the life of our neighbor in such a way, then he can master his life less and less. Every one of us is in the school of life called Earth, and each one needs his own energy to master this school of life. But if we draw energy from our neighbor, he may not be able to recognize many things because he has to deal with us because he has to fulfill this or that for us, so that we are content. In the meantime, many impulses of the day pass by him—his impulses that he cannot perceive because we lean on him and demand of him.

The one who leans on another, bears the main guilt. The other one who fulfills the desires is also guilty. This is how both burden themselves. In so doing, they are bound to each other—the one who demands and the other one who lets himself be used. They have to clear this up together. Even if the situation has passed, it all remains in our soul as pictures, until it has been cleared up. Every one of us will one day recognize himself in the pictures of his soul-film.

Every thought is a component of a picture or it is an entire picture. The pictures stay in us and are also stored in the stars. Thus, we are registered. In due course, our pictures will come back to us. We experience ourselves in the forest of pictures of our human ego. Then we cannot say: "This is not me" or "That was not me." We experience ourselves in the role of our humanness.

The one who recognizes himself today in the moments of the day and clears things up does well. In the soul realms, he will not have to live and suffer through the pictures of his ego.

Gabriele:

To no longer keep the order of the temple means that we no longer remember the Ten Commandments and the Sermon on the Mount. In so doing, we forget that we are heirs to infinity and that the divine heritage is in us. Then we live for the day and soil our temple daily more. Day by day, we burden ourselves more. To keep the order of the temple means to live consciously, to fulfill the laws of God more and more, so that our temple may cleanse itself and we gradually find our way to the inner light.

To find the way to the holy of holies, we have to follow the Inner Path because it is only in this way that we establish communication with the All-Holy One in us.

Once we have accomplished this, by working on ourselves, by overcoming our base humanness and by actualizing and fulfilling the eternal law, we do not have to ask anymore: "How is this or that?" The divine in us knows about all things because it is the Self of the All.

The divine always communicates. Christ in us is always ready to help us, to serve us, to give us an answer. But for this, the communication with Christ is necessary. Through the Inner Path, we draw closer to the communication with Him, step by step.

The one who does not keep his own temple pure builds external temples or maintains these through his energy by affirming rites, dogmas and cults, and with his talents and money. He then becomes the prisoner of an order that is not the holy Order, God.

Gabriele:

The order of an institution, for example, is not the holy Order. Where there are customs such as rites, dogmas and the like, it is said in many cases: "you must." It is in the nature of customs that they use and often abuse people. Customs often become compulsions. But in the Spirit of God, there is no compulsion. "We may," that is the law of freedom. This is why we may walk the path within to draw closer to Christ. The "may" gives us courage, the "must," on the other hand, always pulls us down. This is why all customs will fall apart.

Anything that is based on force is not divine.

Only the weak soul that lacks energy wants to adorn itself with outer wealth. The mature soul that is filled with life force is fulfilled and rich within. It is undemanding. The undemanding person will receive what he needs and often more than that because God gives to the one who gives himself to Him.

Gabriele:

Every robbery is sinful and this sin has to be expiated.

When we pressure our neighbor, when we urge him, we take energy from him. If he does what we want, our neighbor will not come to know his own thoughts and desires. He passes by his path through life. When sin breaks open in him, that is, when the causes become effective, then we, who have invaded the temple, will be burdened with twice as much.

If our neighbor has to fully bear the effects of his causes, like suffering or illness because—on our account—he was unable to turn to the tasks which life had given him, then we are partially to blame for the suffering or illness because we contributed to the fact that his causes have now become fully effective.

If our neighbor dies from his illness, then it is possible that we share in the guilt of his early death. This can grow into a larger mountain of guilt that contains the sin against the neighbor, that is, the binding.

Day after day, we receive so-called admonishing impulses, so that we recognize in time the complexes of sin that could lead to suffering or illness. If we clear up in time what the energy of the day reflects to us in the form of feelings, sensations and thoughts, then the Spirit of the Christ of God in us transforms the negative energy into positive power. Then the cause no longer has to become effective.

Respect the temple of your neighbor, for he, too, shall learn the order of the temple and recognize himself through his weaknesses and faults—which he sees only when you do not block his view—and he shall clear up what he is aware of, so that he, too, may enter the holy of holies, his temple, which cleanses itself more and more.

Gabriele:

With our urging desires, with which we again and again invade the temple of our neighbor, we block his view. He then has to look to us and cannot recognize himself. As a result, we contribute to the fact that our neighbor passes his life by, that is, that he cannot master the Earth's school of life.

If you heed the laws of the order of the temple, then you respect yourself and your neighbor.

The one who does not respect himself does not respect his neighbor either because he does not keep the order of the temple, himself, the law of the temple.

Gabriele:

The one who does not respect himself does not monitor himself. He speaks everything that comes to mind. In this way, he wastes energy and lives more and more externally. He does not cleanse his temple because he does not pay attention to himself, and is satisfied with the stimulation of his senses. Because of this externalization, he does not respect himself and will not respect his neighbor, either.

From this we can conclude that the one who respects himself, monitors himself. He curbs his speech. He speaks only what is essential. He lives alert and concentrated, focusing on the situations and moments. In this way, the inner life builds up in him and a spiritual aura around him, which means strength and protection. He will also respect his neighbor, since he respects himself, and he will find the positive in everything and in everyone and will build on this. He is the spiritual person who is selflessly active.

The law of the temple is the holy Order. It is the divine Will, the divine Wisdom, the divine Earnestness, the Patience of the Eternal, His infinite Love and Mercy. These are the seven basic powers of God.

The order of the temple is the law of the temple. It is the eternal holy law. It is the life in God and with God.

The one who keeps the law of the temple raises his feelings, his sensations, his thoughts, his words and deeds to God. Thus, he is fulfilled by God, and what he feels, thinks, speaks and accomplishes bears divine power.

The one who keeps the law, God, is one with his neighbor and with all Being because the one who keeps the eternal law is the Being.

Gabriele:

The divine power that is in all things is active in the light-filled feelings, in the ennobled sensations and thoughts, as well as in the selfless words of the spiritual person who is permeated by the divine. His word has substance because it is permeated by God.

The Being is the law. As pure beings, we, the Being, are compressed law. This means that everything is in all things, and as compressed law, we are in the flowing Being, in the stream, God, as the drop of infinity.

Gabriele:

Let us become aware that the One, the Holy One, God, dwells in us.

Since He dwells in us, we are sanctified ones, as beings in God, as pure beings because we are His holy law, which is our spiritual heritage.

Let us see ourselves as this temple. Let us sense and feel deep into our inner being—what concerns come to us?

Are they still the human desires, the wanting to be and to have, or is it what our soul desires because it yearns for purity, clarity and for the light of inner life?

If we strive earnestly toward God, then the desire to sin less and less comes more and more often.

Everything is consciousness. It is also consciousness to sin less and less. If we decide to do this day by day, then one day it will take hold in our conscious mind and we will be reminded of it again and again—especially when we fall into old faults and habits again or when we are on the verge of creating new causes.

Through a conscious life, our consciousness begins to expand very gradually. We see and register more. We recognize ourselves in what we see and very gradually we find our way to the innermost part of everything that we meet.

Our life comes alive, it gets interesting. If we are alert, we discover that everything wants to tell us something.

Light and shadow speak to us. Light is happiness and peace. Shadow is what oppresses and what we should clear up. If we clear it up, then we have again taken a step toward God, our Father.

If we follow the impulses that the day gives to each one of us according to his consciousness, that is, if we change and no longer commit the negative that we have recognized, then, when our neighbor needs help, we can also have recourse to the actualization potential that we have worked out. We can then understand him and do him justice because we have experienced and overcome the same or similar thing.

The Absolute Law is the pulsebeat of infinity, God. The pure beings, the pure nature kingdoms and all heavenly bodies follow this pulsebeat. God is the Being and the stream that flows throughout everything. He is the power that encompasses everything. He is the life; He is our movement; He is our Being.

Let us take up communication with the depth and vastness in our soul, and we will feel that the mighty All is in us, the all-encompassing law, our true being, our eternal existence, our eternal life.

aily anew, become aware that in you dwells the All-Wise One, the Eternal, who knows about all things, who is with you, who speaks to you, who knows every answer and solution.

Gabriele, the teaching prophetess
and emissary of God, explained about this:

If these words have penetrated us, we sense what wealth lies in our inner being, and that we are children of the inner kingdom, heirs to infinity because God, the infinity, dwells in us and speaks to us.

God, the omnipresent Spirit, is in every question, in every answer, and in every solution. God is everywhere. He helps us give the right answer. He helps us find the solution in a problem.

He, the All-Wise One, is always there, and we, as beings in God, are wise because we came forth from the power of divine Order, of Will, of Wisdom, of Earnestness, of Patience, of Love and of Mercy.

As beings in God, as the human being who lives in the inner sanctum, we know about all things. In the divine, the knowledge about all things is the eternal wisdom. Thus, we are rich. If we become aware of this, then we have to say: How poor, yes, how pitifully poor, we are when we sin again and again, when we occupy ourselves with the same problems over and over again, thinking this is the most important thing. Let us take note that in the problem is the solution, God, the Eternal, who dwells in us.

In us is God, who knows about all things. If we become aware of this, then there is only one aspiration: to become one with Him, to draw from the source of infinite wisdom and to give from the love and wisdom because that is what endures, that is truth and that is our life.

Gabriele:

If we want to reach the point where the great Spirit, God, speaks through us, then this means for us to withdraw from our ego, our all-too-humanness. It means for us to turn into the inner temple and to ask God for guidance and help.

God does not make us wait for Him. God helps. God, our eternal Father, serves all His children. His Spirit, which dwells in each one of us, serves each one of us. Serving is God's infinitely eternally giving love.

Perhaps we may say: "I do not feel or hear Him." Why not? Because of our externalization. Because our senses are oriented to the external world and demand more and more. Because we work more with our intellect, instead of going within and actualizing the laws more and more. This is possible for every one of us. Who does not know the excerpts of the eternal laws, the Ten Commandments and the Sermon on the Mount? Figuratively speaking, they are the Inner Path that leads within, that builds the bridge to Him who always serves us because He always gives.

Gabriele, the teaching prophetess
and emissary of God, explained about this:

What we move in us for a longer period of time settles firmly in the conscious mind and in the subconscious. If a thought comes and we constantly move it in us, then we intensify it. The thought then becomes a program because we add more and more thoughts to it. This program goes into our brain cells, into our conscious mind. It moves us again and again. If we let this happen, then we are literally drawn into the world of the senses. We are drawn into our sinfulness, so that it is often very difficult for us to go into our inner being.

The one who lives consciously is alert and knows the vagabonds that insinuate themselves, to tempt him.

Gabriele:

Not all thoughts that touch us are important for us and should be analyzed. Often, they are merely vagabond thoughts that we accept. The one who is not alert nourishes them.

These vagabonds are thoughts that may remind us of situations that we have already cleared up, but which still lie in our world of memories. If we move the memory for a longer period of time, then we bring it into our conscious mind. It is then active there. It sends and will also receive from there. What was a memory has again become a correspondence, a negative energy potential.

I repeat: If we take from our world of memories, from what we have already cleared up long since—all the occurrences and events—and play them out in our thoughts and feelings, then we again create programs in our conscious mind. According to the law of sending and receiving, we may then possibly experience the same or similar things that we had already cleared up. Why? Because we nourished the world of memories and thus created a new program. The one who does not live consciously may thus build a new karma, new guilt entanglements.

Gabriele:

The whip of inner strength consists of the law of God, of the seven basic powers of God, from Order to Mercy.

By overcoming our humanness and by actualizing and fulfilling the spiritual laws, the inner life unfolds in us. We increase in spiritual strength, which we are more and more able to actively put into practice. We then oppose the temptations of the all-too-human with decisiveness and firmness and send away the vagabond thoughts that insinuate themselves. What touches and moves us in the way of human aspects, we immediately overcome by mastering ourselves with the help of the transforming power of the Christ of God.

By mastering your thoughts and senses, your inner temple has become pure.

Whatever insinuates itself, every temptation, drive it away from you!

However, before you drive the temptation away from you, greet the good in it and allow the good to move in you.

The movement of the good in you causes anguish in the evil, in the tempter who is behind the temptation.

Gabriele:

With this, Christ is telling us that in everything is also the positive, even in the temptation. When we affirm the good in everything and move it in us, then we experience the help of the Christ of God.

When we say: "I affirm Christ in my soul," then we feel His help, and we become free of this temptation.

Gabriele:

We know that Christ is also in the tempter. Everything negative is transformed into the positive through the power of Christ.

Selfless help never interferes in the neighbor's sphere. It offers itself because everyone has free will.

The positive stimulates the positive in us. The negative stimulates the negative in us. If we are alert and clear up the sinful, then we are liberated. We will then become the liberator who irradiates the good in the evil. Thus, we come into communication with the innermost being—with the good core, with the light of Christ—in the evil, and in this way, we also stimulate the tempter to reflect and to possibly change his ways.

If we are in our temple, if we are oriented to within, we will also live in an alert manner, and withstand the temptation and the tempter.

The same happens through you, the liberator, only in a reverse sense: The good in you knocks at the door of evil, to move it to see reason, to recognize itself and to turn back.

Thus, if evil approaches you, then step before the gates of your inner temple and bring the gifts of goodness to the evil.

By the reaction of the approaching thoughts that you have perceived, you notice the reaction of the tempter. If you feel that your selfless gifts found resonance, that is, were accepted, then, give even more. Then call the tempter's attention to the consciousness of the Christ of God and again enter the inner sanctum, your temple.

Gabriele:

We recognize the reactions of the tempter when we watch the behavior of the approaching thoughts, the thought vagabonds that knock at our door. If they continue to urge, then the tempter was not accepting. If the approaching thoughts leave us, if we feel an inner liberation, a sense of well-being, or even a subtle feeling of happiness, then our positive powers, the gifts of goodness, entered the tempter, who now moves them in himself. He has then accepted them.

If the approaching thoughts continue to beset us, then we will surrender them to Christ and, at the same time, we will look at ourselves to see what we may still have in us as correspondences. Once we have cleared this up, then we should again enter our inner temple, the inner sanctum. This means that we go within again and remain linked with God.

To constantly abide in the inner being, to live linked with God, the I Am, is what identifies a spiritually mature person, the one fulfilled by God, who lives in the fulfillment of the laws of salvation. As long as we are on the way to this and practice the actualization of the laws of God, the great cosmic teachings of the Christ of God set the goal for us and, at the same time, give help along the way.

There, in your innermost being, allow no human thoughts and reactions. Maintain the good of the tempter in your innermost being, and move it from time to time. In this way, you are sending the All-law to him. You are thus sending gifts of selfless love to him. You, however, do not go into a receiving mode. Leave this up to the Christ of God and His child, the tempter.

Gabriele:

Therefore, we should not allow any human thoughts and reactions into our innermost being. If human thoughts come, if problems or difficulties move us, then we should very quickly step before the temple, look at them, clear them up and again enter the inner being.

We should move the goodness of the tempter in our inner being because the positive is in the tempter, as well, just as the positive, the light of the Christ of God, shines in each one of us. When we affirm the good in the tempter, then we are sending selfless thoughts, divine energies, to our neighbor again and again. The tempter is also our brother, our sister, our neighbor.

But we should not go into a receiving mode. This means that we should not curiously inquire and ask whether our positive thoughts were accepted. At the moment we think "Have our positive thoughts been accepted?" we

are already tuning in to receiving, through the principle of
sending and receiving.

*How your neighbor behaves and what he sends con-
cerns only the eternal Father and His child.*
Keep, you, the order of the temple: be silent!
To be silent means to be in the stillness.
*God lives and speaks through the one who lives in the
holy of holies, in God.*
*In the temple of God, no human thoughts can exist. So
linger within, in you, without thoughts, that is, in silence.*

Gabriele:

All-too-human thoughts come from matter, are related
to matter and are thus, of the Earth. They cannot enter
God. God is spirit and not matter.

To be able to be silent, we have to learn to discern
when we should speak and when we should be silent. Let
us keep in mind: What is important? What aftereffect can
a conversation, a statement or an action have?

The wise one thinks before he speaks because he lives
in the inner stillness where no human thought can enter.

»You keep the order of the temple: be silent!«, means that we should not immediately speak out whatever comes to mind. We should think about it and place what we want to say into the eternal law, into our divine heritage, with the question: Is what I want to say significant? Why do I want to say it? If I say it, what consequences can it have for me or for my neighbor?

The prudent one very gradually finds his way into stillness because he strives to draw from the inexhaustible wellspring, which is God in each one of us.

And when you think, then think divinely.
And when you speak, then speak the law of God—speak divinely.
Speak only divinely, and only when your neighbor desires gifts from the law of life.

Gabriele:

This means for us to speak only when we feel that we can give our neighbor gifts of life to take with him. Anything else is human, and what is human, is a waste of energy.

To think and speak divinely establishes communication with God in our inner being. If we no longer want or expect anything, if our ego is no longer involved, if we are embarrassed about a human talent, then we are giving selflessly. Only then, and solely then, do we speak the law of life. Only then, do we think divinely.

From the viewpoint of our shadowed human consciousness, it often seems difficult for us to find our way into the divine law again. And yet, one day we will have to immerse again as a drop in the ocean of God. And we will do this because our origin is divine.

Take note: Your pure sensations and your pure thoughts are divine.

Your selfless, noble, that is, ethical, senses are finely attuned. They are the antennae into the All, which reach into the heavens because you live in the Being, in heaven, and thus receive from heaven, as well.

Gabriele:

Our eternal heritage is light. Therefore, we are beings of light—light of His light. If we penetrate everything with our light, then we feel our divine sensations, our pure thoughts.

The light is the heavens. The one who is in communication with the light is in communication with heaven and with all those who are in heaven.

»Your selfless, noble, that is, ethical, senses are finely attuned.«

For us, these words mean that we have to refine our coarse, human senses, to find our way to the ethically fine senses of the soul.

If we refine our sense of sight, our eyes will be light-filled. Wherever we look, thoughts of God and of the divine in all things will come.

When we look here and there, and human thoughts come, then our sense of sight is not yet refined. Then we have shadows in our eyes—our human ego. Our eyes still bear the darkness.

Once the light of God is active in us, then we perceive the divine in everything. Then we have the light in our eyes. Then the melody of love sounds in our heart, the melody of thankfulness toward God, who is the power, the light, in all things, who goes with us and radiates toward us in all things.

If we hear only what we should hear, that is, if nothing urges us to listen in, and if what we hear brings thoughts about God and if we find the divine principles of the law in what we heard, then we have activated the light, God, in our sense of hearing. Then the light guides us. In the same way as it guides the eyes, it also guides the sense of hearing.

If the perception of our senses of smell and taste causes us to remember our divine origin, then the light, God, is alive in our senses of smell and taste. Then we will not stick our nose into different containers to absorb the smells of the human-earthly life because our senses are ethical.

We will also sit at a nicely set table and dine in a well-mannered and ethical way. We will not rest our elbows on the table, but will make sure to dine with decency and consciously. We will chew well the bite that we have in our mouth and let it glide into our digestive organ, and only then take the next bite. Nor will we gulp down the content of a full glass all at once, but will take the drink in single sips. We will not speak with a full mouth, either.

When we eat and drink in an ethical way, that is, a well-mannered way, then the light is with us and we will establish communication with the food and drink, which contain the Creator-power, the light. Thus, we nourish not only our body, but we also nourish our soul because our soul bears the inner light. The soul, insofar as it is light-filled, longs to be in constant communication with the light.

Once we have raised ourselves to the divine, we will also not touch everything because our sense of touch and all other senses, as well, do not react with wanting to have, that is, they do not crave anymore.

The one who does not rest in himself wants to touch everything. He wants to reach for everything because he is unable to reach an understanding of himself, since he has not learned to recognize and overcome himself.

If we refine our senses, then we are ethical people with higher morals, with higher values. Only in this way, do we gain access to the eternal Being and to the ethically pure senses of our soul.

Here, too, we recognize again that on the Inner Path, first comes the journey to within, from without to within, the cleansing from without to within, until the drop, the divine being, is once again perfect and immerses in the ocean, God, and is one with God, eternally. Then the light-filled consciousness radiates from within to without through the person who is permeated with the light, and the person is a spiritual person, through whom God is able to work.

ever look at your neighbor, or you will look only at yourself.

Only when you have learned to see through yourself, from your innermost being, from the holy of holies, will you also penetrate your neighbor.

As long as you cannot penetrate your neighbor, you have not taken him into your innermost being.

Gabriele, the teaching prophetess
and emissary of God, explained about this:

If we look only at the shell, the human being, then we always see only the humanness—and what upsets us about this humanness is what we are, ourselves. Then we are looking only at ourselves. As long as we look at the faults of our neighbor, we are seeing only our own faults. Then our eye is sinful because we see only the sinful and perceive only the sinful.

To gain access to the inner being of our neighbor means to fulfill the laws of God. Then the positive sides of our neighbor awaken in us and we also establish communication with God in our neighbor. This is the taking in of our neighbor. Then we penetrate the shell and experience our neighbor deep in our soul because we are in communication with the innermost spheres of our neighbor, with God.

Without the Inner Path, without journeying within to the kingdom of the inner being that is in each one of us, we will never be able to take in our neighbor. When we accept him casually on an external level, aware that he is a human being just as I am a human being, then both will look only at the humanness, and will thus not find the way to one another or be in unity with one another. They may admittedly have many things in common, however, they are not in unity, in God's unity because they both look only at the shell and therefore, at the humanness.

Our path goes within, to the divine in us. The more we open the divine in our inner being, the more we can see through our neighbor. He suddenly becomes transparent to us, since we, ourselves, have become transparent because our soul shines and radiates the glimmer of our homeland through our physical garment.

Gabriele:

We get to know our neighbor as our brother and our sister only once we have recognized ourselves, that is, once we have defeated ourselves, our human ego. Then the sense of communality awakens and then unity awakens. We become transparent because we have hardly anything more that is negative. We have no more secrets because we live in a lawful way.

When we vanquish ourselves, we become purer, our nature finer, and we find our brother and our sister in ourselves. Our neighbor will be close to us. Even if we do not know him externally, we feel his inner being and it is close to our nature because we have become one with our pure being.

Gabriele:

As long as the Absolute Law, our divine heritage, our innermost nature, is foreign to us, we are also strangers to ourselves. We do not know our true nature, nor do we know the eternal homeland. In this world, we will be lonely and after our physical death, we will be a stranger in the other world. We will live far from God, and not recognize that God is so near to us. We will not behold Him because we did not behold our neighbor in the temporal. We saw him as a mere human being and not as a being in God. We are strangers here as well as there because we are not near to our divine nature. Our divine nature is our spiritual heritage.

Gabriele:

When we no longer live in the narrow, egocentric, human consciousness, when, for instance, we are not controlled by an external thought that says: "My neighbor is a stranger to me, I don't care about him," then we penetrate our neighbor with our spiritual consciousness and are with him. Our soul then bears hardly any shadow of our human ego. The light of actualization then radiates through our soul, and the divine light penetrates everything, including matter, and our neighbor.

Everything that exists is imbued by light. Once we have become light of His light, we penetrate our neighbor. We penetrate every problem, every difficulty, everything that comes toward us because the light always communicates with the light. Since the light is in everything, the light will connect with light again and again. Because of this communication, we will think, speak and act in a lawful way. We will think about what we will say because we are in communication with the light.

Let us remember: God is light.

Let us remember: God is in us.

Let us remember that we are all His children and thus, all brothers and sisters.

Let us remember that the Kingdom of God is in us and that the fullness of the eternal Being lives in each one of us.

Let us remember that we are free beings, children of the unending love.

Let us remember that our neighbor, the positive in him, is a part of us, and that the positive in us is a part of him.

Let us remember when we are in nature: As essence, the nature kingdoms are a part of us, and, as essence, we are a part of the nature kingdoms.

Let us remember when we see the stars that they are a part of us and we are a part of them.

Let us remember that the All is a huge communication network because everything is communication.

Let us remember that positive, selfless thoughts achieve the heavens because they are thoughts of heaven, and negative thoughts can cast us into hell, into our dismal consciousness.

Let us remember that the law of God is our true Being, our divine heritage. If we live according to the laws of God more and more, then we will feel secure, enveloped and protected by our loving Father. He, the great Spirit, who loves us above all things, sent Christ, His Son, to us human beings. As Jesus of Nazareth, He pointed out the laws of life. He lived according to them.

Let us take Christ into our daily life as a role model. Let us think of Jesus of Nazareth again and again. When something is hard for us, let us ask ourselves: How would Jesus have done it? How would Jesus have spoken? How would Jesus have acted? Then we will feel that the light draws nearer to us. In time, we will also immerse in the light, thus renouncing this world with its enticements because we have everything, all of infinity. This inner possession is the treasure that we may bring to the light.

Gabriele:

We then look only at the shell of our neighbor, at their burdens, and do not accept and receive them as brother and sister. As long as the person is merely "known" to us, we have sympathy or antipathy for him. If he is a stranger to us, then we are indifferent to him. Both give evidence that we live in separation from God, and not in unity with God. In God, all are equal, and in Him, all people and beings, and all Being form the unity.

*Think about the following spiritual principle:
You have spoken with a person, whom you know only by name, for you do not know what he consists of. Your neighbor, too, who lives only in the external, does not know himself because he does not know what he consists of, either. That is, he does not know himself, and you do not know him, either. If you both do not know yourselves, then you do not know God, either, and therefore, each of you is alone. God, the eternally loving Father, knows every single one because He loves each child and carries it in His great Father-heart.*

Gabriele, the teaching prophetess
and emissary of God, explained about this:

As long as we do not know ourselves, we have not examined our human ego and have not conquered it, either. When we speak with those of like mind, who also have not examined and recognized themselves, then each speaks only what he has not examined, his human ego. It is true that both speak to each other, but they speak past each other because both do not know themselves.

*verything is in you. The life is in you and you fulfill it of your own accord.*

Since everything first takes place in you, the eternal Being is without shadow. This is why there is no above and below, no in front and behind, no right and no left.

The All-unity is a mighty crystal that sparkles in all facets of inner life, and each radiation permeates every facet.

The human being speaks of »above« and »below,« of »in front« and »behind,« of »right« and »left,« because he sees only with his external eyes and registers only the reflections of the truth.

Gabriele, the teaching prophetess
and emissary of God, explained about this:

»Since everything first takes place in you, the eternal Being is without shadow.« Let us call to mind that the pure beings of the eternal Being live in the eternal stream, in the law. In the eternal Being, there are no projections. The law is eternally flowing, eternally permeating radiance. It is absolute. It is the mighty stream, in which the being lives and has its existence, from which it draws and gives—being, moving and acting in the stream. Because of this, there are no shadows.

Only the human being creates shadows. He creates them through his projections because he abuses a part of the powers that God gave on loan to His Fall-children to take with them. He takes these positive powers, the eternal law, and reverses them, from the divine love to self-love.

The aspects of our self-love are projections. The shadows of our sins lie on our soul. From our soul, they radiate into our body and, at the same time, into the stars of the computer system of the purification planes. These are the projections of our human ego. Each one bears other shadows, depending on his burdens.

The shadows of our soul show in all the human expressions of our life. Light and shadow look through our eyes. The way we see is the way we see our surroundings. This is how humankind creates its world, which consists of nothing other than the sum of all the projections of the individual people. Over countless generations, from the beginning of the Fall, we created shadows and thus, our world because the human being and the humanness are density, transformed-down energy, that is, God's energy, metamorphosed.

What radiates toward us is likewise reflections. We again perceive only what we have emitted. This is how we see our neighbor. This is how we hear our neighbor. This is how we smell, taste and touch. Everything consists of our projections and the reflections of our projections, which radiate toward us from our surroundings, and are, in turn, the ego, the human aspects.

This is why, in matter, there is an above and below, an in front and behind, a right and a left because everything is density and we always look only at the walls, the density. But the Spirit of God penetrates the density. For Him, there is no above, no below, no right, no left. Let us imagine that we are in a crystal that is constantly moving. Where is the above? Where is the below? Where are the right and left, the in front and behind?

The whole universe is like a crystal. Everything permeates everything else. This means: The whole universe, the pure Being, is all-permeating radiant power, the eternal law.

Through human wrongdoing, he created density, by which emerged the three-dimensional way of thinking, since with his physical eyes he can see, in turn, only the walls of his self-made cocoon-world, and accepts this as real and as the quality of his life.

Density, matter, is nothing but transformed-down divine energy, the reversal of light into shadow.

The soul of the person who lives in this human world of shadows is shadowed and is on Earth as a human being to expiate what the soul has contributed to the shadowing of the whole—unless the being of light comes on behalf of the Almighty to show the ways how the human being, the shadowed soul, can find the way out of the labyrinth of his dark ego.

Gabriele:

Our cocoon-world is the plasma, our aura.

The shadows of our soul radiate through our body and surround us like a cocoon. We live in this cocoon-world, that is, in a plasma. When we speak, then we are addressing our plasma. The answer is what lies in the plasma, namely we, in turn, ourselves. Via the plasma, let us also call it the aura, we are connected to the stars of the purification planes and to the material stars.

It is said: "Just as we call into the canyon, so does it come back to us." Spiritually speaking, this means: Just as we emit our ego, so it comes back to us. When we receive an answer from one of our neighbors, it is also this way because it is only in our plasma that we hear what our neighbor says, and we hear from it only what we have stored in our plasma—and thus, also in the soul and in the stars. This is our narrow world, and many people are so proud of this narrow world!

It is our task and our path to dissolve this plasma. The soul garments are this plasma of transformed-down spiritual radiation, of base human aspects. We have to lighten our soul garments more and more and, in time, dissolve them. Then the divine will radiate through our soul, and we will also be connected with the divine. Our aura will then be the divine, the law of the All, and with this, we will be united with the eternal homeland. Thus, we are conscious beings of the cosmos because we are one with the All, one with the eternal stream, since we live in the stream, in the eternal Being, in God.

Therefore, we have to dissolve our plasma with Christ, to be able to see more deeply. Only then, can we look into the problems of our neighbor and help him. Then we look not only at the shell, not only at the person—we see through him, grasp his feelings and thoughts and know how we can help him, what we can say to him, and how we should deal with everything we encounter.

If we are in our plasma, in our human aspects, then we speak past one another. Each one speaks himself, according to his plasma, according to his shadows.

If you want to keep the order of the temple, then be aware that life is a whole: It is, as a whole, above and below, in front and behind, right and left. If you have recognized this and live in the innermost part of your temple, then you also draw from your innermost being.

What for the externalized person is above and below, in front and behind, right and left, is for the inward-looking person the life, the whole, in himself.

Gabriele, the teaching prophetess
and emissary of God, explained about this:

Let us feel into the words: *»Life is a whole. As a whole, it is above and below, in front and behind, right and left.«* Right or left, in front or behind is always the whole. To wherever we look is the whole because God is indivisible. He is always the whole—in all things.

When we look to the front, then we see the whole. When we look behind us, we again see the whole because God is everywhere. What then, is in front? What then, is behind? What is right, left, above, below? If the whole is in us, in front, behind, right, left, above and below, then there is only unity, and only the whole—present everywhere, and thus, in us.

In the eternal Being, our homeland, there is no in front, behind, right, left, above, below. We human beings have created this three-dimensional world through our thinking and willful striving in the mine and for me. The in front, behind, right and left are a result of externalization. Through our human aspects, we have separated ourselves from our inner being. We have turned away from God and created our own world, the world of our human thinking and feeling, of our wanting.

Consequently, with our humanness, we again look only at the external world, at matter, in the question: What is in front? What is behind? What is right? What is left? What is above? What is below? The spirit being does not ask. Only we, the human being, ask: What is where? What is in front, behind, right, left, above and below? We ask because we do not know ourselves.

Once we experience and know ourselves, our true being, then we may very well still use the terms above, below, in front, behind, right and left because we are human beings and live in the three dimensions—but we see through what is in front, just as we see through what is behind. We see through what is to the right and see through what is to the left, as well as what is above and what is below. Then our language is merely a use of terms, a means of communication and orientation in the spheres of matter. Yet we penetrate everything because the law of God permeates everything.

Once we penetrate everything, then our world gradually changes. Then the material structure becomes brighter and loosens. In time, density will no longer exist because we dissolve it together, by actualizing the laws of God.

It is the task of the beings in the earthly garment to bring not only themselves, but also the environment, the entire planet Earth, into higher vibration, into a more light-filled, finer structure. The spiritualization of life leads to transforming the life forms higher. This is how the spiritual evolution of humankind and of the Earth takes place. With this, the confinement in the limitation of time and space will also diminish.

It is still difficult for us to comprehend this because we still live in these programs of in front, behind, above and below, right and left, in the program of the three dimensions. Our earthly human programs run their course in these three dimensions. This is how we have created this world since the Fall. This is the way we see it now, and this is the way we believe it is correct and in order.

In reality, this world is merely a realm of shadows, consisting of the many shadows of the many people. This world consists of the projections of countless beings and people, who have been willfully emitting and receiving since the Fall, thus creating density. We incarnate into this density and continue to create, according to what we brought with us in the way of light or shadow. We create our density or our finer radiation. By way of light-filled thinking and living, we help to lighten the life in this world and to brighten our planet Earth.

We have to change our way of thinking, otherwise we will not understand the law of God. We have to become aware that what is in front is also behind because God is in all things. He is the whole—indivisible. Let us grow into the following awareness more and more: The one who calls us has, in turn, the whole in the call. The one who speaks to us has, in turn, the whole in the question. The one who approaches us comes toward us as the whole. No matter where we look, we always behold the whole, if we are turned within and keep the temple order, that is, if we fulfill the law of God more and more.

All these are pointers. They cannot directly give us the awareness, the understanding, that "everything is in all things, God—the whole." It is not like one brings a neighbor a gift, which he accepts and then calls his own. These indications want to encourage us to unfold this spiritual dimension within ourselves. This will be possible only if we open ourselves to this, if we allow our inner spheres to be touched by it, for the inner life is the life of our soul. The human being, the shell, the human mind, is unable to grasp it.

Once the desire has taken hold of us to draw closer to the divine in us, once we recognize ourselves in the moments of our day and free ourselves little by little from the ballast of humanness, then we will also take into our daily lives what is given to us in the teaching of the Absolute Law.

Let us try it out! In the days ahead, when our fellow people approach us, let us become aware in our hearts that the whole is coming toward us—God because He is indivisible. Let us likewise become aware that the whole is in what we hear because God is indivisible. The whole is in whatever we see because God is indivisible. No matter what we hear, smell, taste and touch, it is always the whole because God is indivisible.

If we do these exercises again and again, we will get to know ourselves. When we get to know ourselves, the result will be that, in time, we will know our neighbor. We will gain respect for life because the whole is in all things.

In the little ant is the whole. In the butterfly is the whole. In the grain of sand is the whole. It approaches us and shows itself to us in the ant, in the butterfly, in the grain of sand. And what does the human being often say? "A grain of sand, so what? It's lying there; it is insignificant." This is how we think and speak because we look only at the shell. When we learn to look through the grain of sand, we grasp it in our inner being and perceive that more lies in it, indeed, everything—the whole, God! Then we understand that what is lying there is merely the shell. In the shell, from the shell, the Being radiates toward us—God.

Let us practice grasping the whole, the life, the inner life, even in the smallest things, and then we will feel more and more that the power is in us and in all things. If it is alive in us, then what is "in front," what is "behind," what is "right, left, above and below"? When the whole radiates through us, radiating through us from all pores, as it were, what is "in front, behind, right and left"? They are terms that are meant to help us to feel, to sense, our true nature. They are terms that should encourage us to immerse in this beautiful, noble, fine, pure Absolute, to become free, free of our human ego. And as we become free, we also allow our neighbor his freedom.

If you keep the order of the temple, then you live in the temple, in the holy of holies of God in you, and you experience yourself. If you have experienced yourself as the Being, then you know your neighbor because you know the All, the Being,

Then you do not need to seek—you have received because the Being gives eternally. It gives in you. It streams through you and reveals itself in you and in this world.

Gabriele:

The one who knows himself has ultimately overcome his all-too-humanness. With what he has overcome, with the positive power he has gained, he also sees his neighbor.

With this power to overcome, we see our neighbor in the right light. We have vanquished our humanness, and our neighbor is in the process of overcoming the same or something similar. Because of this, we can understand him; we feel sympathetic toward him. Through this inner understanding, through the sympathy, we also have access to our neighbor and can help him as much as he wants to be helped.

If we live in the temple of the inner being, then we also know to what extent we can help our neighbor, what we can say to him and how we should encounter him. The innermost being knows about all things, and the one who lives in the innermost being receives for himself and for his neighbor.

Therefore, the one who knows himself also knows his neighbor. The one who has overcome himself also knows the steps for his neighbor to overcome his humanness. We cannot vanquish our neighbor's humanness for him because each one has to overcome his humanness himself, with Christ. But if we are the conqueror of our base nature, our ego, we know the way because we have followed it, away from the humanness, away from the sin.

If you recognize yourself as the Being and live in the Being, then you do not need to look around to find the truth, the Being because you know that what is behind is the same as what is in front. You do not need to look to the right or to the left because you know that what is right or left is the same as what is in front and behind. You do not need to look either upward or downward. You know that what is above and below is the same as what is in front and behind, right and left: the life, the large in the smallest and the smallest in the large, in you, the Being.

Take note and carry it with you at all times:

God is present. God is everything, everywhere.
In the largest is the smallest; in the smallest is the largest, God.

If you have found yourself, then you have found God, and you are at home in the All. Then you do not need to look around for the All nor look to the right, or to the left, nor upward or downward—the All is in you; God is in you; your neighbor is in you; all the forces of the kingdoms of nature are in you.

If you have found yourself, then you behold everything in you because you are everything in all things, yourself.

Again, take note and bear this consciously in you:

If you keep your temple pure, then you have opened everything in you, and you also have respect for the temple of your neighbor and reverence for the All-Holy One who dwells in you and in your neighbor and in all life forms of nature.

You are rich, for the All is in you. Therefore, you find everything in yourself—the smallest in the large and the large in the smallest.

Gabriele:

»If you keep your temple pure«—For us, this means that if we strive daily to purify our temple, then we will gradually open up the eternal law. Then we will gain respect for our neighbor's temple and reverence for the All-Holy One.

Let us practice this, being aware of the following: Do we respect our neighbor's temple? Do we let our neighbor have his freedom or do we force him to think as we think is right? Do we force him to act the way we think is right?

Let us ask ourselves again and again: Do we feel reverence for the All-Holy One, for God in us? Let us remember that each one of us is the temple of the Holy Spirit; that God, the All-Holy power, the Absoluteness, dwells in us. Let us bring this to mind again and again. Especially when we want to fall back into our old habits and our old thought patterns, let us bring to mind that in us dwells God, the All-Holy One. Then we will also sense the inner wealth and, at the same time, notice how poor we really are when we nurture our all-too-human aspects.

We will then very gradually realize that everything is in us, and that we ask many questions on an external level—"What is when and where?"—only when we are far from our inner being. Then we are merely in our human consciousness and see everything superficially, not grasping the core, the essential in the situation. If we use words like: "When is what? When and where?" merely because we live in the temporal, then this is based on our life as human beings. If we, for instance, ask what time it is so as to orient ourselves, then this is our language, our means of communication, to find our way around on this Earth.

Let us practice the order of the temple! Let us experience ourselves! Let us gain respect for our neighbor! Then we will attain freedom because we also leave our neighbor his freedom.

Let us remember: We are the temple of God, and God dwells in us. Let us develop reverence for God, the All-Holy One—and we will sense that we are images of our Father.

Let us take this awareness with us into our further days on Earth, and let us always remember: God is our Father and we are His children. If we actualize what we bear in ourselves, the beauty, the purity, the fineness, the nobleness, the good, the absolute love, we will draw closer to God and to our true being. Then we will experience what it means to receive pearls from the very basis of the Being. Then we will be pearl fishers of the inner life, treasure seekers, who find their way to the inner wealth.

, *Christ, as Jesus, taught this and more details of the eternal law to those of My apostles and disciples who could understand them. But again and again, I also had to explain to them the path to the eternal Being, as well as the Fall-law, the law of sowing and reaping.*

The Fall-law is transformed-down energy of God, which the adversary reversed and wanted to use against God. This fallacy bore the turning point in itself because what the human being sows as human aspects, he will reap— and not God or his neighbor.

Gabriele:

Nearly two thousand years ago, Jesus of Nazareth already struggled with His apostles and disciples, so that they would learn to understand the law of sowing and reaping, the Fall-law, and the eternal Being.

A great step lies behind us: nearly 2000 years. Many people are still struggling to discern sowing and reaping and the eternal Being.

In this radical change from the materialistic time to the age of the Spirit, more and more people comprehend what it means to live in the causal law, in the Fall-law, and to go into the eternal law. The law of sowing and reaping brings the fall of the base ego again and again. The eternal law brings inner peace, the nearness to God and the ascent back into the Being.

Gabriele, the teaching prophetess
and emissary of God, explained about this:

With this axiom, we temporarily look into the causal law again, to understand what humanness is—to then grow out of the humanness, into the eternal substance, into our eternal cosmic being.

The inner values are the divine Order, the divine Will, the divine Wisdom, the divine Earnestness, the Patience, the Love and Mercy. If we are lacking in these aspects, then we look for something new. However, this search for something new is merely a seeming search. In reality, the soul seeks the eternal One because the awakened soul is constantly on the lookout for the light of God. It is constantly seeking, to again immerse in the origin of life, and return to God.

How difficult it is for the awakened soul in the human being if the person still nurtures his human programs! There are often dissonances, discrepancies between the awakened soul and the human programs. The person becomes restless; he seeks. He seeks, as he thinks, for new things. In reality, it is the seeking soul, which longs for the light of the Father and conveys to the person: Clear up your humanness and find God in me!

The curious one is the desire, the greed. He sees and hears only himself.

The curious one, who curiously looks to the right and left, to in front and behind, above and below, is also the fearful one, who sees danger for himself everywhere. He does not rest in God and therefore, does not live in God, either, and through this, creates for himself what he is afraid of. He lives in the world of limitations and of density.

Gabriele:

The frightened and confused soul that is poor in light is also the frightened, bound and spiritually blind person. If the soul has awakened, it is no longer afraid. It feels the light and yet cannot reach the light because the human being violates his soul. He puts brakes on it, so to speak. He does not allow it to draw closer to the light.

If we strive to make everything safe for us in the external world, to look to the right and the left, in front, behind, above and below, to avoid all danger, then we will not escape it by doing this—we will encounter it. We attract the danger, what we are afraid of. Whatever we are afraid of will sooner or later break in over us.

We know and can experience on ourselves at every moment: No matter where we look, from there, we will be stimulated to think. And every thought can become the starting point for a complex human program.

If we are curious to see this or that, things that we perhaps should not see at all, then these things that are not yet a part of the energy of our day will stimulate us to think. Then it can become very hard for us to follow the Inner Path because by doing this, we prematurely call up sins that we then become aware of via our thoughts. This negative potential, which we may not even be able to clear up yet because the day had not yet foreseen this and had not yet brought the energy to solve and redeem it, can now become a trap for us.

The sins, our burdens that were awakened and summoned too early, break in over us and leave us no peace. They force us to keep thinking about them. If we continue to think, and are unable to control them, then we will be controlled by them. Through this, we create further programs. The more human programs we create, the more limited, that is, constrained, we are in our way of feeling, thinking, speaking and acting.

This is why we should look at our curiosity. What are we craving? What are we lacking? The lack shows itself in our way of feeling and thinking.

If we feel vaguely uneasy, then we should briefly pay attention to this feeling. It comes up and reveals itself in thoughts. We can grasp our thoughts better than our feelings. In this way, we can also figure out our curiosity and overcome it.

Let us live consciously! Whenever we look around, let us ask ourselves right away: What are we looking around for? Why? What are we calling up? All this wants to tell us something. Our life is interesting—if we monitor ourselves!

The one who is afraid of others is afraid of himself. He has no confidence in himself. To him, density is reality, and at the same time, threatening. In his fearfulness, he is constantly concerned with looking around himself, so that nothing may happen to him. Curiously, he looks in front, behind, to the right and to the left, upward and downward, thus lulling himself into thinking he is safe because he is of the opinion that this way he has everything in sight.

Gabriele:

If we have mastered our curiosity, that is, if we have cleared up what our curiosity had for a goal and content, then we will find our way into our temple. We will go ever deeper into our inner being, to the All-Holy One, to God, who dwells in us.

May it be clearly said once more: The human being, the inhabitant of the Earth, also needs his sense of sight for his orientation on Earth. Our physical eyes look to the front, to behind, to the right and the left. We have to turn around to orient ourselves. This is because we live in density. This is not curiosity.

As human beings we have to look back and to the right and the left. In the end, we are always looking at the walls of the three dimensions, at the walls, as it were, of the human ego. On the other hand, the pure being, the divine Intelligence, our true self as substance and power in God, beholds everything in itself. This is how our inner being sees everything that approaches us. Everything that vibrates in infinity is also in us.

The impulses from the All arrive in the inner being of the pure being. The pure being is not, as we human beings, dependent on being addressed from without. It perceives the impulses in its inner being, and at the same time, sees the picture that the impulse-giver sends, and knows what the impulse-giver wants, as well as immediately knowing the task and the solution.

For us human beings in density, it is necessary that we look around for the sake of orientation, not out of curiosity. However, when we rest in our temple, in our inner being, then we will also receive the impulses that we need for today, for this day. Then we will not need to look around curiously. We will learn what we need to learn. We will see what we should see because our five senses are purified, ethical, fine and are aligned with the perfect consciousness in us. In this way, God, the All-Holy One, our eternal Father, can guide His child.

To attain this direct guidance from God is the task of the soul in the earthly garment. On the way there, a mighty power is at its side: the power of the Christ of God.

As long as God, the Father, the Absolute Law, cannot yet reach us, cannot yet guide and lead us directly, Christ prepares our way. He is our helper and Redeemer. Through His »It is finished,« He holds out His hand to us at every moment and guides us over cliffs, valleys and heights, over stony paths, to God, our Father, to the light, to the perfect pure being that we, in reality, are.

The truly wise one is the prudent one who remains in the holy of holies and maintains the stillness there. In the temple of stillness, the truly wise one, the prudent one, receives direct instructions from God and salvation from God.

If you are experienced in the law of inner life, then you feel and think in a divine way and speak His word, which you are—divine.

Gabriele:

When we have attained this, then we are perfect consciousness, perfect intelligence, perfect substance in the perfect life—God.

Gabriele, the teaching prophetess
and emissary of God, explained about this:

All the drops in the ocean, God, permeate one another because each drop is the eternal law. The drop in the ocean, God, is the condensed law. It is the divine, the perfect substance in the stream of the All, in the flowing law. This flowing law is the light. It permeates and radiates through each drop, and each drop permeates, in turn, the other.

This means that there are no shadows in infinity, but only light. And there is no night and no so-called day, which shows itself to us human beings, only because the light of the Earth's sun radiates that part of the planet Earth that turns toward it. In the eternal Being, there is only the eternal law, the light, which streams eternally and radiates throughout everything. Because the eternal law, the light of God, sets everything aglow, there is only the day of God and no night because God radiates eternally.

God is light. God is harmony. God is the infinity. God is the All. God's harmony is eternally flowing, rhythmic life. The rhythms of the eternal Being are absolutely harmonious. They are the sounds of the spheres of eternity.

We are all beings of eternity because our spiritual body is immortal. Our immortal, pure being is the law of the All; it is harmony, symphony; it is sound, color and form. God, the Eternal, created us. Just as He is—harmony, selfless love, peace, symphony, unity, beauty, purity, selfless love—so are we, as well, in the eternal Being. Consequently, we are the being in God, the Being. God is flowing life—we are substance of life, embedded in the eternal stream, God. We are the drop in the ocean, God.

Our soul, which bears in itself the drop from the ocean, God, often has to suffer under the rigidity and intransigence of its person. So that the radiation power of our innermost being can help to soften the shell of our humanness, we should frequently make ourselves aware of, and affirm, where we come from, who we are and what our task is in this life on Earth.

Our eternal Father gave Himself form out of His All-Law, the stream. He is the Being that has become form—just as all of us, as pure beings in the eternal homeland, are the Being that has become form, substance of the All. Through our spiritual form, we are the images of our eternal Father. We are not merely a tone, a sound, a component of the

All, not a hovering something—we are heirs to infinity, streaming Being that has become form, the drop.

Everything that vibrates in infinity is in us. It has assumed form in us as the pure being. The pure form is the consciousness of the All, which tirelessly radiates, which tirelessly communicates because God is not standstill, but flowing life.

Each one of us has to again find our way into this eternal, holy consciousness, into our true being because our true being is immortal—it is from God, since God created it. This immortal being in us, the All that has become form, is the spiritual-divine body that each of us bears in ourselves. The divine body, which has become form, the substance of the All, became shadowed through our wrongdoings, through our offences against God. The shadows, that is, the sins, surround the spiritual body, our sublime, sanctified consciousness.

We are on this Earth to clear up or expiate the shadows with the help of the Christ of God, our Redeemer, so that our pure body, the substance of the All, can again come to the fore.

All people have a soul, the fine-material substance that is effective in us. This fine-material, burdened body permeates the physical body. It permeates us by way of our neural pathways and via all the functions of our body. Depending on how we react, our soul also reacts. Depending on how we think, our soul also reacts. Depending on what we say and how we speak, our soul also reacts. Our thoughts imprint our soul and our soul, in turn, imprints our body. All facets of our soul, all movements in the soul-garments, all changes are registered in the stars.

If we are aware that we are on Earth to become divine again, then we also take the first step to put order in our life, to unravel our human thoughts with the question: "What am I thinking?" If we put order in the world of our thoughts and clarify it step by step, then we will recognize ourselves more and more and experience who we are. Only self-recognition can tell us who we presently still are. It points out our human aspects that we should clear up with the help of the Christ of God.

If we have cleared it up with the help of the Christ of God, then it is necessary that we no longer commit the human aspects, the sins we have recognized. We don't always manage this step, to implement the positive, right away. By clearing the sinfulness up with the help of the Christ of God, the negative potential of this sinfulness that we have recognized and cleared up has left our soul. It has transformed into positive power—but the corresponding negative programs are still in our brain. To no longer sense, think and act as before, we now have to reach the application of higher, lawful principles. We have to resolve for higher values and higher ideals, so that we are able to take the next step toward God, toward our divine heritage.

Christ, our Redeemer and divine Brother, gave us insight into our true heritage, into our true being. Once we take the first steps toward our divine nature, we will already recognize to where the path is leading. It leads back to what we were and are in eternity: eternal law, eternal Being that became form.

Christ gave us His great cosmic teachings. In them vibrates the eternal law, our eternal homeland, our true being, the highest goal, the unification with God, our Father.

The All-law, God, is the holy of holies in you. Absolute stillness is there.

Gabriele:

The Inner Path to God, to our true being, is the path into absolute stillness.

The inner stillness is peace. In the inner stillness there is nothing that urges, nothing that wants, there is no mine and me.

est in yourself—you are.

You are the Being that does not chafe at anything, that does not get annoyed about anything and does not take offence at anything. You are the Being—you see through all things and everyone. For this reason, you also penetrate everything and everyone.

Gabriele, the teaching prophetess
and emissary of God, explained about this:

Once we have become calm, once we have cleared up our humanness with Christ, then we rest in Christ—and we are. The law is—and has no questions. It does not need to ask because it is. And the one who is the law knows about all things because he is perfect intelligence, that is, the image of God.

As long as we take offence at anything, this shows us that we lack something. We see something in the wrong way. We do not have an overall view. We take offence at what we do not see through. The perfect intelligence, however, the wisdom of God, has an overall view. It sees through the density. It recognizes and knows about the depths. It also sees what the density consists of and what takes place behind density.

The path to God is the way to overcoming the density, the sins of the soul, in order to immerse in the perfect life, to become the perfect intelligence, the perfect consciousness that knows about all things, that sees through everything because it is the being in the stream of Being. On the Inner Path, we take these steps to our divine heritage, to our being, to our true life, which is perfect.

Jesus said, and Christ speaks again today: "The Kingdom of God is within, in you." Therefore, we should go into the inner kingdom, into our homeland because the external realm, this world, passes away. Only the Spirit of the Christ of God and the Kingdom of Peace in us are lasting.

Let us grasp what a treasure Christ has again revealed to us, the kingdom of the inner being, the Absolute Law, our divine heritage! We no longer need to seek. We no longer need to ask: "Who are we? What is our homeland? What are the laws of the eternal homeland? What is our divine heritage?" Christ has given us the answer. He gives us insight into our true life, into our true being. He also gives us the strength that we need to enable us to open the inner kingdom, our spiritual heritage.

Christ wants us to become peaceful, that we live with one another and are for one another. As it is in heaven, so should it also become on Earth. It can become on Earth only if we become and mature in Christ, if we fulfill the commandments of life—ultimately, our true life, so that we are again fulfilled beings, beings in God, our eternal Father.

We are called upon not to misuse any energy because the reaction to this will be much greater. Much energy is wasted in this world. The results are the reactions that we heard and hear about daily, that we read about, see and experience.

This is why we human beings should pay attention to our words. Before we speak, we should grasp the words in their depth and weigh them by asking: Are they lawful—or do we want to show off? Do we want to draw from the wellspring of life, from the eternal law, from our spiritual heritage—or do we want to attain something for ourselves with this?

Something to note down: Let us awaken each word in us to life—only then, will we experience what words mean and what they bring us. We awaken the word to life in us, when we examine it: Is it all-too-human—or is it selfless, divine? Words, be they divine or not divine, crystallize into energy forms; they turn into pictures. In the pictures, what we have placed into the words takes on form—our feelings, sensations and thoughts. Thus, our words take on form; they come alive. They remain in our aura and radiate. They attract what vibrates in our aura: the thought-forms, that is, thought-pictures, that are also active in our aura.

For this reason, we should strive daily to awaken our words to life, so that we experience what words mean and what words bring us.

Something more to note down: We should accept and receive what we hear or see only after we have placed it in the truth, in the eternal law. However, this will be possible for us only once we know the eternal law, our divine heritage.

Christ gave us the eternal law. He gave us the preview of our true life, so that we know our goal. He also gave and gives us the signposts that lead to it.

Gabriele:

As long as we are occupied with our humanness, we speak ourselves. We cannot speak or talk about anything other than ourselves because our words, our terms, all our thoughts, desires and ideas are in our brain as programs and in the repository system of the stars. We are in constant communication with what we have input. It is our human self.

What we have input is our repertory. This is available to us when we talk to each other. This is what we talk about. This is what we are, and beyond this, nothing is possible. This is the limitedness of our human ego.

We thus speak only of ourselves. When we talk with our neighbor and if we both live in the causal law, in the law of sowing and reaping, then each one speaks only himself. This is why there are the many confusions, the many misunderstandings because no one is able to be responsive to the other. Both understand only the surface of their words. They cannot look through them to grasp the content because they have not yet found their way to the divine law, to the perfect consciousness, that knows about all things, that sees through everything, that grasps everything, that knows every answer and solution.

We speak ourselves and speak past each other because we don't understand one another. We hear so often: "You don't understand me." Our neighbor cannot understand us because he, too, speaks only himself. And likewise, we speak ourselves, and at that, according to what we have entered in our soul, in our brain and in the causal computer, as well. Day by day, we reel off our human programs. This continues until we clear up these human aspects and attain the perfect consciousness that knows about all things, that sees through all things, that is in all things.

Our world of thoughts that greatly moves us today is also our yesterday. If we don't clear it up today, then it is also our tomorrow.

We are on Earth to become divine again. For us, this means that we should recognize our humanness each day and clear it up with Christ.

When we look at what we were thinking today alone, then we can ask ourselves: Were these also our thoughts yesterday, the day before yesterday? Were they the thoughts and desires that we have harbored already for weeks, months or even years ago? With an honest answer to our question, we tell ourselves what we have entered in the repository system of the law of cause and effect.

What is registered comes back to us. We are in communication with these programs because we have the same programs in our brain—that is, in our conscious mind—in our subconscious, in our soul and in the repository stars of the causal sphere. This is our human heritage, our personal ego-world. This is what we live in, what we communicate with, what moves us, what burdens and controls us.

Once we have grasped some of what is in the memory bank of our humanness, we should not move it in ourselves for very long or push it away from us. We should clear it up right away with Christ because at the moment of recognition, the strength to overcome the negative is given.

Once we no longer commit the fault, the base humanness, then it is transformed. The negative energy, the sinfulness, became positive energy through the transforming power of the Christ of God and is erased in the repository system of the causal computer.

We are again and again in communication with our base self via the inputs we have entered in the computer system. We cannot even see, hear, smell and taste anything at all, other than ourselves.

Let us return to the eternal law, God, and bring to mind the high principle: Every spirit being is the law of God, speaks the law of God, moves in the law of God, and has its existence in the law of God. The principle reversed by the adversary is the causal law. In this law, each one speaks himself—his base self. He senses himself, thinks himself, smells himself, tastes himself, namely, everything that he has entered in the computer system of the stars. This is then the person-law, which is anchored in the causal computer and controls everyone who lives in this reversed principle.

Thus, we see that the darkness has turned the high principle around and transformed it down to the world of humanness. Just as in heaven, in the highest, every being is the true self, the eternal law, and speaks the eternal law because it, itself, lives as a being in the stream of Being—so does this also take place in the lowest, only reversed: Every person speaks himself, thinks himself, hears himself, until the soul has immersed again as a drop, as the true self, in the ocean, God, the Being.

Gabriele:

Dear fellow people, we cannot understand each other in depth because each one has created his personal existence, his person-law. Therefore, each one thinks differently, speaks differently, feels and senses differently. Our person-law, we can also say our individual law, is hardly related to the individual law of another. As a result, each one speaks only himself and both speak past each other.

We often say: "We understand each other." Did we really understand each other, or did we merely hear our words? Or do we think we understood our neighbor because we like him or because he flatters us? And that is why we say: "We understand each other." All this is thinking in personal terms within the individual law.

All pure beings understand each other. The spiritual body is the substance of the eternal law. It is the divine heritage of every pure being.

We are on Earth to become divine again, to find our way out of this confinement, out of this limitation of our human ego, of our mine and me, so that our consciousness may expand and break through the limits of the human ego and enter the divine unity and freedom, our spiritual heritage.

The spiritually alert soul has many opportunities to lead its human shell to where the person is able to perceive some of the aspects of that life, for which the awakened soul longs.

Gabriele:

»*The true and the all-permeating takes place only in the innermost part of your temple, in the holy of holies— with the All-Holy One and through the All-Holy One, God.*« What does this want to tell us?

Each one of us is the temple of the Holy Spirit. By actualizing the Ten Commandments and the Sermon on the Mount, we enter the holy of holies, which is in us. The more often we enter the holy of holies, the more intimate is our communication with the Spirit of God in us. In this way, we free ourselves from our person-law, from our individual thinking, which, in the end, is focused solely on ourselves, on our base ego. Then we draw more and more from the wellspring of life, which is our spiritual heritage.

Through the unfoldment of our spiritual heritage, our spiritual eyes also open, the eyes of our soul, which then penetrate matter and the words of our neighbor. For the person whose soul moves in the light of God, words are mirrors. All of matter is mere reflection, not fact. It is only the result of our deeds, of our projections, of our conceptions.

The one who sees through the mirror, the projections, grasps his neighbor in his inner being and, at the same time, knows what he can give him as gifts of love. The wise one who draws from the source of life knows the amount. He knows how much he can say. He also knows what he has to say because he sees through the things, the thoughts, the words, everything that exists—and sees through the person because everything is merely reflection.

The mirrors deceive! Our physical eyes see merely the reflection and deceive our senses. Deception classifies and makes judgments. The clarity of the soul, the eyes of the Being, behold what is real because the person whose soul has become a clear wellspring does not classify and make judgments—he is understanding and of good will.

Gabriele:

»If you have become the Being, then all things and
everyone are in you.« For us, this means that our soul
has again attained a high degree of nobility and fineness.
The noble, the fine, is the pure. The noble and fine is the
beautiful. The nobility of the soul sees through everything
because the soul is again in communication with God.

Therefore, we are all on the path to again become what
we, in truth, are. No one of us can avoid again becoming
as God beholds us.

Once this has been achieved, then we are the Being,
and the Being is unity. Then the stars are no longer distant

from us because God is near us. Then the substance of the nature kingdoms, the life, is no longer distant because God is near us. Then we are conscious heirs of infinity and conscious images of our Father. God is the wellspring, and we are the well, from which we draw and give.

The one who lives in this noble, fine and pure consciousness will not wantonly destroy any external form of life because he then disturbs this part of life in himself, thus becoming the disturbed one who destroys everything that he believes does not serve him. Through this externalization, war, murder and discord emerged.

Recognize: This means that what you kill wantonly—people, animals and plants—is what you shadow in yourself. You disturb your own life and remain the disturbed one, the ego-person who affects his environment in a destructive manner.

Gabriele:

Let us look into our world. There are very many who find really a lot disturbing. This means that we are disturbed by our inputs in the causal computer system because we are no longer the Being, but the mine and me.

Our disturbed state of being also destroys because we no longer have communication with the substance in all forms, since we think only of ourselves—always only: "Me, me, me! I am my own neighbor." This is where the disturbance is. Because of this, we are also destroying our world and thus affecting our planet Earth, the Mother Earth.

Only within yourself do you behold the Being in all things. For this reason, you do not need to look around. You have the circumspection in yourself.

Gabriele:

To look around and to have circumspection also means foresight and insight into things.

Gabriele, the teaching prophetess
and emissary of God, explained about this:

We learn more and more to understand and grasp the selfless, impersonal love.

The impersonal is the All-law. It is the wellspring and the strength, it is the stream—we also call it the ocean—in which all beings have their existence, out of which all beings draw, and from which all beings live. It is the ocean of impersonal love.

The pure beings do not need to be personal. They have everything because they all live in one and the same stream. To them, it is natural and a matter of course to be impersonal because they do not want anything. They possess everything because they are heirs to all Being. The light-poor soul wants because it no longer lives its heritage, and therefore, the person wants everything for himself because his human ego is no longer the divine I Am.

The law of sowing and reaping came about through self-love, through the person-oriented love. This implies that the one is closer to me than the other. The one who is closer to me receives more—the other receives less. This is the person-oriented love, the self-love, the selfish love.

What is in heaven is on Earth in modified form. For this reason, the Earth, the material universe and the planes of purification are merely the mirrors of the eternal Being. The law of sowing and reaping is to be regarded as a mirror image.

Heaven is the Being, the pure, the law that radiates throughout everything, God. The law of sowing and reaping is the »being« of the human being, which consists of the mine and me that came and comes out of the base ego.

The pure is the Being, the Self, the I Am, the impersonal life, the law, God. The pure beings are the pure, the Self, the Being, the impersonal, the I Am, the law, God. Their feeling, their word and their action is the law, God, the Self, the Being, the impersonal, the pure. They, the law— since their ether-body is law—feel and speak themselves, the pure, the Being, the Self, the impersonal, the law, God.

The law of sowing and reaping can, in general terms, be called the law of burdens. It consists of the many components of the human ego, which have become the egoity-law of the individual. The egoity-law of each indivi-

dual consists of his negative feelings, thoughts, words and deeds. The egoity-law can also be called the person-law because it relates to the person who emits his ego and receives again the same sending potential.

The one who has created his person-law lives in it, and, through his soul, he calls it up from where it is stored, in the stars. Your neighbor cannot adopt your egoity-law, unless he creates the same or like things through the same or like negative feelings, thoughts, words and deeds.

Gabriele:

If we still move in the egoity-law, in the person-law, then this is not worth being called life. However, in the recognition of our human aspects lies the chance to overcome them and discard them, and again reveal the impersonal life, step by step.

Every single one of us is on Earth to become divine again. The divinity of our nature is the Absolute Law, the life in the eternal Being. We should strive for this life. Through the teachings of the Absolute Law, we may learn about the goal, the goal of our journey: our life, our eternal being, our high consciousness—the All-Being in God, the impersonal.

he pure beings move in the eternal law. They speak the law and are themselves the eternal law.

Every burdened person moves in his egoity-law, in his small world that he created with his ego, the mine and me. He speaks his small world, with which he built his egoity-law. According to this law, he senses himself, thinks himself, speaks himself and acts as he feels, thinks and speaks. Thus, he feels, thinks, speaks and acts according to his base self, his base being.

The human self, that is, the base ego, has no eye, no ear, and no sense for its neighbor, only for itself.

The human self finds no entry into the divine Self, into the holy of holies, and thus, cannot sense, recognize, see through, and experience its neighbor because selflessness is not yet developed in the externalized person.

The human self, the base ego, has nothing in common with the divine Self, with the All-permeating I Am.

The pure one speaks the pure, the eternal law, God. The impure one speaks his impurity, his egoity-law, the base self.

Therefore, each one speaks himself: the pure one, the absolute Self, the I Am—the impure one, his base self, his base ego that is oriented only to the person.

Gabriele, the teaching prophetess
and emissary of God, explained about this:

How poor a world, which resembles the poor, that is, light-poor souls, the light-poor human beings!

If humankind fulfilled the laws of God, then God's heaven would be on Earth!

God said: "I make a new heaven and a new Earth." A new humanity, people in God, is a part of the new heaven and the new Earth. The Inner Path means to discard the clothing of the old Adam and to envelop oneself in the garment of the eternal law.

The one who applies the Absolute Law to himself joins with others to bring heaven to Earth.

e still.
In the inner stillness, you become aware that you are a being from God, which is in God because the All-Eternal Father and you, His child, are one. You, the pure being, live in the holy of holies, in you, the self, for you are the temple of God, and the All-Holy One dwells in you.

Gabriele, the teaching prophetess
and emissary of God, explained about this:

The inner stillness is the eternal law, which, in perfect harmony and symphony, communicates with all life forms, with all beings, and with all people who immerse in this stillness, in the Absolute Law.

A person who wants nothing more than to please God will begin to grow calm very gradually. The urging of the human ego then stops because the one who longs for God, who wants to please God alone, will, day after day, clear up the impure, the human, and thus, become calm. Once a person attains the inner calm, he very gradually immerses in the inner stillness, in the eternal law that unceasingly communicates with the one who has become still.

In our inner being is the sanctuary of God. God dwells in His sanctuary—that is, in us. The innermost being, the sanctuary, is surrounded by our soul and our person.

Consequently, we are the temple of God. In each one of us is the sanctuary, in which God dwells.

When we become aware of this, or even, when we bring this to mind each day and thus resolve for it, then very gradually the longing awakens to please God alone. Then we will also gradually cleanse and sanctify our temple, by no longer allowing anything negative. If there are still negative, that is, sinful, aspects in us, then we will quickly clear them up, so that we please God alone, our Father, and again become His image.

Be still.
In you is the stillness and you are in the stillness.
Once you have become still, then you no longer have human feelings, thoughts, words, stirrings and inclinations; you are imbued by the All-stillness, God.

Gabriele:

»Be still. In you is the stillness and you are in the stillness.« This is the process of becoming aware. The person who becomes aware that the stillness dwells in everyone and that the quiet, pure person lives in the stillness, God, will be born anew. He will be born in the Spirit and apply the laws of life, the laws of the Spirit, more and more.

There is no way to the stillness without becoming aware. Therefore, this means for us to become aware daily, by the hour and by the minute that you are substance and power, a being out of God. Be still and entrust yourself to God at every moment. Then you will also grow into the inner life because you become aware of where your faults lie, of what your faults are and how you can clear up your faults, that is, your sinfulness.

God is the All-stillness—the All-radiation. God is the crystal of infinity, as it were, for the pure heavens are the crystal, and those who betake themselves into the pure, the eternal, are, in turn, the crystal in the stream of life.

God, our Father, is compressed life, compressed Being, the crystal of infinity. Since He gave us everything as substance, power and life, we are, in turn, crystals of infinity, whose facets radiate the eternal life, radiating into all realms because the crystal bears as substance all the powers of creation and all the forms of Being.

Nothing is closed to the crystal. It moves in the rhythm of the All; accordingly, it radiates the facets of the eternal law. In the depths of the soul, each one of us is a crystal in the eternal Being.

Sanctified feelings and thoughts unfold in you; you speak inspiring words and act impersonally for the great whole.

Gabriele:

A person who has largely reached the goal of the path of purification speaks what the crystal radiates to him. He feels as the crystal feels. He thinks as the crystal conveys it to him.

People who daily strive to cultivate these sanctified feelings and thoughts have a sense of responsibility and a sensory awareness. This sense of responsibility has its effect not only on the individual, but a mature person's sense of responsibility is comprehensive. It spreads to all of infinity.

Sensory awareness is clarity. Wherever the matured person looks he beholds the light. He also beholds the shadows and knows how he can help and give. What he hears, he hears in his innermost being. He hears the voice of the All and perceives the murmuring of the human ego. The senses that are purified are in God, and are like the finest antennae that are able to feel into all things—into the pure Being, as well as into the human ego. From his sensory awareness and his sense of responsibility, the matured person can communicate lawfully with his neighbor. He beholds the depths in his neighbor. He sounds them out and looks at, and into, the shadows. He is the spiritual investigator who recognizes all things.

The true Self, the all-encompassing, mighty I Am, communicates with you, and you are the radiance of beauty. You are the pure, the noble and fine, the sublime—because you dwell in yourself, in the eternal Self, in the Being, and because you are what heaven is: beauty, purity, the noble, the fine, the sublime, the kindness, the selfless love.

Gabriele:

Our pure spiritual body consists of all that was conveyed to us through the teachings of the Lord, in which the entire Being vibrates. Every one of us will again find his way to the inner beauty, the inner purity, the inner nobility, the fine and sublime, the kindness and the selfless love.

We often find it difficult to apply this high, absolute standard to ourselves. A picture could help us, so that these aspects of the eternal inner life become a more tangible reality for us. In the picture, we can resolve for the highest ideal—and likewise create it in ourselves.

The highest ideal is what we are in the eternal Being: beauty, purity, nobleness, the fineness, sublimity, kindness and selfless love. We resolve for this, but it is not yet what we are. We will create it in ourselves, by resolving for it over and over again.

This highest image is our true being. If we want to attain what it contains, then the Inner Helper and Advisor, Christ, will support us. Each day, He points out to us our weaknesses, our shortcomings, our sinfulness.

To develop the longing for this sublimity of our true nature, we should bring to mind what we are striving for. We consciously orient ourselves to the highest ideal, the Being, by resolving for it. While doing this, we should not give room to any negative thoughts.

If we think negatively, then we should immediately set up a warning sign for ourselves: »Stop! I do not want to move this negative thought anymore.« If we ask Christ for help and support, we will recognize what the negative thoughts—that is, our sinful aspects—want to tell us. Perhaps they want to tell us that we should clear up several things, that we should ask our neighbor for forgiveness. If we do this as quickly as possible, and again resolve for our ideal picture, then we have not granted any room to these human thoughts. Through this, no further negative thoughts could take hold in our conscious mind.

The more often we move negative thoughts, the more they intervene in our life and become our life. This means that they become programs in our brain cells, which then burden us again and again, which bestir themselves again and again, and which stimulate us again and again to think the same or similar things. The more often we think the same and similar things, the farther we remove ourselves from our ideal picture, from our true being.

If we give room to the negative, then we fill ourselves with unlawfulness and no longer grasp who we are deep in our soul: the beauty, the immortal, the eternal youth, the heaven, the purity, the eternal law, which unites all beings in God, the inner nobleness, the fine, the sublime, the kindness and the selfless love. Then we feel ourselves far removed from the words "our true being," because in our life we have given more and more room to the negative. We have filled ourselves with negativity—now it fills us up. To wherever we look or listen, we call up only our unlawful aspects. The result of this is that our life becomes ever harder and ever darker.

So that such a thing cannot happen, we should consciously give room to the positive and divine in our thoughts and life. A help for this can be to make ourselves aware of this highest ideal picture, our true being.

Gabriele, the teaching prophetess
and emissary of God, explained about this:

»The sun of love has the language of light.« We heard about the crystal that radiates the law, the Being, from all its facets. The crystal with its facets is the sun of love, for the law of God is love. The one who has become a crystal in God is without shadow because infinity, the true Being, knows no shadows. The one who fulfills the law, the shadowless, eternally flowing, radiating law, is permeated and aglow with what God is: love.

»Your nature is the radiance of the sun, of selfless love.« These words tell us that we are the All that has become form. All the heavenly bodies are in us as essence and form our true being.

»Be still, completely still. Nothing and no one stirs in you.« Let us allow these words to vibrate in our inner being. *»Be still, completely still. Nothing and no one stirs in you.«*

Nothing and no one can do harm to the innermost being. There, in the stillness in us, in the holy of holies, with God, is safety, is security. It is our homeland.

We human beings long for safety, but we will never find it in this world. If we think that now we've found secureness, we can be sure that it will soon disappear. Where is there security? Who can offer us security? People? Assets? Money, power and prestige? How quickly all this fades away. Then our security has also vanished. Then we stand there, like beggars on the street, as it were, wondering: "Where is the security? Where is the safety? I am homeless."

Safety, security, and a home can be solely with God—nowhere else. We are wayfarers on the way to inner security, to inner safety, to our true homeland. No matter what we do on Earth, no matter where we seek a hold in human aspects—in time, we recognize that there is no hold anywhere—solely in God. Once we become aware of this, then we will more frequently seek out our innermost being, the sanctuary in us, in which God dwells.

Whatever you intend to do and to fulfill—the true Self in you, the Being, feels, thinks, speaks and acts through you.

Gabriele, the teaching prophetess
and emissary of God, explained about this:

»The true Self, the Being, feels, thinks, speaks and acts through you«—it is, again, the crystal in us. It is the Intelligence, God, who knows about all things, who is all things.

The Intelligence, God, dwells in us. We are heirs to this Intelligence. As pure beings, we are divine intelligence, ourselves. Therefore, this all-encompassing and all-permeating Intelligence is in us, also in this form of existence, the human being. However because we have covered up this high consciousness in us, having overlaid it with our sinfulness, having constricted it with our egocentricity, we have developed the intellect, the puny humanness—instead of the divine, which can no longer become sufficiently effective. The intellect is the reversal of divine Intelligence, a substitute.

We see in this world what all has already been done by the intellect. Certainly, we need our life programs—for example, the program of our occupation, our language. We need these programs to live—however, they alone are not suitable for changing or even improving the world.

The intellect intervenes ever more in the event of creation, in the intelligence of God. We experience what comes of this: destruction and downfall. The intellect is limited. It is focused only on the external, the shell; it does not know the core. It always changes only the shell and each of these changes brings more changes. Humankind has to suffer because of this. What does it get from so-called prosperity? It briefly revives—then things go downhill again because the intellect scratches only the shell, the surface, and does not allow for the Intelligence.

The Intelligence of God does things differently than the intellect. The ego of the human being has the wanting. It wants to create itself. It wants to govern—it wants to be God. Thus, the human ego has transformed down a part of the divine I Am and has compressed, hardened, this substance. It is our human ego-law, the shell, which we have to gradually soften, to again find our way to the inner being, to the divine.

Gabriele:

God is omnipresent. God is in everything negative. God is the helping power in every matter that comes toward us. God is in our planning. God is the order in our disorder. God is the power to clear up what we have not cleared up. For us, this means that we may turn to God in all that comes toward us. If we turn to Him with an honest heart, He will help us, for Christ in us is the Inner Helper and Advisor. He is our Redeemer and Liberator.

In every difficulty is the solution. In every problem is the divine, the help, the liberation—but we have to solve it with the help of the Spirit in us. With each difficulty, with each problem, we can go into our inner being, to Christ in us, and ask Him for help—He will help us. But we may never say: "Lord, solve it as I want"—but always: "Your will be done!" He knows the ways. He helps us as it is good for us.

Our ego urges. It wants the quick solution. We could resolve to practice patience, to take back our humanness, so that in difficulties, problems, and in our planning, we ask God, Christ in us, for help. Then we should not entertain the thought of whether there is indeed a solution or not. These thoughts block the inner help. We should live consciously, which means that in every situation we should bring to mind God's help and concentrate on doing our work.

The alertness of our existence causes us to receive the solution from our inner being. Suddenly, sensations, thoughts rise up, which show us the solution to our problem or difficulty. Sometimes it is merely subtle impulses. Often, it is not the immediate solution itself, but merely the way to the solution or the first step toward it. If we entrust ourselves to Christ, He will also lead us further. The beginnings tell us: "Have trust. I will guide you further, so that you are able to solve everything."

Then we should not carry out the negativity that we have recognized in ourselves. In it is the picture of what we will do instead in the future. To then actualize this in the deed is the next step toward a lawful life.

Gabriele:

Let us realize that in every question is, at the same time, the lawful answer. The question is energy and in each human energy is the divine energy, the Helper that is always present. If we develop the Intelligence, our spiritual, divine heritage, by putting order in our life, by recognizing the will of God and fulfilling it more and more, then we grow into selflessness, into God's love and into His wisdom.

Wisdom is the Intelligence of God, His deed.

*Once you are in your innermost being, then your temple
is pure and you are in communication with the pure.*
You hear what others do not hear;
you behold what others do not see;
you know what others do not know;
you recognize what others do not recognize;
you sense what others do not sense;
you smell and taste what others do
not smell and taste;
you perceive what others do not perceive—
because you are the truth,
the stillness of the temple,
the selfless love,
the law, God.

Gabriele:

If our divine consciousness has opened to the extent
that it can feel and sense into all things, then the soul is
largely filled with light and the divine is active in us. Our
consciousness expands through the actualization of the
eternal laws. It radiates into infinity and into the realms
of the eternal Being.

No sphere in heaven is foreign to the divine consciousness. If we have opened it again, then it radiates and illuminates all spheres of the All because the All has become

active in the soul. The person has then returned home. He has found his way to God, the origin. The soul is pure once more and has become the crystal of life.

Therefore, we must again become what we already are in our innermost being: purest substance, noble and fine, the divine law, the selfless love. Bit by bit, each one of us must divest himself of his garments, that is, discard his human aspects, transform the garments—to then stand there in the garment of eternal life, of selfless love. Therefore, we are on Earth to become divine again.

Recognize:

Every issue, every matter, every difficulty, every problem, every situation, every conversation, indeed, every word, speaks itself.

The Being in the issue, in the matter, in the problem, in the difficulty, in every situation, in every deed and in every thought, speaks, in turn, the mighty Self, the Being.

Gabriele:

Every problem, every difficulty, has three aspects; let us call these three aspects the three tongues. They are the conscious mind, the subconscious and the spirit consciousness. The conscious mind is what we grasp with our reason at the moment. In the subconscious is what we have an inkling of, what still lies in us as human weaknesses, faults, and what has not yet been cleared up and forgiven, which could thus be the cause of the difficulty or the problem. The third tongue is the tongue of truth: It is the eternal law in all things. It is the solution that lies in every difficulty, in every problem. If we accept the lawful solution and clear up our wrongdoing with Christ, then it is also solved in our soul, that is, dissolved.

Thus, every difficulty and every problem speaks to us. With which tongue? We have to find that out for ourselves. We experience it in our thoughts. When a problem appears, then we ask ourselves: What are we thinking? What does it want to tell us? But if we pick the problem to pieces and blame our neighbor, then we have neither grasped nor solved the problem. We speak with the tongue of the conscious mind or the subconscious, and do not let the tongue of truth speak, which is the solution in all things, the Spirit of God, through which everything is solved in the soul.

This is why we should briefly examine everything that comes our way, every unpleasantness: What does the matter, the problem, the difficulty want to tell us? If we ask Christ—who is in all things—for help and support, then in time, we will sense ever more often and more clearly what the lawful solution is.

Ask and it will be given to you. Seek and you will find. Knock and it will be opened to you. In every situation, in all that comes to us, we may call on Christ. If we affirm Christ, the Being, in all things, then Christ, the Being, the eternal law, will support and help us, so that we can lawfully solve the problem, the matter, the difficulty, every situation.

We should make it our task to address ourselves again and again: "You, the person, take yourself back! The solution in everything is Christ." If we become aware of this, then in time we will feel His closeness, and we will also think about each word, and place what we want to say in the law—again, with the request: Christ, help and support us! Only in this way, will we gain access to the inner kingdom, to our divine heritage!

So even in this troubled time, in which the world has a destructive and demoralizing effect on humankind and on nature, we will find Christ. We need Him. Without Him, nothing will function in the future because the "for or against," the "either—or," the decision for or against Christ, is inevitable. Each day we are faced with the decision "either—or," "for or against, Christ."

The shell, the human, speaks itself. The power in the shell, the Being, also speaks itself; it is the I Am.

The one who has become the Being, the selfless Self, is in communication with the pure. He beholds with the eyes of truth. He clarifies, makes order, clears up, plans and speaks from the eternal Being, the selfless Self.

Gabriele:

We have already heard quite often that every one speaks himself. The pure beings speak the eternal law. The impure beings, the human beings, speak their impurities, their person-law, that which is impure and stored in their soul, in their brain and in the stars of the law of cause and effect.

The impure one is connected with his impure aspects, that is, he is in communication with his causes. The pure one is in communication with the eternal law. The impure one is without peace; he constantly seeks approval of his base self. The pure one is peaceful; he does not seek—he is in constant communication with his true self, the divine in him.

We are on Earth to become pure. Particularly in the present time, this is a concern of many. Many sense that this world no longer provides a hold for them, that they can no longer persist in this world. Many comprehend that only One can help. It is Christ, our Redeemer. He helps. He draws ever closer to us.

Let us put this to the test day after day. Let us call on Him, Christ, in every situation, and ask Him to help and support us. Christ is always with us. When we leave our house or apartment—Christ goes with us. No matter what we do, we affirm that He is with us, that He helps and supports us. Let us affirm this repeatedly.

Once we feel and sense into our inner being, by saying yes to Christ—who is the light of our soul and the law of infinity—then our days will become more light-filled and we will become freer day by day. We feel the courage and strength to clear up the human aspects that the day points out to us because we call on Christ, since we ask Him for support and help in every situation. Through this deep communication with the Highest in us, we become more certain and more joyful. Joyfully and thankfully, we will then clear up the human aspects. In this way, we mature into our spiritual heritage more and more, into the life that brings us security, peace, joy, selfless love and thankfulness.

The base ego does not know the I Am; but the I Am knows the base ego because the I Am, the Being, permeates all things.

The pure one, who keeps the order of the temple, will endeavor to clarify every situation from the perspective of the law, to carry on every conversation in a lawful way, to solve every issue, every matter, every problem and every difficulty from the perspective of the law, God.

Gabriele:

This could be a task for us.

Let us become the pure one who keeps the order of the temple, who examines his thoughts more each day! As we have read, thoughts and words create forms, they bring about effects. And the thought, which we think—perhaps imprudently and carelessly—is a sending potential, an action, as it were. The reaction is much bigger because the potential of the feelings and sensations inherent in our thought is part of it, as well.

If we consistently turn to Christ in every situation, that is, if we count on Him and use every moment for clearing up and turning back and changing our ways, then already within a few days we will sense how the stream of positive power embraces us and carries us upward and forward.

431

By consistently turning to Christ, we experience inner tranquility and stillness and from this, experience self-possession. Through this, we take a step back from our human ego and see it from a higher position. The effect is that we are able to resolve it more quickly and easily.

If the human ego wants to resolve the issue, the matter, the difficulty, the problem, the situation or the conversation with its base ego, then it either remain unresolved or it lead to chaos.

Gabriele:

When we look into this world, we recognize what the intellect has accomplished. The intellectual person wants to solve everything himself. The result is worldwide chaos.

Therefore, let us turn back! If we dissolve our personal chaos with Christ, then very gradually we find our way to the I Am, to our divine heritage.

Gabriele:

Let us realize that God, our eternal Father in Christ, speaks to us unceasingly. Every movement of our body, every word, every thought could not exist if it were not for the power of God.

Let us wake up! Let us live more consciously, and we experience the nearness of God, the eternally speaking God, for the divine law is eternally flowing, eternally giving, and reveals itself eternally.

Everything is consciousness. The pure is consciousness, and the impure is consciousness. The pure speaks in the holy of holies—in you, to you and, at the same time, out of you.

The impure speaks the impure. It speaks the burden; it speaks out of the disorder. It speaks the disorder, and thus, there can be, in turn, only disorder in the world.

Gabriele:

Though we have disorder in the world—in our innermost being, in our heart, there is order. Therefore, let us immerse in the holy order, which is in us, and we will create order around us—in our families, in relationships and marriages, at work, everywhere. Let us create order, by no longer feuding with each other, by repenting and forgiving and understanding each other. Then there will be peace. The Inner Path, which leads to eternal life, to peace, goes from without to within.

The more we find our way into our inner being, into the kingdom of the eternal Being, which is in us, we sense the Being, the heavens. Heaven, our homeland, cannot be described in words. If we were to imagine that the paths are made of gold, that all buildings are the finest porcelain or purest gemstones and everything radiates mightier than all suns and stars together—then all that would be merely a reflection of our homeland. That is the splendor of our Father and that is the splendor of our eternal homeland.

Therefore, it is worth it to open up our inner homeland, so that after the death of our body we can again be there, in the eternal light. This is the goal for all of us. This is the path for all of us. Christ helps and supports us. Often the Lord says: "You are children of the fullness." Or: "You are children of a king." These are words—but we human beings can hardly comprehend what they signify in their depth.

Nevertheless, let us allow this to have its effect on us, for if it is touched by the light of our eternal homeland, it will light up in our soul.

Your eyes are the light of the soul.

You see only yourself. You hear only yourself.

With your feelings, sensations, thoughts, words and deeds, you draw the picture of your soul.

The picture of your soul is your consciousness.

Every state of consciousness perceives what corresponds to its state. This is what goes into it. This is what it is. This is what it radiates and this is what it passes on at the same time.

Gabriele:

»Your eyes are the light of the soul.« Light or shadow look through us. Our soul looks through our eyes. In this way, it perceives the physical world into which it was born. Soul and person see their surroundings according to light or shadow. The person reacts accordingly.

We see, hear and register what our senses signal to us. Our reactions are in accordance with our perception. According to the light or shadow of our soul, we react either lawfully or unlawfully. There is nothing between the "either—or"!

We see and hear according to the character of our soul. We see ourselves and hear ourselves only as long as our soul is shadowed, as long as it looks through our eyes, hears through our ears and acts through our other senses with the limitation of our human ego.

Everything is consciousness. We perceive our environment based on the momentary condition of our soul, which tends either toward light or toward shadow. This is how we see our environment and how we react.

We express what we see and what we hear. Is our expression reality or illusion? If the light of the soul looks through our eyes, then we speak the truth, the law. When the shadows of our soul, our correspondences, look through our eyes, then we see only what corresponds to our human ego. Beyond that, there is nothing for us. We live either in reality, the Being, or in unreality, in deceptive illusion.

Therefore, what we are, reality or illusion, is what we emit. What goes out from us comes back into us. We cannot comprehend more than that! It is the state of our consciousness. Beyond this, we perceive nothing. Therefore, for us, this means to develop and unfold ourselves on the path of spiritual evolution.

We are placed in the day so that we clear up the human aspects we have recognized, day after day. As we dissolve our sinfulness, our consciousness expands. We see more and perceive more deeply. We hear more and listen more deeply into the reasons for the materialistic. Through this, we also grasp the deeper correlations of light and shadow. Through the transformation of our shadows into light, we gradually find our way to the origin of our life, to God, to our existence as a being in God, to our divine heritage.

Can your neighbor see the same picture that you have drawn with your world of feelings and thoughts, with your words and actions?

Even what you describe is seen differently by each one—all according to their pictorial awareness.

Every person also sees his surroundings differently, again, entirely according to the pictures of his consciousness, which he has predetermined himself.

The sounds, too, which come up in your pictorial life, are also heard differently by each one.

Gabriele:

We can experience that this is so. Let us try it out—at home, in our families, in our living communities, in our circle of friends:

Let us take a picture. Each one looks at one and the same picture. The individual writes down what he perceives in the picture, including his feelings and sensations. We will see that each one sees something different. Each one will also have different sensations and feelings.

After a vacation together, we can also see that each one has felt the vacation days differently and has seen the landscape in a different way. We could test this and see that it is so. We note down: What did each one perceive? What did he see? What did he hear? What did he feel and think? With this test, we recognize that each one noticed something different. Something different moved each one. Why is this so? Because no one has the same state of consciousness as his neighbor. We perceive our environment according to our state of consciousness, according to the light and shadow of our soul.

Noises, as well, let aspects of a person's world of thoughts, which consists of colors, forms and tones, be discerned. Let us do another exercise: Everybody listens to the same melody. What does each one feel? What does each one think? How does he react? Each one perceives different resonances, which, in turn, trigger different feelings, sensations and thoughts, according to the individual's state of consciousness.

If you call your neighbor's attention to certain sounds or colors or forms, then despite your description, he will perceive the sound differently than you, and he will also see the colors and forms differently than you.

Gabriele:

When we hear these principles of the law, we should ask ourselves: What is our life on Earth? Is it the eternal life, the truth, or is it an illusion?

With our words, we have created terms for ourselves. For example, the color red is simply red to us because everyone has affirmed this term. Is what we describe as "the color red," the tenor of consciousness, really red, or have we merely given this color a name?

What is this color called in other cultures? When someone coins this term, then others copy it. And so, our human terms are an agreement according to the appearance. One says "red." Others adopt this term and think it is reality. But according to the laws of God, this doesn't have to be so.

The same holds true of forms. We have our terms for this, which we affirm, and based on this affirmation, we think it is so. But according to the law of God, this doesn't have to be so.

We human beings coin a term for a certain tenor of consciousness because we presently conceive of it this way and not differently. We call it this because we see it this way and we see it this way because we—our soul, our person—are conditioned this way.

We thus realize that our world is relative and not absolute. We live in a world of terms, in a world of illusions, in the world of our programs.

What we have programmed into ourselves is what we comprehend, what we understand. We set up our pseudo-reality for ourselves with terms.

For instance, we say that we are sick. For us, illness is a term. According to the law of God, illness is merely the outflow of disharmony. However, the word, the term "illness," connects us with all other terms that were programmed into our brain in connection with the term "illness." In this way, we reinforce what we call "our illness." We bind ourselves to this term, to this program.

Thus, when the outflow of the disharmony takes place, we call this disharmony "illness." We imprint it with the stamp "illness." We affirm this imprinting, thus expanding on it and manifesting it in our body. Then we speak of "our illness." In reality, it would be an outflow of our disharmony, a movement, in which the positive power is already active in order to have a healing effect. With our term "illness," we bind the outflowing disharmony in our body.

In the eternal law of God, there is no illness because there are no terms, no illusion, but solely the truth, which is reality. The Spirit of God is truth and not illusion. All pure beings are in the truth and understand each other because they live the one law—the Absolute Law, the law of God.

We people live our person-law, what is personal to us, which for us means our personhood. But we have to gradually raise ourselves above our personhood, above our ego-law, to find the truth. According to human terms, we are the person, but according to the law of God, our eternal being is manifested law.

As long as we live in our person-law, we speak past one another. Each one may speak his mother tongue, but in reality, each one speaks his own language because each one places into his word a completely different way of seeing things, a completely different tenor of consciousness. This is why each one speaks his own language, despite having the same mother tongue. Therefore, what we place into our word corresponds to our state of consciousness.

We now understand what human limitation means. It is the constriction of our human self, of our personal thinking, feeling and wanting. As long as we relate to our patterns of thinking, that is, to our terms, to our human aspects and programs, we live in limitation—and limitation is illusion.

Therefore, we have to get out of the confines of the human ego, out of the limitation, out of deception and illusion! We have to look more deeply. We have to listen into the words. We have to see through the external, in order to experience in its depths, the eternal Being, the positive, the divine. Only then, will our life become interesting. Only then, will we sense what limitation means, and what it means to live without bounds.

The unlimited consciousness, the divine, is in each one of us. The unlimited in us knows about all things, sees through all things and hears what is lawful in everything.

That is our life in the eternal Being. Our path leads us there. Each day we have to make the decision: light or darkness. The path into the light is the path of expanding our consciousness.

Gabriele:

If we believe the statement of the Lord, then the question is posed to us: Who is right? Many say: "I am right." But each one sees and each one hears something different. The one perceives more sounds, the other, in turn, sees other colors. And so, who is right?

Can we prove that we hear more sounds than our neighbor? Can we prove that the color red is really red, and that the other color is yellow? Can we prove it? We can prove it based on our terms because we have the term "red" in our awareness. Whether it really corresponds to the color vibration as it is in the eternal law is an open question.

We thus recognize that all terms are relative, and the relativity of the term is never the truth.

*Can a person really prove that he was stolen from—or
was only that taken from him, which he had stolen from
his neighbor in a former existence?*

*Both, the one who was stolen from and the one who
stole, violated the law of God, for neither one should take
something from his neighbor and call it his own.*

*You say that you can prove that your neighbor lied. Did
your neighbor really lie—or did he merely say what you
move in your world of feelings and thoughts and what, in
the last analysis, you are, yourself?*

*Recognize that everything has two sides—unless you
are divine. Then you are the truth and live All-consciously.*

*Then you will not get upset, either, but will speak the
truth. You will clarify everything and leave it at that.*

Gabriele:

We often see only the momentary situation and say:
"Of course, I am missing my wallet, and my neighbor has
it. This means he stole it from me." The one who knows
the causal law will not be satisfied with this external point
of view.

When someone steals from us, then that is the harvest,
behind which is a seed, a cause. When we apply the spir-

itual law—"what the person sows is what he will reap"—to ourselves, then, when our feelings surge, we recognize what cause may lie behind the harvest because the surge of our emotions is brought about through feelings, sensations and thoughts. These are aspects of a former seed. Now it depends on us. Do we want to look at ourselves and repent and clear up the aspects of our seed, or do we just disregard them? Then we continue to sow.

These occurrences are small things in the law of cause and effect. Just as it functions on a small scale, so it is also on a large scale. Collective guilt is also a part of the law of cause and effect, for instance, when a million people are part of an event. Each one has his share in this collective guilt.

The one who, as a human being, ignores the impulses of grace from God, the admonishments and warnings because he has completely turned to the world and its temptations, has to bear that part of his guilt he may have created in a former life. These causes that were created on the Earth are magnetic. They may possibly draw us again to incarnation and to that country where the causes become effective, perhaps in the chaos of war or in natural disasters and so forth.

According to the law of cause and effect, we suffer only what we, ourselves, have caused—nothing beyond that, not one bit more. That is the justice of the law of cause and effect and not of rights.

If we argue, by claiming that the other is guilty, then we strive to push through our supposed rights. In this way, we close ourselves off to self-recognition. The guilt remains and may possibly continue to build up and will hit us as an effect—if we do not come to our senses in time.

Gabriele:

These words from the Christ of God refer to the law of correspondence, an aspect of the causal law. We recognize ourselves in our neighbor when we disparage, accuse or condemn him, or reproach him for mistakes and, at the same time, are annoyed with him.

A person who takes such things as a reason to look for the causes in himself and to clear them up decreases his burdens. He walks and transforms himself in the light of the Christ of God and becomes free.

I give you an exercise for self-recognition:

Each one looks, for example, at the same area of a landscape. Each one sees different aspects in it. What the one sees, that is his picture, and not the picture of his neighbor.

A small animal moves in the landscape picture. Each one registers the animal—and yet, each one sees and senses it differently.

The perception of the individual is part of his picture and not that of his neighbor.

The picture of each individual is the picture of his state of consciousness.

Just as the individual sees and hears, feels, senses and thinks, that is his state of consciousness, with which he registers the picture, sees the colors and forms and hears the sounds.

Who can prove that the little animal looked as he perceived it? Everything is relative since each one sees, hears, smells, tastes and touches from his viewpoint, from his present consciousness-radiation.

Since each person has a different state of consciousness, he perceives the reflections which he calls matter accordingly.

Recognize that the one who heeds the many aspects that lead to freedom brings peace to himself and to his neighbor. For this reason, never influence the consciousness-radiation of your neighbor by thinking that you have to put order in his home, in his room, according to your consciousness.

Remember the following spiritual principle:
Leave to your neighbor his kingdom. That means, do not change his consciousness-radiation. The consciousness-radiation of you and of your neighbor also affects the rooms that you or your neighbor live in. Leave to your neighbor his small kingdom, for this is how he wants to feel at home. If you heed this spiritual principle, then he will be glad when you visit him.

Enter his room only when you are welcome and leave everything in the room the way your neighbor arranged it because that is the perspective of his consciousness.
If you sit on a chair or take an object, put the chair back as it was and put the object back in its place—just as it was before.
Do not change anything, even if you would like it better otherwise, and if you think it would be nicer as you see it. With this, you influence the consciousness-radiation of your neighbor and with your seeming order you bring disorder into his life, into his consciousness-radiation. Just as your neighbor sees it, that is how it is good for him at

present. He does not want it changed by you—unless he asks you to.

The one who heeds this spiritual principle respects his neighbor and himself, too.

Even in the smallest things, the following spiritual principle applies: What you do not want others to do to you, do not do to others, either.

Gabriele, the teaching prophetess
and emissary of God, explained about this:

Everything is radiation. How we furnish our little kingdom, our realm, the arrangement of the objects, corresponds to our consciousness. An object radiates to us according to how we place and arrange it. This is equal to our consciousness-radiation, from which results the communication with the object. For our present state of consciousness, that is the radiation of harmony and peace.

If we like certain objects very much, then we put them in a certain place in our home. When we enter this room, it is possible that our eye falls on this object that is placed so that it please us. It radiates to us and a possibly depressive mood becomes lighter. Friendly and joyful vibrations affect us and embrace us. And so, in our little kingdom, we can build ourselves up again and unfold positive powers.

We thus arrange our little kingdom according to our state of consciousness. We have chosen the colors and forms in our room according to our consciousness-radiation. This is how they radiate to us and please us. Our neighbor, in turn, furnishes his room, his little kingdom, differently. He decides for other colors and forms than we do, all according to his consciousness-radiation.

When we now rearrange the order in our neighbor's room, we bring in our consciousness-radiation which, however, is not in accord with his consciousness. Thus, we interfere in our neighbor's sphere with our human ideas. This results in disharmony.

When we speak of our little kingdom, which should be harmoniously and beautifully furnished according to our consciousness, this has nothing to do with external wealth, with splendor and magnificence, with prestige and the like. Each of us has a home, and in our home, a room or at least a corner that belongs to him, which has his vibration, and which conveys to him the feeling of being at home there. This place, whether large or small, is what we call "our little kingdom."

According to the law of God, every one of us should dwell and live as it corresponds to his consciousness. Everything that opposes this state of consciousness also opposes the peace. And everything that is far beyond this, for instance, great wealth, splendor and the like, is unlawful. Through this, we cannot become children of God, but instead, want to be gods.

We should also respect the inner sphere of life, the inner temple of our neighbor. For us, this means to be silent and alert. Take your neighbor into yourself, and then you will know when you can address him and what you can say to him because then, in your consciousness, you grasp where he is at that moment.

Many people have the habit of thoughtlessly and abruptly addressing their neighbor when they meet him. They say everything that is on their mind without asking whether their neighbor wants to hear it. Do we know where our neighbor is with his awareness at that moment? It could be that he is in an inner prayer, in a deep dialogue with God, in his inner temple. When we suddenly address him, then we disturb him and push him out of his inner being.

The alert person who really wants to visit his neighbor in his inner being will first consciously accept his neighbor and receive him. He feels him in his inner being, and weighs the situation: Can I now say something to him? He then knows when and how he can address his neighbor and what he can say to him.

ever be curious. Do not look behind, to the right and to the left out of curiosity, to see and to hear. You are responsible for what you see and hear.

What you saw and heard stimulates you to think—and you are responsible for every thought. What you saw and heard stimulates you to speak and to act—and for this, too, you are responsible.

The pure one will not look around curiously. He will not produce thoughts. He will not look for words or think about how, what and when he should act and work. The pure one has everything in himself, and is in all things because he is the truth, which, in turn, is in all things.

If you behold your neighbor, then you behold the All, and you behold the eternal Father in you and you behold your neighbor in you. You are the image of the eternal, sole holy Father because you are divine in Him, His created children, whom He beholds in Himself, through Himself and in the All.

If you have beheld your neighbor in you, then you have beheld your eternal Father, for the Eternal and His pure child are one.

Since you know and behold your neighbor as a part of you in you, you also know the eternal One, the Holy One because you are His image, the eternal law—which you know because it is what you are, since you are divine.

Gabriele, the teaching prophetess
and emissary of God, explained about this:

Through curiosity, we distract ourselves from the energy of our day, from what the day wants to tell us. Then we do not live in the present and do not pay attention to the impulses that want to call our attention to what is waiting for us to clear up here and today.

Instead, we see and experience things that can call up much in us that we are not ready for, that we cannot yet master and therefore, not overcome, either. We see and hear a lot that we may not be able to come to terms with because it does not belong to the energy of our day. But we think about it. We have ideas, emotions surge. We might value-judge and reject our neighbor. Since every sensation, every feeling, every thought, every word and every deed is energy, we will also burden ourselves with it because to wherever we send, from there we receive.

Our thoughts, which we send to our neighbor, can also set some things into motion in him and awaken or intensify a negative potential at an inopportune moment. It is possible that in this way, a cause reaches its effect too soon in him. A burden in the soul breaks out too soon, so that he is hardly able to deal with it and clear it up. Thus, he may have much to bear with this complex, and conceivably develop more guilt. We are now bound to this person, to this soul, to whom we have emitted thoughts or sensations because of our curiosity. We will have to meet him again someday, to clear up what needs to be cleared up and to make amends for it. For we will reap what we sow.

Curiosity not only prevents a conscious life in the present, but is, already, the result of externalization. If we lack energy in our soul because we are not true to ourselves because we do not use the energy of the day, then curiosity awakens. We are then constantly concerned with finding out and hearing about everything. Why? Because we don't know ourselves. The one who daily finds himself in his thoughts and clears these up on a daily basis, attains spiritual energy, the divine power of light. His consciousness-radiation increases. He can be true to himself because he has found himself and will no longer be eager to eavesdrop or to spy things out, believing that he will miss something, thinking that he has to achieve and experience something.

The peace, the stillness and the fulfillment of our soul cannot be chased after, spied out or eavesdropped. We do not find ourselves in the external world and do not find God in this way, either.

Jesus of Nazareth spoke to His apostles and disciples in the following sense: The Father and I are one. If you have seen Me, you have seen the Father. His words mean the following: If you have fathomed Me in the depths of your soul, then you have perceived My radiation and have recognized and sensed the radiation of the Father. The eternal Father was not personified in Jesus of Nazareth. The Christ in Jesus, however, was the image of the Father, His Son. As pure beings, we are also sons and daughters of God and the image of the eternal Father.

Once we have found ourselves in our neighbor, once we have truly recognized and beheld Him in ourselves, then we have sensed the radiation of the eternal, holy Father because the pure soul is one with the eternal Father. Then we understand the words of Jesus in their depth: The Father and I are one. If you have beheld Me, then you have beheld the Father. You have thus perceived His radiation and sensed Me as a pure being, as the image of the eternal Father.

In His great cosmic teachings, Christ speaks to us:

»If you have beheld your neighbor in you, then you have beheld your eternal Father, for the Eternal and His pure child are one.

Since you know and behold your neighbor as a part of you in you, you also know the eternal One, the Holy One because you are His image, the eternal law—which you know because it is what you are, since you are divine.«

If we know the eternal law, then we also live the eternal law and live in the eternal law. The soul is then divine and united with the One who is eternal: God, our eternal Father. Then we are consciously in Him and with Him, and are eternally united with Him in all eternity, for He, the great All-One, beheld us. He created us and thus, He beholds us in Himself.

This is why we will also find our way back to Him as pure beings because He has never, and will not, let us out of His heart. He beholds us as perfect beings. That is the great All-magnet, which radiates into the astral planes and to us on this Earth. This All-magnet, the love of God, radiates to human beings and souls and attracts us again.

God, our Father, does not release us from His love and care, even though we, the human being, may resist ever so much. He gives us the freedom to live as we want. But at some point, our soul awakens, as well as our person. Then we will feel the great, mighty All-magnet, the unending love that attracts us more and more. Through Christ, our Redeemer, we will then find our way to Him, back to His eternal Father-heart, from where we went forth.

Let us allow this awareness to unfold in us, so that it totally envelops and lifts us up!

The great love-magnet, God, the All-magnet, our Father, emits through all soul realms and to the human beings, to this Earth. This great All-magnet of love calls and guides us through Christ, our Brother and Redeemer. And through Christ, we find our way again to Him, in His heart, in the eternal homeland, where peace and happiness are—the eternal Being.

It is necessary, however, for us to do the following: First, open the Kingdom of God in you and, through the inner kingdom, through the Kingdom of God in you, you will find your way again into the eternal kingdom, into the eternal homeland. The inner kingdom is the law of love in us. Once we have opened it, then we are in God, and are also united in Him and with Him.

he innermost being is the stillness that beholds itself and sees through all things. The stillness is the true life.

Therefore, be still. The stillness is the All-wise word, the law of the All. It reveals itself as the stillness in the stillness. It beholds itself in the stillness as the stillness.

Everything is the law, which is the sublime, unending stillness, which speaks itself, the I Am.

Gabriele, the teaching prophetess
and emissary of God, explained about this:

We find our way to the stillness only by going within. We are on the path to within, to the kingdom of the inner being, if we monitor our words, our actions, our thoughts and sensations, as well as our feelings.

The inner stillness shows itself in the world of our feelings. How often do we believe that we are still—but are we really still? What does it look like in the world of our feelings? Has this sphere of our inner being already become clear? Does it signal the clear stream, the pure Being? Is the omnipotence of God present in our feelings? Or are our feelings still marked by longings, desires, by wanting?

Our feelings lie deeper than our sensations and thoughts; therefore, they are harder to grasp. But if we have walked the path within conscientiously, and if we continue to walk it diligently, then we reach the world of our feelings. We can then also immerse in our feelings with our thoughts and sensations because there, we sense much more clearly what is still in us as human aspects.

In our world of feelings, we are even able to recognize aspects that have not yet risen to our conscious mind, aspects that are still in us as karma, but which are already stirring in our feelings. Although we will not recognize the entire guilt of our soul in our world of feelings, we will be able to raise parts of them into our awareness, clear them up and thus erase them.

The basic tasks of the Inner Path are: Put your thoughts in order! Curb your speech! Master your senses! The five senses of a human being are nothing more than the reversal of the five divine-atomic powers of the eternal Being. Thus, we have reversed and twisted the eternal Being, which consists of the powers of the five kinds of spiritual atoms. We have turned the lawful into its opposite. By reversing the five divine senses of our soul, we have shaped the world of our human senses, which is, for the most part, in accord with our feelings, sensations, thoughts, words and actions.

Once we put order in our thoughts, curb our speech and master our senses, then we take the first step to becoming still in our conscious mind, so that we immerse ever more deeply—toward the inner stillness, into the Absolute Law.

If we turn more and more within, by clearing up our wrongdoings, then calmness draws into the world of our thoughts, sensations and feelings. Our soul breathes the breath of life more and more, which streams to it by way of the unfolding spiritual consciousness. The senses of the soul, the types of spiritual atoms, then increasingly align again with the divine core of being, the source of life in us, so that we attain the inner perception. The loud person is silent. It becomes still in us. We have found the way into our inner self, which is the I Am, the stillness.

The depth of our being, the stillness, the ocean, God, is the eternal law. This stillness is not being silent, but is harmonious, eternal, cosmic All-rhythm, the movement of the eternal Being, the sounds of the spheres of infinity.

If we really want to become still, that is, if we want to immerse in the lawful stillness, in the streaming All-law, which gives and communicates untiringly, then we have to go from without to within, in order to then live in the pure world of our feelings, through which the Absolute Law flows into our conscious mind, into the word and the deed, by way of the purified world of our sensations and thoughts.

The level of our feelings is essential for our spiritual development. If it is covered over or blocked, we no longer have access to the deeper layers of the unconscious, and thus, no longer find what is still in us as human aspects.

Our self-recognition and clearing up remain superficial, so that only a small part of our burdens can be erased. The deeper things are revealed especially in the world of our feelings. There, we are shown where we stand and who we are at the moment. There, we experience either our actualization, the Being, or our non-actualization, our humanness, our wanting to be, to have and to possess.

If our thoughts can be grasped by us more easily than our feelings—we can fool ourselves with our thoughts, and likewise with words and with deeds. Our world of feelings is more realistic. It does not let itself be easily fooled by us. What momentarily marks us, either our true being or our humanness, lies in our feelings.

»Therefore, be still.« These words hold true at all levels of consciousness. First of all, they can say to us: "Be still. Do not worry! Entrust yourself to God, your Father, in every situation."

They can also say to us: "Be still, live in a concentrated and alert way. Grasp what the day wants to tell you, so that you can clear up your humanness, and thus go deeper and deeper, going within to the stream of stillness more and more."

»The stillness is the All-wise word, the law of the All.« The true stillness is the constant communication of the being that became form in the stream of the Being. This is the uninterrupted communication of the spirit beings

with infinity. The law of God »*reveals itself as the stillness in the stillness.*« The stillness is the symphony of the All. It is the word that speaks to us. It is the law that communicates itself untiringly. We experience this only in the depths, in the very basis of our soul.

»*It beholds itself as the stillness in the stillness.*« To behold means to receive images. The pure beings experience all impulses as images in the divine particle structure of their spiritual body. Wherever they move, wherever they go, wherever they are, the impulse that reaches them is absolute. It is thus perfect and shows itself in the perfect image. Thus, the being of the heavens receives all messages as images in the particle structure of its spirit body.

For us human beings, the sending and receiving station for impulses is the brain. What comes into our brain cells is conveyed to our body. Our body is a sounding board. Just as it sounds in us, that is how we vibrate. And just as we vibrate, that is how we show ourselves in our thinking, speaking and acting. This is how our stirrings are, our inclinations, our gestures and our facial expressions.

Gabriele:

For us, this means we have to become the divine again. We have to go inward, to again immerse in the eternal stream, in our true being.

We need not be afraid in this world. The one who proves himself as a child of God, by endeavoring again and again to recognize the laws of God and to actualize them each day, may be sure that he walks at the hand of the Christ of God. Christ calls us and He knows that we are not yet perfect. The daily effort of consistent actualization makes us joyful and happy, and gives us the security in Christ.

»The stillness is the law and the wisdom of God.« The wise one has immersed in the law. He knows about all things because he sees through everything. He lives in the purified world of feelings, and thus, in the soul that is pure for the most part, and he draws untiringly from the source in the innermost part of the soul. This fount of life flows through the soul into the person's world of feelings, rises into his world of sensations, shows itself in thoughts and communicates itself in words.

Therefore, to know what it is like in our inner being, we need only to critically consider our words and what lies in them.

As long as our words are not selfless, our thoughts are not selfless, our sensations are not pure and thus, neither is the world of our feelings. Therefore, cleansing and going from without to within is called for.

We are able to penetrate all things only once we are able to draw from the forces of the eternal Being and live in the largely purified world of our feelings. The inner source, the inner light, radiates and streams throughout all things. The soul of the person who lives in the Being also radiates through all things.

Many will say: "That is still a long way off." But let us be aware of how near God is to us! God is the wisdom. He is the law—and we are divine in His heart. If we try to draw closer to God each day, if we take the steps, then, day by day, we will feel how close Christ is to us, how close God, our Father, is to us. We then recognize that the Absolute Law, our true being, is not so very far away anymore—it is in every thought.

Our turning back and clearing things up allows the positive, the divine, to rise in the negative. For instance, if we are envious and turn back and clear it up and no longer do it, and if we counter the negative with positive powers, the powers of peace, and keep peace with our neighbor, then we have already raised one or several aspects of our true being, of the eternal law, out of the darkness of our humanness and into the light. That is a step toward the actualization on this Earth of the Absolute Law, of the eternal Being.

Thus, we are not far from the sublime Absolute Law. It is not far away; it is very close to us. Each day shows this to us, for the positive, the eternal law, is in our problems and difficulties, in everything that is negative. If we clear up our wrong behavior with Christ and no longer commit what we have recognized as negative, fulfilling instead the principles of the law of inner life, then we experience the nearness of our divine heritage, parts of the eternal Being.

Let us take courage! Each day is a great gift to us. This should give us hope. We should nurture it every day, by affirming the good, the law of God, in everything and by developing it through actualization. Then the days will become more light-filled because we recognize that in the difficulties, in suffering or in joy is the eternal law of love. It is present everywhere. Let us apply it, hopefully and joyfully, and we will draw closer to our true being. The awakened soul longs for this, and we human beings should follow this inner longing, by discarding daily what we have recognized as human.

With this, the following can be a help for becoming aware:

Be still.
Think before you speak.
Monitor your thoughts.
Look into your world of sensations.
What wishful pictures are still present?
What do our feelings tell us?
Are our words in accord with our thoughts? If not, why not?
Are our words in accord with our sensations?
Are our sensations, thoughts and words in accord with our feelings?

If we want to fathom our world of feelings, we have to tell ourselves again and again: Be still! Experience yourself more deeply! Be still and be honest with yourself. Look at yourself in the world of your feelings!

Let us resolve to think again and again about the statement: God is love.

Selfless love does not punish. Selfless love does not chastise. Selfless love helps untiringly. It gives us strength and wants to lead us out of our humanness, out of the chaos of our still existing human thoughts, sensations and feelings.

Let us draw hope in Christ! Let us draw hope in God, our Father! Let us realize again and again: We are not forsaken! Christ is with us. Our true being is not far away. Let us actualize the laws of God and we will experience aspects of our divine heritage.

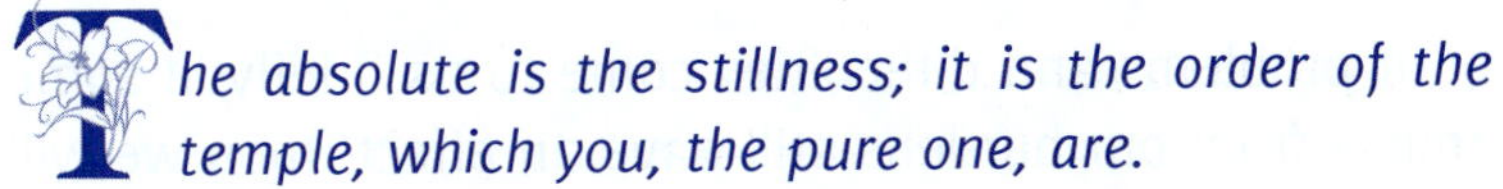

he absolute is the stillness; it is the order of the temple, which you, the pure one, are.

Gabriele, the teaching prophetess
and emissary of God, explained about this:

Let us listen to the breath of stillness! The breath of stillness is the breath of God that streams through our soul and through our body. It is the eternal law of the heavens, our true being, our divine heritage.

The breath of God, the eternal law, is able to stream unhindered through our soul and our body only if we clear away the hindrances, our human ego. Our breath falters again and again until we have purified our soul. Once our inner being has been cleansed for the most part, then our life takes its course more calmly because it flows in the pathways of the inner being and we move in these pathways of the inner being.

As long as our breath falters, our sensations, feelings, thoughts, words and deeds are still impure. Once our feeling, sensing, thinking, speaking and acting is largely in accord with the divine-eternal laws, then the breath of God streams through us. The power of God carries us and the stillness of the divine fills us. Then our breath no longer falters. It goes easily and in a flowing rhythm. We don't get irritated anymore because we are above the human situations, above the problems and difficulties.

If problems and difficulties come to us briefly, if some things from our burdens still have an effect, then we will clear them up as quickly as possible because we have learned to approach everything human with the power of God, with the breath of God, to clear it up and no longer do it. Quickly, we again turn into the temple of the inner being, the stillness, where we are, from which we receive, from which we give. This is living in the awareness of the I Am.

If you know who you are, and if you know that the awareness of the I Am is the life, then you live and will not take offense at anything. Nor will you break through anything because you see right through and penetrate everything that is density, hindrance and offense in the eyes of the world.

Gabriele:

What good does it do when we always take offense, when we constantly value-judge, criticize and are out-raged? With this, we don't change anything for the better. We have to be decisive about how we want to act. If we have decided for our spiritual life, then we will no longer take offense at our neighbor because we can see things more and more impersonally. We will address the things that move in the world, the human aspects. We will enlighten, yet not take offense at them, but continue on our path to the kingdom of the inner being.

The one who takes offense at his neighbor and lets himself be hindered on his path has to ask himself the questions: Have I taken offense at something in myself? Were my correspondences triggered? What is behind this in me?

The spiritual person explains and perhaps offers his help. If this is not accepted, then he continues on his way because every one is free to think and to live as he wants.

Gabriele:

Many are seeking solutions. Often, we say that we have found a solution. Nevertheless, it would be a question to ask if it really is the true solution that gets to the core of the problem? And with our »solution,« is the problem, the difficulty, the disharmony already solved?

Only with Christ, can we find the lawful solutions and then also solve the matter accordingly, that is, clear it up. Knowledge of a worldly, as well as spiritual, nature can make many a thing possible for us. To grasp the essential, however, is possible for us only by way of our daily actualization, when we have figured ourselves out more and more. Then we can see to the bottom of the situations and matters. As long as we look only at the surface of the problem, of the difficulty because the light of our consciousness does not reach any further, we will not go into the depths of the problem to solve it with Christ, with the power of the spiritual consciousness.

The Spirit of truth helps untiringly. It is always there for us, ready to help and to serve us. Christ is the present power.

But we have to learn to be aware. This means that we have to practice concentration, in order to be focused on the day, on the situations that the day brings, so that we can solve what the day points out to us.

The one who is not wise is also not quiet, that is, still because he keeps wanting until he has found himself in the very basis, in the stillness—that which he is, the self, the wisdom and the beauty from God, the all-knowing law, God, the wisdom, which is the same as truth.

Gabriele:

»The one who is not wise is also not quiet, that is, still.« Everything that the outer world reflects addresses the person who is turned without. Unceasingly, via the stimulation of the senses, his world of thoughts, sensations and feelings are kept in motion and stimulated to emit more human aspects, to desire and to want.

The pressing, egocentric and wanting human aspects draw us without again and again, into the world of sensory stimuli, of the intellect and of deception. It makes us restless and brings us more burdens, more causes and more effects, more blows of fate.

For this reason, we walk the path from without to within. We clear up our human aspects and set them aside, so that we become still.

The stillness is God. It is deep in the very basis of our soul. Only out of the stillness of our inner being, will the salvation for our life be born, and not because we want it.

Your neighbor, the one, is just as near to you, the pure one, as the other because no one can be far from you and a stranger to you, since God is in you and you are in God, and your neighbors are in you and you are all in God. That is unity. The one is in the other and both penetrate each other and penetrate everyone—and everyone penetrates both. That is the All and the law of love and unity.

Gabriele:

If our consciousness-radiation penetrates our neighbor and the nature kingdoms, then our neighbor, in turn, is also able to penetrate us and the nature kingdoms also penetrate us because we have become transparent.

We become transparent only by fulfilling the law of life. Otherwise, we remain the density and delimitation.

If we say about one of our neighbors: "I like this one less than the other one," then we will never become transparent. In this statement, we judge and condemn because we reject the one and affirm the other. But before the face of God, all are equal. If we do not strive for equality, we will never find our way into unity with our fellow humans and with the cosmic Being, and will not attain the brother-sister-hood, the brotherhood in Christ.

As long as we consider our neighbor to be a stranger because we don't know him, we are a stranger to ourselves. We don't know ourselves. Only when we have experienced ourselves, will we experience and get to know our brother and our sister in ourselves. Only then, will we draw closer to the unity in God.

If we say: "I like the one, and the other is less important to me," we bind ourselves to people because we hold the one in esteem and reject the other. That is human, and against the divine. In the law of God there is no binding, no being bound. In God it is: All things are in everything and everything radiates through all things. Every single being penetrates all of infinity, and all of infinity penetrates the one being. This is the unity in God, and in this, is freedom. No pure being will say: "I don't know this or that. I know this place" or "He is a stranger to me" or "This sphere of heaven is unfamiliar to me." Everything is in the spirit being. Everything penetrates the divine being and the divine being, in turn, penetrates everything. That is the All-communication with all Being. That is our conscious heritage, the life of the pure being, which we are deep within. This is what we have to strive for.

In the words "have to" lies the meaning that sooner or later, we will all walk this path, and there is no other path because our soul is immortal. Each one of us bears the spiritual substance of life, the spiritual body—which we call soul, since it is shadowed—and this is what is immortal.

If the one were closer to you than the other, then you would look to the front, to behind, to the right, to the left, to above and below, in order to see him because you do not behold him in yourself.

Gabriele:

Density is a product of base humanness. It came about by looking into the external world, through the negative principle, through our human expressions of life.

Our human will created and creates forms. We want this and that—this is always connected with human thoughts, sensations and feelings—and already we create thought-forms. If we continue to want, to think and sense with the same or similar content, then these thought-forms condense. They take on a clearer and clearer contour and structure and, in time, they crystallize.

This is how our world emerged. Let us look back at the past epochs: Their characteristic always developed through the formation of certain forms. One generation after another passed their thoughts, their feelings and sensations on to the next one. From this developed density, the variety of the forms of life on Earth.

This shows how the demon used the humanness and the human beings to attain what he wanted and still wants. The adversary wanted matter that had become form; he wanted density.

The adversary of God wanted to be creative himself. He wanted to create his own forms. In heaven, the eternal pure Being that became form is unchangeable and in continual evolution. It is the divine nature, the divine buildings, the divine beings, all of the pure life; that is the eternal Being that became form. The adversary of God did not find an inherently new principle for his plan to found his own realm, on which he could have built his own. God is everything in all things—there is nothing that does not have its origin in the divine. This is why everything that was caused by the Fall, all density, will be transformed into pure, fine-material, eternal Being, and will return to the eternal heavens.

The one who is against God believed, and still believes, in the possibility of his own creation. He took the principle of the divine Being and said: "I will create my forms." And he created them through the human thought-forms, which became density, that is, matter.

It is said in the following sense: "God thought—and it became." God is the flowing primordial power; He is the primordial sensation. He places the "Let there be," His holy Will, into the streaming, flowing law. Out of this emerged and emerge the divine forms.

The adversary seized that part of the life energy that God had given His fallen children to take with them on their Fall-path and reversed it. He himself created, so he believed. In reality, he only misused what was given as a loan, a part of the positive life force from God.

The pure Being remains eternally. The pure energy that God gave to His children was transformed down more and more. It became density, matter, with its forms. As a result of this, we, too, the human beings, are transformed-down energy—a thought-form. We have formed ourselves just as we felt, sensed, thought, spoke and acted.

Generations ago, the form of the human body was entered into the world of the stars, into the causal computer, through sensations, feelings, thoughts, words and actions. According to the principle of sending and receiving, the radiation came back, intensified, and the burdened soul surrounded itself more and more with this thought-radiation. The human being emerged—thought that became form.

In the eternal Being, the Eternal created and creates the divine beings from the eternal stream, the Absolute Law, the pure, flowing Being. "Let there be"—and the spiritual beings emerged and emerge—pure, eternal law that became form, substance from His power. What do the components of egoity, the human aspects, see and create on the Earth? Impure, individual law that became form. We recognize that the adversary reverses everything.

But he will not achieve his goal of causing the principle of infinity, the eternal law of the heavens, to fall, thus conquering God. For God is absolute—this means, perfect.

There is nothing that would be greater than God. He cannot be surpassed or conquered. He is the almighty power in everything, the positive nucleus that leads everything to perfection.

The impure one, the unenlightened one, often wishes for his neighbor what he does not have, himself: the beautiful, the good, the peaceful, the happy—facets from the eternal truth, whose actualization he still lacks in himself. What he wishes for his neighbor does not enter his neighbor because it is not imbued with power, truth and love. These are soulless wishes that return to the impure one, the unenlightened one.

Gabriele, the teaching prophetess
and emissary of God, explained about this:

Everything that is not actualized, that does not radiate from the very basis of our soul, is not vivified. It is not filled with divine power.

How often do we wish our neighbor happiness, health, contentment, prosperity? Every time that we wish all this for our neighbor, we should ask ourselves: Are our words vivified? Do they come from the very depths of our soul? Are we, ourselves, happy? Do we have inner peace? Do we really feel well, that is, are we filled with inner dynamism and life force? If yes, then our wishes go into our neighbor's heart and move his soul, so that he is stimulated to reflect and will, himself, feel the happiness and sense the peace.

On the other hand, if our words are not vivified, that is, not permeated with the power of actualization, they do not enter our neighbor's heart. They are empty phrases, turns of speech. They are an abuse of words and of the divine law because happiness, health and peace are aspects of the eternal law. These statements, spoken without actualization, come back to us again. They become a boomerang for us because they admonish us and demand of us what we have entered into the atmosphere as affirmation.

This means for us, for every person, to be watchful and pray. This means nothing more than to be alert, so as not to continue to commit sin. Therefore, we should pray consciously and fulfill the laws of God more and more, so that we do not succumb to temptation.

The All-unity is the wisdom of God. God is everything in all things, the law of life.

The pure one addresses the whole in everything that he says, the large in the smallest and the smallest in the large.

Gabriele:

»The All-unity is the wisdom of God.« This wants to tell us that the All-unity is the closeness with all Being, with everything pure. The pure is in everything that we encounter. Let us examine ourselves: Do we feel close to it? Can we affirm it? Are we for the most part in communication with the pure or with the external aspects, the humanness?

Let us become more and more aware: The pure is in everything because God is everything in all things, the law of life.

»The pure one addresses the whole in everything that he says, the large in the smallest and the smallest in the large.«

God is omnipresent, that is, the whole in everything. He is indivisible. The entire law is contained in a speck of dust, in a grain of sand, in the smallest. Certain aspects of God are developed in the speck of dust, in the grain of sand. This is why it, too, radiates the divine. It radiates the facet of the whole that is developed in it. However, all of creation, the entire law, is in the speck of dust, as well as in the grain of sand and in the tiniest microbe. Thus, all spirit beings address not only facets of the law, but always the whole.

We people often disregard the small. But a spirit being respects the smallest just as the great, the mighty All, just as every spirit being, every human being, every soul. Why? Because the great All-One, the indivisible God, is the whole in everything. God is the principle: Link and be. The adversary created his principle for himself: Divide, bind and rule. With this, he is subject to God.

Let us call it to mind again and again: In everything, even in the smallest, is the greatest, the whole—God! Whatever we see—and be it ever so insignificant to us—let us remember: In the smallest, in the most insignificant, is the whole, the entire creation, the All-Spirit, and thus, the perfection.

Let us bring this to mind again and again, then we will increasingly experience how rich we are in our inner being. The innermost wealth is the Kingdom of God, the law of God, which is in us. Some day, we will open this law, this inner wealth, in us because each of us is on the way. Wherever he may be at the moment—whether he still has the whole path before him, or whether he has already mastered a part of the Inner Path—he is always on the way that leads home, to the Kingdom of God. Through Christ, each and every soul will find its way back to the Father's house.

It depends solely on us: Do we want to go on, toward the eternal Father, or do we want to go backward on the path, into density, into the quagmire of the human ego? Each day shows us: Either forward or backward; either for God or against God; there is nothing in between. For this reason, the decision is required at every moment.

Let us be aware of the following: No matter what comes to us, we consciously or unconsciously always make the decision: for God or against God, for the light or for the darkness.

To be able to take further steps toward the divine, deep self-recognition is required.

Everything is color, form and sound. Our soul and our physical body are also bodies of sound. Just as we sound, that is how we behave, that is how we breathe because our feelings, sensations, thoughts, words and deeds determine the rhythm of our life. They also determine our breathing.

The breath of life, the stream of Being, which wants to stream completely through us, knows no interruption, no faltering. If we are in harmony with the Spirit, the life, we are also in harmony with ourselves, and our words and thoughts are the same as our sensations and feelings.

Let us compare our thoughts with our feelings and sensations! If they are in accord, that is good. However, if our sensations and feelings tell us something different than our thoughts do, then we should figure out what is still in us.

Therefore, let us understand ourselves as a body of sound! We can get to know our body of sound—as an exercise—by consciously perceiving what we encounter and use our reactions to it for self-recognition. In this way, we can also sense into a word or several words that we read or hear. We feel into what the words want to tell us. We examine the thoughts that come to us to see whether they are in unison with our actions, our sensations and our feelings. If this is not so, then we have to say that it was merely our conscious mind that manifested itself in our thoughts, but not our level of feelings that tells us much more clearly what it is still like in us, in the depths of our human nature.

For example, let us take a word from the Christ of God in His great cosmic teachings and allow it to fall deeply in us. We let it reverberate in our inner being. The thought that comes up, which we can also note down briefly, wants to say something to us very personally.

Thus, we are not satisfied with the one thought, nor with the shell of the word, but we look into it. If we draw to us the thought that can consist of one word or several words and take it into our inner being, then our thought-word splits as if automatically, so that we can recognize one or more aspects of our humanness, which are waiting to be cleared up today.

Examining our inner landscape is often accompanied by the joy of discovery. What still lies in us in the way of the all-too-human aspects and is not yet recognized, cleared up or settled works like a jamming transmitter. It can be the source of much uneasiness, worry, anxiety or many wrongdoings. Once we have found what weighs on us, makes us anxious and torments us, then we also know what we have to clear up, to forgive and to make amends for, in order to be free. Becoming free from a part of our human aspects is at the same time a step toward inner purity.

The one who wants to go deeper, to get to the bottom of his burdening human aspects, will not leave it with the answers that he finds for himself. He will again look into the words that came to him and will work out why this and that still exists in him. We will again receive the answer to this question because the answer for us is already in the words.

Thus, we find our way to the root of our evil, more and more, to our human aspects, to the root of the narrowness, of the depression, of the lack of freedom, to then work on the root system. In this way, we increasingly come to our level of feelings, to examine ourselves in these depths of our human aspects, so that we can clear things up more quickly, and draw closer to the holy law, God, our Father.

The access to ever deeper layers is opened up for us with the little word "why." It is the question about our motivation, about what impulses from our level of feelings contributed to our behavior.

We should heed one thing. If we recognize, for example, an aspect of our base humanness through this exercise, then we should also work on it today and clear it up today.

If, despite knowing better, we continue to nurture arrogance or the wanting to be, if we plunge into the noisy world, if we continue as before, it is possible that we burden ourselves twice as fast because we do it despite our insight and knowledge.

The help is always there. If we go earnestly and honestly to Christ and pray deeply, then at every moment He helps us to reduce these dissonances of our human ego.

In the morning—already when we first wake up before we get up—let us go into deep prayer. Even before the human thoughts come, we should pray deeply into ourselves and ask for help, and help will be granted to us.

Our awakened soul senses that it is on the way and draws ever closer to the longed-for goal, the light, the freedom. If, for example, a part of arrogance, of wanting to be is still active, then our soul calls for humility, stillness and modesty. Let us always remember that our soul calls us, and thus, God calls us. He calls us in the words that especially touch us, that call up a warm echo in us, that awaken the longing in us.

Therefore, let us pay attention when we hear or read something. One, two or three words, or a sentence can cause us to vibrate; our body of sound begins to vibrate. It took in impulses that are sounds, as it were. Through this, our body began to vibrate more strongly, to sound. We notice this because the rhythm of our breathing changes. We feel a movement in the world of our sensations and feelings.

If we are alert, if we write these words down to then look at them more closely and compare them to the world of our feelings, then we will experience more. We experience ourselves.

Let us learn the language of words, and we will get to know ourselves better. In time, we will also sense that words as such have hardly any significance—unless we let them take effect in us, so that they show us what we need to recognize or who we still are.

»The pure one addresses the whole in everything that he says, the large in the smallest and the smallest in the large.« This also means that when the Spirit of God reveals Himself to us, He never speaks merely the word, but places the whole law into each word. For example,

in the words "the wisdom of God," lie the seven basic powers of the heavens from Order to Mercy. We simply call them the seven times seven energies. In reality, they are the infinite planes of the Being—and the whole law in the smallest.

This means that a pure being places the whole law into each word that it speaks. From this whole, the corresponding facets of consciousness become active and reveal themselves. God is indivisible. That is why the whole is in everything, also in each impersonal, lawful word.

The word of the heavens is the law of God. The whole, the great, the infinite, the law, is—as we already heard—in a speck of dust as well as in the mighty Primordial Central Sun. That is God, the life. It is also our life.

For us, this means that we have to again open up the true life in us because it is our divine heritage, our eternal being. Once we grow accustomed to feeling into the words again and again, then in time we will sense the individual aspects of our narrowness and yet, at the same time, we will sense the vastness. In the Spirit, the vastness is infinity, and thus, the eternal law.

Let us bring to mind that in God we are great beings because God, the great, mighty Spirit, created us, and because we live in His heart as His children. If we are aware of this, we will distance ourselves from the narrow, petty human feelings and thoughts.

God is the infinity. He is the greatness, and we may be divine in God because we bear His greatness in ourselves. We are children of God, sons and daughters of infinity, equipped with the whole, eternal, infinite law. That is our divine heritage. Let us go through our days in this awareness, with this affirmation, and we will experience them differently and we will experience ourselves differently. Then we will realize what great wealth lies in us, and we will recognize where we can start today, to open it up step by step.

The one who speaks to, or wishes, his neighbor only facets from the eternal law, thus placing only parts of the eternal law into his word and into his action, also favors only parts of the eternal law and expresses that he is imperfect.

With this, he bears witness of himself. He favors certain people, while disregarding others. This means that he makes exceptions in relation to himself and to his neighbor.

The language of the law is the whole law, since everything is in all things, the greatest in the smallest and the smallest in the largest. The pure one always speaks the whole law. If he wishes his fellowman selfless love, then he addresses all the facets of the eternal law. That is the language of the law.

Gabriele:

In everything is the whole, also in the smallest. It is hard for us human beings to grasp this, but it is so.

Let us feel into a grain of sand or a speck of dust! The whole law is in the grain of sand or in the speck of dust, and this consciousness is in all things, in the smallest and in the large.

If the speck of dust were to limit itself to being a mere speck of dust, if it would rigidly persist in this consciousness, there would be no evolution in the speck of dust.

What the speck of dust radiates is its consciousness, the developed facet of consciousness from the whole in it.

However, the various consciousness aspects of life radiate the developed facets, the whole is nevertheless contained in everything—the whole law. Evolution is the result of this.

If God had breathed only one, two or three facets of life into the speck of dust, the grain of sand or the smallest forms of life, then these small forms would remain imperfect forever. There would be no evolution for them.

When the All-Spirit breathes out, evolution takes place in the respirated planes of infinity. The whole law is more intensely activated in all the forms of the planes that are being respirated by the All-Spirit. The result is evolution, and a further facet of consciousness becomes active.

If instead of the entire eternal law, only one facet of consciousness would be contained in the smallest particles of infinity, then the All-Spirit could not guide this component to evolution. If the indivisible, God, were divisible, there would be a standstill in the individual spheres of the All. God is not standstill, but eternal motion, eternal evolution.

The facet or facets of life that the speck of dust or the grain of sand or a microbe, that is, the smallest form of life radiate is in God and lives in God. The speck of dust is. It does not ask when it will evolve further. It knows. It does not ask because it rests in God and is aware of evolution.

In the speck of dust are the predispositions for a perfect divine being.

Spiritual evolution is the unfoldment of consciousness. The one facet of divine consciousness raises itself in individual steps and levels via the various spiritual minerals and via the species of plants and animals. By way of this great event starting in the mineral kingdom and going through the plant and the animal kingdoms, the nature being emerges, which, after it has reached full maturity, is raised by God to the filiation. It then becomes a fully mature spirit being.

With His first exhalation, with the first formation, God placed everything into this first exhalation—all the way to the perfect spirit being—including its name. The spiritual name also develops. The smallest form of life, the smallest, most inconspicuous spiritual mineral, already has a name, an active vibration potential, which radiates. It develops via the mineral, the plant and animal kingdoms, and further, via the nature being to the spirit being. Then its name is completed.

Everything that lives in the pure Being moves and develops, increasing in consciousness, light, radiation and power. Let us become aware that God is eternal movement. Life is constant movement. The All is infinity. No limitation, no standstill exists anywhere in the All. The All can expand into all eternity without limitation.

As human beings, we can hardly imagine this because we always reach our limits. In God, everything is without boundaries—infinite. We should let the word "infinite" simply vibrate in us because it cannot be grasped with the intellect.

Infinity is God. He is also eternity. God is perfect. He is absolute. God is the eternal law. There is nothing beyond that.

The entire evolution is predetermined and is contained in the two primordial particles, in the principles positive, negative—we human beings would say male, female. It is the primordial principle of life: giving—receiving, giving—receiving.

The activity of the spiritual life form is movement in the cycle of giving and receiving. Stone, plant, animal—everything receives the divine power of light, pure energy. Every life form also gives according to its state of consciousness. It shines; it radiates; it moves. It gives in the law of God, in the great garden of God, the eternal Being—for the great totality.

Although the life form may still be small, containing one single facet—by giving, that is, by being active, the facet that was activated by the All-Spirit develops. Thus, the life form does not remain inactive, waiting until its facets have formed. God, the life, is the active, creating law, the activity. Let us think of the ants; they work and work. And through this, they themselves develop the already activated facet in them. Once the entire facet of the law, for example, the consciousness of the ant, has unfolded, then the next step comes.

This can be an example for us. We, too, are in the process of evolution toward the Father. If we are lazy and negligent, then we do not develop the steps toward the law of God. Standstill persists, and finally regression and fall.

No matter on what level of consciousness we may presently be, out of our selfless activity, our actualization of the divine laws—which the day brings to mind for us—ensues the energy for evolution, for reaching the next higher level. This is life. This is the principle of giving and receiving. This is how the smallest little animal lives and matures. This is how every form of life lives and matures. This is how God set it up.

As long as we do not give and speak from the law of life, we are also at a standstill because we are not willing to accept the light of God, the breath of God, in order to enter the evolution leading to the filiation to God.

As long as we do not live the principles of equality, freedom, unity, brotherliness and justice, we are still lacking in spirituality. As a result of this, we make exceptions again and again because we will accept the one and reject the other. We will understand the one and not show understanding toward the other. Then, the one is worth more to us than the other. This conduct is human and thus, not divine.

As long as we live in this humanness, we cannot reach the law of God. We will come to the eternal Father only via our neighbor, and with our neighbor and Christ, into the eternal Being. There is no other way.

It is impossible to reject a component of life and still believe we are fulfilling the law of life. If we reject animals, plants and minerals, we are rejecting the law of evolution because the law of evolution is in the minerals, plants and animals. If we say no to this, then we will not address these facets of inner life in the very basis of our soul. On the contrary, we will burden our soul. The more we are burdened, the more we speak our person-law, our base ego.

The language of the law, however, is always the language of the whole because the whole is always evolution. All pure beings live in this awareness.

Gabriele:

Peace is in all areas of life. Peace is in the principle of Order, of Will, of Wisdom, of Earnestness, of Patience, Love and Mercy. Peace is stillness. Peace flows from gentleness and kindness. Peace flows from selfless love. Peace flows from a selfless gift.

If deep from our inner being, we want to give our neighbor something, we can do this in the following awareness: "In the gift of God, the gift that I now give, are contained all seven basic powers of God, the whole law." Speak and live in this way: "Father, You are the whole law in this gift, and so I pass it on as Your child. I thank You that You are great, infinitely great, and that I may be Your child."

Once we are in this high consciousness of selfless giving and receiving, then we know what our spiritual heritage is. We experience ourselves as our self, in our sensations and feelings. The true Self is the eternal law, our eternal homeland, our life. It is in eternity. Everything else passes away.

The pure one always speaks the whole law, even when he wishes an ill person health.

If he were to wish the ill person only a facet of health, for example, the health of an ill organ, then he would be addressing only that part of the law that is overshadowed by the illness. By doing this, he would ignore the effectiveness of the whole eternal law. Through this, he could perhaps hinder the effectiveness of the eternal law in the ill person.

The one who wishes for only the physical recovery of his neighbor addresses the illness itself, which he may even intensify, if the ill person relies on this statement. With this, he disregards the will of God, who knows about His child and wants to guide it in such a way that is of benefit for its soul.

Selfish thoughts influence merely the surface—that is, the effect, the symptom, the illness—and prevent the eternal law from becoming effective.

Gabriele:

Therefore, when we wish our neighbor health, then we wish for him that the entire divine law may become active in him and guide our neighbor to what is good for his soul.

Gabriele:

We hear again and again that matter is reflection because it was not created by God, but shaped by us human beings. Through our negative feeling, sensing, thinking, speaking and acting, density emerged. Density is merely the mirror of the Being.

We human beings are also reflection. What is in our soul radiates to without; it marks and shapes us. Thus, our radiation corresponds to our feeling, sensing, thinking, speaking and acting.

If we recognize that everything material, condensed, is only reflection, we will at the same time become aware that it cannot be reality. Reflection is not reality. To us human beings, it merely seems as though it were reality. It is the world of appearances and illusions, but not of the Being.

The law of God is all-radiating, all-penetrating, for there are no shadows in the eternal Being. As long as shadowed human beings exist, there will also be density and thus, reflection, which we consider to be reality.

From the beginning of the human race, all generations have played a part in the emergence of these mirror images, in the emergence of our world of appearances and terms.

We know that everything is based on the principle of sending and receiving. Our unconscious also sends and receives. When we wish our neighbor peace, then we have to ask ourselves, whether we ourselves have peace. If we are without peace, then we radiate solely our strife. If the one to whom we have wished "peace" is also without peace, then, according to the principle of sending and receiving, he can take in only strife.

Thus, our words can be »hollow.« In the inner part of the shell, the meaning is often different than what the external word says. Then the external is nothing more than illusion. It is not filled, not vivified. The shell, the word, speaks of peace; the core of the word, the inner being, however, is strife. It is not the shell that is significant, but the core.

The whole of infinity is communication. If we merely seem to wish our neighbor peace, then, in reality, we radiate our strife to him. Through the communication principle of "like receives like again and again," we can activate our neighbor's strife with our sending potential, and perhaps stimulate him to negative thoughts or to acts of violence. This means that in this case, we are the main culprits and burden ourselves accordingly, and our neighbor likewise incurs guilt.

As a result of the principle of sending and receiving, which is the same as communication, we are bound to our neighbor, whom we have caused to sin. Thus, through our hypocritical greeting of peace, our neighbor can become even more discontent and unhappy—and we, as well.

As a human being, the truly wise one needs the language of the world to make himself understood. Despite the limitation of words, the wise one will address the whole, the all-encompassing law, God, in words such as »health« and »peace.« Then the eternal law, God, will prevail, which leaves every person his free will and guides him in such a way that it serve his soul and not solely the shell, the person.

Gabriele:

We have read: *»Despite the limitation of words, the wise one will address the whole, the all-encompassing law, God, in words such as "health" and "peace".«* The whole, the all-encompassing law, God, is contained in everything, also in each word. "Lord, Your holy will alone is done in my neighbor and in everything." The wise one lives in this awareness and this is what he radiates into what he addresses.

When we wish our neighbor health, for example, then we should vivify the word, in the awareness: "Lord, Your holy will is done in my neighbor." However, it is important that we move in our heart the positive, the divine, which dwells in each person, for every person and all Being are a part of us. Only in this way can the entire eternal law of health and healing become effective. And it is effective, as it is good for the soul of our neighbor.

Gabriele:

The one who is ill himself and does not examine and fight against the symptoms of the illness, and then wishes his neighbor health, merely addresses the illness in his neighbor and possibly those aspects that correspond to his own illness because his conscious mind and subconscious are filled with thoughts of illness.

Our human feelings, sensations, thoughts, words and actions, to which our illness, our worries and hardships also belong, are our personal inheritance, that is, what we have acquired for ourselves. We radiate, or emit, this. The one who is receptive to this takes it in and moves it in himself. Since no energy is lost, no thought or word is lost either because everything is energy. This negative energy can, according to the law of plasma, enter the person to whom we emit, and in whom the same or like things exist.

The shadowed person lives in his plasma. The plasma that surrounds us is our aura, also called corona. It corresponds to our present radiation-picture. Our plasma, our aura, radiates only what we have entered in our soul. This vibrates in us. It goes out from us, and we attract corresponding things. Thus, we enter the programs of the sinful, the strife, the disharmony and the illness in ourselves.

Via sending and receiving, we are thus in constant communication with what we have stored in our soul. Only what is in our memory bank is our human potential of recognition. We can neither think nor speak beyond this, unless, by conquering ourselves and clearing things up with the transforming power of the Christ of God, we have already opened spheres of our spiritual consciousness.

When we wish our neighbor health and we are ill ourselves, what is in our memory bank? Health or illness? Since illness is in our memory bank, we also radiate this consciousness "illness."

If we use the word "health" and do not ourselves make an effort to clear up with Christ the causes that led to our illness, that is, our sinfulness, our wrongdoing, then the word "health" is merely a shell. However, the aspects of our illness are active in this shell. Consequently, we radiate these characteristics and radiate them toward our neighbor. Through this, we can possibly touch or stir up some things in our neighbor, which then come into movement in him. It can be the same or similar human, that is, sinful, aspects, which may cause him pain, if the same or similar aspects are in him, that is, the condition for a same or like illness or indisposition. With our wrongdoing, we can thus even have an effect on the illness of our neighbor.

We know that every thought and every word presses to be actualized. If we pass on aspects of our illness by radiating them to our neighbor, then our word or our thought wants to be actualized. On the one hand, it actualizes itself in us, by intensifying aspects of the illness in us. On the other hand, it radiates into our neighbor and intensifies the illness or indisposition in him, if our neighbor is receptive for this.

But if we already earnestly strive to clear up with the power of the Christ of God the aspects of humanness that are behind the disturbance in our health, then God's will takes place in us. In our wish for our neighbor's health, we could now also consciously address the will of God, His law: "Lord, Your will is done in us and in our neighbor." Then the law of God will become increasingly effective in us and will point out to us those aspects in which our thinking and acting is not yet in accordance with the divine will.

The one who wishes his neighbor peace and is without peace himself may intensify in his neighbor the aspects that lack peace, if his neighbor is without peace because like always stimulates like and wants to fulfill itself.

The one who wishes love to his neighbor and is, himself, without love may strengthen the lack of love in his neighbor who is still without love because like always draws to like and wants to fulfill itself—again, according to the law »like draws to like and intensifies itself.«

Gabriele:

Before we speak, we should think. Words can often no longer be taken back as quickly as thoughts can because spoken words go into our neighbor more quickly than thoughts do.

Although thoughts cannot be heard, they are still registered by the subconscious of the person and by his soul. The one addressed does not become aware of them so quickly. For us, this means that the one who, with the power of the Christ of God, rectifies his negative thoughts in time, nullifies, as it were, the created cause in his soul and in his plasma, as well as in his neighbor's soul and plasma.

On the other hand, in a moment, spoken words can stir up and inflame much. The one who feels injured by this and does not forgive holds this against the perpetrator and may not forgive him for a long time. The perpetrator and the one affected are tied to each other through this.

Recognize:

Every sensation, every thought, every word and every action is energy.

What a person emits can become effective in his neighbor if the same or like things are in the neighbor. The same and like things return to the person who emitted because the one who emits will receive.

The one who wishes health and peace to his neighbor and is, himself, ill in soul or body or does not have peace in himself, by not having actualized the eternal laws, influences the illness and the lack of peace in his neighbor and intensifies these because he did not let his wishes of peace and recovery, which he offered to his neighbor, become active in himself.

If you wish for your neighbor what you, yourself, have not yet fulfilled, for example, the pure, the noble, the beautiful and the good, it will not reach his inner being because it is not vivified by you—or the surface, the appearance, his base ego, takes it in and feels flattered and honored, and in this way, his base self, his base ego, is strengthened.

Wish your neighbor only what you have in and on you, that is, what is actualized and thus, vivified, and address the whole of the eternal law in everything. Since everything is contained in all things, affirm the whole law, God, in your wishes for your neighbor. Do not look only at the surface, at what should take place on your neighbor's body or in his surroundings. Remember that the salvation of the soul is the decisive factor and that the pure spiritual body is, in turn, the whole law.

What the pure one wishes for his neighbor—that which he, himself, fulfills—comes from the innermost part of his temple and goes into his neighbor's temple. He carries, so to speak, the fruits of the eternal law into his neighbor's temple because he brings the eternal law to his neighbor as a gift of love, which, in turn, is the law itself.

Thus, do not wish your neighbor details from the eternal law, otherwise you address in him and in yourself only parts of the eternal law. With this, you let all other facets of the eternal law lie fallow. This means that you would be satisfied with some facets and through this, you bear witness to your impureness and open the gates to the impure so that it can ensnare you.

Even if you address only a certain area of matter, place in it the whole. That is the true life, that is living in the eternal law, God.

Gabriele:

The language of the Being is the law, which says: Everything is contained in all things. Perfection is the expression of God.

This way of speaking is completely new to us. If we want to make this language our own, then we have to completely change our way of thinking. The one who wants to enter this high consciousness can practice it.

If we practice speaking the language of the law, the language of the whole, we will be raised by the high, eternal vibration of God. The result is inner security, clarity and awareness of God. The "ifs and buts," the "it could be," "perhaps" or "not yet, maybe later" will fall away from us because we speak the language of the eternal law, since we affirm the eternal law, the whole, in each word and strive to fulfill this. Then the will of the Lord is done, and not our self-will.

We should wish our neighbor only the divine aspects that we have actualized, that is, what is vivified. Then we address the whole eternal law in everything.

The one who practices this cosmic language will very quickly recognize in himself what he still needs to actualize himself. The one who discards the negative he has recognized and no longer does it will become a master of the universal, cosmic language, which is an expression of the opened, spiritual consciousness.

The whole eternal law is in everything that we think, speak and do. When we hold conversations, no matter of what kind—even problem conversations—we should realize again and again that the entire law is in everything, and the entire law wants to be effective in everything, according to the eternal free will.

In every conversation, the one who practices this universal, that is, cosmic, language, will address the whole law, which then also helps him to think and speak from the law of God, and to find the lawful solution in the problems.

When we plan for the day, for the week, the month, then in the plan we address the entire eternal law, by turning our plan over to the eternal, holy will of God. Then the eternal law is effective because we let the will of God be effective. However, we should not remain passive, but should keep our plan in our inner being and activate it through our daily activity.

If our life on Earth is lawful activity, that is, lawful action, then we feel the reaction in our everyday life, as well as in our body. This shows itself in our feeling, sensing, thinking, speaking and acting, in our planning, in everything we do.

Summarized, the following can be said:
According to the principle of sending and receiving, the following holds true: The content of what we feel, sense, think, speak and do, also of what we wish our neighbor, is always ourselves. Even when we embellish many things, veiling them with many nice words, the content of what we have embellished is decisive; it is ourselves. What is embellished is merely the shell; the content is significant. What we think and feel, including all our secrets, is solely ourselves.

If we want to recognize ourselves, then we should not look at the shell, but at the content. This shows us who we are and what our plasma, our aura, contains.

»The true life is living in the eternal law, God.«
The law, God, is omnipresent, eternal Being. The omnipresent, eternal law, God, is also contained in the causal law, the law of sowing and reaping. It behooves the person to do the task of clearing up his human aspects and of activating the divine law by actualizing it.

If our human aspects no longer determine our deeds and actions, then we live spiritually. If we no longer think sinfully, then we think divinely, for there are only two laws: the divine law and the causal law.

If we no longer want to live in the causal law, that is, if we change our life, if we change our way of thinking, then we gradually grow into the Absolute Law. If we think the Absolute Law is hard to learn, then we should realize that we already bear it within ourselves and that it is merely covered by sin. Sooner or later we have to become aware of it again, and reawaken it in ourselves. We do not have to actually learn it because we have already developed it in ourselves—namely, once, in the pure Being, in our eternal homeland, as our spiritual body built itself up from the mineral all the way to the filiation to God, according to the many principles of the divine law, and as we learned to activate the spiritual powers in us.

Thus, we already have the eternal law in ourselves: the noble, the pure, the beautiful. It is the law of selfless love. In us is freedom. In us is kindness. In us are peace, dynamism and joy. All these aspects of the divine law are a part of our eternal nature. In their totality, they are our spiritual heritage. To open this up again, that is, to grow into the law of God, we have to betake ourselves out of the causal law, the law of sowing and reaping.

If we become aware that a divine, pure spiritual being is in us, we will also strive to help it break through. When we listen to, or read in, the "Great Cosmic Teachings of Jesus of Nazareth," we are touched by the Absolute Law. Our eternal nature, our divine heritage, begins to vibrate. Then the desire to reawaken our true being grows more and more alive in us. Then we will clear up our human aspects each day and will no longer commit the sinful. Instead, we will enter our divine heritage, by becoming more and more selfless. This means that we cultivate selfless, noble feelings, sensations, thoughts and words more and more. Our deeds become more and more divine.

earn to behold.
The curious person looks curiously to the front, to behind, to the right and to the left, to above and below—and always sees himself because curiosity always calls up only what the curious person is, himself. Like calls to like, in order to communicate with it.

Gabriele, the teaching prophetess
and emissary of God, explained about this:

Let us ask ourselves why are we curious? Why, for instance, do we look around for people? What do we think when we look around for certain people and types of people? What we think is what we are, ourselves. If we have negative thoughts about our neighbors, if we disparage them or get upset about them—what we think toward them is what we are, ourselves. We can recognize ourselves in this.

If envy stirs in us, if we want to copy something from our neighbor, then we lack spiritual self-assurance. We are not true to our true self because we do not rest in the innermost depths of our temple.

To be true to ourselves means to go within, into the temple of our inner being, to go within to God. The more positive energy we have developed in our soul and our body, the more we can be true to ourselves—to our eternal self, the divine in us. We stand more and more in the law of God. We know about His power, we feel His power, which makes our soul strong, which provides each cell of our body with energy, which lets us be alert, dynamic, clear and joyful. Then we are connected with the eternal power more and more.

This gives us inner security and inner independence. Through the continual actualization of our true being, we open our divine heritage each day more. With this divine power, our true being, we live more consciously.

The curious one does not have several things. He lacks energy. The one who lives in the law of God has everything. He does not need to be curious. He does not need energy—he has all the energy of the eternal Being.

Curiosity looks only at itself. When we curiously look to the front, to the back, to the right, to the left, to above and to below, we always see only ourselves. Our thoughts tell us who we are. Curiosity does not speak the language of our neighbor; we speak ourselves. It is our own language. It is what each one of us has stored in his brain, in his soul and in the stars. No communication is possible beyond that.

Curiosity is a kind of greed, a form of expecting something from our neighbor. It is demanding, a wanting to have and to take, a lying-in-wait for something, a weighing of things, a use of tactics. By contrast, the inner perception of our neighbor is straightforward and upright. It does not make judgments and use tactics. It does not lie in wait and does not crave. It does not want to demand anything or bind anything to itself. It does not take anything because it receives.

The one who lives in the innermost depths of his temple is aware of his filiation to God, which he strives for day after day. If we clear up our sins, we uncover our divine heritage again, through which our spiritual consciousness gradually opens, radiating through soul and person.

Learn to look through yourself, to behold from the temple of your inner being, then you recognize the spiritual principle in all things and in your neighbor, as well—and the whole in the spiritual principle. That is the life in the eternal law; that is the language of the law.

Gabriele:

»Learn to look through yourself, to behold from the temple of your inner being« means for us that we must first enter the temple of our inner being. Once we rest in our inner being, once we are quiet in our inner being, we behold with the pure eyes of the soul and perceive what is lawful as well as what is unlawful. However, the one who rests in the pure Being will not tarry long with the

unlawful, but will merely address it, without identifying with it.

Spiritual principles are facets of the eternal law. And yet, each facet contains the whole law. During the teaching hours of the Absolute Law, we heard that a tiny life form, for instance, a grain of sand or a speck of dust, radiates several facets of the law, that which this life form has already developed. They are certain degrees of evolution, which form the state of development.

Through the activity of the life form, its radiation, its spiritual body builds up during the continuous breathing in and out of the All-Spirit. Once the spiritual body is complete, it radiates all the facets of the Absolute Law, and the Absolute Law, the eternal Being, radiates throughout the entire cosmic, eternal body. This is the perfection toward which all life forms strive. The perfectly formed spiritual body is the spirit body of the spirit beings. Since the whole law is contained in every facet, in every spiritual principle that is forming, the spirit being has absolute freedom and the absolute freedom of movement in infinity.

The Absolute Law is the absolute freedom. It is sin alone that makes us human beings unfree, our self-made law, our ego-law, the causal law. However, if we clear up the faults that we have recognized, that is, our sins, then we gradually feel a lightness of soul and body because our load, the burden, falls away from us bit by bit. This lightness is a touch of the eternal freedom.

Learn to listen.—The pure one does not need to listen for something. He knows within himself, in the holy of holies of his temple, what is important. Everything else, what is still pending, is not yet ripe and not yet significant.

Gabriele:

Do we have unlimited trust in God?

If we would completely entrust ourselves to the eternal One, then we would rest in our inner being more and more. Then every bit of curiosity would recede from us because everything is present in our innermost being. What is not yet ripe, what we have not yet uncovered through the actualization of the divine commandments, will become manifest to us when we actualize the laws of life more and more.

»The pure one does not need to listen for something. He knows within himself, in the holy of holies of his temple, what is important.« We will get to know everything that is essential for us at the right time. The condition for this is that we live consciously, that our thoughts do not wander here and there, that we do not preoccupy ourselves every day with our past, but rather live in the now, in the day, in the moment.

If we clear up all that needs to be cleared up, our consciousness expands and we experience in ourselves, in our temple, what is important for us. We experience ourselves and thus, the Being in us—the tranquility and the stillness, which then reveals itself more and more to the pure one or to the soul that is becoming pure.

The one who wants to listen in and eavesdrop will experience only his base ego, which unsettles him and stimulates him to again think, speak and act in an unlawful way—that is, to emit negatively—so that he will receive negativity in turn.

Learn to listen. Never ask curious questions because otherwise you will hear only yourself, your base self.

Gabriele:

Therefore, we should think before we ask, before we speak. Let us ask ourselves again and again: What do we actually want to accomplish with our question? What do we want to bring about? What do we actually want to hear? Is it important for us or is it merely curiosity?

This questioning ourselves helps us in many situations because we recognize ourselves more quickly. If we have recognized ourselves, we can give ourselves the answer, especially when the question was asked out of curiosity or to expose a person or to find him guilty. Then it would be better to clear up what we have recognized and not ask the question because each word can become our downfall.

To »learn to listen« means that we should not want to listen for anything. The one who listens, hears into the words, into the sentences, into the questions and the situations, and hears from this what is behind it. However, this is possible only for the person who actualizes more and more and turns within, to the stillness of God. Only through the inner stillness are we receptive and can perceive what the external word, the shell, is not able to say or does not want to reveal. When we penetrate the shell, then we experience the content of the word, what is behind it and has not been spoken out.

In everything that is being said to you, listen for the spiritual principle of God, and recognize, in turn, the totality in it and, at the same time, experience it in you, in your temple. The spiritual principle contains the whole law, just as the spiritual principle is contained in the whole law. That is living in the eternal law, and that is also the language of the eternal law.

Gabriele:

To learn to listen into the word, into the situation, we have to practice. The first step is to take ourselves back. This means not to think immediately when our neighbor says something, and not to prepare an answer while he is still talking. When we immediately think and get an answer ready, then it comes from our intellect and never from the Intelligence, God. Then the answer does not come from the stillness in us, from the eternal truth. It is not born in us, but corresponds to what is stored in our brain, to our intellect.

»In everything that is being said to you, listen for the spiritual principle of God, and recognize, in turn, the totality in it.« We should make it a habit to first take ourselves back and not want to think or speak right away. Let us allow what our neighbor says to fall into our inner being and bring to mind that the answer and the solution

is in everything. Through this, we will create trust in God. In everything, is the answer and the solution because God is present in all things. When we continue to rest in our inner being, then it is possible that pearls of the eternal truth may rise out of our already opened spiritual consciousness. The answer bubbles up, as it were, from the law of the truth.

If we have a lawful answer, if we sense that what we want to say is impersonal, then we should affirm the whole law in what we say. Even when we do not yet know the cosmic Being, the eternal law, in all its details, we affirm it and affirm God, the whole, in what we say.

Through this little exercise, we will experience what the inner stillness means. We experience more and more that God is very close to us. In time, we sense that He, the great Spirit, our Father in Christ, stands by us and helps in every situation, even in the smallest, the most inconspicuous thing. Often, we think that we cannot go to God, our Father, with a trifling matter. Oh yes, we can turn to Him with everything because we are His children and He loves us.

Let us practice taking into our inner being what has been said and letting the pearls of life come, and let us affirm the whole in our answer. With these exercises we learn what the language of the eternal law is. Through this, we experience our true self, not our intellectual, our human, self.

What we have learned is the intellect, the human self is what we have stored in our brain. The true self is the depths of our soul. The one who immerses into the depths of the Being more and more each day, by clearing up his human aspects and actualizing the laws of life, experiences his true self, himself, as a cosmic being, and he experiences the laws of life.

The one who aspires to listen for the eternal word, the Being, the law, in himself, is not yet the word, the Being, the eternal law. And the one who listens for it—according to his soul's degree of maturity—merely listens and does not yet know it because he has not yet become the law of God.

Gabriele:

»The one who aspires to listen for the eternal word, the Being, the law, in himself, is not yet the word, the Being.« To listen for something thus means that we still have to listen for it, in order to hear it. We are not yet in the stream of God. We are still standing at the edge and looking into the stream. We listen into the stream, so to speak, in order to learn what the stream, the truth, God, the eternal law, may have to say to us.

If we speak the word of God, then we no longer need to ask what the eternal Being is like. We no longer need to search for the laws of life. We know because God speaks through us in every situation. Then we no longer have to struggle to find the truth by asking: What is the content of the situation or question? What does this or that want to tell me? We know it because we have an overall view of things, since we have become the word of God. And the word of God is the eternal law of love.

We are on Earth to become divine again, that is, to again become the word of God, His law. Many still have to make an effort to find an impersonal way of speaking, the answer from the inner being. However, if we have become the law of life, then heaven is open to the enlightened one. There are no more questions because everything is answered in our innermost being, since the law of God knows about all things and we have become the law of God.

Dear fellow people, let us not say, "There is still a long way to go!" God is close to us. The eternal law is in everything that we think and do. God wants to help us in every situation. Let us entrust ourselves to Him. Trust grows by clearing up our human aspects. Then we will feel His closeness, which makes us happy. It is His presence in word and deed, in everything that we think, say and do.

 Thus, this means that as long as we still have to listen for the impulses of our inner being and have to make efforts to grasp the perceptions of our inner being, we do not yet know our true self. Then further steps of actualization into the fulfillment of the divine laws need to be taken, steps into selflessness, into the impersonal, serving life, in order to finally no longer have to listen for the law, but to be it ourselves. And so, we have to let ourselves be permeated by the Spirit of God. Then we are His word.

Is the path to God really as hard as many a one thinks it is? Let us move in our hearts the highest commandment that Christ brings to our awareness again and again in His revelations: Love God, your Father, with all your heart, with all your soul and with all your strength, and your neighbor as yourself. Simple words, but the entire heaven lies in them! Let us resolve to actualize the highest commandment, then we will soon recognize that it is really not so hard to entrust oneself to God and to accept the Absolute Law and put it into practice. Love God with all your heart, with all your soul.

Whenever difficulties come, whenever we want to disparage our neighbor, whenever we believe we know everything better, whenever we want to push our neighbor away from us, we again bring to mind: Love God, your

Father, with all your heart, with all your soul and with all your strength, and your neighbor as yourself.

If we sincerely mean it, then a vibration goes through our soul and through our body. This brings about a quick change in our way of thinking and helps us to go within. Then we will speak the request for forgiveness from the depths of our heart: "Father, I ask you with all my heart for forgiveness for having fallen into my old habits again." If this request comes from the depths of our soul, then the help is already there. In this way, we quickly find our way to the One who loves us unendingly, to the One who is unendingly loved by our soul.

The awakened soul longs for God. Yet often, we do not let it speak. We repress our soul's longing with our intellect, with our ifs and buts or with the thought: "I mustn't show any emotion. I mustn't have any feeling. I have to be strong, manly." Let us allow the inner emotions to come up! Let us allow our feelings to speak for once, let us allow the tears to come—tears of remorse and of shame over ourselves. Then we will sense what the soul has to say to us.

Gabriele:

»And the one who wants to recognize and experience the eternal Being according to the letter reads or listens past the reality.« Why? Because he stays only on the surface.

Let us imagine a word as a walnut. If we nibble only at the shell, we do not recognize the kernel, the nut. Therefore, if we look only at the letter, we look only at the shell and do not experience the kernel, the reality, the content of the word.

»The one who listens for only what his neighbor expresses as truth creates images in his mind from what he hears.« With this, Christ wants to tell us that if we merely listen to the eternal law and do not orient ourselves accordingly, by clearing up our all-too-human aspects every day and living more and more according to the laws of God, then we create ideas. We look only at the shell,

which deceives us. The life is the kernel. And we reach this only when we crack the shell. This is possible for us only when we clear up our sinfulness, which shows itself to us day after day and at every moment. Our five senses bring it to us.

If we cannot plumb the depths of the content of the shell, if we cannot feel into the kernel, into the depths of our soul, then we fool ourselves or, we are fooled. This is why Christ tells us again and again in His revelations: You should not be mere listeners of My word, but should actualize it, in order to be selflessly active.

Through actualization, we experience our divine heritage ourselves. We experience the spiritual law, our true being, ourselves. Then we no longer need to listen for everything, to inquire about everything, to create ideas. We are immersed in the eternal Being, in order to receive from there, from the source of life. That is the wish of the Christ of God. That is why He gave us the great cosmic teachings, the Absolute Law, our divine heritage, in word and in writing.

Gabriele:

If we hear or read words from the eternal truth, we should become accustomed to listening very closely and to taking what we read into our inner being. To bring this about, we do not think right away, that is, we do not think about what we have heard or read, but are alert and absorb it into our inner being. What we become aware of, that is, what moves in our inner being, we let come into our conscious mind. We look at it and make a note of it because it wants to tell us something. In this way, we learn the language of the Spirit more and more. We learn to take ourselves back, to digest in our inner being what we have heard.

If a statement, a word, especially reverberates in us, if we are moved by something, then we affirm the entire law in what moves us, by saying: "Yes, in every statement is the whole, eternal, mighty law."

If deep in our heart we affirm the totality, the life, then we sense that we immediately come into a higher body rhythm, a higher vibration because God is the whole, omnipresent.

We are privileged to affirm the law of God, the whole—knowing well that we are not it yet, that we have not yet completely actualized and fulfilled it. We may affirm it.

Just the affirmation from our heart brings us the resonance and points out the almighty Being, the infinity. We then sense a breath of the timeless and spaceless reality, if our heart, the soul, opens. The awakened soul often longs for God more than the person does because he reacts more sluggishly than our soul does. Through this, a discrepancy often develops between soul and person.

The word of the heavens is His word, the word of God, the eternal law. The one who has become the word of God has become a being in God. He also beholds people, things, events and occurrences in the image of heaven, in the truth, in the I Am—and no longer in the image of his small world, within sight of the »I want.«

Gabriele:

When we let Christ's statement *»The word of the heavens is His word, the word of God, the eternal law«* reverberate in us, then the narrowness of the humanness fades away. What was close to us as thoughts, concepts and opinions recedes. It becomes unimportant. This is based on our not just allowing our humanness free rein, but instead, taking what was said or read into those parts of our spiritual consciousness that we have opened, that vibrate through our soul and our person. With this, we then establish communication and sense the vastness and freedom of infinity. In this distance from our humanness, peace and inner love also resonate. This soft touch is God's answer.

In it we recognize God's nearness. The honest effort to grow into the mighty law leads us into the aspects of the inner law.

Therefore, when we do not think right away, but openly and trustingly absorb what we read or hear, and affirm

531

the divine in everything, then we distance ourselves from our human aspects, from the difficulties and problems. We become clearer and can also recognize more easily and in more detail our still existing human aspects, that which is active and needs to be cleared up. We become much calmer, react in a more composed way, and are thus above the situations more.

Let us realize that God is everywhere, and He is in everything. He is in us, deep in our soul. But He is also in each word, in each thought, in each sensation, in each moment. All that we hear, that we see, is God. He, the great Spirit, lets Himself be heard and be seen, if we regard things in the light of the law, in the light of the truth.

So that we again become the law of the truth, we should first heed the following: Do not take yourself so seriously, you base ego. The I Am is the greatest! If we affirm the greatest, the I Am, again and again, and practice actualizing this mighty All-law, we will also take ourselves back in every difficulty, in every problem and say: Stop! Don't take yourself so seriously. The I Am is the greatest; it is in everything. At the right time, I will learn how I can solve the respective situation or the problem according to the commandments of God.

Therefore, if we take ourselves back, by not thinking right away, but take in what is said to us, we listen more consciously, and our work will also be precise and flow easily because we live in the present.

Once we have become a being in God, a child of God, we are consciously the son or the daughter of God again. When we take these two words "son" and "daughter" and affirm the whole divine law in them, then we feel an instant change in and on us. From this grows respect for our innermost being. The contradictions of the human ego leave us. Once we have again largely become a being in God, we behold what is concealed behind the mask of our fellow people's human ego. The one who is immersed in this deep, inner sensation no longer judges.

Even though we have not yet become the law, even though some faults, that is, sins, have to be reduced, the affirmation of the law of God in the word "son," in the word "daughter," uplifts us, so that we can look at our human aspects from a higher vantage point. But the affirmation from the heart also tells us that since we are a son or a daughter of God, we must also behave like one. This means that now, we should actualize the spiritual principles of the laws of God more and more.

Knowledge obligates. This knowledge also brings with it the strength to put it into practice step by step. If we affirm "I am a daughter of God," for example, we set inactive negative aspects into motion, which let us recognize what still hinders us from being the daughter of God. If we clear up the now active sinfulness, we will experience increased freedom and the awareness that we are mighty beings in God.

This will develop only when—after recognizing and clearing it up—we take steps to ensure we will no longer commit the sinfulness that we have become aware of. The mere denial of the negativity we have recognized is of no use to us. We have to replace the old negative program with a new positive program, by working out a divine law of God from our wrong behavior and making ourselves aware of it.

Many have experienced that it is helpful to note down our unlawful behavior and the divine law of God that we have derived from it. We should carry these notes with us and bring them to mind when we again fall back into old habits.

What we have cleared up still reverberates for some time in our brain cells. We can read the divine laws to ourselves again and again, that is, prescribe them to ourselves, entering them into our brain. We continue to do this until the old program fades away and the new one goes into our thoughts, sensations and into our world of feelings, and we no longer fall back into our old programs. In this way, the negative is successively transformed into positive power. Lawfulness replaces our unlawful thinking and acting.

This is the work on ourselves on the Inner Path. These are the steps into a life in the eternal law, which lead us into our inner being and to God. In this way, we mature in the Spirit and open our divine heritage.

We will not become a pure being in God from one day to the next, or solely by affirming the Absolute Law. But when we affirm the law of God, we affirm the highest power, which becomes increasingly active in us. We feel it to the degree that it can reach our conscious mind through our opened consciousness.

Beings in God live in unity with each other and with all Being. We will find our way back to the unity only when we affirm in our hearts our neighbor's positive aspects and open them in our soul—likewise doing the same with all the nature kingdoms. We are not in accord with the divine principles of equality, freedom, unity and brotherliness when we are favorably disposed toward one person, but reject and disregard another. Likewise, it is incompatible when we love and cherish our neighbor, while at the same time acting against nature and remaining silent about the suffering that is caused to our second neighbor, the animals, and to nature.

Let us also recognize here the great life of creation which essence is in each one of us. Each speck of dust, each tiniest detail of what the mighty Creator-Spirit brought forth, we have to open again in ourselves, to cause it to vibrate in us again, so that we attain the unity with God. In this way, we find our way back to the great event of life, in which we remain integrated because God, our Father, keeps us in His heart.

This is a great and mighty sentence for us.

The image of heaven, so the Lord tells us in His great cosmic teachings, is the truth, the I Am. If we affirm this in ourselves—for in our innermost being is the I Am, since we are the temple of the Holy Spirit—we gradually attain calm and gain inner security, which very gradually lets us recognize problems, things and events in the light of the truth.

The life in God gives us security. The person who looks solely at the external aspects is erratic and uncertain. He lives in constant anxiety that his neighbor could go behind his back. He is always suspicious, mistrusting and filled with doubt. Dealing with his anxiety and his own imagination keeps him in suspense all the time. Thus, he is caught in his anxiety, which whispers to him: "I want" and "I must." The one who lives in God more and more also lives in his inner being more and more, where the light of the truth dwells. In this way, he learns to behold. When he has learned to behold, he affirms in everything the whole law, the entirety. And the entirety, the eternal law, will also help and serve him.

As long as we look at our humanness, we move our worries, difficulties and problems and remain hectic and short of breath.

This is why we should take the following as a permanent task: Take yourself back! Do not react right away. Let what you have heard take effect in you, and only then, speak or act.

If we affirm the whole law, the inner life, in every statement, in every word, then we notice very quickly that we breathe more calmly and deeply. Through the calmer and deeper breathing, we then sense a vastness in us, a breath of freedom.

We can have similar experiences when we compare "I want" with the divine will.

The "I want," that is, the human being, always urges. He urges and urges and wants and wants. And in the end, what comes out is: I must have it now. I must get my way now. It has to be the way I want it now. This results in greed, envy, intolerance, a domineering nature and enmity.

If we affirm that the will of God may be done in and on us and surrender ourselves to God's guidance, then in the moment that we give ourselves over to God, we become calmer and our breathing is deeper.

Through a lawful behavior, we also become self-possessed. We assess people and situations correctly. We know what needs to be done and what is not to be done.

We meet our neighbor with respect and are impartial. We are above things.

Tranquility and self-possession also bring familiarity toward God. We entrust ourselves to God because God knows about all things. He wants only the best for us. He is always close to us. He, the mighty law, the love and justice, is always with us. God is the inner listener, who hears everything.

If the heart of the child speaks to the great Father-heart, then unity and love draw into the person because the heart of God gives constantly.

Gabriele:

In the divine world is the language of pictures. When the spirit being receives an impulse, this impulse turns into a perfect, absolute picture within the being. It is the pure picture, in which the entire event of creation opens up. The inner picture can be seen in the particle structure of the spirit body, and the spirit being beholds in the picture all the aspects that matter.

It is also similar in our world, in our earthly existence: Our words and our thoughts are the language of pictures. These pictures are not perfect, not absolute. They do not correspond to the seven-dimensional world of God. They are merely reflections, converted light that has been transformed down. Therefore, they are not the Being, but merely the appearance, and in many cases, deception.

God is the breath, the life. The question is asked again and again: Why can't we see the Spirit of God? Likewise, the question is raised: Why can't we see the air? We affirm it and yet, do not see it. We breathe air and oxygen and take it for granted without seeing the air and the oxygen. We do see that the air moves the leaves. We hear the rustling of the trees. But do we see who moves the leaves and what makes them rustle? We simply say, "It is the air." But when it is about the breath of God, the eternally streaming energy, then we doubt this almighty presence.

If we link with the Spirit of God, by scaling back our humanness and affirming the mighty omnipresence of the All-Being in us, then the Spirit of life moves in us, too. We feel the calm and stillness. We breathe more deeply.

Let us bring to mind once more: Conscious living means to affirm God, the whole, in everything. We often forget this, and that is why we should practice it. Let us take as a task to again and again affirm God in everything that we think, say and do. Let us bring to mind again and again the following statement: "Yes, Lord, You are in everything. Your Spirit blows everywhere. You are in me, in every situation, in every problem, in every task. You are in my work and with me at my place of work. You are always present."

Therefore, let us affirm the presence of God in all things—and things will go better and better for us. We will become ever clearer, ever freer, and will become the child that God, our Father, desires: the pure, free, noble being in Him.

God is the whole and is undivided. For this reason, the whole is effective in the one who is the divine word. He is the one being in the Being. He is not divided like the person who speaks other than he thinks and feels other than he thinks and speaks.

The eternal law is active and reveals itself in you. Everything is law. You do not see it externally; you recognize and see it as the whole, in you alone.

Gabriele:

Since everything is law, in heaven and on Earth, in the stars and planets, in nature, in people and the person himself, then everything is life because every component is energy, and energy sends and receives, and thus, everything is life. Life is consciousness. Consequently, everything is consciousness because everything is life.

Life can exist only through communication. As a result, like communicates again and again with like. The principle of communication is based on sending and receiving. Thus, everything sends, the divine and the undivine. Each one of us is a sender and a receiver. With our five senses, which correspond to our momentary state of consciousness, and whose activity is connected to our feeling, sensing, thinking, speaking, and acting, we send and receive.

We cannot transmit beyond our self-created frequency range, which consists of our five senses and of our feeling, sensing, thinking, speaking and acting, as well as of our passions, longings and desires. We receive solely what we send.

Through this sending and receiving of human aspects, of undivine aspects, our person-law builds up, the law of sowing and reaping. If we clear up our sinful aspects, our person-law, then we gradually attain the Absolute Law. We become free of our human ego and very gradually establish communication with the eternal law, our divine heritage.

All the sending potentials of our communication network mutually influence each other. Our five senses influence the life of our feelings, sensations and thoughts, as well as our words and actions and our stirrings and inclinations. These, in turn, influence our five senses.

The one who remains caught in this personal communication network is his own prisoner. He sees and hears solely himself. He perceives only the frequencies of his smelling and tasting. He touches only what corresponds to his frequency range. He feels, senses, thinks, speaks and acts solely according to his inputs.

We can dissolve the network of communication of a person—our being spun into our own frequencies—only with Christ, since He is our Redeemer. To dissolve means to free ourselves from our human ego and to turn to the divine laws, which are our true heritage, the communication of the Being.

When we read and hear sentences from the great cosmic teachings of Jesus of Nazareth and let what we have read and heard flow into us, as it were, then this "sending potential" stimulates the world of our feelings, sensations and thoughts, our frequency range. From our own communication network, we then perceive frequencies in which we can recognize ourselves because we receive only what we have stored, that is, what we ultimately are. In this way, we examine our state of consciousness and recognize what needs to be cleared up.

For instance, if the words "God is the whole" and "everything is law" have reverberated in us and called up a movement in us, we ask ourselves: What does this want to tell me? Then our consciousness, to which we have directed the question, may perhaps split open the complex. We can continue to ask:

Where are we still divided? Where do we speak with a forked tongue? Why do we speak with a forked tongue? What are we afraid of? Our honest answers let us look behind our thoughts and fears. We question ourselves to learn what these aspects or sentences have triggered, that is, what human aspects we still have in us.

If the words "God is undivided" move us, perhaps a situation or occurrence that was marked by inner conflict briefly comes to mind. To figure out the aspects of our inner conflict, we ask ourselves: Why did we feel so torn today? What moved us hours ago? What difficulties and problems did we have yesterday? Which of them is still unresolved and not cleared up? What disturbs us? It is possible that our feelings are now signaling a bad conscience to us. Then we ask further: What have we neglected to do? What should have been done a long time ago? What are we avoiding, what have we pushed to the side? What is pressuring us?

By questioning ourselves we can get wise to ourselves. In what is vague and diffuse, which perhaps makes itself felt only in our world of feelings or sensations as pressure, as uncertainty, fear, melancholy or a slight grudge, one aspect becomes tangible, another becomes clearly visible, whereupon a still deeper cause can be grasped and thus, cleared up. It is worth it to consistently keep questioning ourselves and looking for the root. The superficial thought, the fleeting sensation, does not bring a solution and does not make us free.

Often, there is a whole complex of human aspects, which—because we may have not cleared them up for years—can no longer be unraveled so easily. Then, in the way that we have been shown, it is important to find the one frequency in our communication network that the energy of the day puts in our hand today. If we cause this one frequency to vibrate, if we recognize and clear it up, we may possibly experience more frequencies in our communication network. If the complex of our human ego becomes lighter, we come to the root system of our burdens. In this way, we can become free, step by step, by recognizing and clearing things up with the help of the transforming power of the Christ of God in us.

The physical eyes perceive only what is external and not what is manifest in the innermost being, in the pure being, in the temple of God.

The physical eyes perceive only the pale reflection of what is in heaven.

That which is matter is reflection and not the Absoluteness.

The one who beholds becomes aware of God in everything that is—in every flower, in every bush, in every stone, in the stars, in the people. With every blink of the eye, with his ears, with the senses of taste, smell and touch, he encounters God.

Gabriele:

Matter is reflection, the distant echo of the pure Being. If we take the distant echo as reality, then we are in communication only with the echo and we do not develop the organs of perception of the inner being, the fine antennae of the soul. Then, via our five human senses, we are occupied with searching on matter, where we perceive only the distant echo.

If we want to follow the longing of our soul for the splendor of the heavenly Being, we should not be satisfied with the pale reflection. Let us ask ourselves what still makes us cling to matter, to this side of life, to the illusion. Which aspects of humanness are they? What are we still looking for? What do we still want to have? What should matter still offer us?

We attain the inner perception, the access to the radiance of the eternal Being, only when we do not bind ourselves to the reflection.

If we have found where we have such a binding—desires, leaning on others, wanting and the like—then a decision is necessary: Do we continue to seek fulfillment in the reflection, in the illusion, or do we clearly set for ourselves the goal of reaching the radiance more and more each day? Our next steps will show which course we have taken. Are we still controlled by our humanness or are we guided and led by Christ, the might and the light of infinity? By virtue of our free will, we decide this ourselves.

*For the one who beholds, God is present in all things.
When he does his work, God is present. When he has a
conversation, God is present. When he goes here or there,
God is present.*

Gabriele:

»For the one who beholds, God is present in all things.«
As those who behold, we do not look here and there. We let our consciousness, the eyes of our soul, behold. With this, we radiate through our neighbor and through every situation and come into communication with the innermost part of our neighbor and the situation. The innermost part of all things is the divine.

If we have opened our divine consciousness, our spiritual heritage, then we have learned to behold, then we have also become a child of God again. Because God beholds us as perfect, in Him, we are always His perfect child. His heart, in which He keeps us as a free child, is the greatest magnet of the All. It attracts us, even when we take painful paths, paths into the darkness because of our self-will. Even when we linger in the darkness for a long time—at some point, we will feel the mighty radiation of this mighty magnet, God, the heart of love, and we will find our way out of disgrace, defeat, desperation, illness, hardship, hunger, infirmity and much more.

His perfect child, which He beholds as such, is in Him and one with Him eternally. However, let us look at ourselves closely and ask ourselves: Are we one with Him? Are our feelings, sensations and thoughts one with the law of life? Then we can say: "The Father and I are one," because our thoughts are divine thoughts—because our feelings and sensations are divine, that is, selfless, and thus, lawful.

God can then work through us and we can serve Him and our neighbor selflessly. Without wisdom, without the connection to the divine stream, without the communication of our innermost being with the innermost being of our neighbor, with the innermost part of the situation, the difficulty and the like, we are unable to lawfully give, help and serve. The tasks that God holds ready for us in our life on Earth will open to us only when we open ourselves to God, to the inner life and to our neighbor. Therefore, we must first become a child of God and leave to Him how we can serve Him.

The first step into an active life in the Spirit of God is always to become a child. The child gives itself to Him trustingly; it expects nothing. It simply wants to be His child. It wants nothing other than to rest in the bosom of the eternal Father and to walk at His hand. If it has communication with the One whom it loves above all else, God, then God knows how to guide His child and places it where it is good for the child.

We find the guideline for a life in God, for a life in His law, in the Ten Commandments and in the teachings of the Sermon on the Mount. If we follow these spiritual principles, we will become a child of God and grow toward being His son, His daughter. And we will become the ones who behold, of whom the Lord speaks in His great cosmic teachings.

Without togetherness with God, we will not be able to cultivate true brotherliness and a true community with people. Where togetherness with God is lacking, there is always conflict because each one wants to be the greatest.

Thus, we should first strive for togetherness with God. Once we have awakened to inner happiness, then we will also attain the true community with those of like mind. Naturally, we should also cultivate togetherness with our brothers and sisters, but the first step is always the togetherness with God because only then, among those of like mind, is there the alignment that links, and thus, the right kind of communication.

»When he does his work, God is present.« To go through our days with God, means to be aligned with Him, wherever we are, whatever we do. If we are successful in including God in our work, then it goes very easily.

We should get used to consciously including the Spirit of the Christ of God in our life, and to maintaining the connection with Him, by addressing the innermost in us, in gratitude for the alignment, in gratitude that things go well for us. If the awareness of gratitude has come alive in us, then, when we are threatened with facing critical situations, we will call on Christ in us in time, and ask Him for help. He will not be long in coming!

The one who beholds, who loves God, lives in the awareness of gratitude. If our love for God is not yet so great and not yet so constant, then gratitude helps us to strengthen our alignment with God and to anchor ourselves in the awareness of the filiation to God. Even when we realize that in a situation we are far from Him through our human thoughts, let us not fully turn away from Him! Let us remember that our eternal Father stays turned toward us. He is there for us. He helps us to find our way out of our humanness again! If we muster the greatness to thank God for pointing out to us where our human aspects are, then the courage and strength in us awaken to tackle the humanness with Christ and to clear it up.

If we look only at our person-law, at our problem, and talk about our problem a lot, then we do not activate the inner power, the power of God. God is always present. As soon as we ask Him, or thank Him from our heart that we have recognized a negative aspect that we want to clear up with Him, with His help, then we also address the divine in our problem. With this, we establish communication with the divine in the problem. The divine thus becomes increasingly active and shows us the way, so that we can solve the problem or difficulty.

Gratitude contains the affirmation of the divine in everything and causes the positive to be awakened, strengthened and stabilized.

»When he has a conversation, God is present.« Let us remind ourselves of this again and again, and practice attaining the awareness of the presence of God! Let us take ourselves back again and again, affirm the presence of God in everything and ask God for help, and He will support us, if we earnestly want to fulfill His laws.

»When he goes here or there, God is present.« God is always with us. We cannot run away from Him—He is in us. He is in every situation, in each word, in each gesture, in each movement, in each step. And God is always the positive, always the good. He constantly wants the best for us.

If we are aware that God always wants the best for us, then we will also entrust ourselves to Him more and more, and we will ask Him for help, for advice and support. He fulfills the lawful request of His child. This means that if we want to fulfill His laws, then we can be sure that He will guide us. He will help us. He will serve us.

These people have found the philosopher's stone. They let God act through them. The one who keeps the connection with God in everything that he feels, thinks, speaks and does truly walks in the light of God, and God does works of love through him.

In everything, keep the awareness that God is present; God is in all things.

If you have assimilated this certainty in you, then loneliness, desolation and grief will withdraw from you. You will gain togetherness, inner happiness and more insight.

Gabriele:

If our soul has been stirred by the sublime words of the Absolute Law, then the thoughts that formulate themselves as a resonance in us often express the highest wisdom. Nevertheless, we must often realize that the state of consciousness of our human person does not yet correspond to this. Why is this so? Because often, the longing of the soul shapes the words. It has long since wanted to be in the light, in higher regions, in higher spheres, while the person still identifies himself with the base aspects. Therefore, in our world of thoughts, the longing of the soul often gets mixed in with the human ego. This is why we have to feel into our own words, to experience our state of consciousness, and recognize what still needs to be overcome, in order to draw closer to the divine in the deed.

»In everything keep the awareness that God is present; God is in all things.« If we are aware of this and this awareness permeates us, then we will no longer rely on people and place our hope in people. We will rely solely on God. We will never be disappointed by Him.

The one who relies on people will be disappointed. The one who places his hope in people will, in time, lack hope. The one who relies on God receives.

Many people orient themselves to their fellowman. They expect confirmation from him. They want recognition, success, and want to look good. We should take a closer look at these desires and ask ourselves:

What do we get out of recognition, success, and what do we get out of looking good? Perhaps it brings us money and prestige, but let us keep asking: Do money and prestige give us security? Don't we have to worry right away about whether it will be taken from us? And with money, property and prestige, we are often still dissatisfied and unhappy.

If we once play all this through, if we put ourselves into the situations and courses of events, then we feel how it would be for us—and certainly how it has also been for us. Then we are faced again and again with the questions: What do we actually want, anyway? Are we satisfied with the result? Does success bring us fulfillment? Or if we want to look good: If someone praises us today, do we know whether tomorrow he will not already talk differently or whether he is merely praising us with his lips and thinks entirely differently?

We expose ourselves to these human games all too willingly. And then, when things don't go as we want, we become aggressive or depressive. In this way, we get into the entanglements of our causes more and more. Once fate catches up with us, we are surprised.

Let us take the path of self-recognition again and again. Let us analyze our desires, our expectations. What does success bring us? What do we get out of looking good? Where does it lead us? What is the bottom line? There has hardly ever been a person who can rightly say about himself: "Through this, I have become truly happy, satisfied and glad."

And no one has yet to attain selflessness through recognition, praise, success, honor and flattery. The human energy that flows to us seems to build us up. For a brief moment, we feel invigorated and uplifted. But after the brief high flight, things go downhill even more. We have to recognize that, in reality, it brings us nothing. It always leads us into the vale of tears and bitterness.

Success often brings fear, for example, the fear that further success might never come. When we "look good," then we already doubt whether we will still be liked tomorrow, and fear that we could be disparaged. What would be so bad about being disparaged one day? People think this way today and that way tomorrow. Today, someone disparages us, tomorrow, perhaps he has a good word for us again—so that we exalt him. As long as we look to people and expect something from people, we are always in an inferior position.

To rely on God requires first that we trust in Him, that we can entrust ourselves to Him. To entrust ourselves to God means to give up our human ego. Even when difficult situations come to us, decisions with which we may briefly have to depend on our own resources—we have to trust. We have to take the step, even when we do not know what will come afterward. If we rely on God and are sure that God supports us, then we have taken the step of trusting.

If we are faced with the decision of having to give something up and do not know what will come afterward, then we are called to blindly trust God, our Father. Why blindly? If we already knew beforehand what God would do for us, what kind of trust would that be? The true trust in God shows itself in the fact that we entrust ourselves to Him unconditionally, without knowing what the next step will bring. We trust God. No matter what happens, we live in the awareness that God is present. He is at our side. He wants the best for us.

»If you have assimilated this certainty in you, then loneliness, desolation and grief will withdraw from you. You will gain togetherness, inner happiness and more insight.«

This statement from the great cosmic teachings of Jesus of Nazareth can say infinitely much to each one of us. How often do we think that we are lonely and forsaken? How often are we doleful and sad? What is behind this? We rely on people. We place our hope in people.

The one who relies on people, who places his hope in people, will, in time, fall into anxiety and panic because he senses that people cannot give him what he relies on and hopes for. Many people are unreliable. In the word »unreliable« is already the indication of being forsaken.

This is why the person who walks the path to God should constantly be aware of the presence of God. We should always live in the awareness that God is in us and that we can become one with God. Then we will never feel forsaken because God never forsakes us.

The person who strives for communication with the Highest immerses in the divine stream, in which all pure beings live. Thus, he has entered the inner homeland. He will then be with the people and for the people, but he will not rely on them, nor place his hope in them.

Gabriele:

With these words, our Lord, Christ, gives us hope, encouragement, and wants to point out to us the inner strength that lies in the awareness that God is always present.

If it is our goal to become divine again, then we should make ourselves aware each day that God is present. God is in every movement. God is in everything that we see, hear, smell, taste and grasp with our sense of touch.

God is in each one of us. The entire All is filled with His power. If we let His power come alive, by making use of the days, by recognizing our humanness, our wrong behavior, by clearing it up with Christ and no longer doing it, we will very soon sense the presence of God. Fear recedes; strength and assurance replace it. Strength and assurance are motivating, and from the inner motivation, we will day by day take the steps that the day points out to us. And we will draw ever closer to our goal of becoming divine.

»Be still, entrust yourself to Him. He leads you.« If we are angry, if we are agitated, then we should say to ourselves: "Be still. God is present."

If we now become quiet, the brief agitation was merely a touch from without. But if we continue to be unsettled, then we know: "Lord, now You want to tell me something. You are now speaking to me through my faults, through my sins. You are pointing out my faults and my sins to me, so that I may clear them up with You." If we clear them up with Christ and firmly resolve to no longer commit the same faults we recognized, we immediately know which spiritual principle of God we will fulfill. And we will again say to ourselves: "Be still and entrust yourself to God."

God is in each one of us. Are we aware of this day after day?

If our heart has awakened, if we feel the longing to grow closer to our heavenly Father, we will also actively and consistently strive for our goal, our divine heritage.

God is always present, wherever we are, wherever we go—also in an angry crowd of people—God is always present. If we become aware of this, we will grow quieter, calmer and more secure because we say to ourselves again and again: We have in ourselves a mighty compan-ion, the Spirit of God, the unending love.

Remember: God is always present. God is love; He loves each one of you.

Do not leave the recognition that God is present at mere knowledge, that God, our eternal Father, loves you and me, all of us. Only the actualization, this means the spiritual knowledge that is lived, gives you the certainty and dynamism in the Spirit of God—the life in the Being.

Gabriele:

Jesus of Nazareth brought this home to the people of His time on Earth. Christ said it to us in the cosmic teachings: God, our eternal Father, loves each one of us. How often do we hear: "I am lonesome. I am forsaken. I am alone." Externally this may seem to be so, but it is not the spiritual reality. We should not affirm these emo-tional turmoils, for they are nothing more than signs of our self-pity. If we constantly input "I am lonesome. I am alone. I am forsaken," then we separate ourselves more and more from our neighbor and remove ourselves from the great unity.

All that is pure lives in the All-unity of the mighty Creator-Spirit. Nature is in constant communication with the divine. The bush that stands alone, the flower that stands alone, are never lonesome. The beetle that sits alone by the wayside, the horse that grazes alone in a meadow—they are not lonesome. Whether a form of life is here or there, it is always in constant communication with the All, with the stream of the eternal Creator-Spirit. No matter how far a life form may be from others, all are very closely linked through the communication of the Creator-love because the life, God, is in everything.

The one who makes an effort to affirm the life, God, in everything, and to strive for the life in God, comes into positive communication more and more with the positive powers in his neighbor and with the Creator-powers of nature. He feels taken into the great cosmos, into this mighty universal Spirit, into the life. Then the feeling of being lonesome and forsaken recedes. The soul opens like a wonderful rose in summer and spreads its fragrance.

The rose does not ask: What does my neighbor think of me? Does he see me? How does he perceive or register me? The rose does not look enviously at the lily, and the pansy does not want to be the rose. A spring flower does not wish to bloom in summer. Each and every life form feels itself in the Creator-power and, according to its consciousness, passes on what it has developed. That is living in the Spirit of God.

Therefore, let us realize that we are never alone. God is always present. Let us change our way of thinking! Let us drop the words "lonesome," "alone" and "forsaken" from our vocabulary, and instead, practice becoming aware that "God is present. He is always with us because He is in us." Then our field of vision will change. We look deeper and further, and will no longer heedlessly pass by our fellowman. And for his part, he will greet us in a friendly fashion, address us and possibly approach us.

We will also do what God wants, in our marriage and family. We will very gradually build a connection with our neighbor and no longer bind ourselves to him or her. We also bind ourselves to our neighbor with the words: "I am lonesome," "I am forsaken." Let us free ourselves of these binding, divisive words, and have the experience that God is present. God is present in the family, in our marriage, in our occupation and business. Then our vision will expand and we will perceive more. We will also grasp our neighbor as a spiritual part of our soul.

Let us remember that it is not our knowledge that brings us spiritual farsightedness, but the actualization of the eternal laws. This is spiritual knowledge that is lived, which we should carry out day by day, in order to draw closer to our goal of becoming divine again. From the actualization grows the experience and the certainty that God is reality, that God is in us, and that God is present in everything that we think, say and do. This brings inner joy and dynamism. This is the energy and dynamism for

God and for our neighbor. This leads us to refrain from our mine and me, from what binds us, and to attain a connection with our fellowman.

That is the true growth in the Spirit of God. We become calmer, more peaceful, secure, selfless and thus, more loving. We understand ourselves and understand our neighbor. That is the way toward the goal of becoming divine again.

The Being is present. In the Being there is no yesterday, no today and no tomorrow. Matter is transitory. The Being is everything in all things. Through this, matter is refined and becomes the Being because God is the present in all things.

The present in all things is the everlasting, the Being. For this reason, the transitory, the yesterday, today and tomorrow will transform into the Being, which is.

Gabriele:

Yesterday, today and tomorrow are terms like time and space. We human beings have created time and space ourselves, through density. As long as our bodies cast shadows, they cannot be irradiated. And as long as everything that is on the Earth and in the sphere of matter casts shadows, there is limitation. We call this time and space.

Time contains yesterday, today and tomorrow. But if we overcome yesterday, today and tomorrow, if we leave these words in our vocabulary merely as terms, so that we can make ourselves understood in our life on Earth, then the present comes into our life, the divine.

As long as we bind ourselves to yesterday, today and tomorrow, to time and space, we separate ourselves from our neighbor. For example, we say: "Our neighbor has driven away. Our neighbor has gone away." These words separate us. With this, we are saying, as it were, that he has forsaken us and is now separate from us. He is gone and no longer here. This is what our vocabulary signals; this is what our terms in time and space signal.

However, if we have developed the positive of our neighbor in ourselves, then can we likewise say with our vocabulary: "He has driven away, He has gone away," but our neighbor remains close to us in our inner being. Consequently, he has merely left externally, but he is alive in our inner being. This awareness also brings us the closeness to God and, at the same time, the closeness to our neighbor.

We cannot express this in our language. With this, we recognize how limited the human language is. As form, it registers only the divine that has been transformed down, reversed. But as human beings, we cannot get along without words. Let us see the word as a form, a vessel, which we, according to our thoughts, our sensations and feelings, fill with meaning, with the content of our consciousness. Now it depends on the following: What do we put into our words? The meaning in the word is what is significant.

So if our neighbor asks us: "Where is your brother, your sister?"—then we answer, for instance: "He, or she, has gone away." However, into this "gone away," we place the presence of God and thus, the presence of the divine in our brother, in our sister, aware that he or she is in us as a living part of our divine consciousness. Then the connection to our brother, our sister, remains, regardless of our perception of time and space.

It is similar in the eternal Being, and this is also how it should become among the people who walk the Inner Path to the Kingdom of God, to their divine heritage.

A complete change in our way of thinking is necessary. We keep our language as a means for understanding—it merely depends on what we put into these words. That is our present state of consciousness.

»Matter is transitory.« In this time, we are experiencing everywhere mighty eruptions on the Earth and in the Earth. Many are now asking themselves: How long can matter still last? God did not create it. Rather, He permitted it because of the wrong behavior of the Fall-beings. It behooves us to now do the task in density of again recognizing ourselves as a child of God via our human aspects, and of successively refining ourselves, in order to again become the image of God.

As the individual refines himself, he also contributes to refining the Earth, to raising its vibration. However long this process may take—thousands of years or longer—what is that in the Spirit of God? Perhaps less than the blink of an eye? But what was drawn into the depths through the Fall-event must be taken to the heights again, that is, transformed up through the refinement of all that is burdened and through the refinement of the material planets and the planets of the purification planes.

This is contained in the words of the Christ of God, our Lord, when in His great cosmic teachings He says: *»For this reason, the transitory, the yesterday, today and tomorrow will transform into the Being, which is.«* We, humankind, as well as the souls in the spheres of purification, must undertake this transformation. As human beings, we have all contributed to this density. Our sinfulness that has not been cleared up, our contribution to the density, is what we take along with us to the soul realms. There, our part must be expiated in manifold ways, all according to the nature of our contribution.

The Being is the eternal present. It is the now, the to-day. Thus, today is the present. To enter our inner being, the kingdom, our true being, means to fathom, to recognize, ourselves as the being of the eternal Being, and to clear up with Christ what opposes the eternal Being, our human ego. We will be able to do this only if we are alert day by day, if we do not let our thoughts drift into the past or into the future. We should live in the present, so as to recognize and clear up our human aspects. Then we will attain the degrees of purity of our soul. The purer our soul becomes, the more light it radiates into our physical body. This is spiritual evolution, our way into the eternal homeland.

Christ spoke in the following sense: "In My Father's house there are many free dwelling places. Take possession of the kingdom." This means that He is keeping ready for us our spiritual dwellings that we once left. We will be there again as pure beings because we live eternally and will return through Christ, our Redeemer.

The vision of the pure one is the pure that he perceives solely in himself, in his pure temple. There, the most holy, eternal law, God, shines and reveals itself continuously.

Gabriele, the teaching prophetess
and emissary of God, explained about this:

The pure one beholds the pure in himself because everything pure is omnipresent power in the pure. The pure being perceives the divine forms and all divine powers in itself. Therefore, what the divine being radiates reveals itself in the pure Being because also in the pure Being, the law is: sending and receiving. It is similar with us human beings. If our soul is pure for the most part, we grasp in ourselves, in our pure temple, the divine that is also active in the undivine. That is the perception of the pure soul in the human being.

The pure one also registers what is not pure and addresses it, insofar as this is lawful. However, he no longer becomes inflamed about the impure, he no longer gets upset about the human aspects because he has no cause for this, nothing in him that corresponds to this negativity. What the person has stored as negativity is the potential that he can understand. When aspects of this potential are stimulated, then he grasps these only in himself, namely, in his memory bank, in his brain. We often call this memory bank the intellect.

The pure one beholds what the impure one does not see.

Gabriele:

The impure one cannot recognize the pure because the impure sense of sight sends only what is impure and the senses that are turned without receive only the impure. The pure one also beholds the impure because he is above it.

Gabriele:

The divine beings, the souls and the human beings have the language of pictures. The pure being sees the pure in itself, the impure souls and people, the impure. However, everything is movement. It is pictorial life, in which the pure one grasps the movement and the word of the pure. The impure soul and the impure person see the movement and themselves, the impure.

The pictorial vision is, at the same time, a vision of recognition. What you see, you see through and you recognize—and thus, you know about all the details. This is the truth. This is you, the truthful, eternal self.

The truly wise one, the enlightened one, is what he speaks, the law.

The unenlightened one, who is unable to tell black from white, is the blind one who is satisfied with the illusion and believes the Being to be far away.

The true vision is the vision of recognition. You see and know, yet cannot prove it because the innermost being, the holy of holies, does not need to be proved because it is.

Only the illusion wants to prove itself because what is in it, the eternal spiritual principles, is not manifest.

The Being sees what the illusion does not see. This means that I, the Being, behold what you, the reflection, do not see. But when you are the Being, then you are united in Him, in the All-One. Then you will also behold what I behold, and we behold what the illusion does not see.

The spiritual eye beholds—the physical eye sees. Both cannot be brought into conformity with each other because the spiritual eye is the law of heaven and the physical eye is merely the eye of reflection, which passes on the Being as reflection that is many times distortion. The one who is satisfied with this is the fool who has not yet stepped through the gate into the truth.

The eye of the truth is God. The one who beholds with this eye is truthful and divine. He brings the light, the eye of God, the truth, into this world, the eternal law of love.

The eye of truth is the light and the image of your pure spiritual body, which is the image of God.

The physical eye is the image of the soul, of the enveloped spiritual body. It has an eye only for what is enveloped, which, in turn, is the onus and the burden of the soul.

As Jesus of Nazareth, I, Christ, instructed My apostles and disciples from different perspectives of life. Again and again, I pointed out to them the Absolute Law and explained the law of sowing and reaping. I spoke to them in the following sense:

The sea of infinity is the stream of the All. Move more and more in the sea of infinity as the sun of love and justice. Then you will be the life and will no longer ask about life.

Gabriele, the teaching prophetess
and emissary of God, explained about this:

»The sea of infinity is the stream of the All.« It is the eternal law, in which we should move more and more, to be divine again because we are on Earth to become divine again. *»Then,«* as it says in the great cosmic teachings of Jesus of Nazareth, *»you will be the life and will no longer ask about life.«*

The life that the Lord means is the Absolute Law, the eternal Being. It is the absolute life.

The human life is not absolute. The days of each individual differ according to what he has felt, sensed, thought and said in his life. On closer examination, each day is another world, another life. Have we already thought about this at all?

Each of our days is another life, but it is not the life of God. It is the life of our feelings, sensations and thoughts, that which we have entered in our soul and in the stars. We shape our human life ourselves. Just as we shape it day after day, that is how it comes toward us.

The eternal Being is not merely streaming light because God is not merely the stream. From the stream, the Eternal created the spiritual forms, the heavens with their worlds, with the edifices, with the animals, the plants—absolute, perfect, divine. The Being that has become form shows itself to the spirit being in pictures, in its inner being. We human beings also take in the Earth and all that we encounter, then register it in pictures and finally see it in our brain because our pictures are reflected there.

Each day contains different pictures for us, in which we move. That is our personal life, our ego life, but not the life and the movement in the stream of God. However, we should strive for this, as the Lord said to us: »*The sea of infinity is the stream of the All. Move more and more in the sea of infinity as the sun of love and justice.*«
Once more, we recognize that there is only one principle; it is the divine. If it is turned around, reversed, then it is the undivine. But ultimately, it is one principle. We human beings live and move in our ego-pictures, in our person-law, in our self-love. The divine world moves in the eternal law, in the sun of selfless love and justice. We

insist on our rights, by saying: "I am right." The brothers and sisters of the eternal homeland, the spiritual world, the eternal Being, are just. Justice is openness. Rights are encoded and closed.

Each one who insists on his rights encodes his ego because he does not apply openness, the principle of the law of God. This is how we shape our earthly existence, and in this shaping, the day approaches us. The I Am guides. The base ego controls us. This is why each day shows itself differently. One day brings joy, the other brings sadness, all according to what we have entered in our conscious mind and subconscious, in our soul and in the stars. This is the mechanism of control that is active in the day. And so, we are faced with the question: Can we influence this control, for example, our sadness?

An example: We are sad. Thus, the whole picture in us is "sadness." This state of being sad has many aspects that show themselves in pictures. For example, we are depressed, disheartened, despondent, worried and much more. We move in our sadness.

"Sadness" is a collective term for the sum of many feelings, sensations and thoughts. However, our sadness is completely tailor-made for us and our day. We see ourselves in the picture, we see which aspects of sadness have taken hold of us today, and perhaps know why we are sad.

Now, if a friend comes with a small gift or gives us hope, then the picture changes immediately. We are happy. The sadness recedes because we suddenly feel and think differently. What happened?

Our neighbor turned to us and brought us something. This little impetus from without made other aspects vibrate in our disposition, in the world of our feelings, sensations and thoughts. Through the influence from without, our condition was lifted, and already a new picture formed, a picture of joy, in which we now move with our feelings, sensations and thoughts.

Thus, our days are quite changeable, all according to what they bring us and how we react to our neighbor, or to the various situations.

This is then "our life." It is our ego-life, ultimately, always an unsettled life. Why? Because we are dependent on our fellowman. The picture of our days, of our life, is dependent on our neighbor, who gives us hope, who brings us a little gift, who helps us, who gives us a friendly word or an encouraging smile and much more. Thus, we are not determining our life ourselves. We do not act of our own accord. We do not act, but merely react. In this way, we are constantly in a state of expectation regarding how our neighbor will approach us, what he will say to us, what he will give us, how he will motivate us. Through this, our days are very changeable, and we will come out of our self-created ego-life only with great difficulty.

In the end, we do not live our life. We are pulled and driven, one time here, then again there. We are controlled and manipulated by our own weaknesses and human aspects.

If we are oriented toward receiving energy from people, we do not rest in ourselves. As soon as we go into a state of expectation, we are like leeches. Our nervous system becomes tense because our senses are turned to without. The love-stream of God can hardly flow via a tense nervous system. We become restless. Our rate of vibration decreases because we become poor in energy.

If we recognize this, the question arises: How do we attain the inner independence? Where is the hold?

Let us change our way of thinking! Let us no longer look to our neighbor for orientation when we are sad. Let us not continue to nourish our humanness, the sadness, the self-pity. Instead, let us bring to mind the nearness of God. In our sadness, let us create a divine picture: that the stream of love embraces us and permeates us, that God always loves us, that He is our Father, that He is our eternal homeland, that He keeps the heavenly dwelling places free for us, until we find our way back to Him. All this is hope from the Spirit. If we let ourselves be motivated by these inner impressions, we will become more and more steadfast.

Let us give ourselves a little present! Each one of us has little desires. Let us fulfill a little desire when we are sad and let us say thank-you to God, our Father. Then the inner motivation will awaken. And through the inner motivation, which comes from the Spirit of God, from the Spirit of our Father, we will become strong and steadfast. We will become more secure and transform our ego-life with Christ into the mighty life of the I Am.

In this way, we will also very gradually find our way out of our personal aspects, out of our human aspects, out of weakness, out of our sins. We become stronger and are glad when the day again points out something negative to us because we know that the negativity is there so that we can conquer it with Christ.

When hours come in which it is hard for us to turn back and change our ways, then let us bring to mind this inner picture of hope, of the love of our Father, of peace and secureness in Him. There are many situations in the day in which we can create this positive picture, so that we may find our way out of the situation, the difficulty, as soon as possible. Through this positive, lawful picture of life—it is, so to speak, the call to God for support and help—He will also give us support and help, and we will master the situation with Him. In this way, we become stronger in Him. We do not lean on people, but call on God and find a hold in Him.

This is what the Lord wishes from His human children. If we turn to Him again and again in this way, we will very soon experience the mighty I Am, His Absolute Law, and the stream that flows through us. And we will move in this stream more and more because we have become certain that God supports us.

As long as the person lets himself be shone upon by human beings, he does not radiate. Then he is dependent on the shine of his neighbor. If a person is dependent on the shine of people, he does not know the radiance of the sun that dwells in him.

Gabriele:

»As long as the person lets himself be shone upon by human beings« means that if he relies on people, if he expects this and that from people, for instance, that his neighbor help him instead of getting on with it himself, then he lets himself be shone upon by his neighbor, and does not himself radiate. He lets himself be exalted by his neighbor and does not develop the values of inner life himself. Why is this so? Because he does not master the situations with Christ, but leans on his neighbor, who is supposed to exalt him, who is supposed to serve him, help him and make his life, his ego-life, agreeable to him.

Thus, the one who lets himself be shone upon by people does not radiate—because he does not actualize because he does not make use of the days, in order to enter his divine heritage and move more and more in the stream of life.

»If a person is dependent on the shine of people, he does not know the radiance of the sun that dwells in him.«
With this, the Lord wants to say to us: This person does not orient himself to God. He does not ask God for support and help. He does not speak to God, his Father. He looks only to people and expects from people. For this reason, the indwelling sun in him cannot radiate through him and set him aglow. The person then continues to move in his ego-life, day after day in his human pictures, and does not come out of the shadows of the human ego toward the sun of justice.

Thus, we are called to use the days and to daily ask ourselves: Am I moving in my ego-life, which I, myself, have put together through my feelings, sensations, thoughts, words and actions? Do I want to stay in these movements of the human ego? Then I can await only one thing: that fate will catch up with me at some point, for we reap what we sow. Day after day, we may recognize our seed in good time, so that we do not have to reap negativity, but that our harvest will be the actualized fruit of the inner life, of the I Am.

We are not forsaken. We are not lost. We are never rejected or condemned because God is our eternal Father and He loves us. There is nothing greater than God's love. He is the absolute, perfect, selfless love. This absolute love that radiates into the whole universe, and that is also in each one of us, is the enveloping love that cares for us, that wants to free us from sin, from fear, desperation, from depression, from all that is human.

Let us realize each day that God, this unending love, is our Father. Then we will also become aware of the filiation to God. As conscious children of the All-Highest, children of this unending love, we will sense the desire in our heart to grow closer to this eternally infinite love, God's love because God's love is our cradle, as it were. The heart of love gave birth to us and laid us in the cradle of love, in the mighty All, in the eternal law of love.

Although we may have moved far from God and our very own eternal nature—in His heart we are His children. Just as God created us from His heart and laid us in the cradle of the All, in the infinite love, in the law of the Being, this is how He sees us—unburdened. And this is how He wants to have us with Him again, in His heart, in the eternal law of love, in the eternal homeland.

Our soul is striving to go home. In the earthly garment, as a human being, each and every one of us should purify himself with the power of the Christ of God, we should nourish the Redeemer-flame in ourselves and again become the selfless love, to thus again attain the birth into the eternal law, God, into our homeland. There, we will then live in peace again, in joy, in happiness and unity—in the selfless love, in the eternal law.

We are in a special phase of the history of humankind, in a mighty turn of time. This is a time of radical change. In the sphere of the highest material density, in the sphere of the Earth, everything is in evolution. Everything is beginning to vibrate. The base forces are becoming visible—but also the highest powers, the life, God. In this time of radical change from the darkness to the light, Christ gave us the law of the light, the Absolute Law. He revealed it in the human language, to the extent that human beings are able to understand it. He gave us insight into our true being.

In light of the Absolute Law, we also more clearly recognize our human burdens and bindings, and see the steps that will lead us out of the illusory life of the human ego.

Gabriele:

The true self is the selfless love. It is the eternal law, it is us—each one of us—in the pure Being, for God, our eternal Father, beheld us in His heart and created us as beings of love, as the true self, the law of love.

If we are the true self, if we have again become the law of the infinite, eternal love, we radiate the eternal love and are not dependent on the illusion of love, on the transformed selfless love: the self-love. We no longer depend on our neighbor. We no longer stand in the twilight of human, egocentric communication that says, if you give to me, I will give to you.

If we have found our way from egocentricity to a life in God, the I Am, then we are in the light of God and radiate the light of God. This results in steadfastness, closeness to God and communication with the eternal Being. We will no longer shine on each other with our illusion, the base ego. We will no longer want to shine before our neighbor because we radiate the love and wisdom of God. We no longer need our neighbor's praise, his recognition, his human assurance because we are. The person who is does not want to be anything. Nor does he want to have because he possesses the fullness.

Our path leads us to this. Each one of us must follow this path sooner or later—if not as a human being, then as a soul in the spheres of purification because our divine body is immortal, and, in every soul, the Redeemer spark is the way, the truth and the life. Therefore, it is only with Christ that we can reach our eternal Father—and each one will find his way to Him because the Eternal keeps us in His great heart of love.

How long we journey to the eternal Being is determined by ourselves. Whether we go through suffering, misery, fear, worry and illness, or whether we walk the direct path of love, by recognizing our sins in good time, by repenting of them with the strength of the Lord and committing them no more, this, we, in turn, determine ourselves.

In this do-no-more and in the actualization of the laws of God, the infinite love opens for us. Once we no longer commit the sinful, we begin to love God more and more, thus establishing communication with God, the love. This means that we will not have to suffer through our fate because we were and are reminded in good time, before suffering, worry and the like descend upon us.

If we are alert, if we follow the path of remorse and of clearing up, we will not fall into the vale of bitterness. Christ catches us in good time because we are walking the path of remorse and of clearing up and of no longer committing the sins. Thus, we journey on the path of love into the cosmic law, to the cradle, to the birthplace of our life, into the Kingdom of God.

As human beings, we are often oriented to people. We talk about standing together, about being friends that help and support one another. But when we look more closely at this, then we have to ask: Is this truly standing together, the true friendship and help? If we are honest, we often have to admit that it isn't really friendship but chumminess. We shine on each other and think that we have the highest with this because we confirm each other. But we do not affirm each other in our spiritual being. In-stead, it is our ego that communicates with our neighbor's ego. In this way, we mutually confirm and reinforce our human ego.

The Being, the divine I Am, is the truth. Our human ego belongs to the shine, and thus, to deception, to the lie. It hungers for the energy of being confirmed and exalted. To attain these, the ego disregards the true values, the values of truth, of loyalty, of integrity, of openness and honesty.

Perhaps we feel it is a minimal digression from truthful-ness when we say friendly things to our neighbor, which are not vivified from our heart, when we half-heartedly agree with him and flatter him. But what can develop from this is often of great consequence.

If we act in this way, then we deceive and lie not only to our neighbor, but we are not true to ourselves either, to our eternal self, which is the truth. From this grow bindings, disloyalty and much more.

Recognize that shine deceives and the one who falls for this can become a deceiver.

For this reason, do not surround yourselves with illusions, with the shine, but become the sun of love and justice in the sea of infinity.
Many souls and people move toward the Being, but few are in the Being. The one who merely thinks about the Being receives only from the illusion, and not from the source of life, which is the Being.

Gabriele:

The illusion, which deceives and defrauds, is thus our human ego that always wants to show off, that always expects something, that always acts in such a way that it attracts, in turn, humanness. With "humanness" is meant, as stated, the sinfulness against the soul. The one who looks only at the illusion, that is, at the human ego, and occupies himself with the human ego will never find his way to the truth. The one who relies on the illusion, on the human ego, which is deceptive, can become a deceiver because the ego is an obstacle to the truth.

The one who stands in illusion, in weakness because he bases himself on people and communicates with their human aspects, will also become weak when he is approached by temptation. He can become a traitor.

—this means with what is deceptive, by believing in the human ego and expressing what may not correspond to the truth—»... *but become the sun of love and justice in the sea of infinity.*« This means for us to strive for the eternal law, the sun of love and justice. Then we will immerse in the sea of infinity and move in the heart of God, in the law of love.

People who have taken some steps on the path to love will not look at the illusion. They will always seek the Being in the illusion and with the help of the Christ of God they will find it. They will not flatter the human ego, but from the illusion, they will find the Being, the law of life, and will express the law of life. In this way, they will never go astray and will never become deceivers.

Even when our neighbor wants to deceive us with the human ego, when he wants to pretend something to us, when he wants to lead us astray—the one who has taken some steps on the path to love will not let himself be blinded and misdirected by illusion. He will grasp the Being in illusion, and what he expresses will be the law of life. He will not let himself be put off, but will have security and steadfastness in himself.

This is why our path is the path of love, in order to become the sun of love and justice again, and immerse in the sea of infinity.

»*Many souls and people move toward the Being,*« and so, they are on the path to the Being, to the eternal law, »*but few are in the Being.*« Therefore, few, says the Lord, Christ, are presently already immersed in the sea of infinite love, in the eternal law.

»*The one who merely thinks about the Being receives only from the illusion, and not from the source of life, which is the Being.*« If we merely speak about the eternal law and do not fulfill it, then we remain the illusion. Then we radiate our own illusions, by pretending to be close to the law, God, or that we live in the law, God. Thus, we merely speak about the law, but have not yet actualized what we express. The one who merely speaks about the eternal love and does not actualize it is not in the eternal love. He maintains and speaks only illusion.

Illusion has many faces. If it is still important to us what our neighbor or our neighbors think of us, then ultimately, we still strive to pull the wool over our neighbor's eyes, to deceive him.

If we discover this in ourselves, we should take what came to us as a thought or recognition—for example, the words "what others think of me is still important to me"— and let it briefly take effect in us and reverberate in us. Then we will experience in ourselves several aspects of our human ego. We will become aware of them in this statement because we have addressed ourselves with it.

We can now clear up with Christ the human aspects we have recognized and no longer do them. The next step is that we ask ourselves: "Since I now no longer want to do this and that anymore and will no longer do it, what do I want to do instead?" In the earnest question is the answer. It is several spiritual principles of life. We note down these positive aspects. We input them in our brain cells and live accordingly.

In this way, we change our way of thinking. Via the recognition of our negative aspects and our decision to henceforth do what is positive and the will of God, we create a new, positive program, which is a support for us and makes us free.

If we realize that we want to convince others of this or that, then we are also on track of a human weakness, an aspect of our illusion.

If we want to convince, then we do not rest in God's love. We are not in the fulfillment of His will because then, we, the human being, want something. Let us re-member: God never wants to convince us because He is convinced of His love. He is the love. On the other hand, when we want to convince, we are not the law of love. Consequently, we want to prove something to our neigh-bor, which we have not yet proven to ourselves, that is, which we ourselves have not yet actualized.

To examine and to grasp our weaknesses and short-comings, we could ask ourselves: Where is my insecurity? What am I not yet convinced of?

If we beg for pity from our neighbor, then there is also a human weakness, a lack of energy, which our neighbor should fill for us. And the one who in response to our begging for human energy gives us the desired energy of encouragement, confirmation, agreement or pity also acts unlawfully. Both thus bind themselves to each other. Every exchange of human energy leads to binding.

On the other hand, if one of our neighbors is in need and requires help, we will support and help him as much as is possible for us, if our neighbor wants this. Genuine empathy with our neighbor, which grants us strength and wisdom for true help, is an aspect of the divine Mercy.

We will become the »*sun of love and justice in the sea of infinity*« by recognizing our shadows day by day, the aspects of our sinfulness, to then dissolve them with the strength of the Christ of God, so that the sun of love can set us aglow more and more. In this way, we gain the inner strength via our weaknesses through the sun of love.

Gabriele, the teaching prophetess
and emissary of God, explained about this:

We know that words are symbols. Feelings, sensations, thoughts and words bring forth pictures, since our language is the language of pictures. Words, whether heard or read, have their effect on us. If we read with our full attention or if we hear words and, at the same time, our thoughts are with our sense of hearing, then our consciousness is present and feels along with what is spoken. The result are pictures in us.

These pictures are significant for each one of us. They can be decisive for our present life on Earth. They tell us how we are thinking today or how we felt, sensed and thought in the past. Each one of us has different pictures because each one of us thinks differently. Each one of us also felt, sensed, thought and spoke differently in the past, and this results in the different pictures.

Our life on Earth becomes interesting as soon as we study our pictures, that is, look into our words or thoughts because we see ourselves in them. We experience ourselves in our way of feeling, sensing, thinking, speaking and acting. We also see our neighbor with whom we live in peace or enmity. Thus, we can recognize ourselves.

Words radiate their content. They set in motion what is stored in us that is light-filled or shadowed. Let us take the words, *»The one who belongs to the illusion wears many masks.«* Simply the words "illusion" and "masks" can cause many, many pictures to come up in us.

What is illusion? When people live together, illusion often crops up in the form of hypocrisy. For example, we speak sweetly, affirmatively, caringly, benevolently and lovingly, but what are our thoughts, our feelings and sensations like? Perhaps we disparage our neighbor, possibly sending him resentful or even hostile feelings and thoughts. Our words, however, sound friendly, caring and the like. We are thus hypocritical when we speak differently than we think. Our masks result from this.

Sensations and thoughts are creative. This is why they shape our appearance, our facial expressions, our gestures, our whole behavior. This is what we are as a human being. It marks us. It is our radiation. It is the way we behave. It is our appearance, and we also act accordingly—but often only when we are alone and feel unobserved.

In dealing with our fellowman, we often act differently. To conceal our negative, disparaging feelings, sensations and thoughts, we cover them with masks of seemingly positive words, a seemingly positive demeanor, seemingly positive gestures. These are, then, our masks.

The human being has many kinds of masks. Depending on what we do or with whom we are speaking, we act differently, according to the feelings, sensations, thoughts, words and deeds that we have input in our soul, in our conscious mind and subconscious. Either we behave in an upright, clear, assured and selfless manner because we have uncovered these aspects of a divine, lawful life in us through actualization, or we act hypocritically, by pretending to have these spiritual values. Under this mask, we conceal what may still shape us as a human being: the envious, disparaging, domineering traits.

Thus, hypocrisy has many different masks, which we put on according to the occasion. Whenever we act differently than we are, differently than we feel and think, we have put on a mask. And how often do we do this? Only when we begin to monitor our thoughts and our feelings, will we realize how far or near we are to truthfulness.

Therefore, we are not aware of our own mask-like character. We look at the surface of things and do not get to the bottom of things in ourselves. Thus, the one who is satisfied with masks knows neither himself nor his neighbor. He does not monitor himself. He does not examine what is going on behind the mask of his illusion.

Behind the game of hiding behind our masks, there is always the insatiable, greedy ego, the egoism that says: Everything only for me! Our ego always wants and it always wants more. This can happen only at the cost of our neighbor because equality is in the law of God. The human being wants recognition, wealth, exaltation, a good position in his profession and much more. Because he wants to gain something only for himself, he also looks only at his neighbor's masks—observing exactly how the neighbor reacts, how, in turn, the neighbor shapes his masks, that is, how his neighbor acts toward him. He looks only at the masks of his fellowman and weighs which mask he has to put on, to achieve with his fellowman the goal he has set for himself. Therefore, both are mask-makers and neither one concerns himself with his neighbor. They have only their own advantage in mind.

The person who is caught in this world of illusion remains lonely. Preoccupied solely with himself, concerned about his own advantage, he does not move in unity with his neighbor. On the contrary: Through his masks, through suspicion and deception, he keeps himself separate from his neighbor, at the same time creating bindings, that is, guilt. Then the the cleverer mask-maker dominates.

Because the person thinks only of himself, he is against his neighbor. He becomes unscrupulous and hostile. He lives in the satanic principle of "Divide, bind and rule."

Everything that is not divine is our human heritage. We have acquired it ourselves. The human heritage of an individual consists of his human feeling, sensing, thinking, speaking and acting. Under certain circumstances, this can result in external wealth, prestige and much more.

However, the meaning and purpose of our life on Earth is not to increase our earthly prospects and with this, possibly our burden of sin, as well. We should strive to attain our divine heritage, by recognizing our masks, discarding them little by little with Christ, and activating the principles of the inner life: equality, freedom, unity, brotherliness and justice, which, at the same time, are the principles of our divine heritage.

The one who wants to get out of this mask-like character and into a conscious life, into his own center, which is his original nature, and go toward Christ, who dwells in us, begins to recognize his masks. He begins to clear up his human aspects, his sinfulness, and to no longer do it. If we clear up our all-too-human aspects step by step with Christ, our Redeemer, then He will let us recognize in manifold ways what or how we should live. He then shows us aspects of our divine heritage, for example, the aspect of freedom that says: Do not force your neighbor to do what you do not want to do. Do not force your neighbor to bind himself to you and do what you want, so that it goes well for you. Recognize the divine commandment: What you expect from your neighbor, do it first. This results in freedom.

Thus, we experience in manifold ways the impulses from the center, from Christ. We experience them when we are ready to discard our masks and to accept the laws of life. This means, to attain our divine heritage again, step by step because we should become perfect again, just as God created us as His children, and as He beholds us in His heart.

Let us realize again and again that discarding our masks requires self-recognition first and accomplishing the turn from the undivine toward the positive, the divine. It means to let go of the negative and to gain a hold in the positive. Stated again with other words: We change ourselves, point by point and step by step.

If we were to simply take off our masks, that is, correct our behavior externally, then we would not change ourselves. We would put on the same masks, again and again.

If we were to simply put to one side the humanness we have recognized—who would we then be? Our masks permeate us because they are our life. Our feeling, sensing, thinking, speaking and acting—that is what we are! We should not simply cancel our humanness; we should not want to push it away. We should transform it, raising this energy potential out of the darkness and into the light.

This is why it is said: Recognize yourself. Clear things up. Do not do them anymore and instead, fulfill the divine spiritual principles that arise from this. The fulfillment of the spiritual principles of God fills us up again. It fills us with the divine, just as we were previously filled with the human. The illusory flows out of the vessel and the Being builds itself up.

Our masks are also programs that communicate. Life is communication. We could not live without communication. It is necessary to gradually replace the human communication with illusion, with communication with the divine, with the Being. This takes place through transformation, by changing our way of thinking, by reprogramming ourselves.

Day by day, at every moment, we can experience that we live in pictorial communication. At every moment, we can experience ourselves in our pictures. We can sense into our pictures—into the pictures of our feelings, thoughts, our words and actions.

Particularly in the beyond, when we live in the soul realms as souls, the pictures we have created come to us very realistically. In fact, we live and experience ourselves as if in our own motion picture. In the beyond, we experience on our own soul body what we have thought and spoken toward our neighbor, what we have done to him and much more. On Earth as human beings, let us recognize the great grace of being able to look into our film reel, to clear up our human ego, before we have to experience it on ourselves firsthand.

A piece of advice: Let us live consciously! Let us not preoccupy ourselves again and again with our past or with what our neighbor says and does! If we live in the present and if we are willing to recognize ourselves, then little by little we will become aware of what we have created as human aspects. What we clear up day after day, we will not have to suffer.

But the one who lives in the inner world, in Me, the Christ, is clear-sighted and farsighted. He no longer needs masks because he sees through everything and recognizes everything by way of the light of truth. That is the being in the stream of the Being, the personified being, the microcosm in the macrocosm.

Gabriele:

That is where we want to go. We want to be in the stream of the Being. We can take this as a task. In everything that comes toward us, whether we find human or divine aspects in it, we affirm: We want to be in the stream of Being.

We may all affirm the absolute as a goal-picture, so to speak: I am in the stream of Being. Then we will feel the softness, the warmth and the tenderness of the stream. Then we will feel the secureness in the Father, the unending love that sets us aglow.

Everything that you see and that upsets you is your mirror. It influences your person. If you do not follow the path of self-recognition, you perceive only the reflections of your base ego and that of your neighbor. If you continue to do this, then you become ever more entangled in the mine and thine. You then differenciate between yourself and your neighbor. This is the law of the human ego. It is: »Divide, bind and rule.«

Gabriele, the teaching prophetess
and emissary of God, explained about this:

Everything that upsets us wants to tell us something. We get upset because we are hit by a certain sending potential. If we see, hear or remember something that moves us strongly, if we are seized by agitation, bad temper, indignation, irritation or anger, or if we think of an issue again and again, we should ask ourselves: *What upset us?* To recognize this is important for us because this is exactly what we are, ourselves.

Let us start from the eternal law, from our divine heritage. As pure beings we get upset neither about humanness nor about the divine. God does not get upset about our sinfulness because He is perfect. If we get upset by our neighbor's sinfulness, or by a statement, be it lawful or unlawful, then there are several things underlying this in ourselves. Human aspects, sinfulness, in us were set in motion, which lie in our soul waiting to be recognized and cleared up, that is, settled. These sins mark us. They shape our human personality with all the aspects of our ego. They shape our features and our human body.

Recently, the divine world was asked this question: Do the pure beings recognize us, who are now human beings? The answer essentially was: We look at the incorruptible in the person, at his innermost being, what is pure in the center of the soul. We recognize you in this. If we were to look solely at the shell, the human being, we would not recognize you.

This shows us that we have disfigured ourselves through our sinfulness. Our sins mark us. Via our feelings, sensations, thoughts, words and actions, we mark our body, and this is also how we behave. It is how we speak, how we act, how we live with our neighbor. Thus, our behavior is our mirror at every moment.

If we do not look at ourselves in this mirror and do not clear up our humanness, then we look only at our base ego and at the base ego of our neighbor. Therefore, we perceive only the sinfulness, which upsets us again and again. Through this, we create, in turn, causes, sins because the irritation produces many thoughts that burden us. This is why we are given the days, the hours, the minutes, the moments, to look at ourselves when we get upset or when we recognize that the same and similar thoughts move us, again and again.

Each day contains the chance for us to look at ourselves, at how we are, in the many moments. We, the human being, are nothing more than the mirror, the expression of our soul, with its light-filled sides and its shadowed sides. Thus, we can assume that we would not awaken in the morning if the day did not have several things to say to us. Our soul is waiting for us to find its shadows and to clear them up with the power of the Christ of God in us.

If we become aware of a wrong behavior, a sin, then we take the path of remorse, of forgiving and of making amends. In this, what is important is the remorse, that we painfully feel in our own world of feelings our lack of love toward our neighbor. If we ask Christ for the strength to feel remorse, He will give us the strength to repent from our heart. We repent and ask for forgiveness. We, ourselves, forgive and make amends for what can be made good. In short, we clear things up.

If we no longer do what has been cleared up, then what happens in our soul? Sinful aspects are transformed into light. This also has its effect on our body because the body is the depiction of our soul. In time, the person becomes softer, more sensitive. The hard, rigid ego is changed into selflessness and sensitivity—aspects of kindness. The expression of our language becomes finer and our behavior more prudent. From this, emerges a sense of community and brotherliness, more and more.

Therefore, we first have to soften ourselves by feeling remorse. Remorse prepares the soul, so that the sinful aspects give way and what is lawful and light-filled can unfold. Genuine remorse results in a strong will and the strength to no longer do what we have recognized as human aspects in us. Since everything is contained in all things, this results in divine spiritual principles that we fulfill from now on. Divine spiritual principles are aspects from the eternal law. If we do not become aware of a divine spiritual principle, then we remind ourselves of the Ten Commandments and the Sermon on the Mount, just as the Lord taught them to us. We can derive one or more spiritual principles of inner life from them, which we then fulfill each day. In this way we grow into our divine heritage. It is the goal of our life on Earth to again enter the origin, our inner homeland, to open our eternal heritage, while still in the physical body.

If instead of looking at ourselves, we look at our neighbor, we begin to make value-judgments. We disparage our neighbor to exalt our human ego. In making value-judgments, we disavow our brother, our sister: That is you and I am I. Furthermore: This is mine and that is yours. Thus, we separate ourselves from our neighbor and tie ourselves to our views and opinions. If our human ego is stronger than that of our neighbor, we try to dominate him. This is how the satanic principle works: "Divide, bind and rule."

Let us realize that when we strive for domination and power, then—in the long run—we will not gain from this. Of course, things can go well for a certain time, but in the end, we will be in an inferior position because power serves only to assert the human ego. One day we will have to suffer under it ourselves.

The divine principle is: "Link and be." This means: Link with your neighbor in selfless, divine love. Recognize that the positive powers in him are a part of you—and be in God, be in your inner being, be at home there, and draw more and more from the source of unending love.

From the divine "Link and be," arises the harmony of powers, the equality. This results in unity because we are for, and with, our neighbor. At the same time, freedom emerges because we do not make our neighbor dependent on us and do not bind ourselves to our neighbor, either. The unity in God is the life of the community, which is brotherliness and sisterliness. Then there is no above and below.

The one who wants to make room in his life for the basic principles of the inner life begins with equality. Equality means: We are all brothers and sisters, children of one Father. If we integrate these aspects of truth in our life, freedom, unity and brotherliness will result. Then justice will also awaken. We will no longer argue and judge, but will weigh things, to always be just, as God wants it.

To weigh things is to grasp things from within, to grasp the essential. The spiritual person weighs things, by getting to the bottom of the matter, the situation or difficulty. He looks behind the façade of humanness and, in the situation, grasps the positive, the core, the divine spiritual principle, which can be built on. He does not let himself be deceived by the perhaps shimmering, humanly shaped external conditions, and is able to assess them at their true worth. In this way, he finds the answer in all questions, the solution in all difficulties. Thus, he will do justice to his fellowman. He is able to advise and help in the spirit of divine justice, the divine law. He acquires the ability to do this only by the fact that he is just to himself, that is, he recognizes himself day after day and overcomes his human aspects.

Solely the law of God is the justice. All human laws, as we know them in the world, we call our rights. As long as we insist on our rights, we always insist on our ego. If we let the justice of God prevail, then we weigh things and each one will experience justice.

If we immerse into this awareness more and more, then we will no longer judge and condemn according to the word "right," for example, "What I say is right." We will beget ourselves, as it were, into the consciousness of God, in order to attain justice and to be just toward our fellow humans, and not lastly, toward ourselves. It is from justice alone—also toward ourselves—that we gain respect for our true life and respect toward our fellow human beings.

Gabriele, the teaching prophetess
and emissary of God, explained about this:

We attain the connection with the innermost being, with Christ in us, only by clearing away the mountains of our human ego, that is, our sins, in order to immerse in the light that Christ is in us. The connection with the innermost being is the connection with the wellspring, in which all forms of existence live. In this wellspring—we also speak of the »stream«—live minerals, plants, animals, all beings, all souls and people. Nothing and no one is excluded because God disowns no human being, no soul, no form of life.

The origin of the wellspring is the heart of God. The wellspring itself, the stream, is the eternally flowing law—God. God, our Father, always beholds us in the wellspring, in the stream, in His heart. However, we left this, our eternal, inner homeland, by acting against the divine law. Through this, we went onto dry land and now thirst for the waters of life. We are sitting, as it were, on dry land because through sin, we have broken away from our innermost being, from the consciousness of the I Am. Thus, we became hard and are against ourselves because we are against our neighbor because we are against God's forms of creation, for example, against animals, plants, minerals and stones.

Let us realize again and again that if we are against the life, God, then, at the same time, we are against ourselves. What we do to our neighbor—and to our second neighbors, the life forms of nature—we do to ourselves. Therefore, we sin against our neighbor, against our second neighbor and against ourselves. Through this, we divide and rule. If, through a life according to the laws of love and peace, we open ourselves for the wellspring, then we live for and with, our neighbor. We then establish the connection, so to speak, in our innermost being, and there, in the stream, in the wellspring, is all the Being—the nature kingdoms, all the beings of light, all the positive powers of human beings and souls.

If we trespass against a person, then we step out of the wellspring. If we trespass against an animal, we also step out of the wellspring. We separate ourselves from God, as it were, in order to rule over the one person, the one animal.

»Live connected with the innermost being« means: Establish communication with the pure, the incorruptible, in all forms of life—in animals, plants, minerals, in human beings, in fact, in everything that surrounds us. That is living in the Spirit of God. As long as we do not strive for this life and are not in this life, we always feel ourselves as so-called loners. Why? It is because we are not for, and with, our neighbor.

Therefore, if we allow room for our human wanting, our base ego, we are surrendering to our human ego. This means that we forsake the place of fullness, the oasis, the wellspring of the inner being, and go out into the desert. What is the result of this? Our base ego controls us and it is possible that other base forces control us via our ego. These forces are intent on leading us farther and farther into the desert, away from the water of life, away from the bread of salvation. They ensnare us by stimulating our desires and ideas. In us, they slip into arguments for disparagement, hostility and strife. They always steer us toward our neighbor, with the rationale that the neighbor is to blame, the colleague, the partner, the children, the parents. Everyone is to blame, so goes the influencing by the darkness, everyone—only not we, ourselves. Quarreling and fighting emerge from this. In quarreling, in fighting, a lot of divine energy of life is transformed down into still more and more negative energy. The darkness receives this. It lives from it.

Therefore, we have to ask ourselves: Are we also such producers of negative energy? We should monitor ourselves daily. How do we live? Do we live in quarreling, in squabbling, in animosity? Do we live in the desert of our ego and even feel well there? Then we are the donors of those base energies from which the hierarchy of the darkness lives, using them to lead astray and to corrupt.

So that we may find our way out of the quagmire of the all-too-human and go toward the light, Christ gave us "The Great Cosmic Teachings." He helps us to change our way of thinking. He helps us to find our way into our innermost being, to Him.

Who does not want to rest in himself, to be at home in the secure refuge of his inner being? However, we may not think that we can take up residence there by simply resolving: »Now I change my ways. From now on I am in my inner being.« If there is a lot of gravel in front of our house, then we first have to get rid of it, in order to enter the house. It is also this way with our life. Initially this means: Recognize yourself and clear up the gravel lying in front of your innermost being, in front of the altar of love. If we clear it up with Christ and no longer commit the sinfulness, then step by step we will find our way into our inner being, to Christ, our Redeemer and Leader.

Therefore, what needs to be done? Nothing other than to clear up our past, so that we live consciously in the present, in the day. Then we will experience ourselves each day, and recognize from this what needs to be cleared up, in order to find our way into the center, into the stream, into the wellspring, and become one with Christ, one with God, our eternal Father.

To find our way into the center means to be for and with our neighbor. To be in the center means to be in the stream. Then we have returned from the desert world. Our arid soul has received the water of life again.

Only based on our own free decision to fulfill the laws of God will we draw ever closer to the wellspring, the eternal Being, with Christ.

That is the goal of every person, whether he accepts it at this time or not. At some point in time, in the human being or the soul, the awareness will dawn that the goal of existence is the journey home into the heart of God, into our center. So that we can find this path, Christ became our Redeemer, the One who prepares our way to the Father's house. Through Christ, no soul and no human being is lost. He strengthens and inspires. He leads and guides us—if we live in the day with Him, that is, if we recognize, clear up and do-no-more. However, we should ask ourselves: When can Christ take us by the hand and lead us to the Father? When we are ready and willing. He will not force us into anything.

The law of cause and effect, which was created by the adversary—»Divide, bind and rule«—is the person-oriented law, the egoity-law that knows only itself, the base ego.

Gabriele:

The person-oriented law, the egoity-law, is our personal law. Every single one of us, that is, the person, created this for himself. We created it with the human principles of creation, our feelings, sensations, thoughts, words and actions. These five principles: feeling, sensing, thinking, speaking and acting, which were reversed, transformed down from the divine into the human, are those principles of creation or characteristics of creation, with which we create our personal laws. These consist of the aspects of our base ego—of all the negative and unloving aspects that shape our ego.

Thus, we could say that with every violation of the divine law, each one of us forms his own, self-created law. The totality of all person-laws of the individual human beings and souls is the law of sowing and reaping. Based on this, each one experiences his inputs, that is, his personal law, but never the personal law of another. Thus, what a person creates, that is, sows, through his way of living and acting, is what he will reap. In this way, each individual creates his own fate.

The adversary wants division and binding. People should bind themselves to people and things, generate possessions and property, to thus bring about division, the mine and thine. The one who has acquired the most property rules over those who have less.

Gabriele:

Through the fact that we human beings bind ourselves to people, to possessions and property, we leave behind traces, the manifestations of the principle of our personal law. Since everything is energy and everything is based on communication, we are in communication with the people to whom we have tied ourselves, or with the possessions and property with which we are intertwined. Once our physical body passes on, the soul continues to be in communication with what it has left behind, its personal principles of the law. If it does not undo these bindings in the purification planes, where it will be after the death of the body, then it is possible that it will incarnate again in those places, where it once left its traces as a human being, in order to work off what it is still bound to.

In God, in the eternal law, there are no personal possessions and no personal property, no being that binds itself to another being. In God, all are equal and are heirs to the great totality. Infinity belongs to every being as essence, as light and power. It is solely a person's human aspects, his sins, that create the separation and the mine and thine.

If the sins pile up in the soul, then soul and person break away from unity and equality. They separate from the eternal stream of life, God. They become poor in light and wisdom and crave possessions and property. They differentiate into mine and thine. They divide by way of words and terms. They separate—"here we, there, the others"—in their feeling, sensing, thinking, speaking and acting.

From this, emerge the domineering nature and greed. The one who possesses more rules over the others, that is, he is their god. With this, he puts himself above his fellowman and ultimately, above God because God dwells in every person. The one who puts himself above the dwelling place of God, above the person, puts himself above God.

Gabriele:

A majority of so-called Christians and many of other faiths have their holy scriptures in their bookcases merely as decoration and for prestige. Seldom from their own inner initiative, do they read in them now and then. The message of the scriptures was taught, but not lived. So what the great prophets of God and, above all, Jesus of Nazareth, taught was not actualized.

Since with so-called Christianity—but also with all adherents of other faiths—through the fight for mine and thine, ethics, customs and morals are going downhill more and more, the Son of God, the Christ of God, has come again to us human beings—not as a human being, but as the prophetic Spirit. He has come to teach the law of love once again, and to motivate the people to live it, that is, to give it new heart, just as He also did as Jesus of Nazareth.

Christ, the Son of God, who no longer is a human be-ing, now teaches through the prophetic word what He announced as Jesus, and makes true what He promised us 2000 years ago: to lead us into all the truth. In this materialistic world, which is heading for the abyss, He again raises the law of eternal love in willing people. The law of God unifies the people in brother-sister-hood. He, the Spirit of the Christ of God, guides the people who fol-low Him—by accepting the eternal laws, immersing them-selves in them and living according to them—into the New Era, into the Era of the Christ.

Boundaries restrict and lead to hardening. When boundaries remain in force for a long time, people believe they are separated from each other by these boundaries. They then speak about different mentalities that have little in common. From this attitude, awaken indifference and enmity toward the neighbor who, according to the eternal law, is a part of every soul.

Once the adversary has caused division among the people, he then rules and creates more external possibilities for binding people, for example, binding people to creeds, rites, dogmas and cults and, at the same time, to superiors, to subordinates, to husband or wife, to children or material assets, to money and property. From this, emerges the causal law, in which every egocentric person and every egocentric soul has its existence, until they break out of the maelstrom of the human ego and strive for the divine that links and that is.

This world and the planet Earth appear in the divine as a mirror image because the world and the Earth were reversed into their opposite.

Gabriele, the teaching prophetess
and emissary of God, explained about this:

The planet Earth is the Earth as such. The world is what the human being has set up on the Earth. Earth and world are merely mirror images of the eternal Being. They are not the eternal Being because with his person-law, by turning away from God, humankind reversed everything. Thus, everything that we see is merely the reflection of the Being, the side that is turned away from the light, but not the light itself.

The heritage of God to His children can be explained as follows:

That which is Mine is also thine. It is for you and for each child the same, namely, everything from all things, from the One, who is.

The adversary reversed this divine principle of the law and says: The mine and thine belong to me. The adversary believes that through this reversal, he can assimilate everything and be lord over everything and everyone. He wants the power for himself alone and wants to defeat God because he wants to be God, himself.

The materialistic person who is oriented to himself is of the opinion that he is the ruler of the world and of the All. He thinks he is a god because he sees only a small perspective of life and this is, moreover, enveloped by his human ego. This idolatry lends him the arrogance to think he can continue to develop creation, all according to his image and standard. In reality, he leads himself into the abyss and destroys matter and his physical body.

In the number eight lies the Deity, in despising, the adversary, who reversed the holy Being, the eight, and turned it into despising. In this way, he created his Fall-law that will bring him his downfall.

Gabriele:

The symbolic figure eight is the Deity, the Godhead it-self, the origin of all things and all Being. From the origin, from the Godhead, emerged and emerge the creations in all seven basic realms of infinity. The adversary despises this absolute principle of creation, the Godhead because he wants to be creative himself and create his own cre-ation according to his image and standard. With this, he created his Fall-law, the law of sowing and reaping. He will himself be defeated by his law because the one who sows hatred will reap hatred. The one who kills his neigh-bor will be killed himself. The one who despises others will be despised. And the one who thinks he can shape everything according to his image and standard destroys all matter.

We are living in the end time. The one who looks closely at the goings-on on the Earth knows that the adversary of God is falling into the trap. It is snapping shut and he can no longer be effective. He has exhausted his own creation potential and now, the Spirit, the eternal Creator-God, is acting to create heaven and Earth anew, according to His eternal image, the eternal law. This means that the puri-fication planes and matter will very gradually be refined and transformed and again adjusted to the eternal heav-ens, from where the Fall emerged.

Gabriele, the teaching prophetess
and emissary of God, explained about this:

Every one of our neighbors is the temple of God, in which the Spirit of the eternal Father dwells. The one who does not respect this temple, who disdains, robs and exploits it, also wants to destroy the holy of holies, God, in the temple. He thus puts himself above God as the super-god. And since he does not respect his neighbor as the temple of God, he does not respect his own temple, either.

Therefore, the one who does not show respect to his neighbor despises God in his neighbor and in himself. Such a person is always intent on letting himself be honored by others. The one who thinks it is important to be honored does not give God the honor.

The adversary leads soul and person into the world of the senses. He tempts them with the illusion of their neighbor. He shows them what others possess and have, their mine and for me, and makes them greedy and envious. In this way, he leads them away from their inner-most being, the Being, the fullness in God, and toward the external world, to illusion.

The one who allows himself to be blinded by illusion will become like the one who is already blinded: greedy, envious and rapacious. In his craving, he uses all the weapons at his disposal to attain what his neighbor's illusion radiates to him: outer splendor attained through prestige, means and opportunities that are reflected in money and wealth.

In this way, the person moves away from the inner fullness more and more, becoming poor of inner strength and spirituality. He trains his mind and raises it to the intellect, to become an intellectual who has knowledge about the illusion, the deception. In so doing, he no long-er knows the Being, his true self, the reality of life, but knows only himself, his small world where he dominates, rules and binds his neighbor to himself and to his opin-ions, to which he, himself, is bound.

Gabriele:

Realize that the illusion is what is deceptive in the person and in his word. He speaks differently than he thinks. Thus, his thoughts are contrary to his word. He may talk in a friendly manner and, at the same time, think in a disparaging, envious, greedy and vengeful way. This is the forked tongue, with which many speak.

The eternal Being is the eternal law. It is straightforward, upright. It is the selfless, eternally giving love. It is the truth. The thoughts, sensations and feelings of the one who speaks the truth are just as truthful as the word. This is the word of God in the soul and through the person.

Woe to those who use their intellect to idolize human beings. Imperceptibly, such a person creates idols. In this world, he attaches himself to them, and after his physical death, he is bound to them.

Gabriele:

The one who obeys people more than God, the eternal law of love, puts people above God. He is bound to them through this. He will adhere to them in this world and, likewise, as a soul after the death of his body. God will not separate what a person has bound to himself or what binds him to others because each one has his free will to think and do as he pleases. This is his person-law, which will come to him in this earthly existence or in the soul realms. It is the law of sowing and reaping.

The one who is greedy and egocentric, who exalts himself with the splendor of illusion, always wants to be the greatest and the best, and wants to rule over everything and everyone.

The drive to dominate contains, in turn, a flowering of fear that another one could be greater, could attain more splendor, more prestige and wealth. Hounded by fear, he thinks that his eyes and ears have to be everywhere, to ensure that he is not defrauded. If a rival appears, he will be fought. If the rival has abilities that he does not have, then, at the same time, envy and animosity grow, and not least, aggressiveness, the effort to eliminate the rival.

Fear and aggressiveness lead to curiosity. The ego-person wants to see everything, to listen in on everything, to know about everything, to protect himself from dangers that could come toward him from his neighbors, who have more prestige, who seem to be better, smarter and richer. This leads to his constantly having to get his bearings. Curiosity urges him to look to the front, to the back, above and below, to the right and to the left, to see and to listen in on everything. In doing this, he sees and hears only himself because what is driving him, his human ego, drives toward him the same or like things again.

The egocentric person sees himself in every situation. He hears himself in every situation. He meets only himself— people who are, in turn, similar to himself. He and his

Gabriele:

We read that every person speaks only himself and hears only himself. This happens because every person lives in his plasma, which is also called his aura or his atmosphere. The atmosphere of a person consists of his life film. The soul brought a part of this life film along with it into this incarnation.

As soon as a young person can differentiate between good and bad, he clears up the life film he brought with him or he continues to add to it, by enlarging the reel of film with countless pictures from the days, hours, minutes and seconds. In the center of the reel of film is the person and the person's soul. Everything that has formed around the person is his life film. It is his atmosphere, his person-law, also called plasma or aura.

The person is in constant communication with this, his life film. When he is asked a question, he can call up only aspects from the repertoire of this, his own atmosphere, his own life film, passing on only what he has stored.

This is why each one speaks himself. This will continue to take place until the person has worked off his so-called film reel by recognizing his wrong behavior and clearing it up each day. If he no longer commits these sins, the pictures on his film reel will gradually fall away from him. With the power of the Christ of God, they transform into positive, divine energies. With these positive, divine energies, person and soul transmit into the eternal Being and are in communication with the eternal law. Then it is possible for him to give his fellowman a divine, lawful answer to his questions and situations because he can understand his neighbor according to the latter's state of spiritual consciousness, and can fathom his words and situations. He no longer speaks his base self, his human ego, his own repertoire from his film reel, but the eternal, divine law that knows about all things and sees and grasps everything.

Gabriele:

We have read that the life film of each individual also surrounds him. In this life film, in his atmosphere, in his plasma, he breathes and moves. No matter to where his sense of hearing orients itself—he hears only himself because he hears toward without, through his plasma, through his life film. What sounds in his ear is the echo from his life film. He hears only himself because each one can hear only what he has entered in his life film.

The same is true for the organ of sight. The human being looks into his surroundings through his life film. And his surroundings are shaped accordingly. May the one who does not believe this, try it out. Let's ask one of our fellow people how he sees a certain landscape, for instance, or what aspects does he see on a person. Let's also ask him how his food tastes because the senses of smell and taste also correspond to the individual's plasma. When we ask the same questions of another of our fellow people, we will also receive different answers.

The same is true for the sense of touch. Each one can touch the same object and yet sense and feel differently. Each one also has a different breathing rhythm, and this corresponds, in turn, to his life film, that is, to his atmosphere, his plasma, which surrounds him. Each one moves differently than his neighbor. Each one has another way of walking, all according to his life film.

From this follows that the one who curiously watches his neighbor experiences himself in his thoughts and feelings. The one who listens in on the conversations of his neighbor hears from them only what is in his own plasma.

Thus, we live in our own deceptive ego-world and do not know at all that we deceive ourselves and are thus the deceived ones. As long as we live under the pressure of our own causes, that is, in our film reel, we are not consciously linked with God.

This is why the path signifies: Clear up your human ego that you have recognized, your sinfulness. Do not do it anymore. Go within, into the temple that you are, and fulfill the laws of God, step by step. Then you will also gradually reach the innermost part of your temple.

Gabriele, the teaching prophetess
and emissary of God, explained about this:

The human word is not the word of God. Jesus of Nazareth also taught this to those among His apostles and disciples who could understand it. Let us ask ourselves: Can we understand it?

Who are we as human beings? Are we still the self-confident person who is so proud of his human aspects? Or are we the person who is aware of his eternal self, who matures into the awareness of his filiation to God each day more, by fulfilling the will of the eternal Father more and more and ever more joyfully?

If we strive for the awareness that we are children of God, we should act like children of God. We can prove ourselves as children of God by checking day by day whether our words, our thoughts, feelings and sensations correspond to the divine stream, the divine law. When we make the effort to question ourselves daily, we become questioners. We probe our human ego, to clear it up with Christ and to no longer commit the sinfulness we have recognized. Then we devote ourselves more and more to the eternal stream, God, thus becoming children of God because we fulfill His holy will.

The children of God are in the stream, in the law. They are permeated by the law—in fact, the entire, spiritual divine body is the law, compressed, eternal law. They live in the stream, in the law. They fulfill the law and thus prove themselves to be children of infinity, to be children of the eternal Father. Our task as human beings is to again become the children who fulfill the will of God.

Thus, day after day, every hour and every minute, it behooves us to ask ourselves: Are we children of God? Are we aware of what we have thought, spoken and done? Is everything that went and goes out from us in accordance with the eternal law? Have we therefore proven ourselves to be children of the selfless love? Are we in the stream of infinite love?

When we let what lies in these few words fall deep within us, then we sense that it is nothing other than our path.

Let us bring to mind that we are human beings because we rejected the filiation to God, or we still reject it. We think it may be possible that there is a God, whose children we are, but in our thoughts, words and deeds, we are the human being with his ideas and opinions, his desires, his judgments and prejudices. Therefore, if we live according to the dictates of our ego, our ego is our god, our idol. Then the human being wants to be God himself. Don't we want to be even greater than God, when we say, for instance: »That is my opinion. That is how I want to see it and that is how I want it to be«?

An opinion is human. If we express an opinion, this says that we do not know what we are saying. We merely think it could be so, and do not know it. Nevertheless, we make this, our opinion, the standard, the law in our life: "As I think, so shall it be, and not otherwise." With this, we place ourselves above the Intelligence, God. With this, we say: "I, the human being, know better than You." Thus, we reject the filiation to God and betake ourselves more and more out of the eternal stream, out of the eternal law.

If we accept the filiation, we bow before the great Spirit and examine ourselves, always with the question: Is what I thought and spoke the will of the eternal Father?

Am I thus His child—or merely the human being who places himself above God? Am I an idol, or what am I? We should ask ourselves these questions each day because many steps need to be taken from the ego-person to the conscious child of God on the path into the eternal stream, into the eternal law.

Therefore, let us look back. How was our past week? How did we act during the past hours of the day? Did we place our words into the holy stream? Did we examine ourselves, or did we just allow the invaluable days, the energies of the day, to be wasted? Did we really live or were we lived? Did we live in God? Or were we controlled by our opinions, ideas and our intellect? With our feeling, thinking, speaking and acting, were we a part of the Being or of illusion?

If we live in illusion, then we have put up a façade, something external that is deceptive, that is not the way we truly are. Then we may seem to be upright and honest, but behind the illusion we may be false, dishonest and underhanded. Appearances are deceptive. And behind the appearance is, in turn, illusion, behind the façade of sweet words is a sour or even malicious mindset.

Our ego consists of masks, of façades, of illusion. When we recognize this, then we should get going and take off our masks, our façade, step by step, and look at ourselves, at how we are. Whom do we want to deceive? God? He sees into our heart. He sees everything. Do we want to put on an act for our neighbor? What do we get out of it? If our fellowman believes what we say, then, insofar as it is illusion, we are bound to him, thus increasing our burden of sin.

If we have recognized ourselves, if we get going and clear things up, we should not neglect to clearly resolve for a new, positive course. We decide for ourselves: In the future, this is the way we will think, speak and act. If the old program wants to steal in again, a positive guideline for our life—insofar as it is lawful, that is, in accordance with the will of the Father—helps us again and again to quickly come out of our human situation.

»The word of God is the stream of the All.« In this one sentence, Christ tells us what omnipresence is. Let us allow these words to resound in us once more:

»The word of God is the stream of the All.« His holy word streams through infinity and is always present. It is present in every soul, in every human being, in nature, in every animal, in every plant. It is present in every feeling, in every sensation, in every thought, in every word. In every movement of our body, in every stirring of our emotions, in our wanting, in desires and longings, God is present everywhere because the stream of infinity is in everything and flows throughout all things.

Why are we able to comprehend the stream of the All so little? Because we stay too often and too long at the edge of the stream because we occupy ourselves too long with our human programs—with what we have inflicted on ourselves as sinfulness, that is, with what is stored in our soul, and what marks our brain cells and body cells.

If we move our human programs and they move us, we are in communication with the humanness that is our own. We have not only input it into our soul, into our brain and into every cell of our body, but also into the stars of the material universe and into the stars of the purification planes. We are in communication with all these sending stations of our ego. However, this communication has nothing to do with the divine stream, the eternal law, but with our human, sinful principles. As long as we are in constant communication with our human aspects, we do not manage to reach the stream. We experience it seldom or not at all, and we do not grasp it, either. We turn away from the stream and do not activate the divine power. In this way, we are ultimately turning our back on God and telling Him that He should wait until we are ready. God keeps the principle of freedom. He will not impose Himself on the one who does not want to accept Him. In this way, we place ourselves against and above God.

If we do not yet live in our center, if we are oriented to without, oriented to our person, if we still work primarily with our intellect, then we are in communication with our sinfulness and are not in direct communication with God. It may very well be that the innermost part of our soul is unceasingly in communication with the eternal stream because the incorruptible core of being, our true being, the divinity in us, is always in the stream. However, the eternal stream cannot totally flow through all the particles of the soul and all the cells of the body, as long as we develop resistance to Him in us.

We humans talk a great deal. However, our words often actualize themselves in a different way than we want. For example, we talk about health and yet are afraid of suffering, hardship and illness. What is actualized? What we have filled our words with is what is actualized: our feelings, what we are afraid of. We want outer joy, but experience the inner and the outer suffering. Why? Because we do not rejoice in God, but pay homage to the outer joy, to our desires, our longings, our passions. That is the joy that becomes suffering.

»The word that you speak has value and power only as far as you have actualized what you express.« If we have actualized what we say, then the word is a part of God. It is divine. And this word that is actualized in us and around us brings inner joy and the security in God. It guides us to the filiation to God.

Much is spoken about peace, and yet, there is no peace. The more often people talk about peace, the more often they wage war. Why? It is because the word is not vivified. It is neither permeated with the power of actualization, nor permeated by the stream. It is simply spoken from our intellect. Those who talk about peace often do not believe in peace themselves, and do not have peace, either. They are belligerent in their feelings and sensations, and are equipped to do battle. The battle, in turn, brings suffering. The word "peace" is merely the façade. Behind it is a spirit of pugnacity.

»Only what you have fulfilled, that is, actualized, goes into the person.« Our inner and outer life is never limited to ourselves. As we are, that is how we radiate. With every feeling, with every sensation, every thought and every word, we emit energies that strive to generate what lies in them. They are realized.

»This word is empty. It is hollow, as it were, and does not know the depth of the All, which I Am.« The word that is merely a façade, an illusion, has no power and no active divine content. Thus, it is not permeated by the stream of love. It is not filled because the person is not fulfilled.

The human word, spoken without actualization, can become our downfall because we do not do justice to our neighbor with it. We give to him from illusion instead of from the Being. Such words are deception. Binding and guilt grow from them, and we will again become free of these only by recognizing and clearing them up. However, we will become free only if our neighbor, whether soul or person, also forgives us.

The divine stream is always present, whether we experience it, or whether we have cut ourselves off from it, through the barriers of our human ego, our sinfulness. If we are on the path, if we actively strive to draw closer to the divine, to the stream of the Being, then we experience gifts from the grace and love of our Father. Although we are often still those who struggle with their human aspects, we may immerse in the stream again and again. God, our Father, allows this, so that we experience and learn what it means to live in Him.

Once we have cleared up something from our heart, once we have felt remorse from our heart and attained forgiveness, then, for instance, we feel this stream. We feel the liberation. In the soul, we feel the hope, the assurance, and sense how the Spirit of God flows more through us. From this, also grows the longing to draw closer to God, our Father, ever more quickly.

As soon as we have attained forgiveness, a burden, a shadow on our soul, transforms into light through Christ. Then we feel what it means when the stream of God flows through us. If we are then negligent, we climb out of the stream again, onto the edge, and continue to think about our human aspects. At the same moment, we are emitting, and again receiving, only ourselves—our human ego, which we have input. With this, the sinfulness against the soul is meant.

If we move in our humanness for a longer period of time without resolving it, if we think about our human ego again and again, then it is possible that so-called in-jections, the influence from the adversary, will take place. We burden ourselves more and more, and are pushed away from our life of actualization, from the Inner Path, which we should follow and for which we have become a human being.

We should consciously guard ourselves from again igniting the transformed negative communications that want to again entangle us in similar situations. This means that day after day we strive to no longer do the negative things we have recognized. Instead, we strive to build up the positive, lawful aspects, for which we have decided. We gain inner stability only by being consistent.

We will become a child of God only via the daily strug-gle with our human ego, which is our idol. Thus, let us ask ourselves again and again: Are we children of God? Do we fulfill the will of our heavenly Father? Have we vivified our words? What is behind our words? Are we façades, that is, illusion, or being? Can Christ, the stream of love, shine through our soul and through our body?

If we ask these same questions over and over again and examine ourselves in this way, we will gradually be-come sensitive. We will stop ourselves—then, when we are still inclined toward the human. We tell ourselves: Stop now! It can't go on this way. This determination is already the help for a higher life.

Let us once more bring to mind the words of the Christ of God, the statement: *» ... the depth of the All, which I Am. «*

Who or what is this "I Am"? "I Am" is the mighty Spirit of the All, the law of infinity. "I Am" is the stream that permeates and penetrates everything, that breathes through everything. "I Am" is the constant presence. It is God. God is the life. There is no other life apart from the life, God.

If we human beings speak of our "life," we are speaking about the energy of God that was transformed down, about our ego-life—unless we live in the law of God. If we live in the stream, ourselves, in the divine Being, then we rightly speak of "life." In contrast, everything else is the life that has been energetically transformed down.

Let us realize that we have taken a part of the divine energies, of the divine life, and transformed it down, transformed it into our human life. As human beings we also frequently speak the words "I am." However, we relate this "I am" to our humanness, that is, to the transformed-down energies, by saying, for instance: "I am a human being with my faults," or "I am scattered today," or "I am disappointed," and other such things. This human life, which is expressed in our human thoughts, in our human feelings and sensations, is not the eternal I Am.

The life that has been transformed down to the low level of our human aspects must be transformed up by each one of us into the mighty, eternal I Am, from whence we went forth. We—every single one of us—are on the Earth to again change and transform up the humanized life, our sham-life, the transformed-down energies, into our true being, into the eternal life.

We have heard that God is the stream of life that streams and breathes throughout all Being, and provides it with the breath of life of infinity, with the high, pure life force. God respirates every form of life: the stone, the plant, the animal, every being and every particle of our soul. Thus, we can say that God is the breath or the breath of life of the soul. The life, God, flows through the soul and breathes in the soul.

The breath of the soul is a completely different breath than our human breath, the breathing of our body. The soul that turns to God more and more breathes in the infinite rhythm of the All; it breathes in the eons of eternity. This is not the shallow breathing of human beings, but a breathing that we, as human beings, cannot imagine because our brain cells can comprehend only the content of our human, limited consciousness. The breath of the inner life, the breath of spirit beings, is connected to the seven-dimensional life of the pure Being.

The rhythm of our human breathing corresponds to our feelings, sensations, thoughts, words and actions. We control our breathing with these five powers. Every stirring of our body brings about a different breathing. Every feeling brings a changed breathing rhythm, as do each sensation, each thought and each word. The result of this is that each one of us breathes his own specific air. The composition of our own specific breathing air corresponds to our individually varying ways of feeling, sensing, thinking, speaking and acting.

The principle of sending and receiving holds true for all spheres of life—resulting in the fact that like attracts like. Thus, based on our feeling, sensing, thinking, speaking and acting, we attract from the air those particles, those substances that specifically correspond to the rhythm of our breathing, to our physical rhythm of life.

If we think that we all breathe the same air, oxygen, then seen spiritually, this is a limited way of looking at things. The air contains much more that those components that we find listed in our schoolbooks. It is also not only the pollutants and other things that are mixed into the Earth's atmosphere. The air is a complex compound carrier of widely differing vibrations. The human being is also a vibration complex. The vibration structure of the one is not the same as that of another. Therefore, each one of us attracts different substances—all according to his way of feeling, sensing, thinking, speaking and acting. That is his own small ego-world and accordingly, also his breath, the atmosphere that surrounds him.

This means that in our plasma, in our self-created atmosphere, in the aura that surrounds us, are all the substances that we breathe. Since the ego-shell, the plasma, of each one is different, no single one of us breathes the same substances as the other.

Let us realize once more: According to our feeling, thinking, speaking and acting, we take substances from the air that is available for everyone to breathe, and draw them into our body. These substances that we take into our body, breathing them into it, as it were, determine, in turn, our feelings, our sensations and thoughts. And the substances that we breathe out, in turn, that we give off, correspond to this. This cycle is what we call our breathing. This cycle encompasses our small ego-world and is nothing other than what we call "life."

If we monitor ourselves, we can experience this on ourselves on countless occasions. Let us take a pause in the situation and monitor ourselves: The moment we think and the thought becomes more active in us, our breathing changes. Feelings also influence our breathing. The subtlest vibrations of our feelings and sensations attract the corresponding substances from the air. These substances go into our aura, into our plasma. They draw through our body and stimulate, in turn, our nervous system and our disposition. In this way, we create our small world, in which we live and in which we breathe.

We also recognize here the correctness of the statement: We are what we feel, sense, think, speak and do. That is our human, narrow world, our cocoon. It is our ego-law, and it is our breathing. That is what we are as human beings. Once we realize this, at some point we should ask ourselves: Is it worth it to take this little world so seriously, to cling to it so much and perhaps even be proud of it?

Our human life takes its course in orbits, we could also say in rhythms. They are narrow orbits, short rhythms. In the narrow cycle of humanness, we are not in the great and wide stream of the divine. We revolve around ourselves in our humanness, around our human self. We affect our soul and our soul affects us. We affect the air and the air likewise affects us. We affect our plasma, as it were, and our plasma, in turn, affects us. And the more we burden ourselves through this narrow rhythm, the deeper we fall into lower rhythms, and the faster we breathe. We become hectic.

This revolving in a narrow, human cycle is not the life. If we do not take the steps out of this imprisonment, if we consciously choose this life of illusion, then, in reality, we do not live at all, but are vegetating away. Such a condition is what we call spiritual death.

Our life on Earth gives us the task of attaining higher rhythms, by changing and refining our plasma, our aura, which consists of our human feelings, sensations, thoughts, words and actions, in order to attract finer substances from the air, and to become more harmonious, to attain a higher rhythm, a balanced breathing. For us, this means to recognize day after day what wants to pull us down—our sinfulness.

To clear up our sinful aspects and no longer commit them means to attain harmony. If we attain higher rhythms, we attract finer substances from the air; we breathe more deeply, become calmer and are more prudent.

Christ wants us to become aware of all this. He wants to show us our goal, the life, the mighty I Am, in which we are at home. He wants to guide us out of the narrowness of our small world. He wants to guide us to the infinitely eternal stream, which respirates our soul that is becoming more light-filled. He wants to guide us to the seven dimensions of the eternal Being.

We cannot comprehend the seven dimensions with our brain, but we can have an inkling of them and sense them. The first step is simply to affirm them. In the affirmation is the deep trust that God is here. He knows how to guide us. In the trust is also the realization that this earthly world is never our world, the world and the life of the beings that we are, in reality and eternally. Then we also recognize that this world of external things, of humanness, is a created world—created by countless generations of people—which we, every single one of us, whether soul or human being, must transform. The transformed-down energies of life must be transformed up to the mighty I Am.

So that we may recognize where this leads to, so that we—also as human beings—can sense and grasp it a little, Christ gave us "The Great Cosmic Teachings of Jesus of Nazareth."

It is not enough to affirm and proclaim the laws of the All, the laws of God. Only the one who actualizes them brings good deeds.
You must first have actualized, yourself, what you teach. That is the best role model. These words and deeds enter the person's soul because they have substance and power.

Gabriele:

Therefore, it is not enough to read again and again in the book "The Great Cosmic Teachings of Jesus of Nazareth." It is not enough to tell about it and to say: "I know, I read it."

However much we read in this book, it will not bring us anything. It does not bring us the Absolute Law and does not lead us into the Absolute Law—only the daily actualization of what we have recognized gives us the spiritual

644

impetus. And actualization means nothing more than that we recognize our sinfulness, which the day reflects to us in many situations. We repent, ask for forgiveness, forgive and make amends for it. This is how we clear it up and no longer do it. Then we will find the principles of the law of the inner life, our true being, in the book "The Great Cosmic Teachings." We strive for this. We live this. Thus, step by step, we find our way into the life, into the I Am.

»You must first have actualized, yourself, what you teach. That is the best role model.« There would be less strife and quarreling in marriage and partnership, in families, at work, wherever we are, if we were good role models. Role models bring about many a thing, without influencing their fellow people. Good will and harmony enter, if we don't tell our neighbor what to do, wanting to force the laws of life on him. When we live them as an example, then peace enters our own soul first, and then peace also enters our marriage or partnership, our place of work, in all situations of life. Then we don't talk about what we have merely read or heard. Instead, we radiate it. Then we know when it is time to be silent and likewise, we sense when the time has come to be able to pass on a few drops of life. We pass on from our life what has become a part of the eternal law.

Then we do not simply speak a word that we have heard or read, but *the* word because we, ourselves, have become the word.

It is of no use to speak about the light and not be the light.

The one who merely speaks about the light is empty because he is divided. He wants to serve God and thinks that it is enough to serve according to the letter. However, that is not serving, but being servile. He teaches a word, but not the word because the letter kills. However, the light in the letter brings life.

Gabriele:

Let us recognize the difference: A word and *the* word. It can be one and the same word, spoken or written, and nevertheless, it can be "a word" or "the word." It all depends. When we merely speak of life, then it is a word or it is mere "words." On the other hand, if we fill the words with life, then it is "the word." The word is the word of God in us and through us. Not until the person is silent, will God speak. As long as we display our human ego, we do not allow God to speak. We force Him to remain silent in us because we, the human ego, want to talk.

We often wonder: Is our word filled with the life, with the light of God? Or is it merely a word, an empty, a hollow word?

We should deduce this from our breathing rhythm: If our breathing is fast, if we breathe shallowly, we notice that we are agitated. From this, we can already recognize that our word is not vivified. It is a word and not *the* word because our disquiet is the ego. The deep calm, the harmony of the soul and of the body is the I Am.

In a meditation that leads us into the stillness, into our inner being, we can experience ourselves very well. If we tune into the meditation, if we open ourselves to the meditation, then we notice that our breathing becomes calmer. However, at the very moment a thought from us, from the human being, flows in, we become restive: Our body twitches. Perhaps we already breathe more shallowly. Composure, concentration, the state of feeling enveloped all fade away. It is possible that we can no longer follow the meditation.

These thoughts, which act as disruptive elements, come from our subconscious. They point out that we have moved a human thought in us for too long, that we have not cleared it up properly or have even repressed it. If we put off for a longer time something that moves us briefly, if we do not deal with it right away, by clearing it up and then saying: "It is cleared up. I surrender it to Christ and I won't think about it anymore," then it already goes into our subconscious. It is not eliminated, but merely put off. To where? Into our subconscious and from there, after some time, it goes into our soul garments. If we become calmer, for example, in a meditation, such and similar thoughts can rise up out of our subconscious. We will then grasp them and work on them.

We see how important it is that we pay attention to our subconscious, by heeding the impulses from our world of feelings, sensations and thoughts, which signal us that something wants to be cleared up. Only when we do it promptly, that is, right away, will we attain the stillness of our mind and of our consciousness, that is, we will come into harmony and peace with ourselves.

The subconscious part of our person, our ego, must also become quiet because only if the person is silent, will God speak. If the human ego has been overcome for the most part, then the soul is largely one with God and God fills our words.

The negative aspects in our way of expressing ourselves often disguise themselves. For example, we often use the word "hopefully" and think we set a positive impulse with the hope. But when we look into it, we recognize that in the word "hopefully" lies doubt, that is, a human aspect. When we monitor our words more frequently, then it becomes clear to us that our human language is the language of doubt. We seldom speak in absolute terms. It is always: "if," "but," "perhaps," "hopefully"; "it should work out"; "but this or that could happen" and many others. Since our language is the language of doubt, it is satanic.

If we say, or think, for instance, "Hopefully our neighbor will follow the Inner Path," then it will be of no help to our neighbor on his path! In the word "hopefully," lies many a negative aspect. For example, in our world of feelings and sensations, we put our neighbor under pressure. We urge him. Then we have to ask ourselves: Why are we doing this?

Are we, perhaps, placing the uncertainty, the doubt, into our neighbor because we ourselves are negligent on the path to God? If we walk this path consistently, day by day, we have the strength to say: Our neighbor follows the path to God! When this will be is of secondary importance. Whether he follows it today, tomorrow, in years or in the spheres of purification—we must leave to Christ, and ultimately, to our neighbor, as well because he has free will. We simply affirm: He follows the path to the Lord.

God, our Father, is absolute and knows no doubt. What would it be like if He were to think: "Hopefully, My human children are following the path. Hopefully, they are actualizing the commandments." Would He then have sent us a prophet or prophetess, at all? But He is and remains the Absolute.

Doubt destroys everything. The adversary of God also knows this. The most sophisticated arguments of the adversary, who wants to ensnare us and discourage us from the path to God, sow and intensify doubt in us. The weakness is already in the doubt.

God, the Absolute, the Eternal, the All-One, bows down to His earthly children. It may very well be that the word of God through the mouth of a prophet is the word, the language of human beings. But He fills the word with His Spirit. He speaks through a prophet so that we can understand Him. Thus, He has Himself come down to our lowliness and takes our human word, so that He can address us. He places His Absolute Law, Himself, into our word. This is why we hear again and again: Grasp the meaning of the word! The meaning in the word is the divine.

God does not say "hopefully." He has no expectations of us. He is and gives. He serves. In this lies the "Link and be."

We do not serve our neighbor with our human wanting. We place ourselves above him and place ourselves above God. If we do not serve, then we are servile. We tell our neighbor what he wants to hear, to attain with sweet words what we want for ourselves.

The one who is servile is not himself. He dissembles to get what he wants, that is, to dominate. With this, he separates himself from his neighbor, and the neighbor, who allows this servility, also leans on the one who bows and scrapes because this flatters his human vanity. Thus, both are bound to each other. We recognize the satanic principle "Divide, bind and rule."

Every kind of leaning on people invariably brings rebellion, that is, strife, at some point. Therefore, let us recognize: Do we serve or are we servile?

If we tell our neighbor what he wants to hear, then, if we are alert, we notice an agitation in us. We want to tell him something from our ego, from our human aspects. Ultimately, we want him to acknowledge us. If in this situation our breathing gets shallower, if we become anxious, we recognize that we are being servile. The only thing that remains to be done is to examine this recognition more closely, that is, to clear up the humanness and to do it no more. Then we will enter the higher rhythms of life more and more. We come into harmony.

Thus, if we discover that we are becoming dependent on people, that we are being servile, then we should ask ourselves: Why are we servile? What expectation, what weakness, is present in us? Thus, what do we want to achieve? What do we want to cover up?

Once we have left our wanting behind us, we are calm and in harmony.

Harmony, God, serves. It gives without asking, without wanting to convince. God also gives advice in His word. However, this advice is not coercive, but is filled with life. It is a gift. God leaves it up to us whether we accept it or not. This is serving.

To recognize ourselves when we are servile and to clear up our human aspects leads us to serving.

Gabriele:

To journey inward means to clear up the sinfulness that each day points out to us, our faults and weaknesses, and to no longer commit them. Through this, we journey into our inner being, into the kingdom of the inner being, to the light of the truth. Then our words will be vivified, our feelings, sensations and thoughts filled with light. Only in this way, will we find our way to the light and again become the light because we enter our divine heritage, which is our true being.

The one who merely speaks about wisdom and is not wise is in the world and lives with the world and is for the world. Therefore, he is divided. He speaks wisdom according to the letter and yet is in the world. He wants to be wise and yet is not. Through this, he deceives himself and pretends to others what he is not: wise.

Gabriele, the teaching prophetess
and emissary of God, explained about this:

»The one who merely speaks about wisdom and is not wise is in the world and lives with the world and is for the world.« With this, Christ wants to tell us: The wisdom is God. The intellect is the human being. The human programs are the world. The one who wants to fathom God's wisdom and to attain his heritage, the eternal wisdom, has to discard his human ego, the intellect, which frequently displays itself, He has to acknowledge the eternal wisdom, which is in the world, but not with the world, and which is in all that we see, hear, smell, taste and touch. The one who wants to find eternal wisdom has to walk the path to wisdom, by clearing up his sinfulness that speaks against wisdom, and by discarding his inflated intellect, which merely wants to display itself.

Therefore, the one who wants to attain eternal wisdom has to surrender his small ego, in order to attain the great

I Am. Then he not only speaks about wisdom, the eternal law—he *is* wise.

Many call the Bible the book of truth. The Bible is read according to the letter. That is why, until this very day, it remains merely the book, the Bible. The world has not changed through the letters of the Bible. Quite the contrary: It is standing at the edge of the abyss and will fall into the abyss.

It may very well be that the Bible points out much wisdom to us, but the one who merely teaches this and does not act accordingly is with the world. He is with and for all that is against eternal wisdom. He takes the Bible and reads from the Bible and yet, is not wise. If he does not openly admit that he merely talks about wisdom and is not wise, then he is deceiving himself, by thinking that he is wise, and pretending to others what he is not: wise.

The one who merely speaks about a good and loving mindset merely has words about the loving mindset, but does not bring the good, the valuable, into this world.

The one who actualizes, brings spiritual values and spiritual deeds into this world. He is the heart-thinker who gives from the light of life. He lives righteously because he knows: God looks into the heart of each and every one.

hose awakened in the Spirit of God see those who are unawakened. They experience them in their behavior, in their thinking and speaking. They try to help them, as far as the latter want this.

Those awakened in the Spirit know the unawakened ones. They understand them and will be helpful to them to the extent that is good for their souls.

Gabriele, the teaching prophetess
and emissary of God, explained about this:

The awakened one is the person who very gradually immerses in the unending stream of love and becomes the law of love. It is the enlightened one, who sees with the spiritual eyes, who looks deeper, who grasps everything in the heart of the soul, the lawful and the unlawful.

The awakened one, who sees with the spiritual eyes, rests in his inner being and communicates from his inner being, from the divine in him, which he has opened for the most part.

The divine does not judge and condemn. This is why the awakened one takes in his neighbor's total radiation, also the total radiation of every problem, of everything that comes toward him. The divine in him sorts the divine from the not divine and communicates itself to the awakened one.

The awakened one then recognizes—by the radiation, by the reactions, by the entire behavior of his fellow people—whom he has before him, and knows how he should behave. The divine in him reveals to the awakened one what the person standing before him does not recognize himself.

The clarity of the divine consciousness is the mighty sea in which the unawakened one is merely reflected. From this reflection of his neighbor, the awakened one infers what marks the unawakened one, and what he could say to him and how he could help him, if the latter wants this. The divine also conveys to the awakened one, who lives in the stream of love, whether the unawakened one wants it.

Gabriele, the teaching prophetess
and emissary of God, explained about this:

We find the word "uncanny" in people's vocabulary. For the intellectual, unawakened person, the awakened, the wise person is uncanny. The world-oriented person hears the words of the awakened one and cannot apply them to himself because his consciousness is unable to immerse in the depths of the words of the wise one. Then the world-oriented person says: "This person is a provocation! He says things that don't fit in this world. He gives suggestions that are unacceptable."

Thus, the awakened one is a provocation to the unawakened one because he doesn't understand him, or he is something uncanny that one may not heed, or he is an eccentric because he doesn't run with the pack, of which there are many in this world.

If the intellectual person does not understand what the wise person says, then he thinks he was provoked by him, that is, teased by him. That is why he simply turns away from him with the inauspicious word: "provocation." In actuality, God spoke to His child through the wise one and wanted to guide it onto the path of wisdom. If the intellectual remains arrogant, then he places himself above God and therefore, doesn't want any suggestion or help from God.

Those who live daily with an awakened one look solely at the person and do not comprehend what radiates from him.

Gabriele:

The awakened one who lives in the stream of the divine wisdom has no reason to display himself. He lives in the mighty I Am and remains a person among his fellow people. The awakened one, the person, is, however, not human. He is a human being because he is enveloped in flesh.

With his human consciousness, the person who still lives his humanness sees the person who, however, does not speak in a human way. The human one sees the humanness of the person. He grasps only what he is himself: human—and thinks that he can measure the awakened one, the person, with his measure of humanness.

If an unawakened one wants to teach and guide another unawakened one, then both remain unawakened because they speak only empty, that is, hollow, words, in which the fire of love that makes them bright and seeing does not blaze. Both are the blind ones who will fall into the pit.

For this reason, be alert and pray, and let your words become filled with light. Indeed, let them become divine, so that you live in Me, the Christ, and are one with Me, the Christ, for the Eternal has sent Me to humankind to proclaim and bring the light and salvation to it.

The one who has devastated his inner temple builds ever greater and more splendid dwellings. Through this, the awareness of the presence of God and the sight for the true life were lost. I Am come to erect the inner temple again and to cause the holy works of God to become visible.

With My power, I Am among the people, to again proclaim the light and the salvation to them. Blessed are the ones who find Me in their hearts. They do not need external temples anymore—they have become the temple of salvation, themselves.

Gabriele:

»The one who has devastated his inner temple builds ever-greater and more splendid dwellings.« The inner temple is the light-filled soul that rests in God. Consequently, the person is the temple of God, in which God dwells. The one

who sins day after day, who disregards his neighbor, who rejects him, who does evil to him in his thoughts, words and actions has burdened the inner temple, that is, made it a desert because he belongs to the desert world and disregards everything that does not promote his well-being.

In this way, the person has devastated his temple and disregards his true life. He lives in the illusion that he calls life, which, however, will afflict him in due course, so that he may recognize that the Eternal dwells within, in each person.

The one who has taken the step to respect himself as the temple of God will cleanse it and keep it clean. He will then also recognize that he does not need any splendid houses of God or any external »dwellings« of the Holy Spirit. He knows that he is the dwelling of God, himself because God dwells in him.

Jesus, the Nazarene, taught the order of the temple and that God dwells in each person. He wanted to establish the inner temple and not build temples of stone. Jesus essentially said: "Tear down this temple and I will rebuild it in three days." With this, Jesus indicated the temple of the inner being and the resurrection of life in Him and through Him.

Christ, the Redeemer of all people and souls, is again at our side with His power. He teaches us the path to the heart of infinity, so that we cleanse our temple and establish it with the power that is in us: the Christ of God.

I Am the freedom. Do not let yourselves become bound, neither to dogmas nor to statutes.

Realize that in heaven there are neither dogmas, statutes, ceremonies nor superiors and subordinates. In heaven, you are all equal among one another—brothers and sisters. The one who does not strive toward this goal or who lets himself be dissuaded from this goal is a fool and spiritually dead, as it were.

The awakened one strives to reach his inner being, the kingdom of life—the unawakened one strives toward the external, toward the things that are reflected in the materialistic world and that rule the one who is with this world.

ever let yourselves be integrated in institutions and taught by Pharisees and scribes. They do not have the keys to the Kingdom of God, since they have not entered the life, themselves. As a result, they do not let those enter who want to come in because they do not know the lock, since they are not practiced in carrying the key that I Am, Christ.

he pure one sees through everything. His beholding eye is the perception of his divine consciousness. Everything that takes place in his divine consciousness is the truth. Everything else is merely a mirror, a distant echo of the truth, a reflection, the illusion of truth.

Gabriele:

The perception of the divine consciousness in the pure one is the communication with the divine in all forms of being, for all forms of being bear within the divine consciousness. The divine consciousness is the truth, eternity and everlasting.

Everything that is outside of the divine consciousness is the shell. This, in turn, is the mirror image and thus, merely a distant echo of the truth, that is, reflection, illusion.

Gabriele, the teaching prophetess
and emissary of God, explained about this:

We could compare the human body with modeling clay. Our feelings, sensations, thoughts, words and actions knead the clay and bring it into the form that corresponds to them. This means that we bring ourselves into this form. We are, ourselves, the shapers of our body. We are, ourselves, the gestures, the facial expressions, the entire behavior. We react according to our feelings, sensations, thoughts, words and actions.

If our neighbor addresses us, then he transmits to our sending potential, to the programs stored in our brain. Our reaction, our behavior and our answer correspond to this. Thus, we could say that when two people converse, then it is telepathy because with his words each one has an effect on the program world of the other one. The latter reacts accordingly.

If we no longer have any negative programs, if the Spirit of God can flow through us, that is, if we are totally oriented to God, then we have no human reactions or counter-reactions. We stay calm and give the answer out of the stream that flows through us, out of the divine.

Your inner being, as well as your outer aspects—your word, your behavior—speak themselves. The fulfilled one speaks the self because he is the self in the All-Father-Being. The world-oriented one speaks his base self. He speaks the language of his ego—that which he is, himself. The world-oriented one is the one who is wrapped up in the world, who is content with what he sees, with the reflections of his little world, which are his own mirror image.

Gabriele:

The All-Father-Being is the life of the pure children of God. They are the Self, the Being because they live eternally present in the Father-Mother-Consciousness, in the All-Father-Being.

The eternal Self is the law of God, which is everlasting. Every pure being is the embodied eternal law, the Self. The world-oriented person is his base self, formed from what he has felt, sensed, said, thought and done in his incarnations.

The base self is the sin. If a person has not cleared up his sins, neither in previous incarnations nor in this one, then he is the sinful one. That is his self because it belongs to him. It is the base self. It is the potential from which he draws. And what he draws is expressed in his whole behavior.

The world-oriented one does not know the eternal Self, but only his base self, his ego. He is content with the reflections of the eternal Self because he does not know anything other than his own self. This is how he sees himself, how he hears himself, how he smells himself, how he tastes and touches himself. This is how he feels, how he talks, how he acts.

What you, the pure one, the light in the primordial light, say is substance and power, since it is spoken from the holy of holies, from you, the Being. That is the language of God in you and through you.

Speak the language of the true Self, and you are divine. The language of the true Self is the God-filled word. It flows from the innermost part of your temple.

Gabriele:

A person attains purity when he daily clears up what the day points out to him as sinful aspects. Thus, the cleansing of the soul means to clear up the humanness. The one who does this also fulfills the law of life consciously. Once he has largely cleansed his soul, he draws from the primordial light. Then his words are filled with light and power. Then the true Self, God, speaks through him because his words are substance and power from God.

The eternal word flows in the innermost part of your temple. If you have entered it, then you are in the stream, which is the word, God.

The divine does not defend itself, nor does it debate because it is. The »Is« beholds and sees through everything and knows the innermost part of the person and his outer aspects, as well. The one who knows the eternal law because he is it, will not debate.

Gabriele:

The divine law does not defend itself because it is creation, itself, as well as all the details in creation. The divine does not need to debate about the truth. It is the truth. Only the one debates about the truth who has not found the truth and, therefore, does not know it.

Gabriele:

God is impersonal life. This means that God is impartial. He does not favor one of His children and reject the
other one. He loves all equally because He, God, is the
principle of equality.

God speaks to the people and sheds light on their behavior. Jesus lived this as an example for us. But He does
not harass His children. Therefore, we should not harass
our neighbor either, but explain and put right, again and
again.

Christ said: »*If the unregenerate one continues to
speak, despite the explanation or despite knowing better,
then he talks himself into trouble.*« For us human beings,
this means that we deliberately set causes and will experience the effects on our own body.

You, the truly wise one, be silent. If you have put right what is not right, if you have shed light on the untrue with the light of the truth and if, despite everything, you are rejected, then be silent because you know the true Savior, God—as well as the judge who speaks solely of himself. He is the person who through intransigence, through revenge and greed, delivers himself to the law of sowing and reaping, by sowing into the field of his life that which judges him. It is his small, base self, his egoity-law.

What you speak outside of the holy of holies is not always the language of your personal ego because your thoughts and words are not always your thoughts and your words. When you speak so-called thoughtless words over years and decades, then it may be you who is speaking, but another is speaking through you. This is the outside control via your sensory world in which you then live. The programmer, the one who, or which, controls you, also controls others through you. The one who allows this is a slave to sin and a sinner.

Gabriele:

We live in the world of sin. The one who does not clear up his sins each day, will continue to sin, thus making himself available to other sinners who, with their sinful sending potential, activate his sending and in this way, gain access to his earthly existence. Then he is lived. It is thought and spoken through him. Then it is not his thought and his word, but the dream world of one or several souls. This is, then, the outside control. Through this, the person has forfeited his own life on Earth and placed his earthly existence at the disposal of invisible forces, which then live through him and control him.

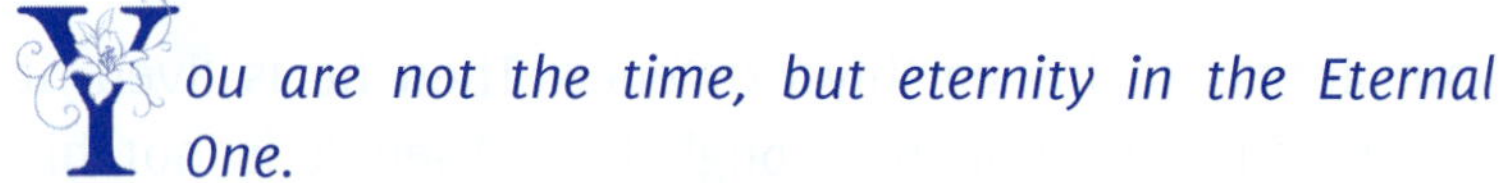

ou are not the time, but eternity in the Eternal One.

Gabriele, the teaching prophetess
and emissary of God, explained about this:

Thinking under the limitation of humanness created the constriction of the consciousness. The constricted consciousness is our life in time and space.

Through time, which we have given ourselves—with the terms today, tomorrow, day after tomorrow, days, weeks, months, years—we think that our life is passing. But that is a human view, not reality. Our life does not pass. We are eternal because the Eternal created us.

We should not take the thought that we live only a certain length of time as a measure of our being. It may very well be that we need the earthly measure of time to arrange our life, our actions, to plan our work, so that our life on Earth takes an orderly course. But our awareness should be: We are eternal life.

If we no longer take our shell so seriously, but daily become more aware of the life of our soul, then things will also go well for our shell, our person.

If we think of our soul every day, then very soon we will sense what eternity means. We breathe more deeply and calmly. We grow more relaxed. We plan our time on Earth, our earthly existence in the shell, and work well.

We place our planning into the will of God and are active day after day—in a similar way to the spirit beings, consciously with the strength from God, selflessly, in God, for our neighbor, for the great totality. We clear up what the day points out to us, and then we experience the breath of eternity because the Eternal breathes in us. We become quieter, calmer, more prudent. Our trust in God grows, and we trust that He can guide us.

When we do it this way, then we do not want to control our life. We make our plan for the day, the week and the month and place it in the will of God, so that He can guide us day by day. We do not sit back and take it easy, but rather do our daily work, always aware that God guides us.

At first, it may not be so easy because we do not yet sense what the will of God is and what our will is. But if we place our planning in the Ten Commandments, in the Sermon on the Mount, that is, in the law of God, again and again, if we ask Him, the great Spirit, for support and help again and again, then it will become clearer in us. Our consciousness puts itself in order and cleanses itself. So many useless and pressing thoughts no longer pulsate through our brain. Then we feel that the Eternal respirates us, and that He guides us.

The material shell, our human body, is nothing more than the garment, the vehicle of our soul for this life on Earth. For each one of us, the day will come when this shell falls away from our eternal body because it is not the material garment that lives in all eternity, but the spiritual body in us.

This is why the body of eternity is important, and we should see to it that it becomes pure and—when the physical body passes on—enters eternity.

If we live more and more in the awareness "We are beings of eternity because the Eternal is the life in us," we no longer take our human aspects so seriously. Then we are also ready to clear up our human aspects and no longer do them.

We should take as a task to no longer take our egocentric person so seriously. Then we will identify ourselves more with our eternal being, with the life of our soul, and will tackle our human aspects with the power of the I Am—and from a higher vantage point—in order to overcome them with Christ.

Gabriele:

The order of the temple is God because God is Order. In Him, everything is in good order. If we put order in our life, we will also put order in our thoughts. Our humanness, the negative, the ego-life, shows itself most clearly in the world of our thoughts. Once we have put this in order and aligned it with God, then we will go into the kingdom of the inner being step by step. Soul and body then become one, more and more. They become the temple of God's love because we fulfill the law of love.

Gabriele:

If we have read these sentences in a calm and collected manner, then we would have to say to ourselves: How limited we are! How much we restrict and limit ourselves! God is the unlimited stream, the life. God in us wants to help us in every situation, in our planning, in our thinking, in our feeling and doing. He is always ready to support us. The only question is: Do we want to accept His help? If we do not, then He does not coerce us because He has given us freedom.

What is freedom?
God is freedom. He does not force His children to anything. Love cannot practice any coercion. Love gives itself—it gives itself.
The infinite love of God is the heavenly law, our divine heritage. The principles of our divine heritage are equality, freedom, unity, brotherliness and justice.
Freedom comes from the principle of equality.

We are all equal before God's countenance. He created us, His children, in this way. He, the great Spirit, God, our Father, kept nothing for Himself. He gave us all His love, the eternal law. In its structure, every spiritual body is the eternal law of love. God created us this way and this is how the spirit beings live in the stream of love. They fulfill the law of love. None is greater, all are equal.

The spirit beings have different mentalities and different capabilities, corresponding to the plane of heaven in which they live as beings of the light. Just like the basic power of Order, so do the spirit beings of the heavenly plane of Order also have a certain mentality. Likewise, Will, Earnestness, Patience—also called kindness—each have their respective mentalities, from which the capabilities ensue.

The spirit beings are active in the eternal Being with their capabilities. They work according to the law of love because they are, themselves, compressed law of love. They are completely free. They do not need to make any determinations. They are determined to fulfill the will of God. Actually, they are the will of God, themselves because the Will is also a basic power in the law of love, which is their life.

Since God, the divine law, the law of love, is in everything, everything is energy because the law of love is energy. The spirit beings work with this energy, and they live with this energy. It is the life.

The life, the energy of God, is present in all things without exception, even in each atom of matter because God also gave Himself to the Fall-children—who did not want to be divine, but to be God themselves—to take along with them. In each atom, in each stone, in each blade of grass, in each animal, in each particle of our soul, in each cell of our body, in each star, in each sun, everywhere, is God, the life, the love.

We human beings and souls now have the freedom to accept this love of God, or to continue to reject it—just as the Fall-beings did: wanting to be God themselves.

Everything is law. The law is the cycle of giving, the same as sending and receiving. Just as the spirit beings are active in the stream of love, in the law, and remain the law of God, so does the law of love come, in turn, to them, flowing through them and maintaining them in the eternal Being because God is immortal.

The Fall-beings turned against God and His law of selflessly giving love. But since everything is law, the principle of sending and receiving is also active in the Fall-realm. There, each one creates his law, his ego-law, which is not the law of God and does not correspond to the will of God.

Let us ask ourselves: Does God make us think negatively? Does God make us act against Him? Is it God's will that we have feelings and sensations that are against Him? Does God make us be against our neighbor? Whose will is such conduct? Who determines it? In the end, it is we, ourselves. We determine it, ourselves, from one single Fall-thought, the thought: "I want!" From this one single Fall-thought—"I want!"—emerged our wanting, emerged the "being against God."

God gives us the freedom to be against Him or for Him. But with this, each one determines his life, himself, according to the principle of sending and receiving.

God sends and receives. It is the eternally dynamic principle of life, the cyclical breathing in and out. God breathes out energy. The spirit beings work and create, causing the energy to increase. God breathes in energy, which intensifies in the Primordial Central Sun, and He breathes out again. The spirit beings live in this principle.

We humans also breathe. We breathe out—we send—and we breathe in—we receive. *What* do we breathe out?

God leaves us our freedom. We breathe—we send—our thoughts out and fetch them back again based on the principle of sending and receiving. Thus, every sinful thought is a boomerang, whether we want this or not.

The principle of sending and receiving exists in the eternal Being, in the pure spheres, as well as in the realms of the Fall, in the law of sowing and reaping, in the causal law. The eternal rhythm of the Being, the inhaling and exhaling of the eternal Spirit, the sending and receiving, is the life, which is constant movement. This is how it is on the smallest scale. This is how it is in or with each one of us.

Therefore, what we breathe out in the way of feelings, sensations, thoughts, words and actions, comes back to us. If these, our feelings and sensations, thoughts, words and actions, are negative—that is, if they originate from the egotistical "I want!" to which our shallow breathing corresponds, the "mine, only mine"—then we attract the same thing again, namely, that which is ours, that which we have exhaled, that is, sent out.

If a person does not know about these interrelationships and spiritual principles, or if he does not want to accept them for himself, then he complains: "Why does God allow that I am sick, that I suffer, that I am hungry, that I live in need, that I have to suffer this fate?" Let us realize: That is not God! God is freedom. He does not force us to anything. In the eternal Being, He gave us as pure beings the freedom, and this is also how He keeps it, even when we are against Him.

The law of God, the sending and receiving, is unchangeable. If *we* digress from the divine law, that is, if we change ourselves, by being against God, the law remains: What a person sows, that is, sends, is what he reaps, receives. The person sows and the person receives—but not God.

Thus, we ourselves get to feel the effects of our own causes. If we have reason to say "My neighbor does not love me. My neighbor is against me" or "My neighbor does not do what I want him to do," then we should, in each case, ask ourselves: What is behind these statements in me?—especially when we get annoyed in the process. If we get annoyed, then this wants to tell us that the same or something similar is in us. If we don't get annoyed, we will explain things according to the law of life. We will give indications, compare positive and negative, address the negative—but we will not get upset.

God does not get upset when we are against Him. He always remains the same because He is perfect. Unceasingly, He sends out His law, His infinite love. In His heart, He sees us as perfect—just as He beheld and created us. And this is how He radiates His love to us.

Let us become aware once again that God is freedom. He does not force us to anything. This is also why we human beings should not put any pressure on our fellow people, neither on a small, nor on a large, scale. This also holds true where belief is involved—there may be no coercion. Each one should decide freely how he wants to strive toward God or whether he wants to. This is how God acts with us. He lets us decide freely, but His will is that we again fulfill His will and are with Him again.

We should think of this more often. With all His heart, God wants us not to torment ourselves, not to suffer, but rather to be with Him, in the light, in the love. God, our Father, sent His Son, so that we know the way to love, so that we find our way to the love. And to where did Jesus, the Christ, point us? He said: "The Kingdom of God is within, in you."

That the Kingdom of God is in us, and not tied to an external place, to external conditions and circumstances, means for us that every one of us has the freedom to cause the inner kingdom to grow and develop each day. Then we don't need any external forms, any rituals, any external religion—we need the community of brothers and sisters, in which each one says: "I go into my heart. I open up the Kingdom of God in me day by day, so that after the death of my body I will again consciously be in the Kingdom of God as a being of the light." In this lies the freedom.

Universal Life also stands under this spirit of freedom. Universal Life means living in God. It is the same way with the revelations of our Brother and Redeemer, Christ. God leaves us our freedom. For this reason, in Universal Life there is freedom. God does not force us to any ritual. God does not force us to any dogmas. He wants us to be free and to decide freely. Freedom is living in God. Therefore, we can say that Universal Life *is* freedom.

If we live this way, then we come together as free people in the spirit of love, who seek community and blossom in the community because community is the same as unity. Unity is freedom. Freedom and unity make us strong in heart and strong in the love for God and for our neighbor.

Original Christianity means: community, unity. From the original stream came the Son and brought us the life, the Redemption. The Son of God is our Redeemer. This is why we call Him Christ. Since the true teaching, the law of love, which Christ lived as an example for us and taught us, came from the original stream, we call ourselves Original Christians.

Original Christians are free people. They seek community, but they do not bind themselves to any person. Original Christians are people who love each other more and more selflessly, that is, without value judgment. Selfless love means: I do not place my neighbor higher nor do I demean him. My neighbor is a part of my eternal life.

In a true community there is the common good. Common good means: the good of all. The common good is based on true brotherliness, sisterliness and selflessness. If all brothers and sisters keep that part of their neighbor, which is in them, in their hearts, and activate it, aware that: In my neighbor is God, in me is God. We are one in God—then each one will see to it that things go well for his or her neighbor. That is active Original Christianity. That is the common good, the good of all.

On Earth as it is in heaven. If we are aware of this and if we become more aware of it each day, then the longing for our divine heritage, for the eternal law, awakens. The longing for God reminds us again and again to discard our ego-law, our person-law, the confining law of "I," of "mine" and "me," in which our neighbor has no room and no place. Then we discard the "my well-being" and grow into the common good.

The common good is also the shared good, in which each one has a share. Each one puts his strengths to work for the common good.

No spirit being will say: "The other one should do it. I am resting now. Perhaps my neighbor can do it better." Every being in God does everything in the Absolute Law. It does not rest at the cost of its neighbor's energy. According to its capabilities, it works in the great totality for the good of all.

On Earth as it is in heaven. Universal Life means freedom—freedom in the Spirit of God. Universal Life means: Open the Kingdom of God in you, and you will find your way to a free community of brothers and sisters, who give honor solely to God. They honor God by daily letting God work through them more and more, through their selfless feelings, sensations, thoughts, words and deeds.

If we strive for this day by day, we find our way into our divine heritage more and more, into the Absolute Law, which is our true life, which makes us free, which makes us happy, which unites us.

Living in the law of God means to live in the will of God. In thoughts, words and deeds, we send out what is the will of God, and the will of God, His law, comes back to us. Then we are in the stream of life. The good, the kindness of God, also determines our earthly existence.

But if we want that whatever happens is what *we* want, then we are sending out our personal law, and we receive accordingly. What is important here is what lies *in* our words or *in* our thoughts, not what we—perhaps with nice words—pretend. What lies in them marks us and comes back to us—and in many cases, it assaults us.

If we become aware of the kindness and love of God, then we would have to tell ourselves each day: Away from limitation to unlimitedness, to our *life*, to God. God in us, the Christ of God, wants to help, to serve; He wants to guide us, lead us, plan through us, work through us, think, speak and act through us. As soon as this is possible for Him, it goes well for us. Then our days are brighter and happier. The "we" will then become community, the good for all.

Then, at the right time, you speak the word that is rich in content, the word that is divine, and you do what needs to be done at the right time, which, in turn, is divine. Then your daily work runs in accordance with the will of the All-Holy One who is in you, and in whom you are.

Gabriele, the teaching prophetess
and emissary of God, explained about this:

If we feel into the words of the eternal law, then we may sense a breath of the eternal homeland. We should keep this subtle stirring in our inner being and not immediately let it be drowned out by the loud, hard vibration of externalized life. If we are touched by this breath from the eternal homeland, let us consciously allow it to keep vibrating in us! Let us take it along into our daily life, by frequently bringing the following to mind:

God, the All-One, who loves us, breathes in me. God, the All-One, helps and supports me in every situation. He desires us to again be consciously in His heart as pure beings. If we strive daily for purity, if, day after day, we clear up what the day points out to us as human aspects, then our daily work will proceed according to the will of the All-Holy One, who is in each one of us. Then we will feel the freedom because we come into unity with our neighbor and with God, more and more.

Particularly at this time, which is so turbulent externally, many people are being touched in their inner being by the Spirit of life, who gives revelations, who teaches, who is effective in many a way and causes His power to flow increasingly into matter and into the hearts of all people. Here and there, the longing for God is awakening. We should not let this delicate, fine stream promptly seep away again.

Particularly when the vibration is raised, we should note down our own longing thoughts and read them now and then, think of them frequently during the day, express them frequently and speak them toward God. It may be that He already knows everything, but if we turn to Him, if we speak or think our feelings of profound love toward Him, we establish communication with Him. What we receive—from the ray of His grace—vibrates into our inner being. It uplifts us—our daily life becomes more filled with light.

The moment we take ourselves back and think or speak these fine stirrings, movements and thoughts of love and thankfulness from our heart to Him, to God, our Father, to Christ, our Redeemer, our consciousness is raised. We receive more energy and everything proceeds more easily.

A help for us all!

If the day brings a lot of turbulence and if this enters our inner being, then we should withdraw in time for a few minutes, and go to Him as His child. He, the great Spirit, knows about everything, but when we talk to Him, then we ease our soul and our mind. We again create the connection to God, our eternal Father, if, from our heart, we say something like the following:

Father, you know that I love You. I feel that I am Your child, and I know that You are in me and that you strengthen me.

If, for several minutes and from our heart, we speak this in this consciousness of the child to its Father, if we linger in this vibration of grace, then the connection with God, the life, reestablishes itself, and the stillness of the Being draws into soul and body.

As Jesus of Nazareth I traveled a lot with My apostles and disciples. On the paths and byways from one place to another, I taught them the following:

When you walk, then walk upright; when you stand, then stand upright; when you sit, then sit upright.

Each one of you is the being in the stream of the Being.

Every harmonious movement is the rhythm of the stream, the rhythm of the All.

The stream knows no bending, no curve. It does not give way to anything or anyone. It flows unvaryingly through the All and flows throughout everyone and everything.

When you walk through this world with long strides, then you walk bent over. Your eyes look to the earth, to the ground, from where you absorb what adheres to the ground. Everything that is heavy or burdened crawls on the ground and burdens, in turn, those who direct their looks and thoughts solely to the ground.

Gabriele, the teaching prophetess
and emissary of God, explained about this:

An example for better understanding: When we place a delicate feather on our hand and blow it away, then it does not fall to the ground like a stone. We can watch the lightness with which it floats for a long time. While we do this, our eyes are not directed to the ground, but to the distance. When the feather falls to the ground and doesn't get burdened by dirt, then the wind will carry it upward again, and we see it flying again.

If our feelings, sensations and thoughts are divine, then they will never stick to the ground, but will rise up and go into the divine worlds. They also go into our soul as a power of light and, via the soul, are connected with the life that is God.

The image of the feather wants to tell us that we should become light and buoyant, by clearing up with Christ what makes us heavy and downcast, and no longer doing it— our sins. Then we will no longer walk bent over, loaded with the burdens of sin, but our eyes will again and again be directed upward and into the distance, like the flight of a feather. Then we perceive the ground merely to watch and see where to place our feet. We then look into the distance and heavenward. Our eyes and our consciousness will rise up again and again, just like the pure feather that the wind drives heavenward, again and again.

Recognize: A heavy gait is, as it were, a crawling gait. Such people see only themselves and what they, in turn, are—that which radiates to them from the ground.

Gabriele:

We all know about gravity. Everything heavy falls directly to the ground. Everything that is lighter floats for a time before it falls to the ground.

If our soul is heavily burdened, then we feel this heaviness. We cannot define it, nor can we readily fathom it, but we feel the burden. This puts pressure on our body and on our senses. Through this, we become lazy, that is, negligent with ourselves and in our conduct toward our fellow people. Consequently, we lower our heads and our gaze sticks to the ground, again and again. Our steps become bigger and very gradually, our back bends. Listlessly and ponderously, we go our way, without paying attention to our neighbor or what is around us and above us. This is, then, our crawling gait, which keeps our gaze directed to the ground because everything heavy and burdening falls like a stone and stays lying there. Thus, the heavy thoughts also stick to the ground and to objects that are on the ground.

What is close to the ground is of low vibration. From there, negative energy potential radiates again to the one who, via his posture and via the burdening of his soul, calls it up.

Our eyes, our ears and other sensory organs are the antennae to our environment. Via our senses, what corresponds to our active sins comes to us because like attracts like again and again.

Therefore, walk upright. You then gain foresight and insight and an overview. Then you are linked with the cosmic powers more and more. These point out to you what still needs to be cleared up, so that, in time, you behold cosmically, you hear cosmically, you feel, think, speak and act cosmically.

Gabriele:

The cosmic powers are the powers of God, which flow throughout all of infinity. They are the omnipresent powers in human beings, animals, plants, stones and the stars and planets. They are the law of the heavens, the flowing light-ether, which, when manifested, forms the spiritual body of the pure spirit beings.

If we want to be connected with the cosmic powers, with the eternal presence, God, then we have to clear up our sinfulness with Christ. Christ in us then transforms the negative energies, the sinfulness, into positive, cosmic powers. By way of these pure energies, the divine in us, we are in communication with the pure, cosmic powers, which form the stream of infinite love, God, the stream of the Being. These pure, divine energies then touch us more and more, and, in time, point out our human, our sinful, aspects to us, so that we clear them up with Christ before our causes, our sins, become effective in and on our body and in our surroundings.

The more sinful aspects we clear up—and we can do this every day, every hour, in fact, every minute—the more our soul will become light-filled, lighter and freer. We enter in communication with the pure, cosmic powers more and more. We draw closer to God. The more the soul purifies itself, the more we feel, think, speak and act in a finer and purer manner. In this way, step by step, we open up the cosmic life in us.

When you stand, then stand upright. Do not lean against objects and things. The one who leans against objects and things will also be emitted to by these objects and things. You then absorb whatever adheres to the objects and things.

The one who leans against objects and things also leans on his neighbor and takes from him the humanness that he radiates.

Gabriele:

Everything is energy. Since everything is energy, everything is law.

There is the Absolute Law of God. It is the omnipresence, the life in all things, in the large and in the smallest. The Absolute Law is universal, the light-filled, high radiation of the Being. As long as we human beings are still afflicted with our ego, we still live in our ego-law, in our individual principles of sin.

We shape our lives according to our feeling, sensing, thinking, speaking and acting. These energies, which go out from us, also come back into us again. They liberate our soul or burden it—all according to which principles we feel, sense, think, say and do—either divine or not divine.

What lies in our soul—the divine or not divine—is what we emanate. It is also the magnetism with which we attract either the divine or the not divine. Therefore, every person is a radiation-body, an energy-body, as it were. He transmits his energies to the objects that he touches or breathes toward—because the breath is likewise energy and carries the particles of what permeates us. Even by thinking intensely toward objects, we charge them with the corresponding vibration.

What we have touched also radiates some aspects of our daily behavior—the positive as well as the negative, according to how we feel, think, speak or act.

If one of our neighbors has a similar radiation-body, an energy-body similar to ours, and leans against objects that we have leaned against, or picks up objects that we have already had in our hand or have breathed upon, then his magnetism can attract a part of what we have left behind, and at the same time, our neighbor can leave behind a part of his radiation. Thus, the whole world is one big radiation-picture of all people.

If we don't want to infect ourselves with the negative energies of objects and things, then we have to clear up our sinful aspects with Christ and no longer commit them. Through this, we will magnetically attract less and less negativity, which, among other things, urges us to think and to do what we have absorbed. Our magnetism for negative things becomes ever weaker, the more divine laws we actualize.

Thus, if our soul grows more light-filled, we will also be more sincere and thus, more just. We will lean against fewer and fewer objects and things because we have learned to think in a straightforward manner, to stand straight and to account for our personal life. Then we will no longer lean on our fellowman either because we know what we want: to fulfill the laws of God, and do them.

If you lean on your neighbor and your neighbor leans on you, then, in time, you will both become tired and weary of each other because the energies that you transmit and draw from each other will soon be exhausted. What then?

The results are strife, quarreling, discord and disunity. Once you are weary of each other, then each one seeks his next victim, on whom he again leans—and perhaps the victim, in turn, leans on him. The result will be the same as before.

Gabriele:

Living in the Spirit of God means to rely on God, to entrust ourselves to God and to be with our neighbor and for our neighbor.

Thus, we should not use our neighbor in such a way that we demand from him what we don't have and what he cannot give us, either. If we rely on God and entrust ourselves to Him, we receive what we need and are for and with our neighbor. Instead of strife, quarreling and discord, unity comes into play. Weariness transforms into togetherness. Instead of rejecting our neighbor and turning to another, we remain true to him, so that we break the cycle that would lead us into more temptation and more sin, into more disappointment and more weariness.

Therefore, stand upright. Do not lean against anything or on anyone. Then you will gradually become cosmic antennae that reach into the heavens and receive from the heavens.

If you sit, then sit upright. Your spine is not curved. It is perpendicular and shows you that you should sit upright, to receive from the stream of the Being.

You have heard that the stream of the Being, the law, knows no bending and curving. A healthy spine, too, knows neither bends nor curves.

If you lie back in your chair, then it is as if you were lying on the floor and receiving the vibrations that crawl along the floor.

If you cross your arms and legs, then you block the flow of the Being in and on you, or you direct it away from you and attract other forces.

Gabriele:

We human beings have many habits. Our external posture constantly gives us hints about our inner attitude. If we don't sit straight, but negligently, by lying back in our chair—we would say, we sprawl in it—this shows us that we are likewise negligent in our inner being. We give in to our sinfulness, by nurturing sinful feelings, thoughts and words. With this, we are again communicating with the negative energies that crawl along the ground.

We have read and heard that we should be cosmic antennae that reach into the heavens and receive from the heavens. Let us think of our television antenna. It is oriented to the station. What happens if we bend it or change its orientation? We will have poor reception or none at all. It is similar with our body posture. Our posture expresses what we feel, think, say and do. We are transmitting. What we transmit is our image. According to our radiation, we receive, in turn, what we emit. Consequently, each person is his transmitter and his receiver, according to the energy potential of his soul.

Know that the human being should be a cosmic antenna. The one who makes knots in his antenna or bends it can receive neither the powers nor the salvation of the All. It is solely the powers of the All that strengthen and move the person, that make him free and healthy. They give him foresight and insight and the overview.

The one who does not accept and live these spiritual principles becomes narrow-minded and intellectual. In time, he acquires those traits that his neighbors show, who are likewise on the human track.

If you lie down, then lie down to rest. Rest consciously and lie horizontally and be aware that you are resting, then you will perceive the stillness of the All.

If you support your head on your hands while speaking, while eating or doing something else, you will speak only your base self and wolf down the food like a predator with his prey. Then you become a glutton who seeks pleasures and nurtures physical pleasure, sexuality because through his undisciplined behavior, through the bent antenna, he receives corresponding powers, that is, corresponding transmitters.

The stream of the Being is harmonious, rhythmic movement. Therefore, move harmoniously. Harmonious movements are the melodies of the All.

Know that each body is sound; it is melody. Just as it sounds, so is the person.

Every hectic movement is a bending of the antenna that is, in turn, the person, himself. Then the person will lean against things, he will half lie in his chair, cross his arms and legs and support his head on his hands.

Harmonious movements are dynamic movements. They bring about flexibility in thought, speech and action.

Know that the upright person is the one who has straightened up, as it were, who radiates the cosmic sounds in his thinking, speaking and acting, and whose gestures and facial expressions give voice to the cosmic symphonies.

Therefore, sit upright and place both feet on the floor. Then you release tensions and take in harmonious vibrations.

Know that every one of you is the compressed All, and the All is the Being—it is the eternal homeland, the sea of light, God. For this reason, as human beings, behave in such a way that you send into the heavens and receive from the heavens.

If you live in the stream of the All, then you are the essence of the All. Then you live in the fullness and you are the fullness. No person and nothing can disappoint you because you expect nothing, since you are the fullness.

Recognize that the All and the All-stream send unceasingly. Look at the bushes, flowers, animals and stones—they are. They have their antennae directed into the All.

Animals, plants, bushes and trees do not lean on others of their kind, unless the human being interferes in the cosmic course of things. When trees stand too close together, they cannot develop. It is similar with people when they lean on people, objects and things.

Unfold yourselves: Do not lean against anything or anyone.

The ennobled person is the wise person who rests in his inner being.

The ennobled and wise person does not laugh out loud from his throat. He smiles from his heart.

Realize that culture cannot just be put on a person or a country. Culture has to grow out of the person. Where there is no culture, there are many cults.

The You Am I, and you are the I.
Therefore, remember the following:
You are the fine and the beautiful.
You are the noble and the pure.
You are in the You that is eternal, the sublime.

Gabriele:

God is the pure in all things. Everything pure is His eternal law, the I Am. The I Am, the eternal law, is flowing, eternal light, eternal energy that streams through and maintains everything.

From this all-maintaining energy, the streaming light, He took the substance and formed His sons and daughters from it. You are the pure being, eternal law that became form, eternal light—the You. Because you are law that became form, you live in the eternally streaming law, the eternal light, the I Am. Thus, you are a part of the eternally streaming law, God.

You, the substance, the All-law, contain all aspects of the eternally streaming law. Therefore, you are in the I, in the I Am, and in your neighbor, and he is in you because all pure beings are from the one stream: from God, the I Am.

Therefore: *»The You Am I, and you are the I.«* The pure is the fine and beautiful, the noble and the sublime. That is what you are in the I Am, in God.

This explanation holds true for each one of us because each one is the you in the I Am and the you in the you, that is, in your neighbor. Once we are again beings of the light, then we are the eternal law and work in the eternal law. Then we worship solely the sublime because we are sublime ourselves.

The sublime is the One.

You in the You, in the sublime One, are the sublime one that knows about all things because the sublime One is the Father—the greatness, the power and the All itself.

He is the culture and the cultural because He is Creator, God, bearer, mover, giver—the Being.

He is beauty, splendor, the fullness.

He is your Father—you, His child, the heir.

You are the light in the sea of light, God. Therefore, you do not need to hold on to anything or anyone.

Gabriele:

Our divine heritage is the eternal law. It is our compressed, pure, spiritual body. It is what is in all things: the pure. Once we have opened our divine heritage again, we live in the law, in the sea of light, God. We live in the fullness from God and do not need to hold on to anything or anyone, to perhaps receive what we do not possess.

The one who seeks love does not have it.

The one who seeks peace does not have it.

The one who seeks a homeland has not opened it.

The one who seeks wealth has not entered the kingdom of the inner being.

The one who seeks harmony lives in disharmony, in his sins.

The soul of the one who needs people who fulfill his desires is poor in spiritual power.

Gabriele, the teaching prophetess
and emissary of God, explained about this:

People who lean against things here and there, who always need a support and a staff, that is, who cannot stand straight, and whom objects, things and people should serve because they find it hard to serve them-selves, lean against anything they think is more stable than they are themselves.

This means that such people lack steadfastness. They are dependent on people and things. Dependence be-comes insincerity because the dependent person flatters those whom he has made himself dependent upon or wants to make himself dependent upon.

Such people are like flags in the wind, which turn just as the wind is blowing at the moment. The insecure per-son is similar, the undecided one, who thinks constantly of finding a possibility to lean on, where he will get strength. This human insecurity also leads to a lack of steadiness. Such people depend on the opinions of others.

Therefore, do not lean on people, otherwise, you will become dependent and insincere. The one who leans on people also rejects people. The dependent one will become like an appendage of his neighbor. When the latter no longer supports him, he is lonely.

Do not lean against or hold on to things or objects because that says that you rebel against your neighbor. It also indicates the turmoil of your state of mind.

Gabriele:

Therefore, the one who leans on people, things and objects rebels against his neighbor because his weakness seeks a stronger pole, again and again. If the stronger pole, for example, a person, is not willing to be a crutch, then the turmoil of the weakling's state of mind is evident because he doesn't get from his neighbor what he doesn't possess himself: strength.

Gabriele:

The spiritual law reads: Like attracts like. If people and objects radiate what is active in and on ourselves, then we establish a communication with the radiation of our fellowman or with things and objects. Thus, our vibration flows from us to the other pole, and the vibration of the other pole flows to us.

If we are stimulated by what is vis-à-vis us, by people, things or objects, to corresponding negative thinking because the same thing is active in us, then we can intensify our correspondence, our sinfulness. This means to further burden ourselves. That is the law: Like attracts like, or: Like draws to like. The pure attracts the pure; the impure attracts the impure. Each one determines himself what communication he establishes.

Our orientation is significant. Whatever we are oriented toward becomes increasingly active in us.

If we are oriented toward the fulfillment of our egocentric desires, we leave behind our traces and radiation on objects, as well. In this way, we attract forces and people who correspond to our radiation. If we are oriented toward God and toward the fulfillment of His holy law, then even in the material, we will receive the melody of the fine, the pure and good because we have given our inner antenna a corresponding orientation. Then we will also emit fine, pure and noble aspects and awaken and reinforce the light-filled, the pure, in things and people.

Rest in you. Whatever you do, give it your all, with full concentration, focused on the matter and issue.

Gabriele:

»*Rest in you*« means: Do not take the humanness, what you see or what is told to you, so seriously. Recognize in everything that you experience, in every situation and in each problem, the divine spiritual principle, and apply it to yourself. Then you will find your way to inner calm again and again, when external things have drawn you into disharmony.

If you seek in everything the principle of the law of God, you will also find it. And if you live according to it, then the calming pole in you, God, will always support you. In everything that we think, say and do is the principle of the law of God because God is omnipresent. In every activity is God. In every written work is God. In every artisan activity is God because God is everything in all things.

The wise one who lives in his purified temple also keeps the order of the temple while writing. Now, he is writing. His sensations and thoughts are with the writing of his paper. From his innermost being, the holy of holies, in which he lives and from which he gives, he has an effect on the external, on every letter and on every word. Through this, he lends power to what he writes and imbues it with the eternal law, God.

Whatever you do, keep the order of the temple in everything.

Now you go here and there, and you are with you because you are in you.

Now you work at the workbench, and you are with your workpiece and thus, in and with you.

You speak with your neighbor, you are with you and in you and you speak the law in the word.

What you do, you do totally.

Gabriele:

»Keep the order of the temple« means that we should clear up our human aspects each day—what the day points out to us. By consistently clearing up our human aspects, we also attain concentration. Thus, we are attentive, and therefore, with our work. We are ourselves and are not controlled by other forces. That is the order of the temple because the one who consistently clears up his human

aspects, his sinfulness, which he may recognize day after day, and no longer does them, rests in the sea, in God, and lives consciously in his temple.

The person who has found his way to the inner life rests in God, who dwells in him. In so doing, he keeps the order of the temple. Thus, he allows no sinfulness. He takes sinfulness from his soul by way of the energy of the day, clears it up, and in this way, keeps order in his temple, more and more. Through the temple order, he will carry out everything that is lawful, whatever he does, with all the powers of his consciousness because his feelings and thoughts are with what he is doing. Therefore, we can say: What he does he does totally.

When you hold an object in one hand, then you should not hold another one in the other hand, unless both objects are attuned to each other and are not contrary to each other. For example, when you hold a workpiece in one hand and in the other hand the tool with which you work on the workpiece, then both are attuned to each other because the one serves the other.

When you put something in writing, then hold only the writing instrument in your hand. If, for instance, you were to hold a ruler in the other hand, or an object to erase what was written, then you lose your concentration and your attention is divided because these two vibrations, not being attuned to each other, cause inattentiveness and dissonance in you.

If you hold a ruler in the other hand, then, for example, you will frequently underline statements that should not be underlined, or you will underline what you are or are not yet, yourself. With this, you lend expression and emphasis to your human ego because you underline yourself, your ego. When you have the writing instrument in one hand and in the other an object for deleting what was written, then you will more often make mistakes and then erase them.

Recognize yourself in everything and give yourself up, your base ego. Then you will attain the I Am, the Being, that is everything, that knows about everything and sees through everything, that hears everything, that speaks through you.

Recognize again and again: The pure takes place solely in the innermost part of the soul, in the pure—the impure solely in the external, in the world of the senses.

Gabriele:

A draftsman has drawing instruments in his hands, what he needs for drawing. The instruments communicate with each other and with the draftsman—also with his consciousness and with his mental concept. If the communication is positive, the one influences the other constructively. We could say that the instruments make each other and the draftsman fruitful, and help him to bring the drawing plainly and clearly to paper.

A painter needs paper or canvas, as well as brushes, paints and whatever else is needed. If these implements are attuned to each other, then they inspire the painter. His picture will be expressive and the colors in harmony with each other. If the painter had a brush in one hand and a chisel in the other, how would his picture come out? The colors would be hard and the picture could perhaps have an unpleasant sharpness.

Thus, we see that like communicates with like and they make each other fruitful. Unlike things influence each other negatively.

Recognize: The intellect of the human being is not the heart of the soul. The one who speaks from his intellect speaks from his human programs because he is not at home in his innermost being, in the Being that knows about all things, that sees everything, that hears everything, that speaks itself.

Words spoken from the intellect merely go back into the intellect. They have no power. Therefore, they are limited and oriented to matter, which is where they become effective.

Gabriele, the teaching prophetess
and emissary of God, explained about this:

In this spiritual principle of inner life, which Christ reveals to us, we recognize that each person is like a computer that has programmed itself. We program ourselves with our feelings, sensations, thoughts, words and actions. These programs are our own, we, the computer.

We can pass on only what we have stored and are storing—nothing beyond that. The intellect is the memory bank of the human ego. Thus, what the intellect has stored is the person's potential of expression. In contrast, our spiritual body consists of the entire law of God. It gives the law of God and radiates it.

If we purify our soul and place our learning programs—what we have acquired as abilities—at God's disposal,

the eternal law, then the cleansed brain cells are the instrument through which God works. It is then the heart-
thinker who is guided by God. Everything else is the
human consciousness of the intellect, a memory bank of
the human ego, which we call "our life."

*Just as the way of thinking and living of humankind
changes through the ages, so does the word that is
shaped by the intellect. It speaks itself again and again,
from epoch to epoch, only with different words and terms.*

*The human, base self will pass away because it is born
solely in the intellect and is spoken from there.*

*The surface is the intellect which reacts, in turn, su-
perficially. The intellect is thus merely the surface of the
lake, not the bottom. On the surface is merely reflection
and not the truth.*

Gabriele:

In this statement by the Christ of God, we recognize
the process of reincarnation. Times change. The life and
the opinions of people change. That is why each epoch
has its coined words and terms. However, people speak
their human self again and again. They speak from what

their souls brought with them, that is, what lies in the soul and is active. They merely use different words and terms for this than in their previous incarnations because those times in previous incarnations had different coined words and other terms.

The human self, which is spoken from the intellect, changes into the giving self, if the person clears up his sinfulness and no longer does it.

The intellect is what we have input into the brain cells. The intellect can be compared to a lake, whose surface the superficial one looks at and does not fathom the depth because he looks only at the periphery of his consciousness, at his intellect. Thus, the intellect is merely the reflection of what lies in the depths. It is not the truth, but the surface of the truth, the mirror image. If we use only our intellect, instead of grasping life in its depth, this inevitably leads to superficiality.

The word of the innermost being is the I Am, the word of the eternal law. It was not born as was the word of the intellect. The word of God is from eternity to eternity, and the one who speaks it is from eternity to eternity.

Gabriele:

In each human being dwells a soul. In it, is the Eternal, the I Am. The Eternal, the I Am, is the Eternal, the word of God, the eternal law.

In the word of God, the "Let there be," the Eternal breathed the eternal law, the language of the eternal Being, into the eternal, spiritual body that was forming according to spiritual laws. The word of God, the eternal law that was breathed in, is, from eternity to eternity, and the beings of light are from eternity to eternity because they are law from His law.

The brain of a person is the birthplace of the word of the intellect because what the person enters into his brain cells shapes him. This is how he thinks and how he speaks. That is not eternity, but transience. During the phases of transience until it has passed, person and soul may have to endure much suffering and torment, depending on what the person has entered, and still enters, into his brain cells. The sinfulness then falls into the soul. It goes out from the soul into the heavenly bodies of the material cosmos and into the heavenly bodies of the purification planes and comes again and again in rhythmic cycles, until the person extinguishes it. This takes place through the transforming power of the Christ of God by way of the path of remorse, of asking for forgiveness, of forgiving, of making amends and of the do-no-more. Step by step, the person fulfills God's laws, thus coming into his divine heritage again, little by little. With this, he dissolves the cycle of reincarnation for himself, and as a pure being, his soul enters the eternal law, in which it lives from eternity to eternity.

The truly wise one, the enlightened one, speaks the I Am. It is the eternal law, the word that speaks itself eternally in the innermost being of the soul.

The God-filled person never speaks the word of the intellect because he is at home in his innermost being, in the Self, which he speaks.

Let the word first grow in you before you speak.

Whether you think or speak, both are energies that will not be lost.

Gabriele:

»Let the word first grow in you before you speak. Whether you think or speak, both are energies that will not be lost.«

These words from God say that we are responsible for every thought and every word because we have produced these energies, ourselves, through our feeling, sensing and thinking, through our speaking and through our acting. Therefore, these energies belong to us. They are our personal principles of law, as it were because every energy is consciousness and thus, a principle of law that is not lost.

Through this our feeling, thinking, speaking and acting, we create our personal law, which is oriented to us, the person because it went out from us. With our person-law, we again attract what we sent out. Suffering comes back as suffering, hatred comes back as hatred, envy as envy, strife and quarrelling as strife and quarrelling, God's love as God's love, God's peace as God's peace, divine unity and togetherness come back to us as divine unity and togetherness.

What we create is what we emit and, in turn, receive. This is why we should live consciously and prudently and ask ourselves again and again: What have I produced during the past moments, during the past hours, during the past day: negativity, that is, sinfulness, or have I unfolded the divine and expressed it?

That which is sensed in the innermost being, in the sanctified temple, is, at the same time, also the word. The innermost being bears good fruit because the sensation, which gives birth to the thought and brings forth the word, is the divine fruit, the light and the power that come into this world through the Spirit of Christ, who vanquishes the darkness.

The one who has conquered himself with the power of Christ beholds what is, and speaks the Being, the present, God. On the other hand, the external person speaks out of the human past and future because the present of this world is but a breath that, barely grasped, has already faded away.

Gabriele:

»*That which is sensed in the innermost being, in the sanctified temple, is at the same time, also the word.*« The word is God and God is the word. This means, in turn: God is everlasting law.

The one who speaks the word of God sanctifies his temple because he has cleansed it from the refuse of sin. The word of God is the fruit and the one who has found his way to the fruit bears good fruit because his sensations, thoughts and words are divine, that is, fruits of life.

The one who has conquered himself with the power of the Christ of God fathoms the word of human beings because he looks deeper. He does not let himself be blinded by deception because he lives in his purified temple and speaks the word of the eternal present, which is God.— God *is*, and the purified soul, the pure being in God, is divine.

The God-man, who is at home in his innermost being, beholds the »Is« in what is becoming because in his innermost being everything is present and already accomplished. The God-man lives and works out of the presence of God. What for the external person is just becoming, for the God-man it has already been accomplished in his innermost being.

The one who lives in his innermost being also beholds in his innermost being what is taking place and will take place in the external world and how it takes form. With his divine sensations, he accompanies the steps that still have to be taken externally, but which have already been taken in his innermost being. He places the whole into what is becoming, so that it will also be in the external world, as it already is in his innermost being.

What the inner person retains and moves in his innermost being will also be realized externally, in the world of the senses because in his innermost being it already is and is also retained and moved.

Gabriele:

God is present in all things. God, the pure, is also present in sin. If people, indeed, whole nations, create causes and these also come into effect, for instance, in wars, in disasters or when individuals feud with one another in strife and quarrelling, God, the good, is always present.

Even though it seems as if everything negative, that is, sinful, remains, everything belligerent and quarrelsome, the God-man, who is at home in his innermost being, in God, knows that this negativity will one day turn toward the good because in the law of cause and effect everything is already decided, since God is eternal and sinfulness cannot endure.

Whatever took or takes place externally, whatever shape it may seem to take on—God, the pure, knows the outcome, and in the becoming of human procedures, this can only be divine because God is the victor, and one day, the divine will prevail everywhere, for God, the mighty Creator-Spirit, set it up that way.

The God-man—the person who lives in God—knows about this and affirms the eternal presence of God, His holy will. The God-man lets this divine will flow into all situations and events of time. He affirms the Being and not the illusion.

he language of the Being is impersonal. The impersonal expects nothing; it wants nothing. It speaks itself, the eternal Self. The eternal Self is the infinity and the eternal fullness. The pure being is the Self that became form. It is the fullness that became form.

If you are the self, then you are the word of the Self that speaks in you and that penetrates the outside world as sound and tone. There, it speaks itself and vibrates to the ear of the world and into the ear of the Being in the person, sounding in his soul. Thus, much in the world, too, will change for the good of the whole.

Gabriele, the teaching prophetess
and emissary of God, explained about this:

God is the eternal word, the eternal law. It is harmony, color and form. The one who speaks the word of God is the law of God and is one with God and thus, is in the stream of infinity.

God is unchangeable because He is impersonal. He expects nothing from His children. He is everything in all things and each child possesses everything as essence and thus, is in all things and in the All-One.

In the depths of our soul, we are the law that became form. Our sins lie over this. We have become a human being again to wipe out the sins that we inflicted on ourselves in previous incarnations. Therefore, we have incarnated to find ourselves as children of God, by clearing up our human aspects and entering the divine stream, from where we went forth. We are on Earth to become divine again.

Let what you speak aloud stream from you and flow through you. It formulates itself in you because it is the Self. That is the I Am, the word of the Being, the life and the substance of life. It is the Absolute that never passes away, even when the times change and pass away.

Gabriele:

God is the eternal word in all life forms. All that we see—animals, plants, stones and heavenly bodies—is the revelation of God. Thus, God speaks through the nature kingdoms and through the stars. God speaks in the soul of every human being. If the person purifies his soul, he will gradually become the word of God because God will then speak through the purified soul. This means that the eternal law flows through the soul and through the person. The person then also speaks the law because soul and person live in God through the fulfillment of God's laws.

The word, which is the Being, the I Am, the eternal law, and which is in the stream of the All, does not fall back on you like the vapid, energy-poor word of the intellect. The word, the Being, remains in the stream of the Being and flows through you, the being that became form, and through Me, the Being that became form, as well as through everything that is in the stream of Being and has its existence there.

Therefore, speak the word, the Being, in you.

Learn to move everything in your innermost being, to receive it in your innermost being and to speak out of your innermost being. Then you will speak the language of the Being.

Everything that lasts eternally takes place in the innermost being of the soul. That is the truth. That is the constancy. That is the life. That is the stream, the Self, the I Am. It is the life and the substance of life in you.

he one who accuses his neighbor of being untruthful and of lying, without being able to prove this statement, bears witness to himself that he is at the edge of the stream throwing stones at his neighbor—thus stoning himself because his neighbor, whom he accuses, is a part of him in his innermost being.

Gabriele, the teaching prophetess
and emissary of God, explained about this:

God is justice and inherent in justice is equality. Justice is the scale that precisely weighs everything and allots to each one his measure. Therefore, speak only the truth. Explain things and set them right. And if you accuse one of your neighbors of lying because he publicly discriminates against you, you can admonish him and explain that he speaks the untruth. If he continues to speak this falsehood—and all of that publicly—then you, too, speak of the falsehood, which is the same as a lie. For it is written: If you have something to state against your brother, then go first to your brother, in order to clear it up with him privately. If it is not possible to clear it up and your neighbor continues to publicly speak the untruth against you, then he does this, figuratively speaking, in the community. And just as he speaks in the "community," that is, in public, you can also go to the "community," to the public.

Gabriele:

The one who stands at the edge of the stream relies on the knowledge of his mind, on his intellect, on what he has acquired in this world. He believes in this. It is reality for him and he adheres to this until he slips on it and has to recognize that his intellectual thinking is not able to carry him through illness, hardship and fate, but solely God, the eternal stream.

The one who recognizes himself while slipping down into the vale of tears and bitterness, that is, who recognizes his sins, repents of them and no longer commits them, gradually goes from the edge into the stream and becomes one with God. While doing so, his sins fall away from him, which are his illnesses, suffering and blows of fate. However, the one who continues to sin merely bears witness to what he is: a sinful, egocentric person.

*T*he one who speaks the word, the I Am, beholds the truth and the untruth. He explains, sets right, and then goes his way. He knows that the one who changes himself and devotes himself to God walks the path that leads to freedom. But the one who does not change himself walks the stony path into sorrow, to awaken to the truth via the sorrow that is the same as sin, and then be able to enter the truth.

If you do not tire of the search for truth, you will find yourselves by recognizing your faults and weaknesses and by clearing them up in time before sorrow comes over you. For this reason, never tire of searching, otherwise, you will have to endure your sinfulness.

The one who does not want to look at himself always looks at his neighbor. He is of the opinion that he is the good one and his neighbor, the bad one. This behavior brings out the know-it-all, who is of the opinion that he can steer the course of the All, since he considers himself all-round clever.

Recognize that the fool knows everything better. If his neighbor approaches him with his foolishness, then two fools quarrel with each other. Both lack wisdom.

The opposite of truth is foolishness. Very many are occupied with this.

When the soul goes as a fool into the worlds that it has determined for itself through its foolishness, then only foolishness surrounds it because it lives in its illusory pictures of foolishness. Even if the former human being knows about the laws of God and did not fulfill them, he remains the fool and the slave of slavery, of foolishness, which he lived and with which he surrounded himself.

Gabriele, the teaching prophetess
and emissary of God, explained about this:

The divine principle is: Like attracts like. The pure attracts the pure, the impure, in turn, the impure. According to his foolishness, a fool will again attract corresponding foolish ones, and thus, he surrounds himself with foolish ones, just as he is, himself.

The one who does not come to grips with his earthly existence, has no relationship with the spiritual world, either.

Gabriele, the teaching prophetess
and emissary of God, explained about this:

What do these words from our Lord, Christ, want to tell us? We have to come to grips with ourselves, with our thoughts, with our feelings, with all that we say and do because that shows us who and what we still are.

Mostly we deal with our neighbor instead of ourselves. If we invariably look at ourselves, at our thoughts, at what we do, at our stirrings and inclinations, then we have no time to eye our neighbor.

The pure, the fine, the noble and good is still enveloped by the shell of humanness, of the impure, coarse, ignoble and bad. If we burst the shell of our ego bit by bit, then the inner, the spiritual-divine, comes to light, the light-filled being that is in communication with the pure Being, the divine, the spiritual world. If we do not awaken the light-filled forces of our eternal being in us, then we are moved by the communications with our own sinfulness, with what is worldly, human. We then have no relationship with the spiritual world.

Gabriele:

To walk the path to the kingdom of the inner being means to consciously grasp our humanness—that is, the sinfulness against the soul—day by day, in order to bring light into it.

If we do not see ourselves as the temple of God, if we do not want to cleanse our temple, if we look again and again at other temples, at our fellow people, in order to possibly defile them with our thoughts, words and deeds, then we cannot refine our feelings, thoughts, words and deeds, either.

We refine our soul and even the vibration of our body by recognizing our sins, clearing them up and no longer committing them. Then the soul attains a finer vibration because the soul turns to God, more and more. This fine vibration radiates into our physical body and marks us. Our thoughts, sensations, words and actions become finer, that is, purer, more selfless, nobler, kinder. Then we are for our neighbor and no longer against him.

»This side of life« is the temporal. It is the confined, transformed-down life, in which we experience and suffer hardship, affliction, fear, worry, loneliness, grief and finally, death.

We should not cling to this side of life with all the fibers of our thinking and feeling, but should clear up our humanness. If through our egocentric feeling, thinking and striving, we bind ourselves to this side of life, then we sin and create causes on this side of life, burdens of the soul, which work like magnets. These causes, these magnets, draw us again and again to those places where we created our causes, the burdens. If we have then passed on, if our soul is in the purification planes and the burdens become active through the irradiation of the stars, then the causes that we set on Earth may again draw us into the flesh, into another incarnation. The magnet of our guilt is what draws us again and again to the place of our actions.

Whether he lives or dies, whether he is awake or asleep—neither this earthly existence nor death will teach him anything new because he stayed the former, sinful person, despite knowing better.

Gabriele:

Many strive for knowledge, also for spiritual knowledge – and much knowledge is available to many. Nevertheless, not many are close to God, and very few live in God. Why? Knowledge alone does not make you happy, and spiritual knowledge alone does not make you wise.

Even if in our bookcases at home we have many books filled with wisdom, if we also browse now and then in these books filled with wisdom and thus, statements of truth, if we take whole paragraphs and memorize them—it is of no use to us. Quite the contrary: The more spiritual knowledge we have, the more we obligate ourselves before God to actualize this knowledge.

Particularly during this time, much divine knowledge is given to us all. The divine knowledge, the divine law, is given to us so that we fulfill it, so that we become wise and find our way out of our knowledge, out of our intellectual thinking and striving—out of our human obsessions.

Acquiring knowledge about divine-spiritual principles does not bring us higher spiritual development. Nothing will change us if we want to remain the former person. And death, the change of the plane of existence, does not make our soul more light-filled, nor will it expand our consciousness. Without working on ourselves, we do not improve. We learn nothing more.

By virtue of free will, we determine how long we want to let ourselves be led around in circles by our own sinfulness. We will fall down again and again and stay lying there—until we take Christ into our heart and fulfill the Ten Commandments and the teachings of the Sermon on the Mount, which He brought us and lived as an example for us.

Thus, it is about fulfilling the laws of God and not about hearing them. The knowledge about the laws of God is the prerequisite for being able to actualize them. The one who merely talks about divine knowledge, the eternal law, exalts himself with this. He abuses it in his own self-interest. This is a violation of the second commandment, it is the abuse of the name of God, the abuse of the divine.

Gabriele:

»No person can flee from himself.«
Are we aware of this?

Many say: "I will take my life to escape this earthly existence." That is not possible. We cannot escape what is in us. We take it with us, again and again.

Our causes are energy potentials that lie in our soul and will sooner or later come into effect and have an impact—whether we are in an earthly garment as a human being then or are a soul in the soul realms. The effects are similar on the material level and on the levels of the spheres of purifications.

Thus, we take our humanness, our sinfulness, with us. We cannot escape it. But the experiences of what we once caused, filled with pain and suffering, the expiation, does not have to be—if we recognize ourselves in time in the moments of our days on Earth and clear up our guilt with Christ.

This is why each one of us must look at himself. The light, the energy of the day, brings each of us many moments. The day opens our eyes; it opens our senses. By way of our eyes and our other senses, the day shows us what we should recognize and clear up. If we do not do this, then we have to expiate what we have done to others and thus inflicted upon our soul.

The task that life gives us is our human life. What the day points out to us, what it shows us personally, is our life. It consists of our feeling, sensing, thinking, speaking and doing. If we do not make use of the day, if we push aside the learning tasks unheeded, then one day, the task for us will be to expiate what we have inflicted upon ourselves. Inevitably, what will break in over us is the expiation of what our soul has long borne, what we should have cleared up long since. The clouds show themselves in time on the horizon of our life. If we do not dissolve them in time, then their content pours over us. Figuratively speaking, we then stand in the rain and get wet.

Gabriele:

Many of us know that sin first goes into the brain cells. It then stays in the brain cells for a certain time and admonishes us to clear up in time what occurred. If we do not clear up the sinfulness, what we emitted, it goes into the soul and, via the soul, into the repository stars. Therefore, the memory bank of our sins, of our guilt, is the soul and the world of the stars—the stars of the purification planes and the material stars.

What we have entered in our soul and in the stars belongs to us. We are continually in contact with our inputs and communicate with them. And what we entered is continuously lying in wait to break in over us. If the constellation of the stars has the corresponding radiation, then the humanness, our sins, breaks in over us. We experience the effect of our causes, our self-created fate.

As long as the energy potential of our sinful aspects is still lying in wait, admonishing impulses come. Once it breaks in over us, then we have to expiate it. But the grace of God is also in the expiation: to recognize, clear it up and no longer commit it.

»Thus, you are yourself your own danger.« In our words this means: We live dangerously each moment, as long as we are still in the law of sowing and reaping.

Particularly during this time, many people are fearful. What is fear? We sense that something could come that we fear, something unpleasant, bad. What is behind this? In many cases, is it not our own sins, our inputs, which are preparing to be active? Fate knocks at our door before it enters.

Ultimately, no one can take away our fear. There is no help from without because in our fear lies our sense of guilt. In us lie the causes—in us, the help can be found: Christ.

Gabriele, the teaching prophetess
and emissary of God, explained about this:

Therefore, we attain the being in God, the peace of our soul, when we are of good will and put this into practice by working on ourselves. If we want to clear up our human aspects ourselves, by our own efforts, as it were, then it becomes strenuous. We get tired and perhaps lose courage. However, if we turn to Christ, again and again, if we entrust ourselves to Him and rely on Him, then He gives us so much strength that we also do it joyfully. Then clearing things up is lightly done.

»The one who is willing to learn will recognize himself and find his true being in self-recognition. He will actualize—and thus be fulfilled.« To be fulfilled means that our soul fills with light because we recognize the sinfulness, the humanness, and no longer do it. The dark spots on the soul transform into light. Though this, fulfillment awakens in us. We are fulfilled by the One who fills our soul with light and power. We sense more and more the nearness of God, His love.

God's love is the life of our soul and the inner happiness of the fulfilled person, of His conscious child.

Do we already go through our days on Earth aware of God's love? Or does the question still vibrate in us: "Does God truly love me?" That means: "Now I have to still believe that He loves me because that is what I am told. I do not know it yet." Then our faith is merely passive.

As soon as we begin to question, we can already be touched and guided. The soul stirs, longing awakens and the searching begins. We ask ourselves: How can we feel that God is a loving Father? As a child, we want to feel that God loves us. We want to feel His closeness.

If we remain passive in our faith, then it will remain mere faith, and in our heart the fearful question will continue to knock: "Is there a God of love? Does He truly love me?" But we do not have to stay in this vague faith that is riddled with doubt. Christ frequently points out the active faith to us. Active faith means: You should not only hear from your neighbor that God loves you, that God is near you. Instead, you should experience it, yourself. You should feel God, yourself. It is the active faith that ensures that we sense Him, God, our Father, each day more, that we can feel His love more—namely, if we are willing to love Him.

And in what is the love of a child for its Father shown, how does it prove itself? It begins with the willingness of the child to do away with what is an obstacle to God's love. This takes place by the child recognizing the sins it has caused, step by step, by repenting of them, clearing them up with the power of the Christ of God and no longer doing them. The do-no-more also means: Instead, we fulfill the principles of the law of God, as they are presented in the Ten Commandments or in the Sermon on the Mount, for instance. If we take this step of actualization, then we feel God's love in us, ourselves because in our heart, in our soul, it gets better and better.

We feel lighter and brighter because our soul breathes a sigh of relief. Our soul rejoices and is happy that the person clears things up and no longer commits the sinful aspects. Then Christ transforms the negative, the sin, in the soul into the positive, into God's energy of light. That is the touch of God, the happiness of the soul.

We human beings experience this joy of the soul by suddenly being able to give thanks because we sense that our thoughts and our sensations become more light-filled. We experience God, the infinite love and the happiness of our soul, by experiencing that we no longer go through the day absentmindedly, but are aware and clear. We are alert and sense the stirring of our soul, which admonishes us: Pay attention to what the situations, the moments of your life want to tell you. Clear up what the day points out to you today! If we do this, then our soul again receives light and strength from God. In this way, we sense the nearness of God more and more, the love that touches us.

This is our own experience that God loves us, the living, active faith, which makes soul and person happy and fulfilled. Then we are no longer dependent on merely believing that the Father loves us—we know it! The joy of our soul, the thankfulness in our fulfilled heart tell us. Thus, the active faith leads to certainty and, step by step, to unity with the One who loves us and wants the best for us.

The strongest power on our way to God, to our true Being, is the love for God and the longing for our true homeland.

We could take as a task each day to think more often of God, our Father. It can be very simple thoughts. For example, let us make ourselves aware that God, our Father, loves us and that He wants the best for us. We can come to Him at every moment, turning to Him and speaking to Him. He will never turn away from us.

Particularly when we think that we are sinning again, be it in our thoughts, be it with words or actions, we should not defiantly stand in a corner, as it were, and turn our back on Him, as well. Let us turn to Him and say to Him, for instance: "Father, You want the best for me. Therefore, I want to prove myself in such a way that You can guide and lead me." If we realize this in the situation of sin, we will not continue to sin, but will quickly—and perhaps even joyfully—turn back, clear up the sin we have recognized and no longer do it.

Therefore, let us frequently think of God, our Father, and imagine very concretely that He loves us, that He envelops us, that He wants the best for us. Then, it increasingly will be a need for us to devote ourselves to Him more and more, and to make use of our days, so that the good, the kindness and His infinite love can be effective in us.

If soul and person are not willing to learn, that is, to find themselves in God through actualization, the life of soul and person will become harder and more difficult.

Gabriele:

If the good will to recognize and clear up is lacking, sooner or later this will have an effect in our life. The difficulty of life, but also the hardness of the earthly existence comes from the soul. The graver the sins are, the more burdened the person can be—when his sins become active on his body, or are already active.

We shape our life ourselves. We create our living conditions ourselves because each one is his own law. With our feeling, sensing, thinking, speaking and acting, we create our human principles.

In the eternal Being, the spirit beings live the law of love, of unity and of being linked. This goes out from them—and what they radiate and thus emit comes back to them again: the absolute, eternal law of love, of peace, of harmony, of joy, the true Being.

What comes to us human beings is what we emit. If we emit our human aspects, our sins, and if we do not listen to the divine impulses, which are given to us daily to clear up what we have sent out, then our personal life will become harder and more difficult. At some point, fate will then hit—it is nothing more than what we have sent out.

We see that the principle is always the same, on Earth as in heaven: sending and receiving. Through our refusal to clear things up in good time, we have defied our own principles. If the effects break in over us, then it is: An eye for an eye, a tooth for a tooth. Often the person then says: "This hard-hearted God!"

We Original Christians and the many Christ-friends all over the world know that it is different. It is not God who is the author of our fate, but it is our own hard-heartedness and lack of love. It is our sins that have not been cleared up. God is the love that admonishes us again and again, that uplifts us again and again, that shows us the way again and again and helps and supports us to recognize our human aspects and to clear them up. God's love also helps us when we no longer want to commit our human aspects. It reinforces the lawful, the divine, that we have decided for.

Each day, every single one of us experiences God's help in many ways. If we realize this and act according to our knowledge, it will soon become brighter, more light-filled and peaceful in us and around us. However, we may not say: It is up to the others. They should begin. Each one has to take the first step himself, so that God's love can be effective. The one who ignites the light of love in himself is the one who then carries the light into the world.

If you are suffering, then feel in the suffering why you are suffering. Let the sensations and thoughts of the suffering come, for they speak their language. And if you do not tire of fulfilling the eternal law, you will mature in suffering and grow closer to the light that brings you peace and stillness.

Gabriele:

»If you are suffering, then feel in the suffering why you are suffering.« The one who accepts grief and suffering, aware that: "This—and perhaps much more—I have caused myself," will clear things up and bear them in an upright manner. But how often do we wail and complain: The neighbor is to blame. That is why Christ tells us:

»Let the sensations and thoughts of the suffering come, for they speak their language. And if you do not tire of fulfilling the eternal law, you will mature in suffering and grow closer to the light that brings you peace and stillness.«

In suffering, we will mature and grow closer to the light only if we clear up the active sins, which show themselves in suffering, illness and hardship. If we do not clear up our sins, we will continue to sin and our suffering and illnesses will not leave us. They stay with us and come again when the stars reactivate them—in this earthly form of existence or in another life on Earth or if we are in the spheres of purification as a soul.

We determine ourselves how we live, what we inflict upon ourselves and how we expiate this.

The person should neither lament about the path of his life on Earth nor condemn his path through life.

The one who presumes to know his path through life also presumes to have authority over creation.

Gabriele:

Every person determines his life's path himself. What this brings with it, the individual inflicted upon himself. Lamenting his life's path does not change it.

We can change much for the good on our life's path, if we change ourselves by making use of the day, by recognizing our sinful aspects each day, clearing them up and no longer doing them. Each day is a step on the path through life, and each step is different for each one because each one has a different life's path, according to his feeling, sensing, thinking, speaking and acting.

No person can know his life's path because no one knows his future. And anyone who thinks he knows his future is presuming to be the Creator. Only the eternal Creator, God, knows the life's path of each of His children, for each child is His creation.

All the paths that the Spirit teaches lead to the one goal: that soul and person find their way to the Being, which is God.

The hope and the longing for God awaken the fulfillment of hope. Wherever there is hope, the longing for this fulfillment, the ruling hand of God is there.

I, Christ, give you teachings for self-recognition, so that you may resort to them again and again when you become lukewarm:

In each situation, decide for God, then you evade the darkness.

If the person is once warm, then again cold, he is un-decided and serves the darkness. The one who decides for the world decides for the intoxication of the ego. Then the world inspires him, and those who belong to the world will inspire him.

The darkness plays with the human being. It influences him—once for, then against, God. With this, it wants to mock God. It will play this game with the person until the person has decided.

Gabriele, the teaching prophetess
and emissary of God, explained about this:

Many people are in the habit of being excessively enthusiastic when they hear the principles of the law of God, and promise the Eternal, God, our Father, that they will keep His laws, that is, commandments. They then make efforts for several days or weeks. If thereupon, no change occurs in their life, they drop God's commandments, the principles of the law, and commit the old sins, that is, they rejoin the causal chain of the old Adam. Suddenly, they remember God's commandments again and begin anew to fulfill them for several days. Then the good resolutions are again sacrificed to the causal chain of the old Adam.

That is the undecided one who, despite many attempts to fulfill God's commandments step by step, serves the darkness.

*urther teachings for self-recognition:
    Always demand of yourself the utmost, not what is within reach. Then you will come to know the power potential of your soul.*

Gabriele, the teaching prophetess
and emissary of God, explained about this:

In every person lies much more than he can comprehend. Therefore, we should never be satisfied with the obvious, with what is familiar to us, with what we already can do. Although it may be convenient for our person to move and act within the framework of what is easy for us, perhaps with routine steps in the individual tasks—yet, in us, there are ever so many possibilities, other predispositions, talents and abilities that are waiting to be developed.

From what we can do, we should venture to take the next step—at first, it is a step into the unknown for us. If we place our abilities and what still lies hidden in us into the service of the Almighty, we attain inner greatness. Then we also demand the utmost of ourselves, our very best, which goes far beyond what we could formerly do and beyond the horizon of our consciousness up to now.

Admonish yourself frequently by asking yourself again and again what you want to do about yourself.

And when you ask yourself, then you know what you want to do about yourself. Do this, and in you will awaken the eternal self, which you are in eternity as a being of eternity.

Gabriele:

Our day's work can be varied. Diversity always confronts us with tasks that we will look at in terms of our ability. Each task also admonishes us to ask ourselves whether we want to fulfill it, why we want to fulfill it, if we want to benefit from it or whether we want to fulfill it with the power of the Lord. Thus, we fathom the individual facets of our motivation, recognize ourselves and decide how we want to do it.

In every situation and in every task, if we ask ourselves how we want to do it, and look into our subcommunications, into our feelings and sensations, then we know what degree of selflessness we have attained and what our inner devotion to the inner life looks like. We recognize to what extent we are willing to fulfill the will of the Eternal and to act according to the law of God. Then we know which rung of the ladder to heaven we are standing on.

The soul in a person is merely a guest on Earth. The soul has become a human being to develop the inner treasure and to do good. The good comes through people—as does the bad.

Gabriele, the teaching prophetess
and emissary of God, explained about this:

Our spiritual body, which we call soul, is not a part of matter, nor is matter a part of the spiritual body.

The divine essence of matter is a part of our spiritual body. Thus, we are called to cleanse our soul and that part of matter toward which we have incurred guilt, through our behavior toward the Earth and toward the nature kingdoms.

Our spiritual body returns to the eternal Being. The physical body remains on the Earth and will transform into spirit-substance, so that this is again active in our spiritual body.

With a quantum of causes, each one of us has contributed to the density of this planet Earth. We must again transform this quantum of matter, that is, bring it into a higher vibration, so that the Earth, too, can again become fine-material and the spiritual planet can enter the eternal heavens, from where we once went forth as pure beings and where the spiritual part-planet also has its origin.

The good person who lives in Me, the Christ, bears good fruits. The immoral person, who has dedicated himself to the darkness, brings darkness into the world.

Blessed are the ones who bring goodness, through whom the good comes into the world. Woe to those through whom the darkness comes into the world. The one will go to the light—the other will suffer in darkness.

Know and sense in your hearts: The more you love God, the more will God give to you. The more joyfully you share the gifts of love, the more you will receive from God. Only the selfless one receives because he passes it on selflessly. The one who gives selflessly draws from the eternal Being, from the unending stillness that is God. Through this, he becomes more still and God-conscious because he knows that God gives to the one who selflessly passes on the gifts from the treasure of his actualization.

Gabriele:

God is the sun, the force field of infinity.

God is eternally giving love. If we turn away from the sun, the giving love, by sinning against the light, against the sun, then we shadow our souls and turn away from God, the light. We then move in a shadowed existence, in our own world of shadows.

Every shadow is based on self-love, which demands solely for itself, to strengthen the base ego. Thus, the egocentric person strives to augment his shadows.

The more we turn away from the light, the larger and denser the shadows will become. We look only at our shadows and lead our personal shadowed life. We love only ourselves. We become ever more indifferent toward our neighbor. In this way, we remove ourselves from the sun and linger in light-poor regions. If it is then dark and cold, we wonder: Why doesn't the sun shine for me? Where is it?

Only when we turn back, that is, turn toward the sun, will we turn away from our shadows. If we take the path into the light, we clear up the shadows that are behind us and go with us. The more we clear up the shadows, the smaller they become. If we then stand again in the light of God, in the infinite, eternal sun of love, the shadows have transformed and we are light of His light. That is the path into the light, into the eternal life.

The closer we come to the light, the more selfless we will become. The selfless love, the love for God, grows in us and fulfills us more and more. A God-filled heart will love more and more selflessly, and receive all the more from the treasure of life.

Gabriele:

Thus, Christ is the way, the truth and the life. Christ is the light of our souls, which lights our way on the path to the eternal Father, home to the eternal Being. Jesus, the Christ, who became our Redeemer, is also the one who dissolves all sinfulness. Therefore, the one who wants to deliver himself from his sins goes to Christ, the Redeemer, and asks Him for support and help. He then takes the path of remorse from the heart. He asks his neighbor for forgiveness and forgives the one who has sinned against him.

If many things still have to be made good through the deed, this should be done. This results in the do-no-more of this sin and the step-by-step fulfillment of the divine laws, the essence of which we find in the Ten Commandments and in the Sermon on the Mount.

Gabriele, the teaching prophetess
and emissary of God, explained about this:

Day after day, we can recognize to what extent selfless serving has already become our life. Let us monitor ourselves.

Let us look at nature: The eternal Spirit serves every little flower and every little animal; He serves every stone. And we? Do we take the stone and thoughtlessly toss it away—or do we respect and look at it? Do we tear out the little flower, or do we bend down and thank it in our sensations for radiating to us? What about the animals? Do we deliberately tread on the little animal, or do we step around it and let it continue? Or do we take it away from where it is and set it down on another place, somewhat to the side, so that nothing will happen to it?

We can recognize ourselves in our behavior toward our second neighbor. Aside from the animals, these are also the plants and stones. We behave toward nature just as we behave toward our neighbor. If we are against our neighbor, only little strength will flow to us from nature's life forms in woods and fields. We can never rightly say:

"I love the animals," if, at the same time, we despise the inner being of people, by abusing our fellow people for our purposes. This love for the animal is then self-love, that is, self-interest. We want the animal to make us happy.

It should be the other way around! We should be the ones who carry the light of love and selflessness to our neighbor and second neighbor, to the forms of nature. Let us recognize ourselves and behave as children of the eternal light! The powers of our light-filled sensations and thoughts, the positive energies of thankfulness and inner joy flow from us to nature. Let us bring joy to the animal! Let us bring the communication of life to the plants and the minerals! Then we will experience the fullness of God, and we realize that God's life—the Spirit and the love—prevails everywhere. It is everywhere.

Wherever we go, wherever we are, to wherever we look and listen—everywhere is God. He is in all things. Let us establish communication with Him, by letting our heart speak to Him, to God, our Father, to Christ, our Redeemer. Then we will also hear His voice, the subtle tones of the Creator's infinite love, from plants, animals and stones.

The selflessly serving love is the inner devotion. It sets the heart aglow and gives joy to the soul and pulsates through every selfless word and every selfless deed. It lightens and frees the soul and lends wings to the steps because soul and person personify the law of the All.

Gabriele:

We recognize that it is always about the inner aspects. Everything external is smoke and mirrors, as it were; therefore: the inner devotion. Not the mere external turning toward our neighbor, toward nature, but the *devotion*.

In the word devotion, we experience God. God devotes Himself to each one. God serves each one. Nothing is too little for Him because He, the Great One, serves. Selfless serving is not bowing and scraping, but giving. The one who truly serves gives the spiritual gifts of life. That is devotion.

Inner devotion is the inner orientation to the inner life. Not the external, not the shell, the human being, speaks the language of God, but the innermost being. If we have opened our inner being for the most part, if we are near God, then we also live aware of God, with and for everything that surrounds us.

hatever you do, do it from the Spirit because only the selfless deeds are done in and with God.

If you think your works are ever so good—then examine yourselves, whether you have done them from the Spirit, that is, selflessly. If you have done them with your human ego and your benefit in mind, they can have an opposite effect. Sooner or later, you will have to suffer under this.

Gabriele, the teaching prophetess
and emissary of God, explained about this:

All external works are oriented to ourselves, to our ego. The inner works in devotion to the Spirit of life are the works for our neighbor, the works of love.

God shows Himself in manifold ways in the life of nature. We hear Him in the call of the bird. We sense Him in the fragrance of the blossoms and flowers. We see Him in the sprouting of life. We experience Him when the rays of the sun illuminate the stones. At night, we experience God in the stars. We experience Him in the raindrops and in the clouds. The great Creator-Spirit is present. And what we feel in nature, life in its diversity, all that is our divine heritage as essence. That is what we are in our own being, in the eternal homeland.

For this reason, live from the Spirit, and be mindful of the inner light, which is your helper and adviser, Christ:

I, in all of you, and all of you, in Me. I, in you, and you, in Me.

Gabriele:

»I, in all of you, and all of you, in Me. I, in you, and you, in Me.« If we let the Lord's words vibrate in us, if we move them in our inner consciousness, we recognize in this one sentence the infinite greatness of the universal Spirit, of life, of the universal Being.

he truly wise one lives in God, and God lives through him. Whatever he gives is not given by him—God gives it through him. Whatever he does is not done by him—God does it through him.

He speaks, yet it is not he who speaks—God speaks through him. He works, yet it is not he who works because God works through him.

The truly wise one lives in the world for the divine world and is merely a transformer of selfless love, the inner power. He is selfless giving. For this reason, it is not he who speaks and acts, but it is God through him.

Gabriele, the teaching prophetess
and emissary of God, explained about this:

These words of the Christ of God point out to us the goal of our sojourn on Earth, which is also the goal of the soul in the spheres of purification.

There is only one goal: It is to become one with God. That is why we are human beings. That is why we live as souls in the spheres of purification. That is why we incarnate again and become a human being once more.

The wheel of coming and going will continue to turn for each individual until he is able to live in the world without being with the world. Only then, will the incarnations stop. Only then, will the soul go into the eternal light step by step, and become one with the Almighty, from where the pure being—you, as the being from God—went forth.

Safeguard the good, the Being, as the gem of your innermost being, then you will remain in your innermost being and speak the language of the innermost being, the truth.

Gabriele, the teaching prophetess
and emissary of God, explained about this:

We safeguard the divine in us as the gem of our innermost being, by being more and more aware of the divine, of our eternal heritage, and by giving honor to God in our life. The one who thinks again and again of the divine in himself and in his fellow people strives daily to fulfill the eternal laws, the gem of his innermost being. Through this, he will gradually become the truth and give from the truth because he not only cherishes and respects the gem, but also causes it to become the source of strength in his earthly existence.

The one who is begotten by the human being alone, that is, by humanness, will also return to humankind as a soul, again and again, and be born of the human being, of humanness, and speak the language of human beings— until he strives to be born in God, the unparalleled birthplace, which is the Being. Then he will return to God and live eternally in Him, the stream of the Being. Then he will also speak the language of the Being because he is again the Being that has become form, and in which he moves.

Gabriele:

If a body is procreated through the lust of physicality, then the body was not procreated out of love for the partner and for the body-to-be. Such people also attract souls that make demands according to their desires.

If the parents do not discard their physical desires, when the child becomes an adult it will also be very difficult for him to recognize the sensual desires that he brought with him, and to clear them up. Often the parents and children go into the soul realms with these desires and possibly bring their desires again into a new earthly garment, and, driven by their passions, they will find neither rest, nor themselves. Thus, the wheel of incarnation will keep turning for them until they strive for a birth in the Spirit of God and enter the birthplace of the spirit beings, which is the Being.

Speak the language of the Being!
Nothing is outside of you. It is not the flower, the grass,
the plant, the stone, the mineral—you are the being, the
flower, the grass, the plant, the stone and the mineral
because you are in all things as essence and all things are
as essence in you.

Gabriele:

Everything is in all things. This is how God, the Eternal, arranged it. This is how He created the mighty, eternal law of communication. Everything is linked with one another because everything is as essence in all things.

No matter where you go, where you stand, where you
are—be a part of the eternal temple! Keep the order of the
temple. Then you will also be just and attain justice.

Gabriele:

The eternal temple is the infinity of God, in which all pure beings live and have their existence. Each one of us is the temple of God because in each one of us dwells the power of the All-Holy One.

We human beings are called upon to cleanse our temple of impure thoughts, feelings, words and actions, of sensual pleasures and cravings, so that we then keep the order of the temple, that is, fulfill the law of the eternal, mighty temple of infinity. Then we will be just and will attain justice—even if not right way, since God's mills grind slowly, as it were. In the law of sowing and reaping, the effects do not begin from one day to the next, but in the rhythm people predetermined themselves, through their unlawful inputs.

God is just, and the one who relies on God will also attain justice.

Remember: Whatever you do not perceive in your innermost being, in your true Being, you have not developed yet in your innermost being.

You will not grasp and behold what is not alive in you. If your neighbor is not alive in you, then you have neither access to your neighbor nor communication with God.

Gabriele:

We will attain the perception of the innermost being, of the true Being, only once we cleanse our temple of the refuse of sin and no longer commit the sins we have cleared up. By clearing up our sins, we experience ourselves, and at the same time, what we did and accomplished becomes our experience, so that we no longer commit the sins recognized.

All that we have cleared up, which was often overcome through suffering and pain, is now for each of us the positive potential of memory, which we also call a potential of help or experience.

Through the inner communication, through the perception of the innermost being in connection with the potential of memory or help, we can understand our fellow people and see behind their masks. That is, we recognize what they pretend, to conceal their true feelings and thoughts, their true face.

Only once we have overcome our base self, will the positive in our neighbor come alive in us. In this way, we have access to our neighbor and at the same time, communication, that is, perception, with the true Being. The person who does not take this path speaks only his base self. He sees only his base self and has access neither to his neighbor nor to God.

Examine yourself: How you speak shows whether you are in yourself or whether you speak only out of your ego, the surface.

ine in God. Just as the morsels and the drink go into you, they have an effect in you and again radiate from you.

The one who sanctifies his morsels and drink keeps the consciousness of the food and drink alive. It then goes into the soul as essence and strength. The food and drink then strengthen not only the body, but soul and body.

With your awareness, accompany every morsel and every swallow of drink on its way into your body.

The sensations, thoughts and words that you give to the food and drink on its way into your organism have a corresponding effect in soul and body.

Gabriele, the teaching prophetess
and emissary of God, explained about this:

God is the infinite power in all things. Thus, God is omnipresent life. Before we partake of our food and drink, we should raise our heart to God and thank Him for His gifts. Our thanks to God should stay with us while eating and drinking, then the divine in the food will become active and be a fount of health for soul and body.

If you have truly raised your heart to God and thanked Him for the food and drink, then you will also give thanks after the meal and dedicate the following hours to Him, by doing with God what is indicated.

Everything is energy. The food and drink, too, are energy. The way you feel and think—with these forces, you magnetize the food and the drink. It is what you give them on their way into your body.

Therefore, with the intake of nourishment, as well, remain in the innermost part of your temple because food and drink are also a part of the order of the temple, of the law of the temple.

Each aspect of consciousness is the same as its state of consciousness. It has the whole in it and speaks itself according to its degree of consciousness.

The fruits and drinks, too—all food—are consciousness and speak the language of their degree of consciousness. This means that they are in communication with the stream, in which they move and have their existence.

Just as you, the person, treat the food and drink, that is how they will have their effect in and on you. Everything is vibration that makes itself noticeable in and on you, marking you as well.

Gabriele:

The divine communication is the All-consciousness because everything is in all things. Everything is divine and is communication. God speaks from every state of consciousness, according to the degree of consciousness. Consequently, God speaks from countless mouths. Thus, there are countless communications, which can hardly be fathomed by us human beings.

Just as we attune ourselves to the divine communication or cut ourselves off from the divine communication, that is how our life proceeds. Our life on Earth shows itself in our feeling, thinking, speaking and acting, in our eating and drinking habits, in our whole behavior—in our earthly home and outside our apartment or house.

My words are spirit and life, light and truth. The spiritually maturing one, who strives toward the light, toward Me, becomes more sensitive, more permeable for the inner life.

Gabriele:

To become »*more sensitive, more permeable for the inner life,*« means that the person who recognizes his sins day by day, clears them up and no longer commits them matures into the divine consciousness. His soul becomes more light-filled and the person receptive to the inner life.

Thus, to become sensitive means that the soul increases in light and strength because the person clears up his sins and no longer does them. Through this, ever more light radiates through the soul and the person, who has become more permeable to this. In his conscious mind, he grasps what the inner light reflects to him.

Gabriele:

In the words »He does not fill it,« lies an important principle of the law of God for us human beings. It is: What the body is unable to utilize, that is, unable to break down for the physical body because the amount of food is too much, is wasted life energy.

If the amount of food consumed is beyond what is needed, then it will indeed be processed, but not broken down for the organs, for the blood, for the cells of the body. It will be eliminated. The person will have to account for this portion of the food. It is an abuse of nature.

A spiritual person who fulfills the laws of God step by step is also in communication with his body's organs, which convey to him what they need. This is what the maturing person will then give to his body. He does not overindulge; he does not fill his body.

Gabriele:

Many people think that to grow closer to God the body has to be lighter. That is why fasting is recommended in many diets, to perhaps be able to receive divine impulses. This is an error and is misleading.

It is not by fasting that we find our way to God, but through self-recognition, to which each day leads us because each day lets us become aware of parts of our own sinful aspects, of our own sinful programs, our inputs in the soul.

The one who daily clears up that part of his sinful aspects that he may presently recognize will cleanse his soul and his body and will nourish his body as well as his soul. Step by step, he will strive to actualize and fulfill the Ten Commandments and the Sermon on the Mount, and his food will be nature-oriented. He will give his body what it signals and ultimately needs.

A person will find his way to God neither through fasting nor through mortification, but with the right spiritual attitude.

It is not about the physical well-being, but the spiritual attitude, your doing or not doing.

Therefore, examine whether what you want to do corresponds to your innermost being and serves your spiritual growth. Thus, be honest with yourselves. Do nothing that is contrary to the eternal truth, to the eternal Being because nothing is hidden from God. What you have concealed will be evident one day, and you, yourselves, will see whether your thinking and acting was upright and honest.

As long as your eyes are directed toward worldly things, you have not entered the Kingdom of God, and you rely on an external kingdom that is not real.

Should you ask for the recovery of your body, then outer fasting can be salutary only if you simultaneously discard your human thoughts, what you have recognized as human, thus becoming free for the irradiation of the light.

Gabriele:

In His work of revelation "The Great Cosmic Teachings of Jesus of Nazareth," Christ revealed to us: *»As long as your eyes are directed toward worldly things, you have not entered the Kingdom of God, and you rely on an external kingdom that is not real.«*

For us, this means that as long as we cling to worldly things and all our thoughts and energies are caught up in them, we are oriented to the external treasure because all our thoughts and energies, our heart, is there. We build on the external kingdom because our heart clings to these external treasures.

But the inner kingdom is the inner treasure. It is God's word, God's help, the fulfillment of the Ten Commandments and of the Sermon on the Mount. The heart of the person who seeks first the Kingdom of God opens the inner treasure. This person will lack nothing. But the heart of the one who craves external treasures also clings to external wealth. He shuts the kingdom of the inner being to himself.

The external passes away. Therefore, it is not real. The inner remains because it is God's creation.

Our divine heritage is the essence of all of God's creation. Our divine body, which we call soul in its burdened state, thus consists of countless powers, the components of the Being. God's eternal work of creation contains spiritual minerals, plants and animals. Our spirit body is made up of all these consciousness powers.

Therefore, in each one of us is the essence of infinity. That is our divine heritage. Since each person bears within the essence of the eternal Being, and the human being himself is a product of nature—again from the power of creation—each person is the temple of God. Because the same divine heritage is in each person, all human beings are linked with one another as children and thus, as sons and daughters of God. Therefore, each one can say to everyone: "The eternal that you bear in yourself, I also bear in me. The pure that I bear in myself, you also bear in you." That is the spiritual heritage, the essence of infinity.

The divine in your neighbor and every power in the mineral, in the stone, the plant and the animal is a component of your inner temple, in which the All-Holy One dwells.

If a component of your temple is missing, you are in disunity either with people or with parts of nature. Then your temple is also imperfect. This means that you are not in the law of God and are not the law of God, either. Then you cannot enter the holy of holies in you to take up dwelling there.

Then you will not sit at the table of the Lord, either, but at the table of the people who—as you—thoughtlessly partake of the life, the gifts from God. Then you are homeless and an errant sheep that lets itself be led astray, since it is blind and is often kept blind because it follows blind ones who lead it into a temple that was built by human hands.

But if you are willing to establish, cleanse and expand your inner temple through a life in God, then you, too, will straighten up and see clearly.

In the same measure that you perfect your inner temple, you will keep the order of the temple and find entry to the inner temple.

If your temple is perfect, then you, too, are one with all people and all beings, with all Being. Then you are also one with the All and its laws and you also dwell in the holy of holies because you are in the All and it is in you, and you are both from eternity to eternity.

The Kingdom of God is the inner kingdom. You can perceive it only with your inner eyes and you can hear what the inner laws say to you only with your inner ears.

You can hear the true Being, your heritage, only in your inner being. It speaks to you and speaks with you because I Am the »I Am« and the I Am is you. For this reason, you are I, and I Am you, and where you are, Am I, and where I Am is where you are because everyone and everything is in you – you and I as unity in all things.

You and I, the melding of both in the I Am, can be experienced only in the innermost part of your temple, in the holy of holies, in which everything is—the you in I and the I in you. There is nothing where you and I are not as a unity because God is the You and the I, the consciousness of unity. God is the You; you are the divine being. Once you have grasped this, then you will not seek your neighbor—you will not call for him. He is there—in you! Wherever you are, he is with you because he is in you—the you and the I melded in the You, in the law, God, the I Am in you.

Gabriele:

We can meld with the eternal Being, our divine heritage, with God, the I Am, only once we have cleansed our temple. Then our purified five senses are in the holy of holies and experience there what human eyes do not see and human ears do not hear, the I Am. Then the you is the soul in God, and the I Am permeates the you, the soul in God, and permeates the light-filled shell, the purified human being.

If the I Am and the you have melded, then soul and person have found their way to unity in God and are also in harmony with all people, with all beings and the nature kingdoms. That is the melding with the divine, and thus, the fulfillment of the divine heritage, of the divine law. That is the life in the I Am.

The person who is thus united with God and with all Being has also found his neighbor in himself. He does not call him to have him with himself. The divine in the person is linked with the divine in his neighbor and chooses the time of coming together externally.

Gabriele:

Christ speaks: »*The You of God is the duality.*« He says: »*In God, two become one.*« Duality means: A female and a male principle unite in the One and are one in the fulfillment of the eternal laws, which, as a whole, are, in turn, God.

Thus, there are two beings, female and male, which have united in the equivalence of mentality and form the duality—two, which are one in God. This is the melding of the divine male principle and the divine female principle. In terms of polarity, this means: The divine giving, the positive, and the divine receiving, the negative, unite, with positive and negative being seen as the equivalence of energy, joining in the All-family of God, and complementing each other in all things.

The beings in God are images of the Father—who gave Himself form out of His omnipresent, eternal law-stream of love, the Father-form—the visibly shining, eternal, pure figure, the personification of God, that is, the entity, which embodies the all-encompassing eternal power, the flow-

ing omnipresent law of love. The divine beings are em-
bodiments from the eternal law, which, in turn, live in the
eternal law, since they are divine, compressed eternal law
in the divine, eternally flowing law of love.

We human beings are called upon to raise our spiritual
body, which we call soul, and to again be the pure beings,
that is, images of the personified eternal divine stream, of
the Father, which, in turn, are one with the Father in the
stream of the eternal Being, of love. The Father personi-
fies the omnipresent power of the Father-Mother stream,
which can also be called the Father-Mother law of love.

You are My thought, the All-Father thought, the law. The Mine is yours because the Eternal, who I Am, and you are one.

You, the pure one, speak the Self because you are the self. Therefore, you speak your self and you also address the Self in everyone and in all things, you in your neighbor and in all things, occurrences and events.

The word of the pure one is the Self that is in all things. The law speaks itself and brings forth itself again because everything is in all things—it is always the whole.

You address the whole in everything and in every facet of the truth, again, the whole. The corresponding consciousness-radiation, the facet, answers you in you, and you hear again the whole in you.

Gabriele:

God knows no half measures. God is always the whole. His word contains His whole law. The pure beings, the images of God, are the whole and speak the whole in every word.

The sound of the word is the symphony of the heavens. From the symphony, the being addressed senses what it then accomplishes according to the law of the whole. Every state of evolution, for example, a form from the kingdom of the minerals, plants and animals, indeed takes in the holistic radiation, since the holistic radiation, the whole, God, is contained in the life form. It takes from the whole what corresponds to its state of consciousness, and in action and behavior, again radiates the answer of evolution, as it were.

Each one speaks the whole and moves in the whole and yet, gives answer according to its state of consciousness.

You do not need to ask about the state of consciousness. Always address the whole because in the smallest is the large and in the large is the smallest.

Wherever the thought of the law radiates, there it shines again on the law.

What the law-thought contains is already fulfilled in you because the eternal law is the same as fulfillment.

Gabriele:

The Eternal and the divine beings utter nothing that is not in them. They do not speak what should be—they speak what is because they are the fulfillment of the eternal law.

The law-thought cannot be destroyed or diverted. It has already fulfilled itself in you while being emitted.

In the external world, the law-thought fulfills itself according to the law of free will, when it gains entry into the heart of a person.

But the law-thought does not know any hindrances. It penetrates all density and every hindrance and waits until it is received. It also follows the path of fulfillment externally because it is a part of the eternal law that is in the innermost being of the person.

The law-thought does not know time. It is the law, and timeless. The path of the law-thought to a person in the external world can mean a delay for the person because the law-thought knows the moment to act, and stays in the person's field of aura as fulfilled, until it gains entry.

In the lawful sensation and in the lawful thought there is no setback, no dissolution of sensation or thought because they are the eternal law, the All-power.

, *Christ, as Jesus of Nazareth, taught the eternal holy laws to some apostles and disciples who could understand them. Despite their spiritual knowledge, I had to catch them again and again before they fell into humanness, into the »err-reality.« Again and again, I had to make clear to them the holy thought—the eternal Self— which they let out of their innermost being time and again because the illusion, the »err-reality,« the human thought, seemed closer to them.*

Gabriele:

We human beings have the habit of identifying ourselves again and again with our human aspects, the sinful thoughts because as long as we sin, we overlay the eternal Being. This superimposition, the sins, are then closer to us in radiation intensity because they dominate us and do not leave us freedom of thought. They force us to think the way we have created and attracted these energies through our sinning.

So that we become free of the constraints of our own sins, we should call upon Christ again and again, to recognize, with Christ's help, the unreality of the sins, which is limitation and finiteness, to clear it up and no longer commit it. Then we free ourselves from our inputs. We free ourselves from the superimposition of sins, so that the light of the Eternal Himself sets us aglow more and more, and we become the thought of the eternal Self, of the eternal Being. Then God is closer to us because the sins are transformed into His light.

I spoke to them in the following sense:
The holy word that is the power of God and that was born in you can be enveloped by you with the human ego—which builds up in the conscious mind and the subconscious—only if you do not keep it in you as the true Self. If, despite knowing better, you let it out of your innermost being through doubt, fears or impatience.
The core of human thoughts and words is the word of God. It remains divine. But what envelops it directs itself against you and will become a burden for you.

Gabriele:

Many a person is in the habit of blaming others for his wrong behavior. With this, he states the following:

He claims that the human ego, that is, the sinfulness of the other one, envelops the divine in him, the accuser. The negative potential of his neighbor then builds up in the alleged victim, in his conscious mind and subconscious. Consequently, so the one concerned thinks, he cannot keep the true Self in his heart because through doubt, fears and impatience, instilled in him by the other one, he turned away from the innermost being.

The one who assumes that it is so, would have to think about himself personally, by asking where his personal weakness lies so that another is able to inculcate doubt, fears and impatience in him. Not the other one is alone to blame, but rather, he is, himself, also to blame, indeed, he—the alleged victim—even bears the main guilt because the weakness, which he doesn't recognize, and thus, doesn't want to recognize, and which therefore, doesn't transform into spiritual strength, forms a magnet for the suggestion.

The word of God says: »*The core of human thoughts and words is the word of God … But what envelops it directs itself against you and will become a burden for you.*«
This means that our sins and the projections from our neighbors, which we allow into ourselves, contribute to the envelopment of the divine core in us. In this way, we envelop the core of the good, God, more and more, and live our burdens, which are directed against us.

Every law-sensation and every law-thought goes out from the eternal power, God, and from the communication with God. Even if they are enveloped by the human ego, the core, the life, however, remains in God.

The law, God, is: sending and receiving. The eternal law sends itself and receives itself. For this reason, no energy is lost. Thus, the eternal law speaks itself, and the answer is, again, the law, the Self because everything is His law and all pure forms of life are the law and they all have their existence in the flowing law.

 taught My apostles and disciples the law: God is the All-law.

The All-law, God, consists of countless facets of consciousness, which are degrees of consciousness. They are the spiritual life forms—minerals, plants, animals and nature beings—which are led by the Creator-God, the Spirit of evolution, to the next higher degrees of consciousness. The various spiritual capabilities and mentalities, too, are contained in the life forms as predispositions from the Creator-God. This is also true of their spiritual names.

The Eternal leads all forms of Being to perfection. For this reason, everything is contained in all things.

Every degree of consciousness contains the entire All-law. The various degrees of consciousness communicate, in turn, with the same or like degrees of consciousness. Despite all this, the following holds true for the forms of life: In everything is contained, in turn, all things, but not every aspect is already all-encompassingly manifest.

However, everything is manifest in each one of you because your spiritual body has opened forms of Being as the law. Therefore, learn to perceive, to behold in you everything in all things, and to address everything in every aspect of consciousness.

Gabriele:

For us human beings, this means that we should constantly live in the present and not develop any ideas about what could be in the future and how we want to see things and act in the future. We cannot know what will happen in the next minute, or even in the next second. Therefore, it is also unrealistic to plan the future for our human existence. What is important is to plan our activity, and to then place the plan in the hands of God. We should not, however, overdo the planning of our life on Earth and project it into the future. The moment is significant, and thus, living in the present.

If we have learned to live in the present, we will move in our innermost being everything that we encounter, that we see, hear, smell, taste and touch, aware that God shows Himself through the envelopment. God speaks through the word of our neighbor. God is the fragrance of the All: I smell. God is the taste of the fruit and drink: I taste. I touch external things and, at the same time, the divine.—That is present life, which has no room to think about the external form, about disagreeable words, smells and nuances of taste, nor about what it touches, either. The person is indeed aware of what he sees, hears, smells, tastes and touches. He acts accordingly, but he does not judge and condemn. That is living in the present and for us human beings, that is divine life.

I address each one of you: Why do you want to look into the distance, when the Eternal, what you believe to be far away, is in you?

Why do you want to speak with your brother, when he is in you as power and light?

If you have something important to tell him, address him in you. By doing this, you establish a conscious communication with your neighbor and, if it is important for him, he will receive it—if he also bears you in himself as power and light. If your brother is linked with you, then he will answer in you, or you will meet him and make a date for a conversation with him.

But it all first happens in you. That is the eternal law, not the causal law.

I repeat: The prerequisite for a divine communication is that you have opened the divine essence of your brother or your sister in you—and, vice versa, that your eternal spiritual part of life is effective in him or her.

I taught My apostles and disciples: If you want to chase after what is in the distance, you will be pursued and hunted because you live externally, in and with the world, which is mere illusion, that is, the pale reflection of reality. Some pleasant worldly things may come to you briefly—or you will immediately have to struggle with the disagreeable, with what you have sown. It is possible that you will mix new seed, new causes, with the old seed, and through this, attract events and forces that do not correspond to the law of God, the holy order of the temple.

Then you will speak only your human self and will display yourselves in your humanness. You will not speak the eternal word, which is the eternal law, the impersonal life, God because you are personal.

Everything that puts you under pressure and coercion, that does not leave you any way out, is personal. The personal always wants confirmation—whether it presents itself nearby or from a distance. It cannot take the lawful course because what is personal is oriented exclusively to the person and not to the impersonal, cosmic All-Being.

The person, the human ego, is the human self, which sees itself and thus relates only to the earthly life and to the person, to what is transitory and lasts only in terms of years. The transitory human self urges, in order to use the years in which it can confirm itself. Since it is not the unity and the infinity, it urges into the distance, it urges into the proximity. It urges to the right and to the left, to above and below, thus constricting itself more and more because it relates everything to itself, the person.

Every restriction leads to delimitation, to narrowness and to limitation and then to explosion. Everyone who is restricted lashes out. What breaks out is the evil product: strife, war and plundering.

All these aspects are explosions of the human ego, of the human self, which claims more and more for itself. For this, entire armies often go to war, people who are subject to the same or like restrictions and let themselves be ordered about by those like themselves. They then elect their leaders who rule entire nations.

The base ego is insatiable. It wants to possess and to have, until the ego-person passes away. Things then continue in a similar way in the soul realms or in new incarnations. For this reason, beware that you do not decline into spiritual death.

Again and again, I hear you speak about death.

What does death mean to you? To many, it is the end. But death is nothing more than the transition into another form of existence, in which you live in the same way as you lived while a human being.

Death will not take anything from you—nor will it give you anything. The soul that leaves the body is the same one that was in the person and which the person reflected. For this reason, you will not attain resurrection after the death of your body.

Only the one who journeys toward the light, who journeys inward, goes into the light. Just as the soul of a child leaves the inner kingdom to enter the school of life Earth, so should the older person have grown from the school of life Earth into the inner being through actualization and nearness to God.

The one who opens the inner kingdom, the Kingdom of God, will become the temple of salvation and attain resurrection already in his own temple, in the temple of flesh and bone. Then he does not need to taste death. But the one who is spiritually dead is also dead as a soul. The spiritually dead will not resurrect after their physical death. They remain spiritually dead because just as the tree falls, so will it remain lying.

Gabriele:

The spiritually dead are those people who cultivate their humanness, that is, their sinfulness, who do not concern themselves with their spiritual life by asking whether with this thought-radiation, that is, value-radiation, which also imprints the soul, they can enter heaven. The spiritually dead person is the spiritually unawakened person, whose soul, after the death of his body, is the same as what the person was: unawakened and oriented solely to sin.

The spiritually awakening person strives daily to ask after the commandments of God in all that he thinks, says and does, and, during the course of his life, to think, talk and act as God wants.

If he lives accordingly, he will become a spiritually awakened person, whose soul has already resurrected in the human being because it became pure and lives in God. Such a soul is a light-filled, God-conscious soul, which has resurrected in Christ and enters the Father's house through Christ.

For this reason, realize that in the flesh, you should awaken to the filiation to God, and in the flesh, you should attain resurrection because the soul in the person is in the school of life Earth to again become what it is in the Father: divine.

Know that the spiritually dead look only to the letter and do not grasp the meaning. Therefore, verify to whom you speak and what you say because you shall not cast pearls into the grave, but bring them to those who want to awaken.

Gabriele:

Christ revealed that in the flesh we should awaken to the filiation to God and attain resurrection in the flesh because we human beings are in the school of life Earth, to again become what we are in the Father.

Since the whole of infinity is in us as power and light—that is to say, our spiritual body is the essence of infinity—everything is in all things because God is omnipresent.

Heaven consists of seven basic powers, each one of which is contained in the others as power and light. Consequently, our soul consists of seven times seven light-powers of love. The seven times seven powers of God are contained in each soul as essence.

To attain the filiation, we have to have largely opened the first four basic powers of God. They are: Order, Will, Wisdom and Earnestness. If we have opened in ourselves the four basic powers, which in the Spirit are called natures, that is, creation energies, then we grow into the three filiation attributes of God: Kindness, Love and Meekness.

If the soul in the human being immerses in the three attributes of filiation because it has largely fulfilled the four natures of God, the four basic powers, then it has resurrected through the power of the Christ of God and follows the direct path to the heart of the eternal Father. The purified and largely unfolded soul in the human being has experienced, and experiences, Christ. It has found Him, the Redeemer. This soul in the human being has resurrected through the redeeming power and stands in the light of the filiation to God. It is the awakened soul that beholds heaven. The person is peaceful and aware of God. He is for his fellow people and is in the fulfillment of the Ten Commandments and the Sermon on the Mount.

The one who as a human being did not find Me will not find Me after the death of his body, either. The one who lived only in humanness will also live only in a world-oriented way as a soul and again seek out the flesh that to him is the life.

Therefore, recognize: Life is God, and the one who has not found God in himself, has not found Me, the Christ of God, either. After the death of his body, he will go through the gate of death and will remain spiritually dead—until he recognizes himself and finds himself in Me.

The one who recognizes Me knows the All. He is in the All and the All is in him. The one who does not recognize Me is oriented to the Earth and collects external treasures and wealth, since he is not aware of his inner being because he is not oriented to the great whole. Since he does not know Me, he knows neither himself nor the All, the I Am.

Gabriele:

The All, understood as a whole, is infinity and the heritage of all pure beings. The one who daily opens his divine heritage, by recognizing, clearing up and no longer committing his sins and keeping the commandments of God step by step, gathers treasures of the Kingdom of God because he opens the inner kingdom, the Kingdom of God, which is within, in him. His consciousness is oriented to the All and not only to the world. He gathers the treasures of the heavens and is content with what God has given him on Earth. However, these gifts from God do not mean a life in poverty, but a life of moderation: The person has what he needs and beyond that. He does not gather external treasures and wealth because he has unearthed the inner treasure, his divine heritage, which is the All and the great I Am.

The one who has not found his divine heritage knows neither his true being nor his neighbor, who is a stranger to him. As a soul, he will be a stranger in the All because he has not opened the All, his divine heritage, and thus, neither the mighty, omnipresent I Am.

Gabriele:

In His revelation, the Christ of God describes "by fleeing from the world" as the behavior of a hermit, who flees from the world, and goes into seclusion, to grow closer to God.

God, the Eternal, put us into this world at that place where we can recognize what we are supposed to recognize as our sins and clear up in this life. Whatsoever we encounter that upsets us is our mirror and our reflection. How we react because of situations because of occurrences with people, and how we talk and act, is what we are.

In the world, we frequently encounter ourselves, namely, every time we get upset about what the world reflects to us at every moment. A hermit cannot recognize and fathom what is daily reflected to him because he has renounced the mirror, the world. In that place where we have been placed, we human beings should renounce the sin that we recognize during the day. What upsets us day after day is our own mirror image, our reflection. We should get rid of this, to become divine again, as Jesus essentially required of us, when He said: *»Be perfect, therefore, as your heavenly Father is perfect.«*

The world of the incarnated beings, the human beings, is likewise the world of the discarnate beings, the souls. Both worlds penetrate each other. They are places of residence for people and souls, in which people and souls mature by becoming and growing, thus growing closer to the eternal kingdom, to immerse in the stream, God, who is eternal.

*The spiritually awakened ones mature into eternity.
The spiritually dead ones are content with the reflection.*

*This world is the toxic substance for soul and body. The
one who assimilates it falls ill.*

*Every illness is the effect of one or several causes. It
can also be a collective illness, based on a collective guilt,
when several people have sinned against their fellow human beings out of the same motive. If the latter do not
forgive them, then their illness will last, often over incarnations or in the soul realms.*

*The illness is the picture of your soul. It is the mirror in
which you can recognize your world of feelings, sensations
and thoughts.*

*Happy the souls that have taken on flesh to become
divine in the school of Earth.*

*Woe to the souls that have taken on flesh to indulge
anew in the lusts of the body.*

*The soul in the human being is in the school of life
Earth to become divine again.*

*What changes when the soul takes off its mortal shell?
What changes when a flower withers?
What changes when the seasons pass?
Do they go and never come again?
Or is not the Being in the passing, and already again
the becoming, which attires itself in an even more beauti-
ful and lavish garment?*

Humankind calls autumn, the yet-again-becoming in nature, which fashions itself anew and more lavishly: the transitory.

But there is no transience—only change and transformation.

Can there be time in change and transformation?
Time is transitory. What passes on?
What is space if the consciousness is boundless?
What is space if the human being is a sending and receiving station?
What is space if the nature kingdoms are cosmic?
Therefore, what are time and space?

In God there is no time. In Him, nothing is lost. In God, the »cannot understand« does not exist. This belongs to time.

God is the present: Everything is in the One, and the One is in everything. He gives Himself in the one radiation, which He, God, is. Therefore, God can be only »Oneness.«

Multiplicity is time and is the one who determines it and determines those people who strive for quantity and mass and who, in their existence, have lost the measure of all things, God.

When the term time passes away, limitation and finiteness fall. Then the ruling hand of God is visible. The Being then enters the life of fulfilled people—and they live. Death is then broken because time has fallen.

Gabriele, the teaching prophetess
and emissary of God, explained about this:

We have created our "time" through countless aspects of all-too-humanness, that is, sinfulness. Because we do not clear up our sinfulness in the present, it goes back into the past and becomes a burden. In the rhythm of the cosmic clock, the uncleared aspects have their effects as a consequence—it is our future. Thus, through the multiplicity of our inputs, emerged the yesterday, today, tomorrow, as well as morning, afternoon and evening. We even created for ourselves the hours, minutes and seconds, which, in turn, are our measure, our division of time.

In our life's rhythm of past, present and future lies our multiplicity, the countless inputs that shape and control us, which are the volume of our human life. As long as we let ourselves be controlled, that is, driven, by our sinful inputs, others often control us because we have then lost the measure of all things, God, our center. This is because we do not orient ourselves to the Ten Commandments and the Sermon on the Mount with our feeling, thinking, speaking and acting, but take the days as they come, without knowing who we are. We frequently no longer realize that we are not ourselves anymore.

When death enters our earthly existence, that is, when we pass on, then the term "time" falls away, that is, the past, present and future—yesterday, today and tomorrow. The hours, minutes and seconds fall away. The limitations and the finiteness through the term »time« fall. Then we experience our inputs, the multiplicity—or we experience God's ruling hand, if our earthly existence was filled with the fulfillment of the Ten Commandments and of the Sermon on the Mount.

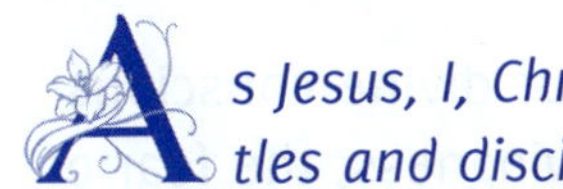

As Jesus, I, Christ, spoke further words to My apostles and disciples in the following sense:

Many people cling to their life on Earth with all the fibers of their earthly existence. They are not aware that already at birth they have put on the garment of death and that the veil of death hangs over them.

You, however, should make yourselves aware that each one of you will die and each one in a different way. For this reason, you should establish a relationship with your dying, so that you are not surprised by your so-called death.

The veil of death hangs over every person. The person can raise it only if he has spiritually awakened—or it will be taken from him only when he has died.

Gabriele, the teaching prophetess
and emissary of God, explained about this:

To establish a relationship with our dying means that in every situation we should realize that we are on Earth to clear up our sinfulness and to no longer commit it.

If we clear up our sins, then the sinful ego dies and the soul rises in the light of the Godhead. Then we will establish a relationship with dying and with so-called death because we no longer fear it. If we clear up the sinful aspects that the day points out to us each day, and if we

no longer commit these sins, then our divine consciousness expands, and the veil of unknowingness, the fear of
death, falls away. It is taken away, as it were because we
live in the face of divine life.

However, if the veil is taken away from our soul only
after our death, then often, we do not know whether we
have died or are still in the temporal as a human being.
As a soul, we do not know our surroundings because we
have sinned each day more, instead of recognizing and
clearing up our sins.

The fear of death is the darkness of the soul in the
beyond, which does not know where it is.

*Thus, take a good look at the fact that every person
dies. What comes after so-called death?*

*I ask each one the question: How do you want to die?
The how gives you the answer with the question: How
have I lived?—Or with the question: How do I want to live?*

*The life on Earth of every person shows him his dying
and raises the veil of death—all according to how the person lived. The earthly life of each person is the measure
for what is concealed from him behind the veil of death.*

*The person determines himself whether he finds himself
outside the wheel of reincarnation or whether he adheres
to the wheel of reincarnation.*

My apostles and disciples asked Me, »How shall we prepare ourselves?« I said to them:

Recognize that each of you is the today and the tomorrow. Each one is a part of every moment, of every second, of every minute and of every hour. Each of you is a part of a day, a part of a week, of a month and of a year.

Because of this, every person has a part in creating what he calls time. Once the aspects for this world—which are effective in the moment, in the second, in the minute, in the hour, in the day, in the month and in the year—have run out, then he no longer is a human being, but a soul.

However, the soul retains the rhythm of the human ego, until it has found the true Being, which is eternal. You can find it only on the path of actualization.

My apostles and disciples said: »Teach us more! How can we fathom the depths of our human ego to become free more quickly, so that we draw nearer to God, the Eternal?«

I essentially explained to them the following: The five senses of a person can be compared to antennae. The one who uses these antennae too little, in order to recognize and sense who he is and to feel who he still could be, does not find his way into his inner being and cannot find himself, either.

Recognize that a person creates his programs by way of the five senses. They are in the conscious mind and the subconscious and in the soul, as well. These programs consist of feelings, sensations, thoughts, words and ac-

tions. Therefore, the person can, according to his degree of honesty, deduce from his thoughts who he is. If he goes with his thoughts to the world of his sensations, then he gets to know who he still is.

If the person takes the finer antennae, which are like feelers, and immerses with them into his world of feelings, he will sense further human traits—or he experiences the wisdom of the soul, the divine aspects that he has already developed.

Gabriele:

The "finer antennae" symbolically stand for the inner hearing. With the finer "hearing," we feel into our world of feelings.

Everything, all of infinity, takes place in cycles and rhythms. Thus, also our feelings, sensations, thoughts, words and actions are cycles and rhythms, which we have determined ourselves, again, through our world of feeling, sensing, thinking, speaking and acting. The heavenly planes with their countless divine solar systems also revolve in cyclic-rhythmical orbits around the Primordial Central Sun. If we fulfill God's commandments more and more, then soul and body attain ever finer and higher rhythmic and harmonious sounds. These rhythmic and harmonious sounds form the fine antennae, feelers, as it were, also called the inner hearing, which can feel into the world of feelings as well as the world of thoughts, but also into the words and deeds of human beings. With these fine antennae, we get to know, for one thing, the deeper layers of our world of feelings, and for another, the deep motivations of our fellow people.

The fullness from God is the life. The one who lives in the fullness of God is and remains fulfilled. He does not need to worry about tomorrow—he is the All and is the fullness of the All-radiation that streams through him and from which he draws because he lives in it.

The fullness, God, knows no privation. It is and gives, and is the wealth, the All, in which the being of the All lives and is as essence. The one who wants to receive the fullness from God has to renounce the world. He may well live in the world and work in the world, but he is not with the world.

The one who disdains the fullness, since he fills himself with the gifts of the world, will live in want, even if he presently appears to be externally rich.

Gabriele, the teaching prophetess
and emissary of God, explained about this:

We attain the fullness from God if we fulfill the commandments of the Lord, step by step. Through this, we cleanse our soul and our body of the dross of sin. Then our soul becomes divine again and is in God's law, which is the fullness.

Such a person knows no fear because he knows about God's justice. Such a person is a peacemaker because he bears peace in himself. Such a person settles quarrels and disagreements and brings harmony into the dispute, so that both parties to the dispute recognize their faults, clear them up and thus find their way to harmony, in which the God-filled person lives, in the All-harmony. Such a person loves his neighbors, but not their sins. He loves the pure in his neighbor and is one with the pure. If it is possible for him, he will address the impurity, so that his neighbor move it in himself and clear it up, if he wants to.

The one who lives in the fullness is in communication with God, and God reveals Himself to the pure soul and reveals Himself in the purified consciousness of the person.

If you ask God for earthly gifts, then you are of little faith and do not recognize your filiation to God, the stream of the All, from which you went forth and in which you live.

Ask for spiritual gifts, for awakening in the Spirit of life, so that you open your heavenly heritage. When you ask for what is your own from the Spirit, indeed, what is given to you, then you will also attain the earthly goods, what you need, and beyond that because God lets no child live in want.

It is the human being who seeks and strives for external things. Through this, he becomes impoverished because he neglects his true heritage.

By worrying about tomorrow, by wondering whether you will remain ill or become ill, or when you will become healthy again, you hinder God, the almighty Spirit, from becoming active in you and through you, and you hinder Me, the Inner Physician and Healer, from bringing you relief and healing by way of your soul.

These human thoughts, desires and longings remove you more and more from God and lead you into a time that is poor in light, into a land that is already poor—just as poor as you have become. Then you will experience your present in the future.

Know that each one of you bears the heritage of the All in himself and is thus the possessor of infinity.

The one who acquires external possessions, who on Earth is the owner of land that he guards and calls his own will keep returning until he has recognized that his true possession is heaven. Let the Earth and a life on Earth become merely a bridge that you cross over. But do not acquire great possessions there—otherwise you will again create a place for your next incarnation.

Recognize Me in you—then you have beheld Me as your brother. Then you will behold heaven because in each one of us is the whole Being as power and light. In each one of us is infinity, the heritage, our spiritual possession. As power and light, we are one because I Am in you and you are in Me.

This is how it is in all of infinity: Everything is in all things. That is the inner wealth—that is our true Being. That is our possession; it is our own.

I say to you, if a person asks you for your shirt, then give him your coat, too. But woe to those who possess a shirt and a coat and deceivingly ask for a second shirt or coat for themselves. Woe to those who could help themselves and yet take. They will be called to account—when their own judgment of sowing and reaping comes over them.

For this reason, actualize the holy laws, so that you may behold—that is, perceive—and recognize the »for and against« in people.

Gabriele:

The words of the Lord say: *»But woe to those who possess a shirt and a coat and deceivingly ask for a second shirt or coat for themselves.«*

Someone who possesses a shirt and a coat should not deceive his fellow people by pretending that he possesses neither shirt nor coat. If you are given a shirt and a coat, then thank God for this and set out to find work, so that you can purchase the second shirt and the second coat yourself. For the one who possesses neither shirt nor coat should receive the shirt and the coat that you deceivingly asked for.

The Christ of God teaches us further: *»Woe to those who could help themselves and yet take.«*

The laziness of a person originates in the world of his thoughts.

If because of his laziness a person does not want to work, so as to help himself out of his hardship, he violates the law of neighborly love, for the one should be helped who cannot help himself, regardless of reason. Someone who deceives others or takes from others because he is lazy will, when the causes have ripened for him and come into effect, experience his own judgment according to the law of sowing and reaping.

od is the fullness. The one who clings to his de-sires, longings and passions is veiled. He wears the garments of his desires and passions—and thus, he does not know the Being, the life, which is the Spirit of God. He entrusts himself to the world and not to the Eternal, who dwells in him.

For this reason, learn to draw from the Spirit of life, by entrusting yourselves to God with all your worries and desires. He, the All-One, knows you and knows how to guide you.

The one who draws from the Spirit of life lives in Me, the Christ, and draws from the Spirit of love and gives from the Spirit of love. He will not be an eccentric, but a spiritually rich person. He will live on this Earth, but will not be with this world.

A person of the Spirit will fulfill his work and give his best. However, he is not only a citizen of the material world—rather, he is a citizen of the Kingdom of God be-cause he lives in God and draws from the source, God.

Take these My words into your life on Earth as salva-tion and life force. Then, as human beings, you will do the works of love and you will stand in the midst of the world and fulfill your obligations with God.

Give your best! You can do this only when you are united with the best, the Being. Never be satisfied with the mediocre or even the defective—give your best.

Gabriele, the teaching prophetess
and emissary of God, explained about this:

To give our best means to give our neighbor not only material help and material goods; it means to not only do our job well at the place of work, but rather to put the divine power into everything, into the material goods, into our work, into our conversations, into every mode of action. Then we keep the right measure in giving—in the material help for our neighbor, in our work, in conversations, in all that we do.

Endeavor at every moment to draw from the works of love and to imbue your work, your thinking and doing with them. Then you are the being in the stream of the Being, and you draw from the All, which is the law, God.

Remember My words: It is not the external that matters, but solely the inner being, that which the temple contains, the fullness, God. Therefore, cleanse your temple, so that you may gain entry to the holy of holies.

ever be indignant. Otherwise, you will be held back by the temporal, by things and events that belong to the transitory.

The one who lives in God lives in the fullness, in the eternal law, God. He will never ask about the how and why because he is the being that knows about all things.

The indignant one bears witness to himself, since he still seeks his hold in external things.

An indignant person is always one who is seeking and has no hold because he seeks security and a hold in the world. In the long run, matter offers the person neither security nor a hold because matter is merely illusion and not the Being.

For this reason, practice keeping the inner calm in every situation, so that you recognize things and events in the light of truth.

God knows about each one. He knows His child and helps him.

Gabriele, the teaching prophetess
and emissary of God, explained about this:

To keep the inner calm, that is, to be composed, means to take yourself back before talking and acting and to first ask yourself: "Why do I want to say that and why do I want to do that? Does my way of talking and acting correspond to the commandments of God, or do I merely want to express my human ego? What do I want from it for me?"

Thus, anyone who doesn't want to take himself back is indignant and unrestrained. Every unrestrained person is a danger to himself and to his surroundings.

The one who has learned to behold does not accuse his neighbor because he knows him. Only the spiritually blind one accuses his neighbor because he knows neither himself nor his neighbor.

Gabriele, the teaching prophetess
and emissary of God, explained about this:

Christ revealed: *»The one who has learned to behold does not accuse his neighbor because he knows him.«* This means that the one who opens his divine consciousness step by step, by clearing up his sinful aspects and no longer committing them, establishes communication with the All-Wise One, the Spirit of truth. The Spirit of truth then flows by way of the person's purified senses and supports the person to recognize, perceive and feel everything in the right way. The one who is in communication with the All-Wise One, God, will not disparage and reject his fellow people, either. He understands them because he knows them and thus, sees through them. God gives to such a person. Such a person sees into the deep wherefores of the divine and of the human existence and knows that God has no mysteries or secrets.

If you are accused, then set things right and point out in general terms what is wrong and insinuated, but never name the accuser. That would be personal. Remain impersonal because when you address him by name and he does not forgive you in time, then it is possible—depending on the cause—that you will have his name in another life on Earth. His name, which you then bear, calls up the causes that bind you to each other. Through the radiation, the soul or the person that you once accused by name can then be attracted. You and your neighbor will be led together by the law of sowing and reaping, to clear up what now, in another incarnation, becomes active.

Gabriele:

If the accuser maintains a low profile, then we should not disclose his name, either. However, if the accuser goes public, then he has disclosed his name, himself. Then his name can also be named by the accused, and the accused has not revealed the name of the accuser, but rather, the latter has identified himself by name.

Therefore, keep the golden rule:

Be silent. Speak only when it is essential and lawful.

For this reason, never be indignant. Take yourself back and remain impersonal in every situation.

Remember: Speak about yourself only if you can explain and clarify the facts or if you can serve and help your neighbor with what you recognized on yourself and mastered. Otherwise, never speak about yourself personally because everything that you say about yourself, at the same time, you are speaking to yourself again. It clings to you and intensifies your ego-complex.

I repeat: Remain impersonal in every situation, then you will find your way to inner stillness and linger in the temple of God.

n the long run, matter offers the human being neither security nor a hold because the temporal is merely illusion and not the Being, the reality, the eternal.

The light illuminates the things and events that show themselves on matter and lets you see them. But if you want to hold on to the ray of light, you will fall. For this reason, learn to move in the ray of light.

Gabriele, the teaching prophetess
and emissary of God, explained about this:

»... hold on to the ray of light ...« means to be content with only the divine words and not to fulfill the words of God, which are the law of life. To move in the ray of light, means to fulfill God's commandments, so that we become the law of love more and more, and thus, move in the radiant light of love.

Gabriele:

To lean on matter means to exclusively take from it, to relate to it and to rely on it. In this way, we bind ourselves to matter and lose the connection to God, the communication with the divine. That is then the separation from God and not the connection with the divine, through the divine.

A binding is like an object. It is shone upon. The connection is togetherness and is radiated through.

If you look at, and listen to, the external alone, then you are externalized and your senses of taste, smell and touch will be just like your senses of sight and hearing.

You determine your life in time or in eternity because you have the principle of the law of freedom and you can thus decide—for the divine or for the undivine. The divine radiates through you. The negative merely shines on you. You decide who you are and what you are, and ultimately, what you want.

You are the light in the light. For this reason, you do not need to hold on to anything or anyone.

You are freedom in the freedom of God.

You are wisdom in the wisdom of God.

The wisdom of God knows about all things. Therefore, you, the wise one, will neither bind yourself to people nor cling to humanness and call it your own.

You are also no longer the personal in the person. You are a human being and thus, a person—but no longer personal.

Gabriele:

The one who walks in the light of God attains freedom and the wisdom from God and the divine love that is his heritage. The impersonal is the ever-giving-of-self that expects nothing. Since it expects nothing, this person will receive in the right measure what is due him.

The personal is the sinfulness, the ego, the "mine and for me" that refers exclusively to one's own person. A person who thinks personally forgets the person at his side or thinks of him only when he wants to have him for himself, and wants to have from him what he does not possess himself, and thus, for which his personal interests urge.

To be wise means to live in a God-conscious way, to not be responsive to the sins, but to the divine in the person, which is impersonal. The impersonal is the equality, since God gives to each one equally. The personal is the inequality. It takes according to its ego, its sin.

If we want to become divine, then we have to strive for the goal of the divine love and wisdom, which is impersonal.

You, the wise one, are All-conscious because you live consciously in God and are aware of all things, of everything that is because you see through everything. The wise one is knowing and has insight into the things that surround him and that come toward him.

he one who rests in God and draws from the eternal law seldom speaks of himself. He is impersonal because he is the one who sees through things, and is the knowable one, and the word of the All, himself. The wise one speaks of himself only when he can thus be a guide on the path, but not to talk about himself.

If a person speaks his personal ego, then he speaks his base self that he speaks out of himself and that he, at the same time, again speaks to himself because the human ego is not divine and thus belongs to the one who is still not divine.

Gabriele, the teaching prophetess
and emissary of God, explained about this:

As long as we human beings do not accept the divine in our neighbor, we will merely talk about God and merely affirm Him as the Father of all children, but not, however, be the children. Jesus essentially said: If you do not become as the little children, you cannot enter the Kingdom of God.—The child gives itself to its father and mother, to walk at their hand. As long as the person does not entrust himself to the omniscient God and let himself be led by Him through the step-by-step fulfillment of the Ten Commandments, he is not the conscious child, the conscious son and the conscious daughter of God. Then the person tends to sin and bows before the sinner, who forces his instructions on him, which he then fulfills, to become like the one who controls him.

Someone who lets himself be controlled by the base ego, by sin, also sins himself, so as to climb higher on the ladder of worldly success, and be what calls itself lord and master in the temporal. Then he speaks only from his sin, the ego, and what he says goes back into him as energy because it does not come from God, but from sin, and this, in turn, attracts sinfulness.

We should frequently bring to mind that neither thoughts nor words or deeds are lost. The sin that goes out from the sinner goes back into the sinner. The light that goes out from a person who is becoming more light-filled goes into the heart of his neighbor. It brings hope and strength and goes back into the one who emitted it, so that this person likewise receives more strength and becomes more light-filled.

The light does not talk about itself, for it illuminates everything and knows about all things. It is the wisdom of God, and it is the wise one who has developed the light of God. A shadow cannot shine. It is dark and can bring only darkness. Since the shadow demands energy, it wants to confirm itself. Shadows attract only shadows, and both shadows confirm only themselves. Light attracts light, and both lights unite and enter the All-wisdom, God.

The undivine, the human ego, which goes out from you, goes into you again. Through this, you expand and intensify your ego-complex, the undivine, in you, thus creating ever greater fields in your soul, into which your ego-seed falls and where it sprouts.

For this reason, before you speak, think about what you want to say because each word is energy that has its echo. Thus, remain impersonal in every situation. Then you will find your way to inner stillness and will linger in the temple of God, the holy stillness, as the wise one.

Gabriele:

Everything that is personal refers to the person, to his thinking, speaking and acting. Since the person's thinking, speaking and acting are often ambiguous, the one side is pretense and the other side, value judgment. This means that the person talks kindly and thinks spitefully. He thinks in a friendly manner and has unfriendly sensations. He preserves the appearance of the selfless deed and expects appreciation and praise. If the expectation is not fulfilled, then follows the disparagement of his neighbor. That is the personal, what comes from the person. That is the egocentricity that constantly wants to take. From this grow envy, greed and hard-heartedness.

The impersonal is the divine, for God does not judge and condemn. He is love, peace and harmony, the sun of justice. God eternally radiates His law of love, of peace and of harmony. Whether the person, the human being, wants to accept it or not, whether the person is against or for God, whether he is a sinner or a purified person—God gives to each one equally.

An example for better understanding: The sun that shines on the Earth gives its rays to the Earth. It irradiates everything and does not ask whether this or that, the one or the other, needs less or more sunlight. That is impersonal radiation. From the Eternal One, eternally flow the impersonal rays of love, peace and harmony. If we turn away from God's love, to build up, to promote, to thus live with our self-love, then this is our personal, our own, our ego.

Is the sun responsible if we go into the shadows and thus receive less sunlight? Is God, the eternally radiating, impersonal love, responsible if we increase our self-love, that is, our ego, and favor it?

Therefore, whatever corresponds to our ego is personal because it is created by the person through a corresponding way of feeling, sensing, thinking, speaking and acting. God, the divine, is impersonal because God gives equally to all people and to all things, and is not oriented to the person.

The truly wise one is not a hermit. He lives in the world, but not with this world. Since he is a human being, he has obligated himself to give to Caesar what is due to Caesar, and he will give to God what is due to God. The one who keeps the laws of Earth that do not oppose the divine can also remind Caesar of his duty, so that the latter gives him what is his due as a human being.

s Jesus, I, Christ, taught the law of God and the law of sowing and reaping to My apostles and disciples in many repetitions. Despite all this, they spoke about unessential things and about themselves again and again to display themselves. I addressed them again and again and made them aware of the unessential, the personal:

If you speak of yourselves, then you express only what you still are, yourselves. Whom do you want to help with this?

Everything that has not been actualized is empty; it is hollow, as it were, and not filled with strength and wisdom. If you have actualized little, you are not filled with strength and wisdom, either, but are filled with the human ego that has its illusions.

The one who is empty and hollow, himself, falls, in turn, for empty, as it were, hollow, words. He looks solely to the word and to the one who is speaking because he does not hear himself and does not see himself, either. He may choose you as a leader and then is the one who is ensnared. Both are then the blind, who fall into the pit of their ego and are chained there to each other because the blind one relied on the blind.

For this reason, first empty your vessel of your human aspects, that is, first cleanse your cups and bowls, your soul particles and body cells, your temple of flesh and bone. Through this, you gain entry into the holy of holies, *from where you are able to give your neighbor what he needs and can offer him selfless service, which helps him on his spiritual ascent.*

In everything that comes to you, first look at the innermost being of the person. Therefore, fulfill the eternal law with regard to each one who comes to you, be it only through a selfless word, a selfless gesture or a selfless helping hand. These small, selfless services are more valuable for the salvation of his soul and for his spiritual life, than if you give him much externally, thus, perhaps helping him to gain in prestige, wealth and power. This earthly burden could lead him to a deeper fall.

From the law of God, the smallest, selflessly offered, is the greatest; it serves the soul and lends it strength. Through the selfless, smallest service, you, too, will remain in the stillness, in the secureness of God, in His fullness because you have given impersonally.

Gabriele, the teaching prophetess
and emissary of God, explained about this:

Christ, the great Spirit in the eternal Father, revealed to us: »*In everything that comes to you, first look at the innermost being of the person.*«

We human beings are in the habit of letting only the external aspects of our neighbor have an effect on us. We know that the inner being shapes the outer and that the outer gives an expression of the inner being, of the person's spiritual state of consciousness. Nevertheless, we should not look solely at the external, but bring to mind that the incorruptible, the divine in our fellowman, is a part of our true being. If we become aware of this, then the question also occurs to us: How do we want to meet our true self in our neighbor? Do we want to disparage it, by dismissing the person, or do we want to peacefully, lovingly, and thus, consciously, communicate with the incorruptible part of our neighbor, which is also a part of our true self? To communicate also means to maintain the communication, by taking into ourselves the inner values of our neighbor as a part of us.

If we realize this, and if we do this in each encounter with our fellow people, in conversations and at our place of work, we will learn to understand our neighbor. We will meet him in his true self, which is also a part of us, according to the commandment of kindness, love and mercy. According to how our neighbor approaches us, we give him a small gift of love, a heartfelt helping hand, a God-filled word, a selfless gesture, or we can also render him a larger selfless service. It depends entirely on the situation and on what our neighbor wants. If we don't let just our neighbor's outer aspects speak to us, that is, if we look deeper, we feel what our neighbor needs. What falls into his heart takes root in him and, at the same time, also enlarges our root ball.

God gives of Himself—but from what God pours out as a whole, each one can receive only as much as he can absorb in his spiritual consciousness. If he thinks that he has to take more, in order to gain capital for himself, then he will lose it—including that for which he has worked so arduously. The one who strives for outer prestige and does business with the divine, the truth, will lose himself and all that he has acquired for himself, personally. For this reason, examine what you think, and reflect before you speak and act.

Maintain the stillness, which is neither human sensation nor human thought.

Be still. Entrust yourself to God. Indeed, trust Him, and you will receive from the stream of life what you should say and carry out in the present.

In everything that God breathes into you is the measure and the quantity. Thus, you receive only as much as you should presently give and speak.

Be still and know that you will be guided. The You of your soul knows about all things. It knows everything—it is in everything.

As Jesus of Nazareth, I reminded My apostles and disciples again and again that all this is given only to the ones who sacrifice their ego, who are no longer the personal in the person, but the Being, the true self.

The one who lives in God lives in the fullness and draws from the fullness because he lives in the source that is God, and he, the being, is divine.

As Jesus, I spoke to My apostles and disciples in the following sense:

Your feelings, thoughts and words are the tools of your body. They are your advance workers. Through the deed you are merely the handyman, doing the finishing work that follows your feelings, thoughts and words. Your feelings, thoughts and words go in advance of your doing and of your deeds.

Without your advance workers, your feelings, thoughts and words, you can accomplish nothing. Your feelings, thoughts and words thus prepare for you what you then carry out—either in a personal way, with your intellect, if your advance workers were of a personal nature, or with your heart, if your advance workers were impersonal, that is, divine.

How you fare today, in this incarnation, you acquired for yourself in your previous lives, through your advance workers, your feelings, thoughts and words, and then through your finishing work, your deeds. Your work, your idleness, your worries, your problems, your blows of fate and difficulties, your suffering and your joys, your health and your illness were all created by you in previous lives. Nothing can come to you that you did not already input beforehand.

Therefore, what you input in previous existences is what you have predetermined for this and possibly future incarnations. In your future lives on Earth, you will then feel, think, speak and do the same and like things. No one else can do your speaking. Each one speaks himself, what he has predetermined in previous lives or in this incarnation, that is, what he has assimilated.

Every human feeling and every human thought, every human word and every human action is, as it were, an assimilation: The person assimilates his humanness into his soul. With this, he shapes his present and his possibly future earthly body.

What you were yesterday, that is, in past lives on Earth, is what you are again today—unless soul and person have cleared it up in good time with the power of the eternal law.

It is possible that soul and person may be in this cycle for thousands of years. They come over and over again and are always the same. Today, they determine their tomorrow. They come again and again with different faces and different bodies, with different first and last names, and in reality, they are the same because they again feel, think, speak and do as yesterday. Their face, their body, *their first and last names correspond to those of yester-day, the radiation of their previous lives.*

What identifies the person today, his thinking, speaking and acting of today, is what he should recognize, clear up and fulfill today. The one who does not fulfill it today, that is, the one who does not use the energy of the day, which points out his thoughts and actions to him, will not successfully complete the school on Earth, either. Today, such a person predetermines yet again what he will be tomorrow.

Each morning, every person is at the mercy of himself. What this day brings to him and what he does with it, determines what his day and his life on Earth will be tomorrow. For the day of every single person is his life, it is what he has input into the stars, himself.

On himself today, every person can deduce who or what he will be tomorrow. Just as he senses, thinks, speaks and acts tomorrow—that is, in a future incarnation—that is how he felt, thought, spoke and acted today, in this incarnation. His activity of today can be his activity of tomorrow.

What the person accomplishes with his baseness, his works, is not the works of eternity. His works pass away, and with them, his base self.

Gabriele, the teaching prophetess
and emissary of God, explained about this:

»Each morning, every person is at the mercy of himself.« When a person awakens in the morning, his soul has undertaken a small reincarnation. The energy, God, has returned to the human shell through the reincarnation of the soul, in order to give the person his day, the day as the person predetermined it for himself in this earthly existence or in previous lives. Thus, in the morning, each person already puts himself at the mercy of what the day brings to him. He cannot change the day, unless he changes himself, by recognizing his humanness, his sinfulness, repenting of it, clearing it up and no longer committing it. In this way, his future will be more light-filled and the path of the soul to God free.

The one who reinforces his own inputs, what the day reflects to him as sinfulness, by again doing the same or like things, can deduce his tomorrow from today. What he senses, thinks, says and does today as sinfulness will be reflected in tomorrow, that is, in the future.

The wheel of reincarnation developed through the cycle of birth and death. Repeatedly, the human being inputs into his soul what goes out from it, with which he once programmed it. The corresponding stars absorbed the respective programs, through which a mighty causal communication network emerged. This causal communication network is the law of cause and effect, which, in turn, forms the wheel of reincarnation.

Gabriele, the teaching prophetess
and emissary of God, explained about this:

Christ revealed to us: *»The wheel of reincarnation developed through the cycle of birth and death.«* Our soul does not experience just one embodiment, but often very many deaths and births. As the tree falls, so does it stay lying. The same species emerges from the still-existing roots. It is similar with our life. The life does not stop with death. Death is merely the disembodiment of the soul. If the person did not make use of his earthly existence, that is, if he burdened his soul with sin, with what is opposite to the divine, then, with his thoughts and desires, he also built up places of destination on Earth, where he will be again in his next incarnations, or births, if, as a soul in the spheres of purification, he does not clear up and pay off what marks his spirit body: the sins.

The wheel of reincarnation, the law of sowing and reaping, consists of countless solar systems of a coarse-material and a fine-material nature. After the death of the body, the soul is magnetically attracted by that plane and that planet that has stored the soul's programs that are active and waiting to be cleared up. The wheel of reincarnation—with its purification planes, which are of a fine-material nature, and the coarse-material matter—is a large memory bank that has registered every uncleared cause of each and every soul and human being, and radiates these back to the soul and person.

The soul, which has cleared up little or none of its soul-guilt in the beyond, again brings into its subsequent life on Earth what still adheres to it. As a human being, it will then be what it was as a soul and as a person in its previous lives. Every person can deduce, himself, from his way of thinking, speaking and behaving, what he once was and possibly still is today, and will be tomorrow.

The slipping in and out of the flesh will continue until the person has successfully gone through the school of life called Earth and until his soul is able to go on, with spiritual-divine gifts and values, to the higher worlds that exist outside of the wheel of reincarnation.

Then the cycle of birth and death comes to an end. The spirit being, the purified soul, returns to its origin, to God, its Father, into the eternal law because it has again become the eternal law, the true Self, which it then speaks again because it is the law.

As Jesus of Nazareth, I gave this and other principles of the law to My apostles and disciples to take with them on their path of life over the Earth. And as Christ, I give them to all people, so that they may walk the path to the inner life, on which I, Christ, go with them.

*everything is consciousness. Thus, you, too, are con-
sciousness. You, the consciousness, are composed of
your aspects of consciousness, of your feelings, thoughts,
words and actions. This is what you are. Wherever your
feelings, thoughts and words go, you are there because
you are consciousness. Your advance workers, your feelings, thoughts and words, and your finishing workers,
your actions, are consciousness.*

*With your feelings, thoughts and words, you emit
yourself, for you are your feeling, thinking, and speaking,
yourself, the consciousness. Since everything is consciousness, you, the consciousness, will be wherever you, the
human being, send to.*

Gabriele, the teaching prophetess
and emissary of God, explained about this:

To this very day, many people have not yet grasped
that their body is energy, which consists of their feelings,
sensations, thoughts, words and actions. The fluidum, the
aura, of the person is his consciousness, which, in turn,
is energy. If a person stays in one place, while his feelings
and thoughts linger elsewhere, then a large part of his
aura, his consciousness, is there. Thus, the body is here,
on the other hand, a large part of the consciousness is
here and there. This means that we send ourselves out;
our shell may very well be present, but not our inner

being. If the shell-consciousness is addressed, then it frequently cannot give an answer to a question, unless it pulls back its aura within a split second, so as to listen and answer the question.

Wherever you send to, that is where you are. You build up your magnetism there, and one day you will be attracted from there.

If you send out a human thought, then your body may be here, but a part of your consciousness is there. It is the part that lies in your feeling, thinking and speaking. Through this, you are multi-divided: here, where your body is, there, where your feelings are, and there, to where your thoughts and words go. Thus, you can be multi-divided because your feelings can be, for instance, with your neighbor, your thoughts, for example, at your place of work, and your words with your neighbor, with whom you are speaking.

This state of being multi-divided can lead to severe disorders in the person. So-called disturbances of the equilibrium can develop. Your nervous system can thus be shattered. Further causes and their corresponding effects can be the result. Through this, the person can no longer think clearly and logically and his actions are then half-measures.

Gabriele:

This state of being multi-divided that the Christ of God speaks of in His words of revelation can lead to an emotional disturbance.

An emotionally disturbed person often lets himself go and often lets everything happen around him because he is indifferent to everything, as a result of his lethargy. But every now and then, he can also fly into a rage and do things that can be preposterous. If he is addressed regarding this, either he falls back into his lethargy or proceeds to a corresponding attack. These emotional fluctuations can lead to disturbances of equilibrium because this often also affects the nervous system.

Through the emotional fluctuations, the life rhythms—since life consists of cycles and rhythms—are also disturbed. These disharmonious rhythms frequently cause totally opposite streams of thought to be released, so that the person lacks any kind of logic. The sentences that he speaks are imbalanced. He stops talking in the middle of a sentence and starts again with another topic. He starts one work, yet does not finish it because while doing it, other ideas and desires urge him, which he listens to and goes after.

Recognize: If you are split by simultaneously sending out human feelings, thoughts and words, you are here and there; you are at this and that place at the same time. Through this multiple and simultaneous sending, which is human, that is, personal, you establish so-called Earth stations. In further incarnations, you will—magnetically, as it were—be attracted there, and you will seek out those places that you have magnetized with your feelings, thoughts and words, in order to clear up there, what you caused in your previous lives, that is, to where you emitted.

If you want to figure out where you will be tomorrow, in another incarnation, then examine your feelings, thoughts, words and deeds of today. And if you want to figure out with whom you will be very close tomorrow, then examine your feelings, thoughts, words and deeds toward your neighbor—that is, examine what binds you to your neighbor and what binds your neighbor to you.

The one who does not build on the temple of his inner being, but lives in an external way instead, lives here and there. As a human being, he creates, in the present, his earthly places of destination and the stations for his next incarnations—where he will then have to live or travel to, in order to remedy what he created in previous existences.

As Jesus, I taught all this and much more to My disciples, and I teach it now as Christ to all people of good will.

The one who has taken up dwelling in the innermost part of his temple will keep the order of the temple that says: What you do, do it totally.

The one who lives in his innermost being, in the holiest of holies, in God, is oriented to the subject, the matter and the situation. His feelings, thoughts and words stream from the holy temple. They are the eternal law. Lawful feelings, thoughts and words are holy forces that move in the omnipresent stream and find access and entry into people, things, matters and situations.

The God-filled one who dwells in the holiest of holies, from where he sends out selfless feelings, thoughts and words, remains in the innermost part of his temple, despite external movement, despite the waves of the ocean world because he lives in God, in the fullness, and is not divided, but is united in God, in the stream of life, in the Being.

Selfless God-filled feelings, thoughts, words and deeds are in the eternal stream and work from the eternal stream and bring the eternal and the lawful into the stream of God again because everything that is pure returns to the pure. The truly wise one leaves to the Eternal when and how the God-filled one will return to the eternal stream.

What the wise one accomplishes, he fulfills for the eternal law, for the eternal stream, in which he lives.

Gabriele, the teaching prophetess
and emissary of God, explained about this:

Transformed-down energies are divine energies that have been diverted and transformed, that no longer vibrate divinely, but sinfully, that are no longer high, but low vibrations. If we sin, then, for one, we are building on already existing like sins, that is, we increase the base energies, and for another, we take the divine word, the high energies, for our base purposes of exaltation, of knowledge and financial gain. In this way, we transform the high energies down into the baseness of sin. We transform them into sin, thus burdening ourselves. That is, then, the transformed-down energies.

God-filled feelings, thoughts and words are the unity-consciousness because they are the law in the stream of Being. On the other hand, human feelings, thoughts and words are loners, which again join with like-minded feelings, thoughts and words, from where they then come back to the sender. However, before they seek out the sender, they have multiplied. They multiply because the receivers think the same or like thoughts, which likewise radiate back. These then return to the sender as a complex and influence the sender as a complex. This means that things will become much worse for him, the person, than they were before.

Such loners are troublemakers. They are the nagging thoughts that want to control the sender. They force themselves on him because they need the sender's energy to remain active and continue to activate themselves. The one who takes in these nagging thoughts thinks the same or like thing. With this, he intensifies the nagging complex, through which, at the same time, the person becomes what he has thought and thinks.

The one who does not sanctify his life loses it and, depending on the burdening of his soul, will possibly have to gain it back through several births into the flesh. He then goes through his own hell, by way of his own torments and suffering, through what he, himself, has entered into himself.

Gabriele:

Christ revealed to us that when we reinforce nagging thoughts with the same or like thoughts, the thought-complex gets bigger. This sinful complex then influences us and turns us into its content. Then we are what we thought, spoke and did: envious, spiteful, cantankerous, jealous, belligerent, aggressive, demanding, ruthless and much more.

For this reason, use the days and hours because you do not know when the soul will be called back and what it will then have to bear and perhaps bring with it again.

If you want to have an inkling of what your soul bears, you can fathom one or more segments of your spiritual ego, by measuring your way of feeling, thinking, speaking and acting against the Ten Commandments.

The person is an unmistakable sign, himself, either of the I Am or of his human ego. He can hide himself only from those before whom he can disguise himself—those who, themselves, are as he is, who shimmer colorfully and embellish themselves with many words and gestures, to draw attention to themselves.

The mask of such a person can be compared to a house of cards. A gust of wind of being disregarded—and the house of cards collapses. What is left over is then the corroding, the biting ego that suddenly speaks another language. The masks have then fallen, and the person be-haves just as he is: disappointed and resigned because he is no longer heeded because his ego is no longer exalted because he is no longer the focus of attention.

f you have something to hide, that is, if you want to hide yourself, then you seek a safe place. You make it your home of choice and call it your concealment where you, the base being, believe you are hidden.

However, being hidden in concealment is evident because nothing is hidden to the stars. You, who want to hide yourself, have entered in the stars what you want to hide from the world. Thereby, you are in constant communication with them, no matter where you are.

From whom or what do you want to hide? The stars, into which you have entered what you are, hit you at the right time—even if you have hidden yourself here or there. There is no place where you can hide from yourself because what you have input in the way of feelings, thoughts, words and deeds is what you are. It is also what you carry with you.

Gabriele, the teaching prophetess
and emissary of God, explained about this:

Our subconscious often serves as a safe place to hide our sinfulness, our human aspects. We often repress our base inclinations and craving desires and push them into our subconscious. Over this, we place the illusion of balance, of courtesy, of many »good« words that deceive the unenlightened one. The deceived one frequently believes the sweet talker and is thus bound to these illusions, until he liberates himself from them and takes the path that is shown to him. This path is plastered with his sensations, thoughts, words and actions, in which he can recognize himself. By clearing them up with the help of the Christ of God, he finds his way to himself and becomes free of what he repressed and glossed over, of what the subconscious had stored.

The enlightened one recognizes the one who repressed and glossed over things because each person marks himself and bears witness to what is stored in his conscious mind and subconscious, and the inputs in his soul. That is why we should not hide our sinfulness, but clear it up with Christ and no longer commit it. The one who does this can talk about his still-existing sins because he is working on this complex, that is, he is working it off step by step with the help of Christ and no longer doing what has been cleared up. He may very well still be a sinner, but already has the sight of clarity, the hearing of the awakened one, the sensitive feeling for nuances of smell and taste and a balanced sense of touch.

Gabriele, the teaching prophetess
and emissary of God, explained about this:

To learn to recognize ourselves means to examine our feelings and our conscience. If we pause and monitor our thoughts as well as the behavior patterns that result from them, the movements of our body, the reaction of our feet, hands and arms, then we sense whether our thoughts are sinful or divine.

Sinful thoughts, also sensations, make us restless. We cross our legs and our arms. We play with objects in front of us, that is, our fingers are always moving. We also constantly move our legs and feet. If these are crossed over one another, then we bob one foot up and down or move our toes. If our feet are on the floor, then we move them. We shuffle about on the floor, bob our feet up and down or move our toes. If we are standing, we shift from one foot to the other and lean against one object and then another. If we are sitting, we fidget around in the chair, that is, we are restless. We experience the same thing when we watch our speech and watch ourselves during our activity, while we work, during conversations or other things. Then we experience ourselves and know who we are. We are the reflection of how things are in our inner being, that is, we are our own mirror. All those who look deeper recognize us in these things.

You are then, yourself, a mirror for yourself and will look less and less into the mirror of your neighbor because you have enough to do with clearing up your human ego. Overcome what you recognize on yourself, then you will unfold toward the divine—just like the flower when the warming rays of the sun touch it.

The one who opens himself to the inner light gains inner beauty because his soul attains purity. Beauty, that is, purity, is an attribute of the true Being. True beauty and purity cannot be emulated because the inner garment is cosmically radiating love.

If the physical body is permeated with the radiance of the inner being, then the person is virtuous and selfless. He gains inner grace, which is then the adornment of his outer appearance. The adornment of the spiritually matured person consists of precious gems: of his selfless thoughts, words and deeds.

he person has to develop the longing to become one with God, only then, will he attain the state of oneness.

Gabriele:

A person develops the longing for God solely by taking steps of actualization, that is, by daily recognizing his own sinful aspects, repenting of them, clearing them up and no longer committing them. In this way, he goes toward the inner light, through which the soul is ever more filled with light and conscious of God. The God-conscious soul and the person striving toward God then feel what it means to be separated from God, and long to become one with God.

On the day that you live completely in Me, you are raised to the truth and you are the truth.

The truth does not need to ask. It does not need to seek anymore. It knows about all things because it is the truth.

If you are raised to the truth, then you are divine.

The truly wise one knows about all things because he has insight into all the things of life, since he has become the truth.

The enlightened one does not need explanations. He lives the eternal law and is the eternal law of love. He is recognized in that he is as he is, upright, honest, selflessly loving—and not by many words of love.

The person who is in the light of truth speaks a different language. What he says is permeated by the light of truth and thus, selfless. The truthful one does not display himself—he is.

The one who sees only the external is blinded by the illusions of this world and believes deception to be reality and thinks he is a realist because he believes in only what his eyes reflect: the illusion of the Being.

On the other hand, the one who beholds, who turns his eyes to within, comprehends the Being, the truth, and sees the external, the illusion.

The one who beholds, sees you in himself as a part of himself. He also sees your external aspects, and sees you as you are, and recognizes you in your world of illusion. He knows where you come from and where you are going because your shimmering shell that strives only for outer splendor is evident to him.

The true Being is the inner radiance. It does not need many words—it radiates. It does not seek oil for its lamp, either—it is because it is the true, the beautiful, the eternal and eternity, the light that never goes out because it is divine. This is what you are in the light of the truth.

The truth does not boast; it is. It radiates and irradiates all souls, people and beings, all Being.

The one who longs for the truth receives sparks from the light of the truth, according to his spiritual maturity.

The more sparks he can receive, the more intensive and far-reaching the light of his soul becomes. It shines for him on the path inward to God, so that he draws ever closer to the Eternal. The light of the truth fills the feelings, thoughts, words and deeds of the person striving toward God with light, so that his thinking, speaking and acting is truthful.

People in the spirit of truth no longer need their neighbor's matchstick, the little flame of aggrandizement and acknowledgment, with which so many people still let themselves be ensnared. The one who needs this little flame is content with this brief flaring up. With this, he is ignited—and with this, he, in turn, ignites others of like mind.

What good to a person is this little flame that briefly flares up? How long does a match burn? It flares up and is readily burnt up.

It is similar with the human ego. It flares up and shines briefly, then collapses. It is again dark in the one who is content with aggrandizement and acknowledgment—until another comes and again ignites for him the little flame of aggrandizement and acknowledgment for a brief moment.

This craving for the little flame of aggrandizement and acknowledgment continues until the soul has unfolded in Me, the Christ, and has become light of My light. Then the soul has ignited itself on Me and shines in God eternally.

The one who ignites himself on My light will become self-luminous again—just as he was as a pure being and will be again as a pure being: eternally self-luminous.

But how poor is the one who offers the match and how poor the one who has to ignite himself on it, to briefly flare up, so that he can briefly display himself, that is, briefly move into the light! Both, the one who offers the match and the one who lets himself be ignited, are souls without light, still poor, spiritually dead ones, who feel sorry and mourn for themselves and briefly rejoice in the little flame of aggrandizement and acknowledgment.

The one who thinks and acts this way and expects the little flame from his neighbor does not live. The one who does not live knows neither himself nor his neighbor, nor does he have an eye for the true and beautiful. He speaks of the Being and means his ego. He speaks of the Self and means himself. He acts solely for himself and gives his all to be seen.

The darkened, the blind, person sees only his base self and does not behold his true self. He will remain a blind one, until he knows who he is and until he lives what he is—divine.

As long as the person does not draw from the truth, he wants to prove himself. If he has become the truth, then he is the truth and the true Being, the life in Me, which is impersonal.

Gabriele, the teaching prophetess
and emissary of God, explained about this:

Christ revealed to us: »The true one does only good for his neighbor and only if his neighbor asks for it.« With this, the Spirit of the Christ of God pointed out to us the spiritual principle of freedom. His words mean that we should not force our neighbor to anything, not even if we think that our help would be good for him. The God-filled person is always ready to help and to serve, insofar as it is possible for him. He will also convey this to his neighbor who needs help, by letting him know this with words like: "I am ready to help you at any time. If you want help, come to me. How and when is left up to you." In this way, the wise one upholds the freedom of his neighbor and thus, the principle of the law of God, freedom.

Even if our neighbor rejects us—the truly wise one remains true to him in his heart and stays ready to serve and help him when he wants it.

If the soul in the person has become the I Am, the truth, the law of the All, then it also encounters the I Am again and again because it lives in the stream of the I Am and is the eye of the I Am.

The I Am is the true Self. It encounters itself again and again because it is divine and all that is divine is contained in all things. You are the bearer of the true Self, of the divine, the All-life.

Gabriele:

To encounter the great, mighty, omnipresent I Am means to live in God, in the I Am, to fulfill His holy laws, so that the eye, the senses of hearing, taste, smell and touch become fine organs of perception, through which the stream, the mighty I Am, flows. Then the spiritual eye beholds the I Am in its neighbor; the spiritual ear hears the I Am in the words of its neighbor; the refined senses smell and taste the divine in the smell and the taste, and the sense of touch that is aglow does not grasp indiscriminately, but is consciously guided by the stream of God. In this way, the truly wise one experiences again and again the I Am in all that he sees, hears, smells, tastes and touches.

He also sees and hears the negative. He does not identify with this, but is ready to help at any time, when his neighbor wants to recognize his sinful aspects, repent of them and clear them up.

The I Am is the true Self, the Being, the truth; it is the law of the All. The I Am is everything in all things. Therefore, it is the Self. If you are divine again, you are the self, the being, the truth, the law of love because you are the heir to infinity and the image of your eternal Father.

On Earth as it is in heaven: The divine encounters the divine over and over again—itself. The human self, the base ego, encounters itself, the base ego, again and again.

y apostles and disciples asked Me how they could become free from bindings and from striving for acknowledgement:

You will become free from bindings and the striving for acknowledgement when you leave your fellowman his freedom and reflect upon yourselves, to attain the conscious sonship or daughtership of God through actualization and fulfillment of the laws of God because in God, all beings live as free beings. They are bound to nothing and no one. They are rich because they fulfill the law of God.

If soul and person do not fulfill the law of God, they become impoverished and bind themselves to people and things that surround them and that come toward them.

The one who lets himself be controlled by the events of everyday life and by people has surrendered the rudder of his life and does not have the gift of discernment. Such people separate from one person and bind themselves to another.

Gabriele:

Anyone who surrenders the rudder of his life leaves the ship of his life to others, who then steer it in the direction that corresponds to their thoughts and striving. Thus, anyone who lets himself drift on the ocean of his life or relinquishes the rudder of his life to others will soon no longer know whether what he thinks, speaks and

does is himself or comes from the helmsman to whom he
has relinquished the ship of his life.

Heed the following simple basic rule:
*Rely on God, the Eternal. Do not expect anything from
your neighbor, then you will not be disappointed.*

*You should not make comparisons with anything or
anyone. Like presupposes like.*
*Recognize that the inner light, the Christ in you, the I
Am, is incomparable.*
*The one who is awakened in the light of the truth no
long-er compares—he is.*

any people are enveloped in the darkness because they are completely taken up by the external. They thoughtlessly pass by their neighbor and do not know that they are passing by God.

Dark, and thus blind as they are, they violate the highest forces of life, the law of salvation. They do not know about their innermost being, the precious treasure, the gem, which is God, out of whom they were spiritually born, thus becoming divine.

Therefore, learn to walk in the light, in the eternal Being. Maintain your life by drawing from the life. Go into the stillness, become still and be active from the stillness. That is the true deed. That is being fulfilled by God.

Gabriele, the teaching prophetess
and emissary of God, explained about this:

Each day is the teacher of a human being. Each day teaches us, by pointing out to us aspects of our pros and cons. The pros are the positive side of our life, the divine. The cons are the negative side of our existence. They are our sins. The sin is the shadow. The divine is the light.

If we want to walk in the light, in the eternal Being, we should listen to the voice of the day, which addresses our physical body by way of our nervous system and our actions and reactions. If we get upset, our day addressed our negative aspects. If we want to find our way out of this side of shadows, then, with the help of the Christ of God, we should find the root of our agitation, clear up this sinful aspect and no longer do it. In this way, we step out of the shadows, the negative, and walk more and more on the light-filled side, in the positive, in the pros.

Thus, the day teaches us. If we learn from it, we become more sensitive and, in time, will very quickly feel whether today shadows are opening up or whether the light, the light-filled side of our life, is showing itself to us.

What the person radiates is what he attracts, and he sees only that. Everyone sees himself in his neighbor, the divine one and the undivine one.

A person encounters what he thinks because like always attracts like, and sees its like.

You see yourself in your neighbor.

What you see and what you get upset about is what you, the person, are. Your physical eyes reflect only you, yourself, and what is around you and what upsets you—and this, in turn, is you.

The one who truly beholds, the true self, beholds and sees at the same time because the spiritual eye sees through, and has the overview of, everything.

The one who truly beholds has an eye for the true Being. He sees into the depths of life and in it, beholds himself and his neighbor and all Being because the spiritual eye perceives everything, since it is, at the same time, the eye of the eternal law: the true Being, the true Self.

The one who truly beholds does not judge because he is the wise one who sees into the depths of life and sees through everything. But the one who looks only at the surface of life judges because he has not yet fathomed the depths of life.

The one who beholds knows no definitions because he does not have to comprehend anything—he is.

The one who beholds has no opinion because he is wise.

Gabriele:

To be wise means to let knowledge be.

The one who merely knows does not see through the background of the earthly existence. He looks only at the surface. He sees only the mirror and does not look through it, that is, he does not grasp what is taking place behind the mirror, behind the egoistical façade that has been erected. The wise one searches through the background. He sees through the façade, through the mirror, as it were, and thus beholds the most concealed things. He does not judge because he has gone through all the lows and highs, himself, and knows the difficulty of this journey. This results in understanding and comprehension. From this, he can help and support his neighbor, who still has part of the journey before him.

However, the one who is merely knowing has not yet gone through the path of the highs and lows. He speaks of the journey and does not journey, himself. He has his prejudices and judgments. That is the difference between »being wise« or merely »having knowledge.«

The wise one lets knowledge be, that is, he leaves it behind him because he has gone beyond knowledge and reached wisdom.

Since everything is in all things, God, everything is also God—in the soul of the person and in every cell of the physical body. If the person feels, thinks, speaks and acts against the Being, the law, God, then he acts against himself.

The one who is against his neighbor is also against himself because God is in his neighbor and God is in him—everything in all things.

If you disparage your neighbor, you disparage yourself. If you insult your neighbor, you insult yourself. If you act against your neighbor, you act against yourself.

Gabriele, the teaching prophetess
and emissary of God, explained about this:

God is in all things as the whole, indivisible, and thus, infinity as essence and power. God, the omnipresence, the pure, the eternal, the infinite One, is the positive power even in the negative, which helps us to dissolve the shell, the sinfulness, that is, to transform it, so that it is solely the I Am that still radiates.

Recognize: If the All-power, God, is in you, then the All-power, God, is also in your neighbor.

You, the Being, the being in God, are the essence of infinity, since the essence of infinity is also in your brother, in your sister. You act against yourself if you are against your brother.

Thus, the one who is against his neighbor is also against himself.

The opposite pole is the adversary who is against God. Thus, you, too, are against God if you disregard His laws. In this way, you create your own human law for yourself— this is what you are, what you live in, and what influences you.

To want to return to God means to return to people, to respect them and to learn to selflessly love them. This is the return to unity because God unites everything.

You are and I am in Him. All people and beings, the stars and the kingdoms of the animals, plants and stones are in Him.

You are mine,
I am yours;
the eternal Being
moves in this consciousness.
I am in everything,
you are in everything;
you are and I am
everything that is.

If your neighbor is close to you, then you are close to God. If you feel distant from your neighbor, then you are distant from God. At every moment, you determine how near or how far you are from God, yourself.

Once you have learned to feel into the soul of every person, then, in yourself, you experience the very depths of your neighbor's soul and know what soul and person need. Only by putting yourself in your neighbor's place, can you understand him and become one with him.

Gabriele:

Our look is limited in our three-dimensional world. "Three-dimensional" means that we are in the existence of time and space, and that we live in boundaries, which we have given to ourselves through our egocentric feeling, sensing, thinking, speaking and acting. Ultimately, we look solely at the externalities. Whether we look up or down, or to the right or left, to the back or to the front—we always see only the external, and ultimately, the walls, our limitations, our sinful inputs. They are our world, in which we have our existence.

The soul—and above all, the very basis of the soul—is beyond dimensions. It knows neither time nor space. It is not bound to hindrances, to objects, to walls. Nothing and no one can stop it, unless it is burdened through sin, which the person commits more and more as a result of his self-made limitation.

Every human being has more or less inserted himself into the three-dimensional world. He is thus a seam in the structure. He affirms this kind of life in the seam and expands it further, by acknowledging time and space as the measure of his life. However, at the moment the person says to himself: "It is true that I am a human being and move in this structure of time and space, but I will not affirm this as my life because God is beyond dimensions," his life on Earth may very well continue to take place in time and space, in the three dimensions, but he will not view it as unalterable. By daily clearing up his sins that he has recognized, which he then no longer commits in his daily life, he expands his consciousness and increasingly uncovers his divine being.

The more the divine consciousness of a person begins to radiate, the deeper he senses. This is the perception of his soul, which does not look only at the walls and objects, which does not see only the façade of the human ego, but is able to establish communication with the very basis of his neighbor's soul, and sense his deeper essence. Like always communicates with like: the surface with the surface, the superficiality with the superficiality, the basis of the soul with the basis of the soul, and thus, the divine with the divine.

By way of his own experience in relation to "Recognize your sins, repent, clear them up and no longer do them," the person activates the divine consciousness, which is able to feel into all things, also into the very basis of his neighbor's soul.

Once you have experienced and beheld in yourself your brother, your sister, then it is just as if you have beheld God, for God is the divine in you and in your neighbor.

When you cut down your brother—be it in thoughts or with the sword—then you cut down yourself, so to speak because the positive side of your brother, the divine, is in you.

If you are against your brother, then you are also against that part of your brother that is in you.

What you destroy today, you must build up again to-morrow.

As Jesus, I, Christ, taught My apostles and disciples to behold, which is, at the same time, the perception because the senses of the soul and the senses of the person are organs of perception.

The one who has spiritualized his human senses beholds and hears the innermost Being, his true self, and his senses of smell, taste and touch are aligned only with what is divine.

The beholding is the perception of the Being in the stream of the Being. If you want to practice the right beholding, the divine perception, to open the eye of truth that is the Being, then affirm—at first, still blindly—the Being, which is in everything you see.

In this way, you experience in yourselves that the Being knows no differences. But it has the gift of discernment and beholds and grasps the various degrees of consciousness of the evolutionary steps that mature toward perfection.

Make no differences between your neighbors because if one of your neighbors is closer to you than the other, then you reject the other and imagine yourselves to be higher than the one who, in the end, is equal to you, the other one. As long as you make differences, you will not attain the gift of discernment and therefore, will also react differently in what you think and do because you do not behold, and cannot perceive, the whole in everything.

Affirm the whole in everything, then you will keep the order of the temple and will also learn to behold the degrees of consciousness and attain the gift of discernment and learn the language of the law, which is not the language of human beings.

Gabriele, the teaching prophetess
and emissary of God, explained about this:

»Affirm the whole in everything« means: God is indivisible. In everything, also in the smallest component, God is the whole, the eternal law. Even if only one facet of the whole shines in a life form because this is the state of consciousness of the form, God, the whole, is indeed contained in this form. It is in evolution, until all facets of the eternal law, God, have unfolded and the form, which then has become a spirit being, is divine.

Since God is the whole in all things, and our soul is the essence of the whole, we should affirm the whole in all things. Through this, we also affirm ourselves as the divine being in God.

The language of the law is the opened divine con-sciousness, the philosopher's stone, which radiates all the facets of truth into infinity, and thus, knows all things because it is the law, the All.

The eye of the law is, at the same time, the ear of the law: What you behold, you also hear.
The one who beholds, hears, registers and reacts all at the same time. What he beholds, he also registers, and what he hears, he also perceives.
He beholds the Being because he is the being, and hears the Being because he speaks the being, which is the life.
The one who is the truth also sees his neighbor as he is. He hears what his neighbor does not say, and when the latter speaks, he perceives from what is said who his neighbor is.
The one who beholds sees through everything because he has the overall view. The light of your eyes is either the light of your ego or of the I Am.

Gabriele:

»You behold the Being« means that you feel the life, which also speaks to you. To behold and to hear is always a whole because God is eternal revelation. If you were to merely behold and not hear, you would perceive only matter, that is, you would merely see it. If a person looks

873

solely at the shell of the Being, at matter, he frequently believes that life forms such as plants and animals are mere objects.

However, the one who beholds the life forms with the eyes of life, feels and hears them at the same time because God is not mute, but constant light and revelation. The same applies to your neighbor. The one who looks solely at the human being may very well see him, but does not understand him. If this person speaks to him, he will not understand him in his words, either.

The truly wise one sees and beholds the person. He senses him as energy, as it were, which imparts itself to him. The wise one knows that everything is the energy of revelation. The divine speaks itself and reveals itself to the divine. The human, the sinful, speaks itself and reveals itself to the sinful—and reveals itself to the divine, which has the gift to discern between the revelation of God and the revelation of sin.

What you see that irritates you is what you have attracted.

What you listen in on that irritates you is what you have attracted.

What you speak is what you are and you are also with those who speak the same way.

The light of reflection of your physical eyes, of your physical ears, of your physical words and your physical desires and passions is the light of your ego. With these reflections of your human ego, you attract solely those people who are the same or like you. You are of one mind with the people who reflect in the same or like way as you. This is human and has no access to heaven.

Gabriele:

God is, and since He is wise, He knows about all things. He also knows that all sinfulness will transform in His light because He does not look at the sin, but at what is perfect in the soul of each person. He beholds the divine, which He is, God, the Omnipresence, in each human being, in all Being. Thus, the form out of God is divine.

God does not get upset about imperfection because He beholds only perfection. Only the imperfect one gets upset about imperfection because he sees with the eyes of imperfection, hears with the hearing of imperfection and reacts to his neighbor with the other senses of imperfection. If his neighbor affects him, then the imperfect one gets upset because his neighbor has addressed the imperfection, the correspondence, which, in turn, is the projection on others. Every correspondence reflects its content in thoughts, words and actions.

The truly wise one does not reflect. He penetrates everything because he is the eternal law that penetrates all things.

The pure penetrates the pure and it makes no distinctions. Pure is pure. It penetrates the All and all those who are pure. The divine principle—sending and receiving—pervades the All.

The impure one always sees only himself—his impurity—in his neighbor. That is what he radiates—that is what he is.

The one who affirms himself, his base ego, understands only himself, his base ego. With this, he is on the human level.

Gabriele:

Anyone who views his human ego as impeccable and absolute revolves solely around his own concerns and has no access to his neighbor. He maintains friendship only with those who reinforce him in his ego, in his sinfulness, and thereby gratify him. These are whom he calls his friends.

The one who is does not need to understand because he is wise. He is the divine essence in his neighbor, and his neighbor, in turn, is the divine essence in him. Both irradiate each other, and both irradiate the All and the All irradiates both. Both and the All irradiate all Being, the Being that has become form, the spirit beings and the spiritual nature kingdoms. And all Being that became form irradiates both, in turn because everything is contained in all things. Thus, there are no differences, only the gift to discern between degrees of consciousness.

As above, so below.

There is only one law-principle: What you send is what you receive.

Nothing that is eternal is outside of you. What heaven is, the eternal law, is in you. That is what you are, the self—and that also surrounds you because everything is contained in all things, and the Being, the law, is effective in all things.

What is on Earth—density, matter—emerged through the reversed principle of »sending and receiving,« through the base ego, which shapes itself with the feeling, thinking and speaking of the individual. What the person has acquired in the way of human aspects is not divine. This burdens his soul and his body; it is what he radiates. Density, matter, which is merely reflection, emerged through the undivine.

The divine principle is the pure—the undivine principle is the impure, from which matter came forth. The divine principle can radiate the reversed, the undivine, the human principle—but the undivine, the human, cannot radiate through the divine.

Gabriele, the teaching prophetess
and emissary of God, explained about this:

Every person has his personal world, which consists of his concepts and are pictures. All feelings, thoughts, words and actions form as pictures, which are in the person's aura; they surround the person and affect him. In this way, the person lives in his world, in the pictures that he created, himself. The one who lives in his world of pictures, lives as if in a closed room because he has no access to his neighbor's world of pictures, and is thus, one who closed himself off and is limited, who is occupied only with his own world, with his own projections.

The one who emulates such a person creates reproductions. The one who wants to do the same as he will never be able to be the same. A reproduction is something copied, which is worth even less than the production by the sinful one. The producer and the reproducer bind themselves to one another because like attracts like, again and again.

Since the divine is in matter and radiates through matter, in time, the mirrors, which as a whole form matter, will become dull. Sooner or later, each mirror will change in the absolute principle because the Spirit penetrates matter, and no shadow can exist in the long run.

Then everything is again the Being in the stream of the Being.

The pure ones who live in the pure principle, in the stream of the Being, and who personify the Being, the Absolute, the pure principle, speak the language of the primordial sensation, which expresses itself in them because they are, themselves, the word of the truth that is manifest in them.

If the pure one sends, he receives the word of the pure in himself because his neighbor—and the language of his neighbor—is divine and is, in turn, a part of the one who receives. The entire law is contained in the divine word because everything in all things is the whole.

The impure principle is the human ego. It is what is outside, it is the density, the human state, the human way of feeling, thinking, speaking and acting—which, in turn, is the one who sends it out himself, projecting it onto his neighbor. He will then hear only the language of his neighbor, which, then again, is his language because like attracts like.

Your feelings, thoughts and words are a part of you. Just as you emit them, in the same way they behave toward you and come back to you. Therefore, just as you send, will you receive, and that is how you will also behave toward your neighbor: positive, divine—or not divine, that is, human.

Your human feelings, thoughts, words and deeds leave their mark on you, which you are, yourself.

The world of your life, which is made up of the sum of your feelings, thoughts, words and actions, and from which your longings, passions and desires follow, compels you to feel, think, speak and do the same and like things again and again. You will continue to be the spiral of your ego, until you move out of this spinning top and reject the tempter—who you are, yourself, and which is your human ego.

The tempter is your small, egocentric world of thought, which consists of the countless threads and cords of your human ego that trap you again and again, binding you to what you sense, think, speak and do. Only with Me, Christ, can you undo the shackles of your human ego, to find your way into the eternal principle, into the eternal law, God, which speaks itself because there is only one principle: sending and receiving.

Recognize and experience yourself as the principle of God. Then you will see through the wiles and the falsity of the adversary. He steals into you by way of your human feelings and thoughts to ravage your temple.

Gabriele:

Every person, the one more, the other less—depending on the burdening or non-burdening of his soul—has an antenna in himself, which can also be called a seismograph. It is the level of feelings, that vibrates in the vicinity of the soul.

To regard a thought means to place it before yourself, that is, to retain it in your awareness, with the request to the Christ of God to support and help you find the root of your thought, that is, the content of the thought or thoughts. If our soul is not too heavily burdened, if we, the person, have developed morally and ethically, our level of feelings, the antenna or seismograph, is more finely adjusted to the divine. The divine in the soul, the Christ of God, will then support and help us by way of our feelings. Thus, He will stimulate our seismograph of feelings, which will open our thought or thoughts like a book, so that we find our way to the root of our thought, page by page. This means that we can look at each page, to recognize how our thought or thoughts have developed. Frequently, we will experience that at the beginning it may have been merely a trivial incident, which, through our sensations and thoughts, we personally built up and expanded, so that it became a thought-complex that burdens us frequently and often makes our life difficult for us.

Therefore, if we leaf through the book of these our thoughts, we should also feel into their content, to see whether here or there we shouldn't apologize to our neighbor for what we said or did. Once we get to the root, we recognize the habits, the wrong attitudes, which we should also go to work on, so that we no longer produce the same kind of thing. That is the deep contemplation of a thought or a thought-complex.

As Jesus, I, Christ, continued to teach My apostles and disciples: Your earthly body is a thought-body. You are equipped today with what you sensed, thought, spoke and did in previous lives and did not clear up.

The cells and organs of your body, which are already formed in the womb, are shaped by the soul that prepared to move into this house. Before your birth, your body is shaped by what you should clear up in this life on Earth. If you want to learn what you have brought with you and what comes from that life, then read your life-picture: the scale of your human feelings, thoughts, words, deeds, desires, passions and longings.

Recognize: The soul thus brings its imprint with it and, already in the womb, shapes its body. Although the child's brain cells do not have anything stored in them yet, what the person will experience in this life is already stored in the body, in the cells of the body.

During fertilization, the soul, which is preparing to incarnate, already enters into the first cell division what it brought with it—what is of significance for it in this life on Earth. Thus, already in the womb, it determines its physical body.

The light-filled soul predetermines the person's fine structure, the noble features, which can first become noticeable in later years, if the body grows and the person has fostered the fineness of his soul. Just as the structure *of the body is, so does the person vibrate; so does he radiate; so is he; so does he behave.*

A burdened soul predetermines a coarser structure that is already recognizable in its early years on Earth, often when the earthly garment enters the development phase of puberty. It is not always the girth of the body that is significant, especially not during the developmental phase of puberty.

However, nothing happens by chance. Thus, it is not a coincidence that one has a finer structure and the other a coarser structure; that one is more delicate and the other one heavier; that one is poor and the other rich; that one is born ill and the other healthy.

Only the fewest people think about why things are as they are. What is important for most people is that all goes well for them. The neighbor who begs by the wayside, who has taken to his sickbed or is mistreated and despised by his fellow humans is of interest only to the fewest of people – and the majority of people act the same way toward the worlds of animals and plants.

Gabriele:

Many people revolve around their own axis, which is forged solely from their thinking patterns. This thinking axis is their measuring stick, and with this, they measure and weigh what they encounter. The one who is not like them is disparaged, and whatever can be had is taken with them. They then call this their property. In this way, the Earth was, and is still being, exploited. Everyone tries to firmly establish his personal axis, by carrying to it all that he calls his property. This consistently becomes his measuring stick, with which he measures his surroundings.

How can a person understand his neighbor by the wayside, if he relates solely to himself, to his measuring stick or standard? How can he understand the Earth with its plants, minerals and animals, when he merely revolves around his axis, and only that is his measuring stick?

Someone who is his own horizon does not see beyond this, and lets himself be shone upon by the sun of his own ego again and again. All this comes under the law: What a person sows, he will reap.

Disinterest, too, is a part of the law »you will reap what you sow.« The one who sees that people mistreat or kill people, the one who sees that people mistreat and kill animals and violate nature, the one who sees that people deliberately violate the laws of inner life and closes his eyes, that is, does not object—is no better than those who do these things. The radiation of his soul, his behavior and the shape of his body will then likewise say who he is.

Although the Earth itself and everything on the Earth is matter, the structures of individual people and of all the other forms of life show considerable differences. Thus, every person brings his soul's identification with him. The structure of his body identifies him since the person shows himself as he is constituted: fine, noble, understanding—or uncouth, coarse and intolerant.

»You shall know them by their fruits« also means, among other things: The person shows who he is—in what he says, how he says it, what he does and how he carries it out, how he dresses and with whom or what he surrounds himself.

In everything, he reveals either attributes of the I Am, of the inner being, or attributes of the burdened soul.

The one who judges his fellow people in his thoughts because he is of the opinion that he is better than his neighbor, is more likely worse. Through his attributes, he displays what he wants to hide in his thoughts and reveals his falseness to the truly wise one. The one talks sweetly and thinks in a sour way, thus showing himself as the cunning one who will himself be conned. People who are marked by falseness sneak around. They are sly and want to listen in on everything to then raise themselves above their fellow people, by talking sweetly—that is, sourly—about them and vilifying their life and existence.

The sincere one who addresses everything clearly and impersonally is not the proud, the arrogant, one. Upright people are honest, clear people who are farsighted.

Erect people who display themselves, that is, people with an air of artificial dignity, are unclear people who hide their narrowness by talking a lot about themselves and by seeming to be kind and busy. They are the domineering and jealous ones who have little inner life—but all the more external semblance.

Those people who are turned without seek external gloss and create for themselves what most people do not have: wealth. They are people with a coarser structure, who then disguise themselves and wrap themselves in crimson and gold, in velvet and silk to veil what they are: coarse, domineering, jealous, envious and intolerant.

Regardless of what the person uses to try to hide himself with, his identification is always his way of thinking, speaking and acting—even when he shows himself as an intellectual and boasts with his knowledge, adorning himself with words that are not typical of the fine person because the latter is fine and shows himself this way, noble. The words of the noble person contain the radiance of the inner being, since his way of feeling and thinking, too, bears the radiance of the light-filled worlds.

I taught this and more to My apostles and disciples. However, again and again admonishing words preceded what I taught: The one who judges and condemns his neighbor is worse than the one who was judged.

I gave My apostles and disciples the teachings from the Absolute Law and from the causal law and further pictorial instructions to take with them on their path through life—for self-recognition and knowledge. The one who recognizes himself and clears up what he has recognized attains the gift to discern between good and evil.

I taught some of My apostles and disciples how to send out feelings, thoughts and words. At the same time, I pointed out to them the dangers that lie in using the energies of feelings, thoughts and words, that is, in sending and receiving.

At the present time [1991], many people hear and read My word, which I Am, the Christ of God, and which I give through My instrument. Likewise, I point out to all those who hear Me through My instrument or read My words, the dangers that are effective in sending and receiving feelings, thoughts and words.

Every feeling, every thought and every word, is a sender that seeks its corresponding receiver, in order to be actualized.

What the person sends will find the receiver, who consists of the same or similar thoughts. Since every receiver also contains the sender, the former is stimulated by the one that sends and, in turn, sends the same or something similar back. Through this exchange of thoughts, an ever greater sending complex emerges, a program that is then also absorbed by the soul as a burden, as a cause. From this, ensue the blows of fate, the illnesses and afflictions that correspond to what the complex or complexes, the burdening or the burdens, consist of.

The adversary strives to direct the person in such a way that he will unceasingly think in a negative way and consequently also receive negativity. Through this, fields of communication build up in the person's brain and in his soul, which he will then use, himself. Via the negative communications, which—as long as the soul is burdened—are also part of his sending potential, so-called injections occur. This means that the adversary lets his desires and his will flow into the person's running negative programs.

The life of a person who allows this to happen will change more and more toward the negative. In the end, he will no longer recognize whether they are his own negative programs or those of the adversary or those of souls clinging to him to fulfill through him what they once could not do in the earthly existence, during their incarnations.

You have heard that all beings and all Being are linked with one another through communication. The principle of communication is sending and receiving.

What the spirit being sends can be seen as a perfect picture at the place to where it sent it, for instance, in the receiving spirit being.

Every cosmic impulse is the law that is revealed as a perfect picture. Every cosmic impulse is the law that is lived, and is therefore, permeated with light and power. The impulse that the spirit being emits never misses its receiver because the impulse, the picture, is the I Am, the life.

In the reversed, the satanic, principle, something similar takes place: The human ego sent out is likewise a picture. The more this impulse, the human picture, is lived by

Gabriele, the teaching prophetess
and emissary of God, explained about this:

In the eternal Being, every lawful sending potential is immediately apparent because sender and receiver are the law of God. In this world, the reversed principle, sinful emitting and sinful receiving, are not immediately apparent because the human being lives in the rhythm of sowing and reaping. What he sows today as negative aspects may possibly sprout only in many years and become the harvest. That is why many people feel they are in the right and believe that what they think, speak and do is right because they don't immediately experience the effects.

Not to have to experience the effects so quickly means to live in a time of grace, which enables us to recognize our sinfulness, the seed, in time, to clear it up, so that there are no effects, no harvest.

Recognize and grasp: The soul that incarnates develops its growing body already in the womb. Even the organs and the functions of the body form the magnets for the material radiation. Once the child is born, then the infant receives its soul-radiation by way of its organs and the functions of its body. In this way, the soul makes a direct connection with the body.

As long as the child is not yet able to differentiate between good and evil, the parents bear the responsibility for their child. How they live with the infant, how they treat it or what they say to it or what they talk about in its presence—the infant absorbs, first, by way of its organs and body functions. In the further course of the soul becoming rooted in the body, the imprint of the body functions then enters the child's brain cells.

Recognize: Like attracts like. It is no coincidence that a child comes into exactly the family it is born into. For this reason, a good or less good development of the child cannot be based solely on the parents, but has to do with the family's total energy-volume. If souls as human beings, that is, in their incarnation, form a family, then all family members have the task to examine their family's sending station and to make of it what will help the individual to become a person of the Spirit.

The family—that is, all family members—forms the birthplace, either for the positive or the negative, the »for and against,« which is then passed on to the following incarnations of the individual soul. Every human being himself decides where his soul will be after this incarnation because each one is responsible for what he has brought with him as a soul from the soul realms, and how he behaves as a human being in this earthly existence.

Thus, the person, himself, has brought upon himself what the soul bears, light or shadow. The members of the family have to expiate, or bear together the same or similar things. This is why the family should be the nucleus for the good, the pure, the beautiful and noble.

The one who monitors his sending and receiving station will apprehend what he sends. He will then also know what he receives. What he receives is what he is today and what he will be in the future—either light and freedom or darkness and bondage, from which, in turn, comes grief, illness and need.

The adversary wants the person to unceasingly send negativity, in order to bind him to himself, the adversary, and to the wheel of reincarnation—in accordance with the law, »what you sow, that is, send, is what you reap, that is, receive.« Through the binding behavior of a person, he also binds weaker ones to himself and pulls them down again, as it were, which means into further incarnations, by way of the wheel of reincarnation. Then it is possible that the present family will come together again in another incarnation, but in another constellation—the father or the mother could then be the children of their former child.

The one who does not recognize himself does not recognize the one he is face to face with, either. Through this, he will be divided in two—one time for God, then again against God. Thus, he remains a swaying reed in the wind whose eyes are closed to the truth.

Those who are divided in two or more parts call out »Lord, Lord,« and yet, are not with Me. One time, they want to belong to Me, then again to the world. They are the lukewarm ones who speak about the light of truth, yet do not live in the light of truth and do not know the light of truth. They speak about the kingdom of heaven, yet are far from it because they live far from God. They are one time warm and then again cold. They cannot be depended upon because they follow the vicissitude of time and those who are as they are: one time warm and then again cold.

Those who are divided in two or more parts have yet little light in their souls. They will remain bound to the wheel of coming and going, until they have attained unity with all forms of life and are thus one with God and with all beings and human beings.

Gabriele, the teaching prophetess
and emissary of God, explained about this:

The word of God, the eternal, holy law of love, is the true, eternal Self. The sensations, thoughts, words and works are divine of the one who has cleansed his conscious mind and subconscious so that they are one with the Eternal, the Self because the divine, God, reveals Himself through the person's sensations, thoughts, words and works.

The person's nature is then divine because he does the will of God. This is truly possible for the human being because Jesus placed this possibility in his heart. The words of Jesus of Nazareth are, essentially: "Be perfect, therefore, as your heavenly Father is perfect."

The perfection is the pure soul, which is the Self and lives in the Self, in God.

Gabriele:

The communication with the true Being, the eternal Self, is the communication with the whole. This means that every divine impulse is the essence of infinity, of the all-encompassing, eternal law, of the entire heavens. In every human sending potential is, in turn, the essence of infinity.

Therefore, the pure always emits the entire law and causes several facets of the law to shine more intensely. That is then the question in the impulse, to which the answer follows in the same way.

Wherever you, the true being, send to, there the radiation of your self builds itself up as picture and form, also in the material world, on the Earth. In time, that which you, the self, have built in the radiation-picture and in the radiation-form comes into effect. What then radiates back to you and your surroundings, thus becoming manifest on the Earth, is, again, the eternal law, the Self, the Being.

Your true self is your divine mentality, your divine abilities, and what you are, yourself, as a being in God. What you are and what you emit is realized because every feeling, every thought and every word ripens to fulfill itself. That is the law of sending and receiving.

Thus, on Earth, the positive, the divine, can build up as well as the negative, the dark. You determine it because you are the determining one for yourself and for your surroundings—and you, yourself, contribute to the buildup of light or to the decline of the materialistic world.

Therefore, recognize what sending and receiving means: In the sending and receiving potential lies, at the same time, the responsibility for yourself. What you send, you will also receive. What flows out of your innermost being enters your innermost being again and builds up as light and power externally.

Nothing that is sent out misses its goal because it was aimed at the goal. The goal lies inherently in everything that is sent.

ll of infinity is built on the Father-Mother-Principle, on polarity and duality, on sending and receiving, on the positive and negative poles. This principle also builds up in the evolutionary steps of the minerals, plants and animals, up to the perfect spirit beings.

Gabriele, the teaching prophetess
and emissary of God, explained about this:

What Christ revealed to us in His great cosmic teachings means: The birth of the spiritual body takes place in evolutionary steps, that is, increments of evolution because each spirit body consists of the countless powers of the minerals, plants and animals. By way of the mineral, the plant and the animal, the communication of the spirit body develops for all of creation, for all the kingdoms of the Being. Once the spiritual body has opened all the increments of evolution and thus, united all the powers of creation in itself, it is complete, to the extent that it can be raised to a spirit being, to a spirit child. This takes place via the Father-Mother-Principle, via the duality of two divine beings. The spirit child activates once more all the levels of the law of infinity and is then a matured spirit being that is one with infinity because it is the essence of infinity, with which it is in communication.

The Fall made the divine principle its own and applied it to itself. It undertook the following reversal: From the divine »Link and be« became »Divide, bind and rule.«

This means that the Fall-thought likewise can actualize itself, that is, bring about its purpose. The purpose then comes back to the sender through the principle of sending and receiving.

The reversed principle will continue to exist as long as human beings are receiving stations for this, that is, receivers, which, in turn, send out the same and like things.

I, Christ, came as Jesus to the people to teach them the law of God—»Link and be«—and to live it as an example for them.

I Am the Christ, the Spirit that reveals Itself, and that again teaches: »Link and be.«

Through willing people, I, Christ, revamp the Fall-law, the law of »Divide, bind and rule.«

I transform all that is negative to the divine. The base energies are transformed up, by which means the Fall-law—»Divide, bind and rule«—dissolves and everything again is the Being, the pure, eternal law: »Link and be.«

The person who is in the process of changing from the negative to the divine, from the »I want« to the »Let there be,« becomes ever finer in his structure. He raises himself to the true Being, which has no thought.

Every thought is the present, the past and the future in one, and is carried by the maintaining energy, the Spirit consciousness.

The present is the conscious mind. The past and the future are the subconscious. The Spirit consciousness is the life. It is the maintaining energy that will again become the flowing power of God through the transformation.

Gabriele:

As long as the person has a burdened subconscious, he will also sin in his conscious mind, that is, consciously. The sinful subconscious prompts him again and again to sin because the conscious mind, as well as the subconscious, can be influenced by the adversary of God, as long as they are in communication with him through sin. The one who cleanses his subconscious lives consciously and purposefully according to the will of God.

To cleanse the subconscious means to daily clear up the sins that have been recognized, to repent of them and no longer commit them. Then many of the sins will become memories that help us to be tolerant, understanding and of good will toward our neighbor. Once the subconscious is cleansed, then the conscious mind is also cleansed and the Spirit consciousness gains the upper hand.

live through the one who lives in Me, the Christ. He has become wise and no longer needs the opinion of his neighbor because he sees through everything and knows about all things. He will then no longer be an opinion-maker because the one who opines does not know. The truly wise one knows and does not opine.

The person who has awakened to impersonalness has found the philosopher's stone. He hears the lawful principle in everything that is spoken—and recognizes, in turn, the whole in it because the eternal, the truth, always communicates itself totally.

Gabriele, the teaching prophetess
and emissary of God, explained about this:

The impersonal has nothing in common with the person. The impersonal is the very basis of the soul, the divine in the person, which does not differentiate between the one and the other. The impersonal gives without expectation. Only the personal, what is tailored to the person—personal feelings, thoughts, desires and the ego—rejects the one and favors the other. They expect from the one and give to the other.

However, the impersonal, the divine in the very basis of each individual's soul, always affirms the good in the person and promotes the good in him, but does not overlook the evil.

Thus, the person has nothing in common with the impersonal. The impersonal is in the person, the shell, and is the divine.

If the person has found his way to the source, to the very basis of his soul, he has discovered the philosopher's stone and has brought it to light. Then the person not only knows, but has become wise because he recognizes the divine in all things, in all problems and difficulties, and finds the solution, which, in turn, corresponds to the law, God.

Every solution from the viewpoint of the very basis of the soul, the recognition of the truth, always contains the whole eternal law. The aspects for the solution or for a true, conscious conversation shine from the whole, and illuminate it in the spirit of the eternal law, so that the solution, the good conversation and much more come to the surface, that is, come to light.

To attain this, it is necessary to clear the jungle of the ego, to reach the philosopher's stone, the impersonal, the divine, the very basis of the soul. This means that the person has found the divine, the impersonal, the philosopher's stone, in the very basis of his soul. The person, the human being, then also lives in a noble and good way, that is, morally and ethically according to the laws of love and justice.

Since everything is contained in all things, you should pay attention to the following to gain knowledge of the All-unity:

What you sow, therein Am I, too.
Wherever you go, I, too, Am there.
Thus, what you sow and where you sow—
I Am in everything.
Wherever you go—I go with you.

The You Am I because I Am in everything;
and you are the I because I Am in everything.

You are here and there, and I Am here
and there.
Therefore, there is no place
where I Am not and where you are not.
For this reason, find yourself in Me,
and I Am the You in you.
Wherever you think toward—I Am there,
whatever you speak—therein Am I.

Whomever you speak to, what you say bears within Me, the Self, the I Am—that you also are, that is in your neighbor and that is in all things, occurrences and events.

This is the law. This is the way the prophets of God thought and think, the way they lived and live.

Gabriele:

The true Self is God, the I Am, which is in all things of matter, in each person, in all material heavenly bodies, but also in all forms and souls in the purification planes. The true Self, the I Am, is indivisible. Therefore, in the smallest is the largest, the entire, divine law of infinity.

Everything is energy. The source of energy is always God. The human being took aspects of the eternal law, for instance, the Order of the eternal Self, and made of it the disorder. He took aspects from the stream of the divine Will and made of it his self-will, which thus became an aspect of the human ego. For this reason, God is the core, the source, the life, the entire law, in all that is bound. The entire eternal law is compressed in every feeling, in every word, in every action of the person. Even if we turned aspects into our ego-self, God always remains the whole in all things and in all beings. Under the aspects transformed by us, which we transformed down to our ego-self, is always God, the whole. Each word we speak contains God, the whole. In each thought we think, God is the whole.

Let us again become aware of the difference between "God is" and "God is in." God is the Being, the Self, and all who live in the Being, in the Self, all beings of the heavens and all pure divine forms are divine. The one who through sin places himself outside of the divine Self envelops the eternal law, the Self, with his sins. Therefore, it is: God is in the human being, God is in the thoughts—and not: God is the thought, God is the word, God is the action.

The one striving for perfection will recognize that God is in all beings and in everything that is coarse-material and finer-material, for instance, the purification planes with their souls. When we speak, think and act, God is always the whole in every aspect.

emember: You cannot serve two masters. Nor can you love two people differently. The one who does this will accept the one and spurn the other.

Therefore, the precept of life says: Love all beings and all things equally. That is the impersonal life; that is the heaven that comes to Earth.

The unified one has become the self, the state of oneness, the light. He is the divine because he lives in the stream, in God. He lives in Me and I live through him, and we know each other because we know God, since we are divine.

Gabriele, the teaching prophetess
and emissary of God, explained about this:

We read that the precept of life reads: *»Love all beings and all things equally.«*

God's love is the source of the wellspring. It flows in infinity and gives to all beings and things equally. Thus, as already described, God's love does not make differences. It does not pay attention to the person—it gives.

Not every person accepts and receives God's love. The one who turns away from it sins, thus building his cellar, which is often a bunker. The person feels totally well in it. This is then his life and the quality of his life. Despite all this, the inner sun shines on soul and person with its whole fullness of light. However, the one who is in the cellar, the bunker, has put himself in the shadows. He has turned away from God, like the part of the Earth that turns away from the material sun in the evening. The night is then the life in the cellar, the bunker. This is the person's personal existence.

Gabriele, the teaching prophetess
and emissary of God, explained about this:

God is eternal and the eternity. The one who sows in God, in eternity, also lives more and more in and with the Eternal because his seed is the faith and trust in God. In faith and in trust, the person fulfills God's commandments and the Sermon on the Mount of Jesus, more and more. That is the good seed that he sows in the field of eternity. The fruit, which he then is, himself, is divine. Everything divine is from the Eternal, for the eternity.

The one who sows in human beings relies on human beings. He believes in the all-too-human and trusts in the all-too-human, in the sins of his neighbor. The one who relies on the sins of his neighbor is a sinner who continues to sin because he does not see through the wall of sins of the person who plants himself before him with his ego and offers himself as a staff and support.

The one who sows in the ego adopts the opinions of others, and others absorb his opinions. Both are bound to each other because one has transferred his undivine seed to the other.

Everything that is not divine is transitory because it is a bad seed, which belongs to a transitory field, the person himself.

The human being and matter are merely projections of the inner being. Just as the person thinks, so is he. That is the projection of his world of feelings and thoughts, his words and deeds.

This is why the illusion can never rise against the Being, nor the shadow against the light. The shadow will shatter on the light.

The Spirit of our eternal Father is the sole reality, the only verity that is and reigns eternally.

On this holy, eternal consciousness, God, matter will be shattered, and all those who bind themselves to matter will break into pieces.

Gabriele, the teaching prophetess
and emissary of God, explained about this:

Let us bring to mind the depth of the words: "God is." In these two words exists neither past nor future but the present. Whatever has no past and no future—that is, what is—is perfect and thus, indestructible and therefore, also irrevocable. What is real for people today gradually goes into the past and becomes unreal because it becomes incidental to the people. What is today for the person can also be his image of the future, which can never be attained to the extent that it was projected into the future—for example, as the ideal image. Either the image of the future changes or it cancels out because the person cannot control his life on Earth, that is, he cannot project it into the future. For each person, his human aspects today become either the past or the future. They then bear merely a shadow of today.

God is, and the "Is" remains the present. The "Is" is irrevocable because it knows neither past nor future. It is written in everything and all beings, like the Ten Commandments that were chiseled in stone.

The human being can govern neither his past nor his future. For a short time, he has regency only over his brief present, over today. This disappears during the next minutes and hours because their content then belongs to the past or to the future. But since God is, and is always the present, He is always the whole in all beings and everything. He is the life and is the Regent of what is pure. The impure disappears because—through the past and the future—it has no reality. Only the eternal present, which is present in all beings and everything, is irrevocable and unchangeable. It is the verity, the reality—the Regency that rules eternally.

As Jesus of Nazareth, I taught My own: The time will come in which more and more people will immerse in the light of the truth, the I Am. They will live in the I Am, in Me, the Christ, and will personify on this Earth the inner light and the inner life, the I Am.

I Am the way, the truth and the life. I come to My own and bring them the I Am. But I will not come in the flesh again. I will be among them in the Spirit—among those who bear the light, the I Am.

Gabriele, the teaching prophetess
and emissary of God, explained about this:

To immerse in the light, in the truth, in the I Am, means to fulfill the laws of God, the Ten Commandments and the Sermon on the Mount, each day, on the plain and simple path that Jesus, the Christ, taught us and lived as an example for us. It is: Recognize daily aspects of your sinfulness, repent of them and clear them up and no longer commit them. Instead of these sins, fulfill more and more the commandments of God, principles of the law of eternal life.

In this way, which is the path to the eternal truth, soul and person begin to live in Christ. They are those people who personify the inner life, which is the Christ of God, by doing the will of God. Once the day and the hour of the return of the Christ of God has come, He will also be among those who bear the light of the I Am, who personify it, as it were.

I, Christ, came into this world in Jesus to serve the people and not their humanness. The same is true of all true prophets. They came into this world to serve the people and not their humanness.

The one who keeps the eternal laws will also act as I and all prophets did. We came into this world to serve the people and not their humanness.

Gabriele, the teaching prophetess
and emissary of God, explained about this:

The great Spirit, the Christ of God in Jesus of Nazareth, and all those who served and serve the Eternal came and come into this world to serve the human being, the person, to announce to the people the principles of the law of love and of peace, so that they keep these step by step, thus drawing closer to God, the eternal and beloved Father.

They did not, and do not, serve the human aspects of the person, which means they do not serve the person's sinfulness, the ego, so that the person increases it. They came and come into this world to foster the good in the person, to teach him to understand God's love and peace, and to apply it in daily life, so that the person raises himself to a spiritual person and does not remain the all-too-human person.

In the language of the Spirit of God, the human being is the person, which envelops the soul. The humanness is the all-too-human, the sinful, which burdens the soul and marks the human being.

The Christ of God wants the human being to raise himself to a spiritual person. Jesus served the people in this awareness, and in the same awareness, all servants of the Eternal served and serve humankind.

Gabriele:

Jesus of Nazareth essentially said: The Father and I are one. With this, He meant the all-encompassing and omnipresent, eternal stream of love and peace, the absolute, perfect law of the heavens. The stream is the one Spirit, which flows through all realms and all Being, which is active in the entire creation. It is active in the material nature kingdoms and dwells in the soul of each human being, as well as in each cell of the physical body.

We have read: God is. Every spirit being, all pure forms of Being are the law of love and of peace. They are not enveloped, but pure and clear as the noblest and finest crystal. God is. He is not enveloped by the pure Being because everything pure is the compressed, radiating, eternal law, the same as a fine, all-radiating crystal.

Every human being and every soul is on a journey to the Eternal, who is. As long as soul and person are burdened, that is, as long as the soul is marked by sinfulness, God, the I Am, is in the soul because God cannot completely radiate through the soul, since the free will has sinned and the self-will, the sin, the shadow, has covered the light. Therefore, each soul and each human being is on a journey, to draw closer to God, the I Am, and to immerse in the stream, the Holy Spirit, which is eternally.

If the soul is again divine, if it has become the law of love and of peace, then it is the all-radiating crystal—shadowless. This means that the soul has again fully blossomed in the Spirit of God. It is the pure spirit being, the All-crystal, in the Holy Spirit, the compressed stream in the divine stream, the divine law itself, the divine form, shadowless, eternally in eternity.

As soon as the soul immerses in perfection, in the stream of the eternal Being, the person, too, will know the truth and express it in thoughts, words and deeds because he then draws from the consciousness of perfection, the eternal Being.

If soul and person have not yet developed the Spirit of the Christ of God who lives in the Father and dwells in every soul, then the person will not understand the eternal laws, which are the truth. Nonetheless, the Spirit is the living wellspring in every soul and in every human being. Despite the darkness and ignorance of the human ego, the Holy Spirit remains in soul and person.

The one who merely accepts Me, the Christ, and does not receive Me in his heart has made of himself his own judge.

Gabriele:

Many people think that when they call themselves Christian, this must suffice in everyday life. Many a church Christian is of the opinion that faith is enough, that he is not responsible for his sins, particularly not if he repents of them at the hour of death, thus placing himself into the hands of the Spirit of God.

The one who believes this has merely accepted Christ. However, in the Sermon on the Mount, Jesus spoke about doing His teachings: Every one then who hears these words of mine and does them is like a wise man who built his house upon the rock.

The one who becomes aware of this statement of Jesus, of the Christ of God, recognizes that faith alone is not enough. The words of the Lord regarding the doing of His teaching say that with all that we daily think, say and do, we should orient ourselves to the Ten Commandments and the Sermon on the Mount. Therefore, we should keep these divine principles of the law. The one who does this and keeps His teachings has not only accepted the Christ of God in a conceptual act of faith, but has received Him in his heart, which means that with the help of the Christ of God, he cleanses his soul and purifies his person—for His Spirit dwells in each human being and in each soul.

The more the soul frees itself from sin, that is, the person breaks away from sin with the power of redemption that dwells in him, the more will the Christ of God radiate through the soul and the physical body. As a result of this God-Christ-alignment, the person fulfills the will of the Eternal more and more. Thus, he has received the Christ of God because he does what God wants.

Gabriele:

The law of love is God and God is the love. The Christ of God in Jesus personified the eternal law of love. He taught us the first commandment, the love: Love God with all your heart, with all your soul, with all your strength, and your neighbor as yourself.

This means that the one who does not strive for this first commandment of love for God and neighbor remains in self-love and thinks solely of his base ego. With this, his base ego, he more or less denigrates and judges his neighbor. Hence, he distances himself from his fellow people and brands his neighbors as "the others," that is, "the strangers."

However, in the Spirit of God, all people are brothers and sisters because we all have one Father. Whether we call this God Jehovah, Allah or something else—it is always the one, great All-love, the one Father, and all people are His children. In this Father-child-consciousness, we are all brothers and sisters among one another.

God, the Eternal, loves all His children equally. He makes no differences between the divine being and the

923

sinner. As long as we human beings differentiate, by loving the one and rejecting the other, we do not love either one. What we call love is merely our self-absorbed love, which focuses solely on ourselves, which thinks solely of itself and wants to gain the neighbor for itself, so that he, the neighbor, serves the egoistical love of our base ego. As long as we seemingly love the one and disdain, spurn, that is, turn our back on, the other, we do not love the Christ of God and God, our Father.

To love your neighbor as God commanded us means to first become aware of the highest commandment of love, to strive for this, that is, to cleanse oneself more and more from the ego-love, in order to gradually immerse in the great law of love.

This causes us to make ever fewer differences between the one and the other. Only then will we begin to love our fellow people, that is, to no longer disparage them, to no longer want to press our ego-stamp on them, to leave them free in their decisions, so that they can freely decide—be it through a wrong decision, which they recognize, repent of, clear up and no longer do.

Therefore, the one who makes differences between the one and the other does not love God; nor is he moving toward the law of love, toward the highest commandment: Love God with all your heart, with all your soul, with all your strength, and your neighbor as yourself.

Love is the law of life. The one who loves selflessly lives. The one who does not love selflessly does not live. He has joined the spiritually dead.

Each one who strives toward selfless love recognizes the voice of love through people and through all things because God is everything in all things, the law, the voice of love.

Abide in My love, for My love is the love of the Father-Mother-God.

The one who keeps the commandments of selfless love abides in My love and is in the love of the eternal Father.

Verily, verily, I say to you: The one who hears and reads these My words and grasps their meaning and achieves what I have commanded him is truly a wise man who builds on Me, the rock, Christ.

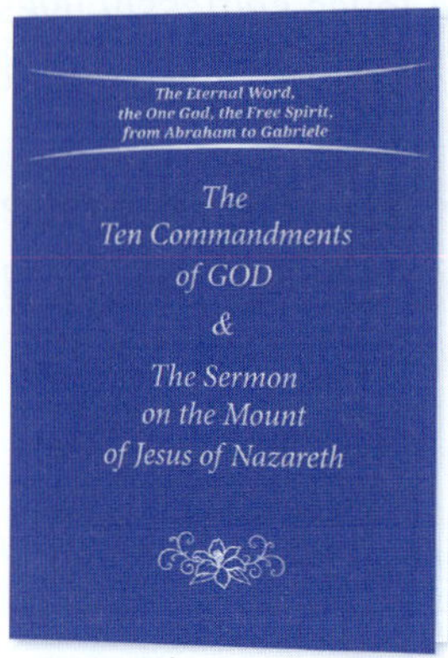

The Ten Commandments of GOD
&
The Sermon on the Mount of Jesus of Nazareth

The Ten Commandments of God and the Sermon on the Mount of Jesus of Nazareth have nothing to do with religion. They are excerpts from the eternal law of the love for God and neighbor. The Ten Commandments of God and the Sermon on the Mount of Jesus of Nazareth are given for every person regardless of culture or nationality. Discover the offer of God, the Free Spirit, for your life and for us all and experience how these simple instructions for life can change our life to the positive. They are the way into freedom and into peace among us people, as well as with all of creation, with nature and the animals.

Read the explanations on the Ten Commandments of God, explained with the words of our time. Deepen your understanding of the teachings of the Sermon on the Mount in the explanations that Christ Himself revealed through Gabriele, the prophetess and emissary of God in our time.

221 pp., SB, Order No. S182TBEN, ISBN 978-3-96446-264-0

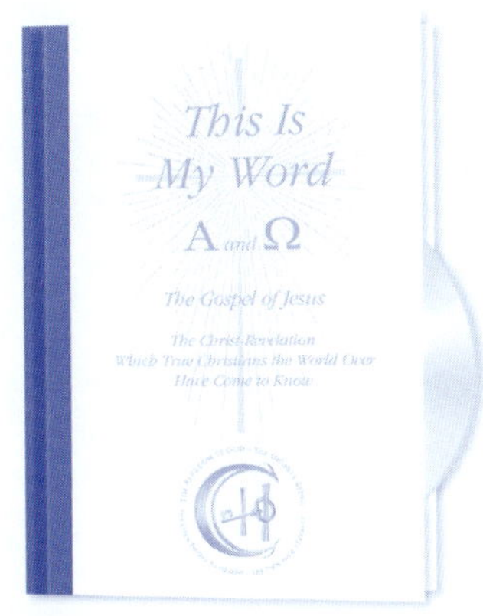

This Is My Word
A and Ω

The Gospel of Jesus

The Christ-Revelation Which True Christians the World Over Have Come to Know

Building on the "Gospel of Jesus," an existing extra-biblical gospel text, Christ Himself revealed the facts about His life and His teachings as Jesus of Nazareth by explaining, correcting and deepening the text through Gabriele, the prophetess and emissary of the Eternal Kingdom.

From the contents: Childhood and Youth of Jesus • The falsification of the teachings of Jesus of Nazareth during the past 2000 years • Purpose and meaning of an earthly life • Jesus taught about the law of cause and effect • Conditions for healing the body • Jesus taught about marriage • The Sermon on the Mount • About the nature of God • God does not punish and condemn • The teaching of "eternal damnation" is a mockery of God • Jesus exposes the scribes and Pharisees as hypocrites • Jesus loved the animals and championed their cause • About death, reincarnation and life • The true meaning of the Redeemer Deed of Christ and much more.

HB: 1116 pp., Order No. S 007EN. ISBN 978-3-96446-313-5
Included with the HB is an audio CD with the Eternal Word from the Kingdom of God: "The Call of the Christ of God" and "The Appearance," given in 2017 via Gabriele
SB: 1116 pp., Order No. S 007TBEN. ISBN 97 8-3-96446-310-4

Gabriele Publishing House – The Word
We will be glad to send you
our current catalog of books, CDs and DVDs,
as well as free excerpts on many different topics

Gabriele Publishing House – The Word
P.O. Box 2221, Deering, NH 03244, USA
Toll-Free Order No.: 1-844-576-0937
www.Gabriele-Publishing-House.com